P9-DWU-570

TRANSFORMATIONS IN SLAVERY

AFRICAN STUDIES SERIES 36

Editorial board
John Dunn, Reader in Politics and Fellow of King's College, Cambridge
J. M. Lonsdale, Lecturer in History and Fellow of Trinity College,
   Cambridge
D. M. G. Newbery, Lecturer in Economics and Fellow of Churchill
   College, Cambridge
A. F. Robertson, Assistant Director of Development Studies and
   Fellow of Darwin College, Cambridge

The African Studies Series is a collection of monographs and general
studies which reflect the interdisciplinary interests of the African Studies
Centre at Cambridge. Volumes to date have combined historical,
anthropological, economic, political and other perspectives. Each
contribution has assumed that such broad approaches can contribute
much to our understanding of Africa, and that this may in turn be of
advantage to specific disciplines.

OTHER BOOKS IN THE SERIES

TRANSFORMATIONS IN SLAVERY

A history of slavery in Africa

326.096
L942

PAUL E. LOVEJOY
Associate Professor, Department of History, York University, Canada

WITHDRAWL

CAMBRIDGE
UNIVERSITY PRESS

LIBRARY ST. MARY'S COLLEGE

Published by the Press Syndicate of the University of Cambridge
The Pitt Building, Trumpington Street, Cambridge CB2 1RP
40 West 20th Street, New York, NY 10011-4211, USA
10 Stamford Road, Oakleigh, Melbourne 3166, Australia

© Cambridge University Press 1983

First published 1983
Reprinted 1988, 1991, 1993

Printed in Great Britain
by the Athenaeum Press Ltd, Newcastle upon Tyne

Library of Congress catalogue card number: 82-12849

British Library cataloguing in publication data

Lovejoy, Paul E.
Transformation in slavery. — (African series; 36)
1. Slavery — Africa — History
I. Title   II. Series
306′.362′096   HT1321

ISBN 0 521 24369 6 hard covers
ISBN 0 521 28646 8 paperback

CE

Contents

v

Contents

Maps

Tables

List of tables

THIS BOOK HAS BEEN PUBLISHED
WITH THE HELP OF A GRANT FROM
THE SOCIAL SCIENCE FEDERATION OF CANADA,
USING FUNDS PROVIDED BY
THE SOCIAL SCIENCES AND HUMANITIES
RESEARCH COUNCIL OF CANADA

Preface

This is a work of synthesis. As such it suffers from the same deficiencies that all studies of its sort do. I have examined some parts of the continent in much greater detail than others in preparing this book, and I have relied on secondary sources extensively, although there has been some use of primary material. Very likely there are points with which specialists will disagree, because the scope of the topic makes it impossible to be fully aware of the debates that affect particular periods and areas. None the less, the study of African history, and more especially the analysis of slavery in Africa, has suffered from the opposite problem to that of over-synthesis. There is virtually no historical framework in which the reconstruction of slave history can be set. The numerous local studies that exist are uneven in quality and frequently are presented in a quasi-historical setting that is fraught with enormous methodological difficulties. Often studies of adjacent areas make no reference to each other. Sometimes, analysis is divorced from all outside influence, as if slavery in Africa existed in a vacuum. There are some brilliant local studies, which have their own implications in terms of the study of slavery in general, but these, too, suffer from a failure to place the particular case in the context of Africa as a whole, or even specific regions within Africa.

With these problems in mind, I set out to write an interpretative essay, 'Indigenous African slavery', which was presented at a conference on new directions in slave studies at the University of Waterloo in April 1979. I uncovered so much material that a more extensive project was necessary in order to consider the issues identified. That essay is in part a bibliographical study that can be used to accompany this book. It is incomplete, even with respect to relatively available materials, and it does not examine the extensive archival information that can be used for a study of this sort, although some archival material has been surveyed. In short, the collection and examination of source material continues, but the present volume is a necessary step in the further study of slavery.

This book attempts a more sophisticated interpretation than was possible for the Waterloo conference. The same basic framework will be evident: an effort to delimit regions within Africa that enable meaningful analysis and a periodization that identifies major turning-points in the history of slavery. It will be clear that detailed studies of particular topics and areas are still essential. This is not a substitute for such research. Rather this book provides a thematic study of African history from the perspective of slavery. Its major thesis is that slavery was transformed, in part because of external influences and in part because of the dynamics of internal forces. On the most general level, it argues that Africa responded to outside influences to a greater extent than it influenced the outside world. The more important questions of how Africans shaped that response and the means through which outside influence was minimized are considered in detail. The implication of this thesis is that slavery was a central institution in many parts of Africa, and the study examines where and when this became the case.

The book should be seen as an introduction to the history of slavery in Africa. More specialized studies already exist that treat particular problems, often for much more limited periods. These include the analysis of the overseas slave trade, the abolition crusade, and the relationship between slavery and imperialism; but even these are often limited even within the general theme of study. The following scholars, whose works are cited in the bibliography, deserve special mention. Philip D. Curtin pioneered the study of the trans-Atlantic slave trade when he attempted a preliminary census in 1969. Now that study is out of date, superseded by more detailed research that is summarized in the appropriate chapters below. Of the many abolition studies, those of Suzanne Miers, Seymour Drescher, Roger Anstey, and François Renault are the most important here, but each has its drawbacks. Miers concentrates on the British and the last decades of the nineteenth century. Drescher and Anstey each focus on the forces of abolition in Great Britain, although their study of the slave trade and the effects on Africa have modified the earlier work of Curtin. Renault provides the most comprehensive examination of French abolition by concentrating on Cardinal Lavigerie and his movement. Renault and Miers provide a good introduction to slavery in Africa during the era of European abolition. All of these studies assist in the historical reconstruction of African slavery, but invariably their treatment of slavery in Africa is of secondary importance to their main purpose: the external trade and European attitudes. These valuable contributions have been particularly useful here because, in the interpretation that is presented below, the external trade and European abolition are both considered extremely important influences on African history and the evolution of slavery.

Humphrey and Allen Fisher, John Grace, and Frederick Cooper have completed book-length studies of slavery in Africa. The Fishers' interpretative essay on the Islamic heritage of slavery in Africa is based primarily on the observations of Gustav Nachtigal from the 1870s. It is broadly conceived but draws on very limited sources. Grace's work is largely on Sierra Leone, with some information on other areas of British influence along the West

African coast. It is historical but not balanced. Cooper's study of plantation slavery in East Africa, summarized below, is the most perceptive treatment of an individual slave-system. This case is unique, for the major slave owners were not Africans but Omani Arabs, and hence some care has to be taken in order to place Cooper's study in the larger African setting.

Essays on slavery in different contexts have been collected into several published volumes, including those by Claude Meillassoux, Suzanne Miers and Igor Kopytoff, James L. Watson, John Ralph Willis, and myself, and others will be forthcoming shortly. These cover diverse cases and present various thematic approaches. The Meillassoux volume contains the interpretations of a dynamic school of French Marxist anthropologists, and Meillassoux has a forthcoming theoretical study that is an outgrowth of his association with the contributors to his volume. Miers and Kopytoff have done comparable work in the English-speaking world; their introduction provides a theoretical perspective as valuable as that of Meillassoux and his associates. The Willis volume includes specialized studies of slavery in the Islamic context, while Watson's collection provides a comparative perspective for Asian and African cases. My own collection focuses on ideology, providing a forum for discussion between those who have been most strongly influenced by the French Marxists and those who are most influenced by Miers and Kopytoff. The trouble with all these short studies, invaluable as they are, is that as the number increases so does the confusion for the non-specialist.

This brings us back to the present endeavour. It is an intermediate stage in research and analysis. Its contribution is intended primarily on the historical level, that is on the plane of chronological reconstruction, although the chronological framework is a bare beginning. Because historical reconstruction has been so minimal in earlier studies, there are bound to be mistakes here. Furthermore, the context of recent research has contributed to the general problem of interpretation in three ways. Firstly, the climate of research has been romantic. The aim of many historians has been to glorify the African past for reasons related to emergent nationalism in Africa and the sentiments of people of African descent in the Americas. This has made it difficult to discuss the inglorious past. Secondly, the development of African history as a sub-discipline has grown from almost nothing to a large body of data and analysis. While this development requires periodic synthesis such as this one, the speed with which new material becomes available inhibits such synthesis and furthermore reveals the thin base upon which much earlier work has been done. Finally, the political climate in Africa has been a difficult one in which to do sensitive, critical research, both for foreigners and nationals. The hazards of examining archival materials and interviewing elders vary as always, but these have often been the least of a researcher's problems in recent years. Police pressure, university censorship, and academic rivalries in close quarters have sometimes been more serious obstacles.

xiii

Preface

This will not be the last interpretation of the history of slavery in Africa. Indeed, my own interest in the subject has grown with the writing of this book. The quantity of material that is available in published and archival form is so voluminous that different thematic studies become more and more desirable. Some of these possibilities will be readily apparent, as will the need for more detailed examination of specific aspects of local and regional history. This book, therefore, is an assessment of the topic in 1982.

The individuals who have assisted in one way or another in the preparation of this book include those who have made material available to me, those who have engaged in an ongoing dialogue on aspects of the topic over the past few years, and those who have read or commented on specific parts of the manuscript. I mention these individuals as a further reference to sources, for in most cases the scholars are actively engaged in research on the topic of slavery: Philip D. Curtin, Joseph C. Miller, David Northrup, Norman Klein, Martin Klein, Richard Roberts, Mark Duffill, David Tambo, Allen Isaacman, Dennis Cordell, Jan Hogendorn, Raymond Dumett, Igor Kopytoff, Frederick Cooper, Suzanne Miers, Jan Vansina, Patrick Manning, and Mordacai Abir. Stanley Engerman, David Eltis, Henry Gemery, and Joseph Miller criticized my efforts to synthesize the material available on the volume of the trans-Atlantic slave trade, and, along with Pieter Emmer and Robert Stein, Miller and Eltis also made available unpublished material. Allen Isaacman, Emmanuel Terray, Sydney Kanya-Forstner, Martin Klein, Myron Echenberg, John Fage, Joseph Miller, and Patrick Manning read all or substantial portions of the manuscript, and hopefully most of their criticisms have been satisfied. John Priestley kindly undertook the translation of several French quotations. Several research assistants were helpful in tracking down material; these include Geoffrey Da Silva, Murray Hoffbauer, Stephen Giles, Mary Pat O'Reilly, and Marc Epprecht. I would also like to thank Michael Craton for the opportunity to present the preliminary paper on indigenous African slavery that provided the foundation for this larger study. Financial assistance for the collection of material has come from York University. It has been possible to devote time to writing this book because of a Faculty of Arts Fellowship from York University for 1979–80, which released me from most of my teaching and administrative responsibilities. York University has also been particularly generous in providing secretarial assistance, and I would like to thank the many people in Secretarial Services, under the direction of Doris Brillinger, who have worked on various parts of the manuscript. Diane Lekkas and Michelle Srebrolow also typed portions of the manuscript. Finally, the Interlibrary Loan department of Scott Library, York University, has been responsible for the tremendous task of locating the often very obscure materials that have been essential to this study.

PAUL E. LOVEJOY
Toronto, Canada

Note on currencies, weights, and measures

A wide variety of currencies were used in Africa during the period of this study. Wherever possible, I have converted local currencies into sterling. The gold equivalencies of Asante, for example, have been converted to sterling. I have also used the Maria Theresa thaler (MT), which circulated widely in the northern savanna and East Africa from the end of the eighteenth century. Cowries were also used in large parts of West Africa.

Unless otherwise specified, all weights and measures are metric.

For Pidge

1

Africa and slavery

Slavery has been an important phenomenon throughout history. It has been found in many places, from classical antiquity to very recent times. Africa has been intimately connected with this history, both as a major source of slaves for ancient civilization, the Islamic world, India, and the Americas, and as one of the principal areas where slavery was common. Indeed, in Africa slavery lasted well into the present century – notably longer than in the Americas. Such antiquity and persistence require explanation, both to understand the historical development of slavery in Africa in its own right and to evaluate the relative importance of the slave trade to this development. Broadly speaking, slavery expanded in at least three stages – 1350 to 1600, 1600 to 1800, and 1800 to 1900 – by which time slavery had become a fundamental feature of the African political economy. This expansion occurred on two levels that were linked to the external slave trade. Firstly, slavery became more common over an increasingly greater geographical area, spreading outward from those places that participated directly in the external slave trade. Secondly, the role of slaves in the economy and society became more important, resulting in the transformation of the social, economic and political order. Again, the external trade was associated with this transformation.

SLAVERY: A DEFINITION

Slavery was one form of exploitation. Its special characteristics included the idea that slaves were property; that they were outsiders who were alien by origin or who had been denied their heritage through judicial or other sanctions; that coercion could be used at will; that their labour power was at the complete disposal of a master; that they did not have the right to their own sexuality and, by extension, to their own reproductive capacities; and that the slave status was inherited unless provision was made to ameliorate that status.[1] These various attributes need to be examined in greater detail to clarify the distinctions between slavery and other servile relationships.

As property, slaves were chattel; which is to say they could be bought and

1

sold. Slaves belonged to their masters, who at least theoretically had complete power over them. Religious institutions, kinship units, and other groups in the same society did not protect slaves as legal persons, even though the fact that slaves were also human beings was sometimes recognized. Because they were chattel, slaves could be treated as commodities. But slaves were seldom merely commodities, and often restrictions were placed on the sale of slaves once some degree of acculturation had taken place. These restrictions could be purely moral, as they were in the Americas, where in theory at least it was thought wrong to divide families when sales were taking place, although in fact slave owners did what they wanted. In other situations restrictions were actually enforced, or persons were automatically granted some degree of emancipation that precluded sale. In Islamic practice and under Islamic law, women taken as concubines could not legally be sold once they had given birth to children by their master. Furthermore, such children were technically free and usually recognized as such. The women became legally free on the death of their master in many cases, and in some they were nominally free as soon as they gave birth, although they could not normally terminate their status as concubine. In reality they attained an intermediate position between slave and free. Other restrictions on sale limited the ability of masters to sell the children of slaves, either because of religious sentiments, in the case of Islam, or because an acceptable kinship or ethnic status had been confirmed. If sale did take place, it was carefully justified in terms of criminal activity, sorcery, or some other ideologically acceptable reason; often these same reasons could result in the sale of free-born members of the same society. None the less, it was characteristic of slavery that the slave was considered the property of another person or some corporate group, despite restrictions on the nature of this property relationship that developed in actual situations.

A digression is necessary in order to establish what is meant by 'freedom'. The term is really relative. People are more free to make decisions for themselves or they are less free to do so. All societies place numerous constraints on individuals, but even when this is recognized we can still understand slaves as people who are particularly unfree. In the context of slave societies, freedom involved a recognized status in a caste, a ruling class, a kinship group, or some such corporate body. Such an identification included a bundle of rights and obligations that varied considerably with the situation but were still distinct from those for slaves, who technically had no rights, only obligations. The act of emancipation, when it existed, conveyed a recognition that slave and free were opposites. Emancipation dramatically demonstrated that power was in the hands of the free, not the slaves.

Therefore, slavery was fundamentally a means of denying outsiders the rights and privileges of a particular society so that they could be exploited for economic, political and/or social purposes.[2] Usually outsiders were perceived as ethnically different: the absence of kinship was a particularly

2

common distinction. A person who spoke the same language as his master, without an accent, who shared the same culture, believed in the same religion, and understood the political relationships that determined how power was exercised was far more difficult to control than an outsider. When differences in culture or dialect were relatively unimportant, the level of exploitation and the social isolation of slaves was usually limited; such situations suggest that slave holdings were small and that political and economic stratification was minimal. Certainly the most developed forms of slavery were those where slaves were removed a considerable distance from their birthplace, thereby emphasizing their alien origins. This uprooting was as dramatic as the transport of Africans across the Atlantic or the Sahara Desert or as undramatic as the seizure of people who lived only a hundred kilometres or less from the home of the enslavers. Both situations helped to define the slave as an outsider, at least in the first instance. Over time, cultural distinctions tended to blur, so that the extent to which alien origin was a factor varied.

When social structures and economies were more complex, then the identification of slaves as outsiders also became more pronounced, so that the acculturation that invariably occurred did not affect the ability of masters to exploit the labour and services of their slaves. For Muslims, religion was a means of categorizing slaves. Those recently acquired were usually not Muslims, or were only nominally so. Even when slaves began to practise Islam, they were usually considered less devout. For Europeans, slaves were perceived as racially distinct; despite acculturation, slaves were even more clearly defined as outsiders, thereby guaranteeing that the acquisition of rights in European society would be severely limited. Other more subtle distinctions were made, including differences in dialect, the accent of people who had just learned a new language, facial and body markings, perceived physical characteristics, and, most common of all, memory.

Slavery was virtually always initiated through violence that reduced the status of a person from a condition of freedom and citizenship to a condition of slavery.[3] The most common type of violence has been warfare, in which prisoners were enslaved. Variations in the organization of such violence – including raids whose purpose was to acquire slaves, banditry, and kidnapping – indicate that violent enslavement can be thought of as falling on a continuum from large-scale political action, in which enslavement may be only a by-product of war and not its cause, to small-scale criminal activity, in which enslavement is the sole purpose of the action. Taken together, warfare, slave raiding, and kidnapping have accounted for the vast majority of new slaves in history. Even when the motives for war were not to acquire slaves, the link between war and slavery was often close. In societies where it was customary to enslave prisoners, the belligerents invariably took account of the possibilities of defraying the cost of war through the sale or use of slaves. When wars and raids were chronic, these resulted in the continuous enslavement or re-enslavement of people, and the incidence of slavery in such situations increased.

While warfare and similar violence accounted for most of the newly enslaved people in history, judicial and religious proceedings accounted for some. Slavery was a form of judicial punishment, particularly for such crimes as murder, theft, adultery, and sorcery. The methods by which suspected criminals were enslaved varied greatly, and often they were sold out of their home communities. None the less, this avenue of enslavement once again was rooted in violence, however legitimate in the eyes of the society in question. The status of a person was radically reduced: the new slave could lose his membership in the community, and his punishment could confirm a status that was passed on to his descendants.

There were instances of voluntary enslavement, particularly when the threat of starvation left the person with no other recourse. None the less, this was not a case of conscious violence by society or an enemy. There may well have been structural causes that placed people in situations where they could not be assured of survival and hence found it necessary to enslave themselves. This structural dimension may well have carried with it a dimension that was ultimately exploitative and violent. None the less, voluntary enslavement was unusual, and it probably accounted for only a small percentage of slaves in most places. Furthermore, the possibility of voluntary enslavement depended upon the existence of an institution of slavery in which violence was fundamental. If there were no such institution, a person would not become a slave but a client or some other dependant. That the status of slave was even assigned in such instances indicates that other servile statuses were not appropriate, either because they were lacking or because they were defined to exclude such cases.

The extent of coercion involved in slavery was sometimes obvious and sometimes disguised. The master could enforce his will because of his ability to punish slaves for failure to comply with his orders or to perform their tasks satisfactorily. Whipping, confinement, deprivation of food, extra hard work, and the ability to dispose of slaves through sale were common means of coercion. Physical punishment could lead to death, and even when there were legal and customary prohibitions on killing slaves, these were rarely enforceable. Often coercion was more indirect. The example of other slaves being punished or sold and the knowledge that the master could do so were usually sufficient to maintain slave discipline. Sacrifices of slaves at funerals and public ceremonies, which were common in some places, were also examples to the slaves. Such public displays were not usually a form of punishment for insubordination; in fact, they were sometimes conceived of as an honour, but most often slaves were purchased specifically for sacrifice. Since insubordination could lead to sale, the risks for the trade slave were obvious. A purchaser might well be in need of a sacrificial victim.

Slavery was fundamentally tied to labour. It was not the only form of dependent labour, but slaves could be made to perform any task in the economy. They had to do what they were told; hence they often performed the most menial and laborious tasks and sometimes undertook great risks. In the case of slaves, the concept of labour was not perceived as separate from the slave as a person. The slave was an instrument of work, and coercion could be used to force compliance with particular orders. The slave was told what to do and, if he did not do it, he was punished, often severely. Slavery could and did exist alongside other types of labour, including serfdom (in which people were tied to the land, and their obligations to the lord were fixed by custom), clientage (voluntary subordination without fixed remuneration for services), wage-labour (in which compensation for work was monetarized), pawnship (in which labour was perceived as interest on a debt and the pawn as collateral for the debt), and communal work (often based on kinship or age grades, in which work was perceived as a reciprocal activity based on past or future exchange). These other forms of labour could involve coercion, too, but usually not to the point at which they could be called slavery.

A peculiar feature of slavery was this absolute lack of choice on the part of slaves. Their total subordination to the whims of their master meant that slaves could be assigned any task in the society or economy. Hence slaves have not only performed the most menial and laborious jobs, but they have also held positions of authority and had access to considerable wealth. The plantation field-hand and the slave general had their subordination to their master in common. Both were assigned a task, but the nature of their employment was so different that they had virtually no mutual interests. The identity of the slave was through his master. Legally, the master was held responsible for the actions of the slave, and this was the same for administrative slaves as well as common labourers. Slaves did not necessarily constitute a class, therefore. Their dependence could result in the subordination of their identity to that of their master, on whom their position depended, or it could lead to the development of a sense of comradeship with other slaves, and hence form the basis for class consciousness. Both could take place in the same society, if slaves and others recognized a clear distinction between those engaged in production and those involved in the military and administration.

Because slaves were fully subservient, their masters controlled their sexual and reproductive capacities, as well as their productive capacities.[4] When slaves constituted a significant proportion of any population, then sexual access and reproduction were strongly controlled. Women (and men too) could be treated as sexual objects; the ability to marry could be closely administered; and males could be castrated. The significance of sex is most strikingly revealed in the market price of slaves. Eunuchs were often the most costly, with pretty women and girls close behind, their price depending upon their sexual attractiveness. These two opposites – castrated males and attractive females – demonstrate most clearly that aspect of slavery which involved the master's power over sexual and reproductive functions. Slaves

5

lacked the right to engage in sexual relationships without the consent of their master. They could not marry without his permission and his provision of a spouse. Their children, once slaves were given an opportunity to have children, were not legally their offspring but the property of their master and often the master of the mother. Biologically, they were the offspring of the slaves, but the right to raise the children could be denied. Instead, slave children could be taken away and, even when they were not sold, they could be redistributed as part of marriage arrangements, trained for the army or administration, or adopted by the master's family.

Masters had the right of sexual access to slave women, who became concubines or wives, depending upon the society. This sexual dimension was a major reason why the price of female slaves was often higher than the price of men. Male slaves could be denied access to women, and such a dimension of slavery was a vital form of exploitation and control. The ability to acquire a spouse depended upon the willingness to accept the slave status and to work hard. Marriage or other sexual unions were a method of rewarding men. The desires of women were seldom taken into consideration. Although men could be given a wife from among the reduced pool of females available for such unions, they were not allowed effective paternity over their offspring. Actual bonds of affection and recognized biological links existed, of course, but these could be disrupted through the removal of the children if the master so wished. The master could reward the male slave, or he could deprive males of their sexuality through castration.

The slave status was inherited. This meant that the property element, the feature of being an alien, and the form of labour mobilization continued into the next generation, although in practice the slave status was often modified. The condition of slaves changed from the initial instance of enslavement through the course of the slave's life, and such an evolution continued into the next generation and beyond. The changed status varied from society to society, being more pronounced in some places than in others. The theory of the slave as an outsider became more difficult to uphold once a slave began to understand and accept his master's culture. While the theory could still define the slave as an alien, slaves were usually provided with the essentials of life, including access to land, spouses, protection, religious rites, and other attributes of citizenship. The more technical aspects of slavery, including the elements of property, labour, and alienness, could be invoked arbitrarily, but in practice these legal rights of the masters were usually not exercised fully. Usually some kind of accommodation was reached between masters and slaves. The sociological level of this relationship involved a recognition on the part of slaves that they were dependants whose position required subservience to their master, and it necessitated an acceptance on the part of the masters that there were limits on how far their slaves could be pushed.

Those born into slavery found themselves in a different position from those who had been enslaved in their own lifetimes, for the initial act of violence became an abstraction. Parents might tell their children of their enslavement, but this was not the children's experience. Children could also learn about enslavement from new captives, and they were educated into a society in which such acts were well known. The threat of violence was also present. Legally, they often could be separated from their parents and sold, even if in practice that was rare. The same insecurity that led to the enslavement of their parents or the new slaves with whom they came in contact could result in their own re-enslavement through war or raids. And if they behaved in a manner that was not acceptable, they could be sold. The violence behind the act of enslavement remained, therefore, although for the descendants of slaves it was transformed from a real act to a threat. As such, violence was still a crucial dimension of social control.

In both cases, moreover, the violence inherent in slavery affected the psychology of the slaves. The knowledge of the horrors of enslavement and the fear of arbitrary action produced in slaves both a psychology of servility and the potential for rebellion. This dual personality related to the coercion of the institution, for memory and observation served as effective methods of maintaining an atmosphere in which violence always lurked in the background. Slaves did not have to experience the whip; indeed they were wise to avoid it.

Slaves tended not to maintain their numbers naturally, and slave populations usually had to be replenished.[5] One reason for this situation was the relatively short life-span for many slaves. Death could result from particularly harsh work, while funeral sacrifices and unsuccessful castration operations took their toll. Travel conditions for slaves destined for distant markets were also a factor, both because individuals were moved from one disease-environment to another and because rations were often inadequate. Another reason was the demographic imbalance between the sexes in slave populations. The number of women in a population is a principal variable in determining whether or not a population will remain stable, expand, or contract. In conditions where the number of males was much greater, as it was among newly imported slaves in the Americas, or when there was an uneven distribution of slave women in society, as in many parts of Africa, the birth-rate for slaves could be too low to maintain the slave population. The situation for populations with an excess number of males led to the general decline in the total population, not just slaves, unless more slaves were imported. When slave women were distributed unevenly, the general population did not necessarily decline, only the proportion of slaves in the population. The women were usually taken as wives or concubines by free men, so that they still bore children. Because the status of concubines and slave wives changed, often leading to assimilation or full emancipation, the size of the slave population decreased accordingly. The children of slave wives and concubines by free fathers were often granted a status that was completely or almost free. Under Islamic law, this was most pronounced. Concubines could not be sold once they gave birth, and they became free on the death of their master. The children of such unions were free on birth. In other situations, the custom dictated that slave wives be incorporated into society, and even when their children were not accorded the full rights and privileges of children by free mothers, custom prevented the possibility of sale and other treatment that was meted out to the newly enslaved. These features of gradual assimilation or complete emancipation contradict that aspect of slavery which emphasized inherited status, but was compatible with the master's power to manipulate sexual and reproductive functions for his own purposes.

This feature of slavery accounted for the continued importance of enslavement and slave trading, the instruments that replenished the supply of slaves in society. The continuation of enslavement and trade reinforced the property element in slavery, but it did so unevenly. Those most recently enslaved or traded were the most like commodities. Those who had lived in one location for many years after their purchase or enslavement were less likely to be treated as if they were simply commodities. The institution as a whole was firmly embedded in a property relationship, but individual slaves experienced a modification in that relationship, until some were no longer property, or indeed slaves.

A brief postscript is necessary to consider the special case of slavery in the Americas, because the American system was a particularly heinous development. Many features of American slavery were similar to slavery in other times and places, including the relative size of the slave population, the concentration of slaves in economic units large enough to be classified as plantations, and the degree of physical violence and psychological coercion used to keep slaves in their place. None the less, the American system of slavery was unique in two respects: the manipulation of race as a means of controlling the slave population and the extent of the system's economic rationalization. In the Americas, the primary purpose of slave labour was the production of staple commodities – sugar, coffee, tobacco, rice, cotton, gold, and silver – for sale on world markets. Furthermore, many features that were common in other slave systems were absent or relatively unimportant in the Americas. These included the use of slaves in government, the existence of eunuchs, and the sacrifice of slaves at funerals and other occasions. The similarities and differences are identified in order to counteract a tendency to perceive slavery as a peculiarly American institution. Individual slave-systems had their own characteristics, but it is still possible to analyse the broader patterns that have distinguished slavery from other forms of exploitation.

SLAVERY IN SOCIAL FORMATIONS

Slaves have constituted a small percentage or a substantial proportion of different populations. While this demographic factor has been important, far more significant was the location of slaves in the society and economy.

8

Slaves could be incidental to the society at large because they were so few in number, but even when there were many slaves they could be distributed relatively evenly through society or concentrated in the hands of relatively few masters. Their function could be essentially social, political or economic, or it could be some combination of these. Slaves could be used extensively in the army and administration (political); they could be found in domestic and sexual roles (social); or they could be involved in production (economic). Often, some slaves in society performed one or another of these functions, although sometimes they were concentrated more in one category than another. Almost always slaves were found in domestic service, but if the social location of slaves was confined almost exclusively to domestic and sexual exploitation, then other forms of labour were necessarily essential to productive activities and hence to the nature of economic organization. Even when slaves filled political functions but were not engaged in productive activities, the basic structure of the economy had to rely on other forms of labour, and hence the society was not based òn slavery.

Slavery as a minor feature of society must be distinguished from slavery as an institution. In those places where a few people owned a few slaves, perhaps as conspicuous examples of wealth but not as workers, slavery was incidental to the structure of society and the functioning of the economy. Slavery became important when slaves were used extensively in production, the monopoly of political power, or domestic servitude (including sexual services). These situations required a regular supply of slaves, either through trade or enslavement or both, and the number of slaves in society became significant enough to affect its organization. Furthermore, when slavery became an essential component of production, the institution acquired additional characteristics. M. I. Finley has stated the importance of this development most aptly:

> Slavery, then, is transformed as an institution when slaves play an essential role in the economy. Historically that has meant, in the first instance, their role in agriculture. Slavery has been accommodated to the large estate under radically different conditions . . . and often existed alongside widespread free small holdings. That both slaves and free men did identical work was irrelevant; what mattered was the condition of work, or rather, on whose behalf andˆunder what (and whose) controls it was carried on. In slave societies hired labor was rare and slave labor the rule whenever an enterprise was too big for a family to conduct unaided. That rule extended from agriculture to manufacture and mining, and sometimes even to commerce and finance.[6]

In Africa, slavery underwent such a transformation at different times and at varying rates in the northern savanna, the west-central regions of Angola and the Zaire basin, and other places.

The transformation in slavery from a marginal feature in society to a central institution resulted in the consolidation of a mode of production based on slavery. 'Mode of production' is used here to emphasize the relationship between social organization and the productive process, on the

9

one hand, and the means by which this relationship is maintained, on the other hand.[7] The concept isolates the social relations of production, that is, the organization of the productive population in terms of its own identity and the ways in which this population is managed. This interaction between the social and economic relations of production requires conditions specific to each mode of production, which allow for the regeneration of the productive process; otherwise there is no historical continuity, only an instance of production. Finally, the relationship between the productive process and its regeneration is reflected in the ideological and political structures of society – sometimes called the 'superstructure' – as a means of distinguishing these features from the materialist base.[8]

A 'slave mode of production' existed when the social and economic structure of a particular society included an integrated system of enslavement, slave trade, and the domestic use of slaves. Slaves had to be employed in production, and hence the kind of transformation identified by Finley must have occurred. This transformation usually meant that slaves were used in agriculture and/or mining but also could refer to their use in transport as porters, stock boys, and paddlers in canoes. Slaves could still fill other functions, including concubinage, adoption into kin groups, and sacrifice, but these social and religious functions had to become secondary to productive uses. Furthermore, the maintenance of the slave population had to be guaranteed. This regeneration could occur through the birth of children into slavery (inheritance of slave status), raids, war, kidnapping, and other acts of enslavement, and the distribution of slaves through trade and tribute. Since slave populations were seldom self-sustaining through natural reproduction, enslavement and trade were usually prerequisites for the consolidation of a slave mode of production.

Slavery did not have to be the main feature of social relations in a society for a slave mode of production to exist. Other institutions could also determine the relations of production under different circumstances (kinship, pawnship, etc.). None the less, when slavery prevailed in one or more sectors of the economy, the social formation – that is, the combined social and economic structures of production – included a slave mode of production, no matter what other modes co-existed (feudalism, capitalism, etc.). This incorporation of various economic and social structures into a single system through the combination of and interaction between different modes of production could occur within the context of a single state or a wider region.[9] Such a social formation could include peasants, for example, who were involved in a tributary relationship with a state, on the one hand, or who were autonomous and subject to raids by the state, on the other hand. The ways in which such different systems were integrated – often called their 'articulation' – could be quite complex. Slavery could be linked to other modes of production through long-distance trade, tributary relationships, or raids and warfare. When the structural interaction between enslavement, trade, and domestic employment of slaves was the most important part of a social formation, it can be said that the slave mode of production was dominant. This occurred when the principal enslavers and slave merchants comprised a class of slave masters who owned a substantial number of slaves and relied on them for the maintenance of their economic and political domination. In this case, slavery became essential to the reproduction of the social formation.

The emphasis on the integration of a productive system based on slavery with the means of replenishing the supply of slaves has significance in the reconstruction of the history of slavery in its African context. This framework highlights three historical situations that were partially related and partially autonomous. Firstly, it provides a perspective for analysing the interaction between Africa and the demand for slaves in the Islamic world of North Africa and the Middle East. Secondly, it emphasizes the connection between Africa and the Americas, where African slaves were essential to plantation production and the mining sector. Thirdly, it allows for a study of the widespread productive use of slaves in Africa, particularly in the nineteenth century after the external slave trade collapsed. In all three situations, a mode of production based on slavery developed, but specific characteristics differed. The framework adopted here – the distinction between slavery as a marginal feature of society, slavery as an institution, and slavery as a mode of production – is meant to facilitate a study of these three different situations.

The debate in the theoretical literature between Marxists and non-Marxists and among Marxists themselves has inspired this conceptual framework, but there are clear differences in my use of 'mode of production' and 'social formation' and their use by other scholars. I disagree emphatically with the approach of Samir Amin, Barry Hindess, Paul Q. Hirst, and others who employ a framework drawn from the interpretation of Louis Althusser, because, as these scholars readily admit, their analysis depends upon ideal constructs that are ahistorical.[10] Rather, I follow the less dogmatic formulation of Emmanuel Terray, whose purpose is to provide an 'instrument of analysis', which I assume means an 'instrument of *historical* analysis'.[11] From this perspective, a 'slave mode of production' is meant to be a descriptive term whose theoretical significance is not developed here. My purpose is to isolate the place of slaves in production as a first step in historical reconstruction.

THE AFRICAN SETTING

Africa was relatively isolated in ancient and medieval times. Before the middle of the fifteenth century, virtually the only contact was along the East African coast, across the Red Sea and via the Sahara Desert. Those places bordering these frontiers were different from more isolated regions further inland. There were exceptions, depending upon natural resources, especially gold, so that five areas of gold production were drawn into the orbit of the non-African world: three in West Africa (Buré, Bambuhu, Volta basin), Ethiopia, and the Shona plateau in the interior of the Zambezi valley. In addition there was internal trade in luxuries other than gold – kola nuts between the West African forests west of the Volta River and the savanna to the north; copper, which was traded south from the Sahara into the lower Niger valley, and which was also distributed outward from the southern parts of modern Zaire; salt from many sources, including numerous sites in the Sahara Desert, the Red Sea coast of Ethiopia, local centres in the interior of Angola, many places along the Guinea coast, and other sites near the Great Lakes of east-central Africa. Despite its probable antiquity, this regional trade was relatively autonomous from the external sector. Furthermore, the other major economic developments during the millennium before the fifteenth century were also relatively isolated. The movement of Bantu-speaking farmers throughout central, eastern and southern Africa, the emergence of pastoral nomadism as a speciality in the northern savanna and down the lake corridor of East Africa, and the spread of iron working and craft production, despite occasional links to the external world, as in the case of cotton textiles, were far more influential regionally than intercontinentally.

One characteristic of regional development was a social structure based on ethnicity and kinship. Although the antiquity of kin-based societies is not known, linguistic, cultural, and economic evidence indicates that such structures were very old. The earliest references to kinship, for example, reveal that matrilineal and patrilineal distinctions were already well formed by the early sixteenth century. Much of the West African coastal region was patrilineal, except for the Akan of the Gold Coast. In west-central Africa, people followed matrilineal customs, as their descendants do today. Such continuity, which broadly speaking also matches ethnic distinctions, suggests that the interior peoples who were beyond the observations of early observers shared these structures. Thus, the coastal evidence for west-central Africa indicates the probable existence of a matrilineal belt of societies stretching across the continent to the Indian Ocean, just as it does today. Nothing in the historical record indicates that this pattern changed abruptly at any time in the past.[12]

Those societies based on kinship have variously been described as ones characterized by a 'lineage' or 'domestic' mode of production.[13] This mode of production had the following features: age and sexual distinctions were fundamental divisions in society, there being no class antagonisms. Elders controlled the means of production and access to women, and hence political power was based on gerontocracy. Since women were often the principal agricultural workers in this type of social formation, production and reproduction were closely associated.[14] The maintenance of society depended upon the fertility of the women and the output of their labour. The crucial variables for gerontocratic domination included the number of women married to elders, the number of children born to each wife, the ability to secure cooperation from junior kin and affinal relatives, and access to the non-human resources of the lineage, including land, trees, wild products, game and water. In this situation, slavery did not alter the essential basis of the social formation. Slaves could add to the size of the population and thereby increase the number of people mobilized by the elders, but slaves performed virtually the same functions as lineage members.

Slavery was one of many types of dependency, and it was an effective means of controlling people in situations where kinship remained paramount. Slaves lacked ties into the kinship network and only had those rights that were granted on sufferance. There was no class of slaves. While they undoubtedly performed many economic functions, their presence was related to the desire of people, either individually or in small groups of related kin, to bypass the customary relationships of society in order to increase their power. Slavery was, therefore, essentially a social institution in small-scale societies where political influence depended upon the size of social groups. If they were allowed to do so, slaves could become full members of these groups, or they could be kept as voiceless dependants, but their welfare was related to the fortunes of their master and his kin. In this setting, people had slaves along with other types of dependants, but society was not organized in such a manner that slavery was a central institution. These were not slave societies.[15]

Besides slavery, there were other categories of dependency, including pawnship, in which persons were held for security for debts, and junior age-sets, in which younger kin were not yet allowed to participate fully in the decisions of the lineage. Even marriage and concubinage were institutions of dependency.

Dependants were mobilized in the interests of the lineage as determined by the male elders. They performed cooperative work in the fields, formed hunting expeditions, defended villages against aggression, and participated in religious ceremonies. Because land was often held in common and because marriage involved payments that were too large for most youths to finance on their own, ties of kinship were strong. In times of difficulty, these connections provided insurance. Junior kin, in particular, were most vulnerable. On the one hand, they needed the family because they often were not wealthy enough or old enough to be on their own. On the other hand, they were the first to suffer in troubled times.

As pawnship demonstrates, ties other than those based on kinship were important because they supplemented or bypassed genetic connections.[16] As individuals held as security for a debt, pawns had kin connections, but not usually with the creditor. Hence their value was based on the expectation that their relatives would repay the debt and thereby release the pawn from bondage. Pawns could be used in this capacity because they were directly related to the debtor. Children were usually the ones to be forced into pawnship, and while they stayed with a creditor their labour was his.

They were redeemed when the debt was settled. Because their family was known, pawns were not usually mistreated. Legally, they could not be sold. They were a pledge, and they expected their term of servitude to be brief. For the creditor, pawns were an investment. Here was an additional dependant not related by kinship who could be called upon to perform a variety of beneficial functions. There was little to lose. If the pawn should die, another had to be provided, as long as there had been no serious mistreatment.

In all societies, a man could have control over many women, including slave, pawn and free.[17] Marrying a free woman required payments to her family, and hence a father with some wealth and authority could augment his position through the arrangement of good marriages for his daughters or nieces, depending upon patrilineal or matrilineal customs. Furthermore, a man could marry pawns and slaves and thereby avoid bride-wealth payments. In marrying a pawn, the debt was cancelled, and usually there were no obligations to the pawn's family. The cost of marrying a slave was the initial purchase price and, since her family was seldom known, the woman was completely dependent on her husband. These unions with pawns and slaves were seldom the most preferred marriages; contracts between cousins were often the most desired unions because such marriages were between free people and strengthened kinship ties. None the less, once a respectable marriage was established, a man could then seek additional wives who were pawns or slaves.

These marital practices explain why servile women were in great demand. The nature of such relationships promoted assimilation not segregation. Women became part of the family. Those whom the master did not marry or take as concubines were given to his male dependants – sons, nephews, loyal followers. In all these cases, female slaves effectively became free dependants, especially after they bore children by a free man. By contrast, the slave wives of male slaves retained their servile status. In these situations there was usually no act of emancipation, nor could there be because kin ties were determined by birth. Full incorporation into a lineage, which corresponded to emancipation, came gradually, depending upon the degree of acculturation, marriage to full lineage members, and individual expressions of loyalty. In the absence of articulated classes, the slave status evolved in a manner similar to the changes in other social categories. Young people eventually became elders; slaves or their descendants gradually became members of the lineage.

Because many domestic slaves were women or girls, these observations on marital customs help to explain this evolution towards full assimilation. Women and slaves born in the family were easily assimilated, and the sale of such individuals was rare. Those taken as slaves when they were children, too, were seldom sold. These slaves were treated very much as members of the household. Their tasks may have been more menial, but they were often granted responsibilities in trade, craft production, or other occupations. Second-generation slaves could fare as well or better.

The emphasis on dependency could be reflected in religious practices; sacrifices, for example, were interpreted as an expression of continuity between this world and the next and the need for dependants in both. The killing of slaves and the quest for outsiders – or their heads – also emphasized dependency through the symbolism attached to such acts. These had no productive function but were indicators of social and economic standing. The demand for victims to be killed at funerals, religious rites, and political ceremonies could be haphazard and hence incidental, or it could become regularized and hence institutionalized. Funeral sites at Igbo-Ukwu suggest that the ninth-century ancestors of the Igbo had already developed a demand for sacrificial victims that could be supplied through the institution of slavery.[18] Archaeology cannot determine the social status of those buried along with nobles – they could be free wives, children, volunteers, or others. At some point in time, none the less, slaves did become the main source for such victims.

THE ISLAMIC FACTOR

The existence of slaves in societies that emphasized kinship and dependency permitted their integration into a vast network of international slavery. This integration probably stretched far back into the past, but only for those areas closest to the Mediterranean basin, the Persian Gulf, and the Indian Ocean. By the eighth, ninth, and tenth centuries AD, the Islamic world had become the heir to this long tradition of slavery, continuing the pattern of incorporating black slaves from Africa into the societies north of the Sahara and along the shores of the Indian Ocean. The Muslim states of this period interpreted the ancient tradition of slavery in accordance with their new religion, but many uses for slaves were the same as before – slaves were used in the military, administration, and domestic service. The names of titles, the treatment of concubines, and other specifics of slavery were modified, but the function of slaves in politics and society was largely the same. Despite the ancient tradition, the principal concern here is with the consolidation of slavery in its Islamic context; for over seven hundred years before 1450 the Islamic world was virtually the only external influence on the political economy of Africa.[19]

Initially slaves were prisoners captured in the holy wars that spread Islam from Arabia across North Africa and throughout the region of the Persian Gulf. Enslavement was justified on the basis of religion, and those who were not Muslims were legally enslavable. After the early caliphates were established, slaves came largely from frontier areas where holy war was still being waged. Hence an early division was established between the central Islamic lands and the frontier, and a degree of specialization entered into

15

this system of slavery. The central provinces of Islam provided the market for slaves; the supplies came from the frontier regions. Slaves were not necessarily black, although black slaves always constituted a significant proportion of the slave population. They came too from western Europe and from the steppes of southern Russia. They were often prisoners of war, non-Muslims who had resisted the expansion of Islam. Slavery was conceived of as a form of religious apprenticeship for pagans. Early on, resident Jews and Christians were given special status as 'people of the book', who were recognized as free men subject to special taxes and limitations on civil liberties but exempt from enslavement. Some Christians were enslaved during war, especially in western Europe, but most slaves came from elsewhere.

The nature of the demand for slaves reveals some important features of the trade. Women and children were wanted in greater numbers than men. They were also more likely to be incorporated into Muslim society. Boys, either eunuch or virile, were trained for military or domestic service, and some of the more promising were promoted. Females also became domestics, and the prettiest were placed in harems, a factor that strongly influenced slave prices. Adult males and the least attractive women were destined for the more menial and laborious tasks, and their numbers had constantly to be replenished through new imports. This slavery was not a self-perpetuating institution, and those born into slavery formed a relatively small proportion of the slave population. Most children of slaves were assimilated into Muslim society, only to be replaced by new imports. Emancipation, concubinage, domestic servitude, political appointment and military position also mitigated against the establishment of a slave class with a distinct class consciousness. Race, too, was minimized as a factor in the maintenance of servile status. The religious requirement that new slaves be pagans and the need for continued imports to maintain the slave population made black Africa an important source of slaves for the Islamic world. Since sub-Saharan Africa was initially beyond the lands of Islam, Muslim and other merchants looked to Africa for slaves. Local warfare, convicted criminals, kidnapping, and probably debt were sources of slaves for visiting merchants, who individually gathered slaves in small lots for shipment by boat across the Red Sea or up the East African coast, or joined together to form caravans for the march across the Sahara. The export trade was relatively modest for many centuries before the fifteenth century and indeed did not really expand considerably until the nineteenth century. Exports amounted to a few thousand slaves per year at most times, and because the affected areas were often very extensive, the impact was usually minimized.

In the Islamic tradition, slavery was perceived as a means of converting non-Muslims. One task of the master, therefore, was religious instruction, and theoretically Muslims could not be enslaved, although this was often violated in practice. Conversion did not automatically lead to emancipation, but assimilation into the society of the master as judged by religious observance was deemed a prerequisite for emancipation and was normally some guarantee of better treatment. One aspect of the religious and related legal tradition was that emancipation as the act of freeing slaves and thereby changing their status was clearly defined. In societies based on kinship, emancipation was a process that was recognized through progressive integration of successive generations through marriage until people fully belonged to the group. There was often no act of emancipation as such. In Islamic practice, there was.

The functions performed by slaves were also different, in part because the structures of Islamic societies were often on a larger scale than among kinship groups. In the large Islamic states of the Mediterranean basin, for example, slaves were used in government and the military, occupations that did not exist in stateless societies. Slave officials and soldiers often proved very loyal because of the dependency on their master for status. Eunuchs comprised a special category of slave that does not seem to have been characteristic of most non-Muslim societies based on kinship. Eunuchs, who could be used in administrative positions and as overseers of harems, were especially dependent, without even the chance of establishing interests that were independent of their master. Under the influence of Islam, this practice spread into sub-Saharan Africa, along with the employment of slaves in the army and bureaucracy.

The Islamic view of slave women was also different from one based on kinship. Islamic law limited the number of wives to four, although only material considerations and personal whim limited the number of concubines. In both Islamic and non-Islamic situations, men could have as many women as they could afford, but the legal setting was different. Islamic custom, again emphasizing a clearer line between slave and free, allowed for the emancipation of concubines who bore children by the master. Legally they became free upon the death of the master, but they could not be sold once they gave birth. In practice, the wives of slave origin in societies based on kinship were seldom sold either, and their status was closer to that of becoming a member of the kin group and hence free. The terms of reference differed, but the practice was quite similar.

In many Islamic societies, slaves also performed tasks that were more directly related to production and trade. Certainly the scale of economic activity in the Mediterranean and Indian Ocean basins involved greater exchange, a higher level of technological development, and the possibilities of more specialized exploitation of slave labour than in most of black Africa until recent times. In fact, slaves were frequently assigned tasks that were not directly productive but instead supported a political and social hierarchy that exploited a population of free peasants, craftsmen, and servile populations that were not slave. Although slaves were most often used for domestic (including sexual) purposes, or in government and the military, occasionally they were employed in production, such as in the salt-mines of

Arabia, Persia, and the northern Sahara. Other slaves were employed in large-scale agricultural enterprises and craft manufacturing. The frequency and scale of this labour, even though it was not the major form of production, was something quite different from the use of slaves in the less specialized economies of those African societies based on kinship.

These different uses for slaves, the more clearly defined distinction between slave and free, and the occasional employment of slaves in productive activities demonstrate a sharp distinction between the slavery of kin-based societies and the slavery of Islamic law and tradition. The most important difference was that slavery in Islamic lands had experienced a partial transformation of the kind that Finley identifies as significant in the institutionalization of slavery. A fully economic system based on slave labour had not taken place in most parts of the Islamic world between 700 and 1400, despite the importance of administrative and military slaves in the maintenance of Islamic society. Slave concubines and domestic slaves were common and indeed affected the nature of marriage as an institution and the organization of wealthy households. The adaptation of similar practices in sub-Saharan Africa involved a parallel transformation there.

THE TRANS-ATLANTIC TRADE

The rise and expansion of the European slave trade across the Atlantic Ocean had a decided impact on the evolution of slavery in Africa, particularly in those areas along the Guinea coast where the influence of Islam had been weak or nonexistent.[20] Whereas the demand for slaves in the non-African parts of the Islamic world had a relatively gradual but steady influence on the spread of Islamic ideas and practices through parts of Africa, the impact of the European market for slaves was more intense over a much shorter period, with a correspondingly different influence. Slave exports rose gradually during the first 150 years of the Atlantic trade, amounting to 367,000 slaves from 1450 to 1600. Thereafter the trade was truly large, on a scale that dwarfed all previous exports from Africa. The total volume for the Atlantic trade reached 11,698,000 slaves (see table 1.1), a figure derived from the pioneering census of Philip D. Curtin and the subsequent revisions of numerous scholars. The pull of the market had the effect of pushing indigenous forms of slavery further away from a social framework in which slavery was another form of dependency in societies based on kinship relationships to a system in which slaves played an increasingly important role in the economy. In short, this change also involved a transformation similar to the one that Finley has characterized as a fundamental shift in the way slavery can be embedded in a social formation.

The opening of the Atlantic to trade marked a radical break in the history of Africa, more especially because that trade involved the export of millions of slaves. Before this commercial development, the Atlantic shores of

18

Table 1.1 *Slave exports from Africa: the Atlantic trade*

Period	Volume	Per cent
1450–1600	367,000	3.1
1601–1700	1,868,000	16.0
1701–1800	6,133,000	52.4
1801–1900	3,330,000	28.5
TOTAL	11,698,000	100.0

Source: Tables 2.3, 3.2, 3.3, 7.1, and 7.5; Lovejoy 1982c.

Africa had been virtually isolated from the outside world. Some salt and fish were traded into the interior in exchange for food, but by and large the coastline was a barrier. The technological breakthrough of ocean shipping had a tremendous economic impact, making available new sources of wealth for local people and facilitating political change on an unprecedented scale. Slavery here was closely associated with this transformation, not only because slaves were a major export, but also because slaves became far more common in local society than previously.

The transformation in slavery that accompanied the expansion of the European demand for slaves was largely independent of Muslim Africa. This relatively separate impact introduced a new force that modified slavery in ways different from the changes that had taken place as a result of the Islamic connection in the northern savanna and along the East African coast. There was no tradition of Islamic law, nor were there other features of Islamic slave practice, including concubinage, eunuchs, and political–military officials with Islamic titles. One important result of European trade, therefore, was the consolidation of a distinctively non-Muslim form of slavery. Slavery underwent a transformation from a marginal feature of society to an important institution, but in most places slavery continued to be interpreted in the context of lineage structures, and this is here identified as 'lineage slavery'.

As an institution, lineage slavery shared the same basic features as all types of slavery: the property element, the alien identity, the role of violence, and productive and sexual exploitation. The striking difference was the remarkable absence of foreign influence on the ideological plane. There was almost no internalization of European attitudes towards slavery, as Islamic theories and practices had been adopted elsewhere. The impact of the market did effect some changes that can be traced to European influence, but this factor operated more on the economic level than in the realm of ideology. Slavery continued to be conceived of in terms of kinship, even as slaves were assigned new tasks. Slaves were increasingly used in government, trade, and the military, in ways that were similar to the use of slaves in Muslim countries. The framework and titles were different, but the

19

function was the same. The same was true in the control of women. Polygynous rules allowed men to have as many wives as they could acquire. There was no rationalization of this practice through laws governing the number of wives and the status of concubines, as there was in Islamic law. Nevertheless, the results were similar. Important men had many wives, some of whom were slaves, and this uneven distribution of women within society was an element of social control, particularly since women were often the principal agricultural workers as aell as the reproducers of kin. Control of women enabled the domination of production and reproduction. This aspect of slavery had an important impact on the export trade. Europeans wanted field-hands and mine workers. They did not really care about their sex, although they perhaps had a slight preference for males. Africans wanted women and children. There emerged a natural division of the slave population, with European merchants buying approximately two men for every woman, and sometimes even a greater proportion of men. The European trade was significantly different from the Muslim trade across the Sahara, Red Sea, and Indian Ocean. Muslims, too, wanted women, not men, as is evident in the higher prices for women in the Muslim trade.

The transformation of slavery in non-Muslim areas was related to the size of the export trade and the extent to which politicians and merchants catered to that trade through enslavement and commerce. As the number of slaves increased and the ability to maintain a sustained supply was established, it became possible to use slaves in new ways, not just using more slaves in the same ways. These new ways were sometimes related to increasing the scale of production, including gold, agricultural goods, craft commodities, and salt. In the nineteenth century, this productive use of slaves became important in many places. Irrespective of the difference in ideology from the European plantation economy of the Americas, slavery became firmly associated with an agricultural society that was based on large concentrations of slaves. There were many places where slavery was still conceived in terms of kinship and where slavery remained marginal to the basic organization of society. None the less, the more intensive enslavement of people and the growth in the slave trade affected the institution of slavery almost everywhere.

The interaction between the indigenous setting, Islamic influence, and the European demand for slaves provided the dynamics in the development of slavery in Africa over the past millennium, but these were not always independent variables. The indigenous setting, for example, cannot be reconstructed merely by stripping away the Islamic heritage or by temporarily ignoring the European market for slaves. That slavery probably existed in Africa before the diffusion of Islam is relatively certain, although its characteristics are not. If we mean by 'slave' people who were kidnapped, seized in war, or condemned to be sold as a result of crime or in compensation for crime, then slaves there were. Structurally, however, slavery was marginal.

20

The influence of Islam and the European market, and indeed many other political and economic developments, has affected the course of slavery. Once such factors had an impact on particular societies, the nature of slavery changed, and the result was a different indigenous setting. In short, the history of slavery was dynamic, and the changes that took place resulted in the emergence of slave societies in places where previously there had only been a few slaves in society. That is, slavery became a central institution and not a peripheral feature. Africa could be integrated into a network of international slavery because indigenous forms of dependency allowed the transfer of people from one social group to another. When kinship links were severed, as they were in the case of slavery, then it became necessary to move people from the point of enslavement to a more distant place. The trend of this movement was towards the external slave markets, those of the Islamic world and the Americas. Slaves tended to go from periphery to areas of more extensive economic and political development, both within Africa and outside Africa. Slaves were not imported into Africa; they were exported. To repeat the crucial dimension of the argument – the integration of Africa into an international network of slavery occurred because Africa was an area of slave supply. In Africa, therefore, there was a structural link between this ability to supply slaves for external use and the domestic employment of slaves.

The scale of this export trade demonstrates its impact. Almost 11.7 million African slaves were shipped to the Americas; perhaps as many more found their way to the Islamic countries of North Africa, Arabia, and India. Though the focus here is on the history of slavery within Africa, not the fate of Africans abroad, the volume of this trade was so substantial that it reveals an essential element in the social control of slaves, and indeed other dependants, in Africa. Export was one possibility that faced slaves; domestic exploitation was another. These were closely related structurally. Slaves were usually sold if they failed to perform their duties, and sale, not only across the Atlantic but also across the Sahara Desert, the Red Sea, and the Indian Ocean, was a form of punishment and hence a threat that helped control the actions of slaves. The trade entailed great risks for slaves, including forced marches, poor food, exposure to disease in a condition of exhaustion and hunger, and bad treatment. Death and permanent physical damage were common, and slaves knew it through personal experience.

As a source for the external trade since time immemorial, Africa was a reservoir where slaves were cheap and plentiful – indeed they were there for the taking. This feature, enslavement, was another dimension of slavery in Africa that strongly affected the history of the institution there. It is inaccurate to think that Africans enslaved their brothers – although this sometimes happened. Rather, Africans enslaved their enemies. This conception of who could be enslaved served the interests of the external market, and it enabled the political ascendency of some Africans on the continent. Warfare, kidnapping, and manipulation of judicial and religious

21

institutions account for the enslavement of most slaves, both those exported and those retained in Africa. Unlike other places where slavery was common, particularly the Americas and the central parts of the Islamic world, enslavement on a regular basis was one essential feature of slavery as an institution. Slave masters in the Americas and the major Islamic states relied on trade for most or all of their slaves. They were not usually responsible themselves for the direct enslavement of people. In Africa, the enslavers and the slave owners were often the same. Europe and the central Islamic lands looked to areas on their periphery as a source for slaves, and Africa was such a peripheral region – virtually the only one for the Americas and a major one for the Islamic countries. Slaves also moved within Africa, from areas that were more peripheral to places that were more central, but enslavement was usually a prominent feature everywhere. There was no separation in function between enslavement and slave use; these remained intricately associated.

This connection reveals a fundamental characteristic of slavery in Africa, and when fully articulated with the use of slaves in production slavery was transformed into a distinct mode of production. The history of slavery involved the interaction between enslavement, the slave trade, and the domestic use of slaves within Africa. An examination of this interaction demonstrates the emergence of a system of slavery that was basic to the political economy of many parts of the continent. This system expanded until the last decades of the nineteenth century. The process of enslavement increased; the trade grew in response to new and larger markets, and the use of slaves in Africa became more common. Related to the articulation of this system, with its structural links to other parts of the world, was the consolidation within Africa of a political and social structure that relied extensively on slavery. Production depended, in varying degrees, on slave labour. Political power relied on slave armies. External trade involved the sale of slaves, often as a major commodity.

2

On the frontiers of Islam, 1400–1600

Slavery was already fundamental to the social, political, and economic order of parts of the northern savanna, Ethiopia and the East African coast for several centuries before 1600. Enslavement was an organized activity, sanctioned by law and custom. Slaves were a principal commodity in trade, including the export sector, and slaves were important in the domestic sphere, not only as concubines, servants, soldiers, and administrators but also as common labourers. The combination of enslavement, trade, and employment of slaves in the domestic economy indicates that a slave mode of production had developed, although the scarcity of source material limits an analysis of the transformation that resulted in this situation. From 1400 to 1600 the geographical area where slavery was most important included a strip of territory along the southern borders of the Sahara Desert, the Red Sea shores, and the East African coast. For the period as a whole, slavery tended to expand; the use of slaves followed trade routes further into the interior from this narrow strip of territory, and the source of slaves for export tended to be south of the desert edge and inland from the Red Sea.

The dominant influence was Islamic, both because the major external market for slaves was North Africa and the Middle East and because Islam had become a strong influence within many of the states and societies in the northern savanna, the Ethiopian highlands and the East African coast where slaves were used extensively. The use of slaves in these places was similar to their use elsewhere in the Muslim world, although in sub-Saharan Africa slaves were more often used in production than they were in North Africa and the Middle East. A secondary influence in this period was the introduction of European commerce into the south Atlantic basin and the Indian Ocean. This contributed to the general expansion of slavery within Africa, in part because Europeans distributed slaves between different places on the African coast and in part because Europeans began to buy slaves on an increasingly large scale for their own use.

THE MEDIEVAL SLAVE TRADE: THE AFRICAN FRONTIER

The export trade across the Sahara Desert, Red Sea, and Indian Ocean was sustained on a level of 5,000 to 10,000 slaves per year for centuries before 1600 (see tables 2.1 and 2.2). Ralph Austen has estimated the volume of this trade to the Islamic world – admittedly on very scanty evidence.[1] The figures cited here, 4,820,000 for the Saharan trade between 650 and 1600 and 2,400,000 for the Red Sea and Indian Ocean trade between 800 and 1600, could be twice as many slaves as the number actually exported or considerably less than the total volume. The time span is so great and the supply area so extensive that the estimated figure (7,220,000) is a rough approximation indeed; a range of 3.5 to 10 million is more accurate. None the less, the thesis argued here would not be changed whether the real figure was closer to 3.5 million or 10 million; hence Austen's rough calculations are used as a convenient measure of the Islamic slave trade. This trade reflected a steady demand for slaves in the Islamic world and resulted in the maintenance of regular contact between sub-Saharan states and societies and Muslim merchants from foreign lands who had an important influence on the spread of Islamic law and its conception of slavery. Although slave exports came from a commercial frontier that stretched thousands of kilometres along the southern edge of the Sahara, the Red Sea, and the East African coast, there were relatively few export points, and consequently the impact of the trade was more concentrated than the distance might suggest. Six major routes crossed the desert: one went north from ancient Ghana to Morocco; a second stretched north from Timbuktu to Tuwat in southern Algeria; a third passed from the Niger valley and the Hausa towns through the Air Massif to Ghat and Ghadames; a fourth travelled north from Lake Chad to Murzuk in Libya; a fifth reached north from Dar Fur in the eastern Sudan to the Nile valley at Assiout; and a sixth passed north from the confluence of the Blue and White Nile to Egypt. Some of these routes were interconnected. The ones north from Timbuktu went to Morocco, Algeria, and Libya, while the Dar Fur–Egypt route, known as the forty days' road, connected with the route north from the upper Nile valley. The Red Sea ports served the Ethiopian highlands and the Nile valley and included Suakin, Massawa, Tajura, and Zeila. The East African towns comprised one route that stretched northward along the coast. In total, therefore, there were only nine or ten outlets for the slave trade to the Muslim world.

When the trade is broken down according to the main routes, then East Africa accounted for a traffic in the order of 1,000 slaves per year in the period from about 800 AD to 1600; the Red Sea ports probably handled something like 2,000 slaves per year in the same period; while the six main routes across the Sahara averaged from 3,000 to 8,000 per year. This suggests an average volume for each route of about 1,000 per annum. The Muslim slave trade involved a steady but relatively small flow over a

Table 2.1 *Trans-Saharan slave trade, 650–1600*

Period	Annual average	Estimated total
650–800	1,000	150,000
800–900	3,000	300,000
900–1100	8,700	1,740,000
1100–1400	5,500	1,650,000
1400–1500	4,300	430,000
1500–1600	5,500	550,000
TOTAL		4,820,000

Source: Austen 1979*a*, p. 66.

Table 2.2 *Red Sea and East African slave trade, 800–1600*

Red Sea coast	East African coast	Total
1,600,000	800,000	2,400,000

Source: Austen 1979*a*, p. 68.

millennium, and despite occasionally high levels for specific points there was not the sustained volume in slaves that characterized the Atlantic slave trade at its height. For the period before 1500, estimates are based on scattered records that suggest that some slaves were always being exported, probably in quantities of several hundred at a time and sometimes a few thousand. Perhaps a majority of these were women and children, but eunuchs were also important. Ibn Battuta, who crossed the Sahara in the middle of the fourteenth century, found that the traffic in slaves was largely confined to females and eunuchs. Indeed, Ibn Battuta travelled in one caravan of 600 female slaves.[2]

In the sixteenth century, slave exports from Songhay and Borno probably reached their peak. Songhay had great numbers of slaves, while the decline in gold exports probably required an increase in slave exports to make up the difference in revenue. Songhay princes amassed slaves in raids to the south.[3] Borno expanded considerably in the sixteenth century and probably increased its supply of slaves to the trans-Saharan market via the Lake Chad–Murzuk route. The Borno kings continued a tradition of slave supply that had been initiated centuries earlier when Kanem was the centre of the state.[4] This era of slave exports ended around 1600, after a final burst of activity that was probably unparalleled in earlier times. The Moroccan conquest of Songhay in 1591 witnessed a temporary increase in the volume of the trade, as thousands of captives were taken. Once the war captives were marched north, however, the trade probably settled back into the centuries-old pattern of a thousand or so per year on each route.

25

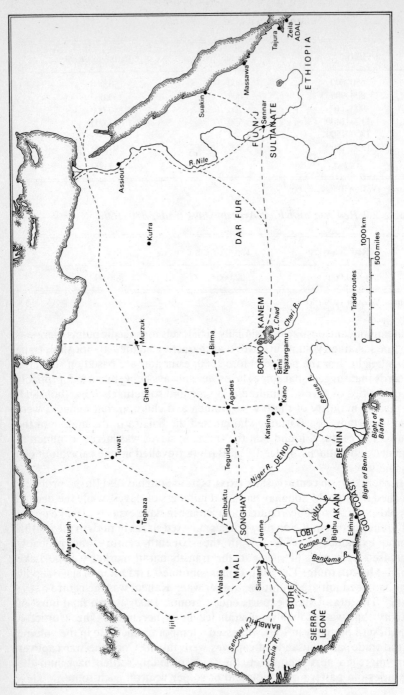

1 The Islamic slave trade in the sixteenth century

Slaves were also a major export from the Nile valley and the Ethiopian highlands in the sixteenth century. Muslim expansion and the reaction to Islam in both areas account for the volume of exports.[5] In Ethiopia, a Muslim holy war, directed from the sultanate of Adal, temporarily overran the Christian Kingdom, so that from the 1520s through the 1540s thousands of slaves were exported across the Red Sea. Thereafter, a Christian revival checked the Muslim threat with the result that more people were enslaved. By the end of the century, the nomadic Galla exploited the unstable political conditions of the region, and other slaves were exported. In the Nile valley, a Muslim state was established at Sennar by the Funj, and its wars of conquest, from which the earlier Christian kingdoms did not recover, resulted in the export of many slaves via the Red Sea and the desert-crossing north to Egypt. The East African coast, although a source of some slaves, does not seem to have been particularly important in the sixteenth century.

The political history of those states participating in the export trade reveals that sub-Saharan Africa was not dependent upon slave exports, even though revenue from the slave trade was probably a major source of income for some merchants and some rulers. The interaction between the external world and such states as Songhay, Borno, and Christian Ethiopia was on a relatively equal basis, at least until the sixteenth century. Portuguese intervention along the East African coast, the Muslim holy war in Ethiopia, and the Moroccan invasion of Songhay shifted the balance in favour of external powers temporarily, but even then the balance was restored by about 1600. The relative autonomy of sub-Saharan African states was reflected in the institution of slavery. Africa became a source of slaves, but not at the expense of its political and cultural independence. The incorporation of Islamic ideas and practices occurred gradually over many centuries in a form that was interpreted within a local context.

This autonomy meant that indigenous developments were more important than external influences in the consolidation of a mode of production based on slavery. The institutionalization of the enslavement process made it possible to export slaves and to use them domestically. Slaves were often a product of war and raiding; certainly very early in the history of the northern savanna and Ethiopia, enslavement of war prisoners became an acceptable practice. Slaves tended to be a by-product of politically-motivated military activities, therefore. The export trade may well have provided some incentive for enslavement, but localized political issues were probably more important. No matter what the relative importance of external and internal factors, both sectors were mutually re-enforcing. This is clear in the account of Cadamosto, a member of a Portuguese mission to the Senegal River in 1455–6, who reported that the king of a small Wolof state raised revenue through 'raids which resulted in many slaves from his own as well as neighbouring countries'.[6] Cadamosto clearly did not understand the reasons why the king had reportedly attacked his own people, probably a campaign related to domestic political rivalry or rebellion, if his information was correct at all. None the less, his report does indicate that the acquisition of slaves through wars and raids was common by the fifteenth century, which confirms evidence for elsewhere in the northern savanna, including Songhay, Mali, Borno, and the Hausa states.

These states shared a structural problem related to the prevalence of enslavement and slavery. Slave raiding could not be carried on indefinitely without depleting the population of the exploited societies. People were either seized or they fled, if they were not able to mount an effective resistance. War parties were forced to travel increasingly greater distances, thereby reducing their chances of successful raids. The consolidation of walled towns throughout the savanna further limited the raiding frontier, but then competing centres could attack each other in the hope of capturing slaves and depriving neighbouring towns of their political independence. Both situations – the withdrawal of people from the raiding frontier and the political rivalries of states based on walled towns – were inherently unstable. Ecological factors also influenced this instability. Firstly, those states in the northern parts of the savanna had the military advantage over states further south through access to better breeding grounds for horses, the mainstay of military superiority. None the less, the northern savanna was more exposed to raids from desert nomads, whose use of camels gave them the advantage of strategic surprise. Secondly, periodic droughts affected the northern savanna severely, and when drought lasted more than a year at a stretch many people were forced to move south. Lands that were sparsely settled were available to these migrants, who might in turn become subject to future raids, once climatic conditions returned to normal.[7]

In this cyclical pattern of history, warriors and politicians could consolidate large empires, as they did in the case of Ghana, Mali, Songhay, Borno, and Sennar. In these cases, political success pushed the raiding frontier back considerably; now rulers were concerned to establish tributary relationships with subjugated provinces and to transform independent farmers into tax-paying peasants and tribute-paying serfs, as well as slaves. The tendency towards political instability, slave raiding, and rivalry between neighbouring towns was temporarily halted. When empires collapsed, however, these tendencies re-emerged.

THE INSTITUTION OF SLAVERY IN MUSLIM AFRICA

In the narrow strip of territory along the southern edge of the Sahara, the Red Sea shores, and the East African coast, the Muslim presence contributed to the transformation of society and political structures.[8] As the political–commercial classes converted to Islam, they adapted things and ways that were identified with Islam to the African setting. There included political titles, for example, although such positions already existed. In Mali, slave officials were appointed as early as the thirteenth century,[9] and slaves were drafted into the army. These uses in the military and government were parallel in function to the employment of slaves in the Muslim countries of the Mediterranean and Middle East heartlands. Not only was the external trade a source of valuable imports, but it helped spread such institutions. Muslims increasingly assumed a role in politics, education, and trade in particular. This consolidation of a Muslim society, often as an island in a sea of non-Muslims, helped structure the political economy.

In supplying slaves, African rulers found it convenient to justify enslavement from an Islamic perspective: prisoners of war could be sold, and since captive people were considered chattels, they could be used in the same capacities as they were in the Muslim world. They could be soldiers, administrators, concubines, domestic servants, and agricultural workers. The participation of such African states as Ghana, Mali, Songhay, Kanem, Sennar, and Adal in the slave trade occurred together with the extension of Islamic influence to sub-Saharan Africa. Similarly, the Muslim merchants along the East African coast – the ancestors of the Swahili – transferred the Muslim conception of slavery into black Africa there.

Muslim attitudes towards slavery were internalized in the African context. In a letter dated 1391–2, Borno's King Uthman ibn Idris protested to the *mamluk* regime of Egypt that Arab raiding parties were enslaving free Muslims, even members of the royal family, and selling them across the Sahara:

> The Arab tribes of Jodham and others have taken our free subjects, women and children and old men of our own family, and other Muslims . . . These Arabs have pillaged our land, the land of Bornu, and continue doing so. They have taken as slaves free men and our fathers, the Muslims, and they are selling them to the slave-dealers of Egypt, Syria, and elsewhere, and keep some of them for themselves . . . Send messengers throughout your country . . . let them examine and enquire and so discover. When they have found our people, let them confront them . . . If they say: 'We are free men and Muslims,' then believe their word and do not suspect them of lying, and when the truth is made plain to you, release them and return them to their liberty and Islam.[10]

Undoubtedly, Borno's king was indirectly seeking support in his wars with Kanem, and by casting his enemies in the role of villains, Uthman hoped to confirm his own allegiance to Islam and thereby that he was worthy of support. Indeed, Uthman argued that he was descended from a dynasty of Middle Eastern origin, which was also an attempt at establishing the legitimacy of the Borno regime. None the less, the letter documents attitudes towards enslavement that became standard in the Islamic belt of Africa. Free Muslims were protected from enslavement, at least theoretically; in practice, free men were enslaved, and little could be done to protect them, despite the efforts of influential men like Uthman.

In the reign of Idris Aloma of Borno in the last quarter of the sixteenth century, one military campaign in Kanem, north-east of Lake Chad, reputedly netted 1,000 female and 2,000 male slaves, who were divided among the soldiers. Another 400 free men, seized in the campaign, were supposedly executed.[11] This suggests that the slave population of Kanem was subtantial, although the actual numbers of slaves reported in this history cannot be accepted at face value, for the court historian, Ibn Fartua, may well have exaggerated to glorify his mentor's exploits. None the less, this report indicates that free Muslims were not supposed to be enslaved; only those already in bondage or those considered pagan were legitimate targets. For sixteenth-century Kanem, which was nominally Muslim, the free population was technically protected from enslavement, and hence Ibn Fartua apparently felt compelled to label all captives who were not executed as already being slaves. The ratio of women to men in the account is also revealing, since more women than men were exported across the Sahara. Not only is this indirectly confirmed, but the availability of so many male slaves suggests that slavery must have been important in production.

Ahmad Bābā, an Islamic scholar from Timbuktu who lived from 1556 to 1627, wrote a book on slavery, *Mi'rāj al-Su'ūd ilā Nayl Hukm majlub al-Sūd* (1614), in which he condemned the enslavement of Muslims but otherwise accepted enslavement as a legal pursuit for Muslims.[12] After the Moroccan invasion of Songhay in 1591–2, Ahmad Bābā was exiled to Marrakesh in Morocco, where he continued to pursue his scholarship and became famous for his relentless campaign to free Muslims who had been illegally enslaved. The collapse of Songhay was a tragic affair in the history of Islam, for both Songhay and Morocco were Muslim states, and many slaves were seized in the course of battle. Although the *Mi'raj* was an indictment of contemporary politics, Ahmad Bābā's legal interpretation was based on earlier scholarly opinions; hence the book also chronicles attitudes towards slavery over many centuries:

> the reason for slavery is non-belief and the Sudanese non-believers are like other *kāfir* whether they are Christians, Jews, Persians, Berbers, or any others who stick to non-belief and do not embrace Islam . . . This means that there is no difference between all the *kāfir* in this respect. Whoever is captured in a condition of non-belief, it is legal to own him, whosoever he may be, but not he who was converted to Islam voluntarily, from the start, to any nation he belongs, whether it is Bornu, Kano, Songhai, Katsina, Gobir, Mali and some of Zakzak [Zazzau]. These are free Muslims, whose enslavement is not allowed in any way. Also the majority of the Fulani, except a group beyond Gao, as we have been informed, who are said to be *kāfir*.[13]

Those countries that Ahmad Bābā considered Muslim formed an almost continuous belt of territory from the headwaters of the Senegal River in the west to Lake Chad in the east. Elsewhere in his book, he condemned these savanna states because they also enslaved Muslims. Ahmad Bābā was as concerned with the illegality of local practices as with those resulting from external invasion. The difficulty facing Muslims of this period was to justify slavery in the context of political expansion and rivalry, when such actions invariably led to abuse. Allowance had to be made for an institution that was well established and commercially profitable, and yet Muslims had to be protected. Ahmad Bābā's attempt to expose particular injustices reveals a fundamental contradiction in Muslim society that plagued thoughtful people for the next few centuries. There was no effective means of preventing abuse. Ahmad Bābā justified enslavement on religious grounds, clearly establishing a boundary between the land of Islam and the land of unbelief. This legalism is instructive of the process by which slavery spread in the savanna regions of Africa. For those who accepted a Muslim interpretation, enslavement was a legitimate activity; war was a normal relationship between Muslims and non-Muslims who did not accept their subjugation.

Slaves were not only used in the military and government, taken as concubines, and exported across the Sahara Desert; they were also employed in production. This use helps distinguish slavery in sub-Saharan Africa from slavery in the Muslim heartlands, where the productive function was not as important in the century or two before 1600. According to Cadamosto, the king of Wolof not only sold slaves to visiting merchants but he also 'employs these slaves [whom he captures] in cultivating the land allotted to him'.[14] These slaves had no opportunity to attain the material prosperity or social standing of the favourite slaves of savanna rulers. Instead, they farmed for merchants and officials alike, producing crops under conditions that bear some resemblance to the later plantations of the Americas or to the contemporary feudal estates of Europe. The more exact comparison, in fact, is with the agricultural estates of southern Morocco and the islands of the Mediterranean, with which they were contemporary and with which they shared a common legal and religious setting.[15] These plantations were a by-product of a political order based on enslavement and the export of slaves. Throughout the borderlands between the Sahara and the more fertile savanna, these agricultural slaves were settled in villages of their own, often under slave overseers. Their absentee owners, be they merchants travelling to distant lands for gold, salt, and other goods, or government officials busy at the capital or some remote post, exploited slave labour for their own benefit. Agricultural output, including millet and sorghum, cotton and indigo, as well as vegetables and tree crops, supplied the large commercial establishments of caravan merchants and the palaces of nobles. The surplus was sold to desert nomads who transported goods from North Africa and who brought salt from the Sahara Desert or the Ethiopian coastal lowlands. The army consumed much of this plantation output; sometimes slave soldiers even contributed to agricultural production.

By the sixteenth century, Songhay masters had settled their slaves along the Niger River, so that the Niger valley had become well populated and agriculturally productive, probably more so than at any time since then. The nature of these slave communities is open to debate. Some historians refer to them as plantatíons, others compare them with feudal estates. But their existence is certain.[16] Gao, which in the nineteenth century was an undistinguished hamlet, was a large city in the sixteenth century, and near it were many estates with several dozen to several hundred slaves each. By the early sixteenth century, there were plantations along the river from Jenne to Dendi at over thirty locations. Some of these concentrations were very large; there were an estimated 1,700 to 2,700 slaves at Faran-Taka, for example. This plantation sector reached its most extensive development under Askia Daoud, between 1549 and 1583.[17] These slave estates demonstrate an important feature of the slave trade; wherever slaves were exported, they were often used domestically in large numbers. As the case of Songhay so clearly shows, exports on the scale of a few thousand slaves per year could reflect the existence of a domestic slave population of considerable size, although usually it is not possible to know the exact proportion of slaves in the population.

These plantations transformed the inner Niger valley into a heavily populated and productive region.[18] With the millet, sorghum, wheat, and rice that came from these irrigated fields, the imperial administration was able to expand militarily and to maintain the empire. The river not only permitted agricultural development, but it also made possible the transport of grain upstream and downstream as needed by the state. The general movement of agricultural goods was northward from the savanna to the towns of the sahel and to the desert market. In locally bad years, grain could move both ways, of course. The river increased the political options of the state, so that control of the Niger was essential to the functioning of a well-managed economy.

Slaves were used in gold mining, at least in the western Sudan, if not also in Ethiopia and the Zambezi valley. The western Sudanese sources included Bambuhu (Bambuk), Buré, Lobi, and the Akan fields. Valentim Fernandes records a report from the Senegalese coast that dates to the first decade of the sixteenth century (*c*. 1507), which states:

> The gold mines are seven in number. They are shared by seven kings, each of whom has his own. The mines are extremely deep down in the earth. The kings have slaves they place in the mines, and to whom they give wives they bring with them. Children are born and raised in these mines. The kings provide them as well with food and drink.[19]

Since gold was a major export from West Africa at this time, the role of slaves in gold production suggests that here was another sector in which slavery had become crucial to the economy.

The same applied to the use of slaves in the Teghaza salt-works in the Sahara, and perhaps elsewhere too. At Teghaza, slaves cut the rock salt into slabs for transport to the savanna markets. Conditions in these desert sites were far from pleasant: it was hot; food was monotonous; and there were few ways to escape the hard work and boredom of the bleak desert. Houses were made of salt slabs. Virtually all the food was imported, but conditions of exchange were closely regulated by the slave masters, the Mossefa Berbers, and by the Tuareg transporters. If the economics of the trade dictated against a satisfactory life at these desert salt-works, the social and political setting assured that whatever profit was to be made would not benefit the slave workers. Slavery was not always an essential feature of the salt trade, for it was possible, as at Bilma and other desert salt-works, for free peasants to be kept in economic and political conditions of servitude that were not very different from those for slaves.[20] None the less, slavery was one answer, and the type of slavery was far more brutal than the usual style of slavery in the middle ages, where slaves could be absorbed into domestic units. Similar conditions prevailed at the copper-works at Teguida n'tesemt.

The pattern of slavery in the Nile valley and the Ethiopian region was similar to that of the central and western Sudan. Despite the presence of Christian states as well as Muslim sultanates, the trend involved the consolidation of Islamic trade and society, and consequently Islamic patterns of slave use prevailed. Most merchants, for example, were Muslims, even in Christian Ethiopia, and hence the export trade across the Red Sea and along the Nile valley remained in Muslim hands. Slavery, too, conformed to an Islamic model that used slaves in the military, harems, agriculture, and government.[21]

The East African pattern was somewhat different from that found along the southern side of the Sahara and adjacent to the Red Sea.[22] Here there were no Islamic empires or strong states actively involved in slave raiding. Instead, the coast was dotted with a string of commercial towns that relayed goods between the Zambezi valley in the south to ports in Arabia and India. Gold, ivory, and slaves came from the interior of the Zambezi valley, and some slaves were obtained locally at many points along the coast. None the less, slavery here was similar to that found elsewhere in the Muslim world. Concubines, domestic servants, officials of the petty rulers of the coastal ports, and plantation slaves constituted the servile population. Plantations were concentrated at several points, including the area around Mombasa and Malindi in the north and on the north-west coast of Madagascar, opposite the mainland.

The absence of a clearly-defined slave class is a significant feature of Muslim Africa during the middle ages. Exploitation was based on a class that had access to political office and commercial credit. Merchants and officials benefited from tribute, taxation, commercial profit, and the output of slaves. Despite the restrictions placed on admission to the merchant community and to high office, slavery was not a barrier. Merchants had to be Muslims, and they identified ethnically. Rulers had to have an aristocratic heritage that showed a clear ancestry. In neither case were slaves excluded. Slave women were taken as wives and concubines, and consequently their children had legitimate claims. Slaves became commercial agents, if they could prove their competence and loyalty, and they were appointed to official positions. Seldom did slave agents inherit, but they could marry the free-born once they themselves were free, and by so doing they established a claim to a legitimate ancestry.

Slave labour was important, too. Without slaves, much of the salt would have had to have been worked in other ways. A significant proportion of farm output also depended upon slaves, and in most households domestic slaves engaged in textile production, mat and basket weaving, and other crafts. Livestock herders used slaves to dig wells, tend herds, gather firewood, and farm. These occupations were also performed by free peasants who paid tax or tribute, participated in corvée projects, and, if they were beyond the confines of the state or were part of a delinquent province, were subject to raiding, plunder, and enslavement. Castes like the blacksmiths and fishermen, though they owned slaves themselves, were subject to special exactions, too. Slavery was only one form of exploitative relationship that dominated African Islamic society in this period.

Slavery provides a key to understanding African history, however varied the relationships of exploitation were. The ultimate threat of the state was the slave raid. Raiding did not just involve enslavement; it also caused death. There was little need for the old or the very young, and many were probably killed during military campaigns. Families were divided, and since there was a greater demand for women and children, men were often executed. Even when communities survived raids, they frequently suffered the destruction of their fields and homes and lost their livestock and other moveable property. The danger of famine and crippling poverty were serious problems confronting the survivors.

For those who were enslaved, the dangers involved forced marches, inadequate food, sexual abuse, and death on the road. The Sahara crossing was the greatest risk for many slaves. The trip was so long, and food and water so carefully managed, that the slightest mishap from a raid on the caravan or an empty water-hole could eliminate whole coffles of slaves. Still other captives, the prime boys, faced castration because the price for eunuchs was always very high – and no wonder the price was high, since death from unsuccessful operations could be as large as nine boys out of ten.

The danger incumbent on enslavement, therefore, was one of the worst dimensions of slavery, for at the time of capture, the enslavers could treat their chattel however they pleased. Victims could be killed or left to face poverty and famine. They could be emasculated. They could be marched to their death, with each point of transfer bringing unknown prospects for the slave. The legitimization of enslavement, therefore, reinforced a tendency towards war and other forms of violence. Because this threat was ever present, people were placed in the dilemma of accepting some type of dependent relationship to political authority or risking enslavement and death. The enslaved themselves were placed in positions that contributed to this cycle of oppression. They made up the armies, fed the political administration and the soldiers, and were the products of trade that benefited the powerful. Slavery infected all levels of society and economy.

34

The threat of slave raids convinced people to pay tribute regularly, while the caste structure emphasized the distinction between slave and free by maintaining a corporate identity for blacksmiths, minstrels, fishermen, and merchants. Despite the absence of a clearly-defined class of slaves, slavery was the cement of the social formation. Slavery emphasized the dependency that characterized all relationships, and as the ultimate punishment for those who refused to submit to a state, it held the whole range of possibilities that existed in the social order, from death to hard physical labour, to high position, to sale abroad. Slavery was the great equalizer, but it revealed the essential inequality of African society.

ORIGINS OF THE ATLANTIC TRADE: THE MUSLIM CONNECTION

The first Portuguese caravels edged down the Atlantic coast of Africa in the 1430s and 1440s, reaching the Senegal River by 1445.[23] In so doing, they opened another route that paralleled the trans-Saharan roads. The Portuguese were more interested in gold than slaves, although they were willing to trade in pepper, ivory, and other products. Their investment in this exploration of the African coast was a conscious effort to bypass Muslim middlemen; initially, the Portuguese only succeeded in expanding the existing trans-Saharan trade by opening the maritime route; later, they participated in internal African trade as middlemen themselves. Structurally, therefore, both the Portuguese and the Muslim traders filled the same functions: they connected sub-Saharan Africa with the Mediterranean world and they participated in the regional commerce of West Africa.

The early slave trade of the Portuguese demonstrates this similarity to the established commercial patterns in four ways. Firstly, some slaves were taken to southern Europe for employment as domestic servants, a demand like that in the Islamic countries of North Africa and the Middle East.[24] Secondly, other slaves were sold to sugar planters on islands in the Mediterranean, and when sugar production spread into the Atlantic, to buyers on Madeira, the Canaries, and the Cape Verde Islands.[25] In both cases – domestic servitude and sugar production – the market was already satisfied to some extent by the trans-Saharan trade. Thirdly, the Portuguese bought and sold slaves along the West African coast, merely transferring slaves from one place to another so that gold could be purchased as a result of the profits realized from the transit trade.[26] Again, Muslim merchants in the interior of West Africa did the same thing. Finally, the link to the trans-Saharan trade is particularly evident in the commodities exported to West Africa by the Portuguese; these included textiles and other goods bought in North Africa.[27] Cadamosto, who participated in a Portuguese expedition to the Senegambia in 1455–6, was well aware of this competition with the trans-Saharan trade, evident in his observation that the Wolof king

35

'sells many [slaves] to the Azanaghi merchants in return for horses and other goods, and also to the Christians, since they have begun to trade with these blacks'.[28]

The total volume of the slave trade was about 40,000–45,000 for the first five decades of Portuguese trade along the Guinea coast (see table 2.3), and the 800 or so slaves bought and sold each year largely fitted into other, established, commercial patterns that the Portuguese were able to tap. In the Senegambia region, for example, the Portuguese were able to buy gold, which came from Bambuhu and Buré in the interior,[29] which were important sources of gold before new and larger deposits were discovered in the Americas. Another reason was that trade was well established in the Senegambia, and the particular geographical features of the region made it easy for sea-borne merchants from Portugal to tap existing commerce. Both the Senegal and Gambia Rivers were navigable inland, and they crossed the routes north into the Sahara to the Mediterranean. It was possible, therefore, to divert some trade to the coast, including gold, slaves, and other goods. Major salt sources were located near the coast north of Senegal and the Gambia. Consequently, Muslim merchants were already moving goods – salt, slaves, textiles, fish, and grain – back and forth between the coast and the interior. It was easy to introduce European commodities in order to buy gold and slaves. This trade continued throughout the whole period of the Atlantic trade, sometimes amounting to a few thousand slaves per year.

Elsewhere in West Africa, the Portuguese found an active trade in slaves on the Gold Coast, where they were also able to purchase gold.[30] Muslim merchants had established commercial links this far south in pursuit of the same gold and, as with the Senegambia, they were on the coast itself. Gold was found in alluvial washings throughout the forest, so that it was easy once

Table 2.3 *Growth of the Atlantic slave trade, 1451–1600*

Period	Imports (Americas, Atlantic basin)	Annual Average	Exports (15% loss in transit)	Exports (20% loss in transit)	Exports (25% loss in transit)	Annual average (20% loss)
1451–75	15,000	600	17,600	18,800	20,000	750
1476–1500	18,500	700	21,800	23,100	24,700	900
1501–25	42,500	1,700	50,000	53,100	56,700	2,100
1526–50	43,800	1,800	51,500	54,800	58,400	2,200
1551–75	61,000	2,500	72,100	76,600	81,700	3,100
1576–1600	112,300	4,500	132,100	140,400	149,700	5,600
TOTAL	293,100		345,100	366,800	391,200	

Sources: Curtin 1969, p. 116; and Vila Vilar 1977*b*, pp. 206–9.

again for the Portuguese to buy gold there. The Muslim network was long established, however, so that the Portuguese dealt with these merchants as well as the actual producers of gold. The Muslim traders took gold north from the Akan deposits towards Timbuktu and thence across the Sahara. They traded in many other goods, too. They brought salt, livestock, textiles, and copper-ware south, and to the north they took kola nuts which were widely consumed in the savanna as a stimulant. The Portuguese imported slaves to buy gold. Perhaps ironically, the first European slave-traders on this stretch of coast became involved as carriers in the domestic slave-trade of West Africa. As was the case in the Senegambia, therefore, the early contribution of the Portuguese to the slave trade was to modify existing patterns of commerce. The Portuguese began purchasing slaves in the 'slave rivers' of the Benin coast sometime in the 1470s, and the 1480 expedition acquired 400 slaves.[31] By the early sixteenth century, the trade between the Bight of Benin and the Gold Coast was in the order of 500 to 600 slaves per year. These were channelled through the Portuguese depot at São Jorge da Mina, later to be called Elmina. These slaves were sold to African merchants for use as porters in the trade with the interior, although a few were kept at São Jorge da Mina as labourers.[32]

In the first two decades of the sixteenth century, slave exports increased dramatically, rising to about two thousand per year, a level that was maintained at least until the mid-century. This increase was related to the inclusion of the Kingdom of Kongo into the commercial network of the Portuguese and to the development of the island of São Thomé, located off shore in the Gulf of Guinea, as a transit point for the slave trade and a plantation centre for the production of sugar cane. These developments were a further extension of existing commercial practices. São Thomé became another in a string of depots: slaves were brought from Kongo to the island for trans-shipment to the Gold Coast, Madeira, the Cape Verde Islands, and Portugal. Between 1510 and 1540, four to six slaving vessels were kept continually occupied hauling slaves to the Gold Coast, for example. Cargoes varied in size from caravels that could carry 30 to 80 slaves, to larger vessels that could transport as many as 100 to 120 slaves.[33]

The emergence of a trade that was independent of the Muslim sector was closely associated with the Kingdom of Kongo, the major state on the coast of central Africa when the Portuguese arrived there in 1482.[34] King Afonso I (1506–45) formed an alliance with the Portuguese crown, through their representatives at the Kongolese capital of São Salvador and on the islands of São Thomé and Principé. Afonso attempted to introduce reforms designed to increase his power, including the acceptance of Christianity and the reliance on Portuguese advisors. Afonso used the slave trade to promote the interests of the state. Through border skirmishes and tribute collection, the state acquired slaves for export. Afonso even managed the transport of some slaves to São Thomé through the agency of two members of the royal household who were stationed in São Thomé in 1526.[35]

These efforts at centralization were only partially successful; indeed the recurrent theme of Kongolese history in the sixteenth century was one of conflict between royal attempts at monopoly and the activities of private traders, both Portuguese and Kongolese. On the one side, Afonso directed trade through São Salvador and the port of Mpinda, near the mouth of the Zaire River.[36] Except for the provincial governors of Ndongo, in the south, the nobility cooperated with these royal efforts. A board of enquiry protected official interests by investigating alleged kidnappings, which attempted to restrain the movement of private traders. Private traders, on the other hand, were not to be outdone. The clients of Fernão de Melo, who had the Portuguese charter for São Thomé, and Antonio Carneiro, who had the charter for Principé, bought slaves wherever they could. By the 1520s, their agents travelled into the interior beyond São Salvador, probably as far as Malebo Pool (Stanley Pool) on the Zaire River and Ndongo in the south.[37]

The principal conflict was between slave traders, official and private, and not between Kongo and Portugal, despite occasional differences over the autonomy of the Catholic Church in Kongo and other issues. This struggle over the control of trade facilitated the growth of slave exports. In the 1520s, exports from Mpinda were in the order of 2,000 to 3,000 per year. By the 1530s, the volume had increased from 4,000 to 5,000 in some years, and in 1548, to from 6,000 to 7,000. Most of these slaves were sent to São Thomé, from where they were redistributed elsewhere or used on local plantations. São Thomé began exporting to the Americas in the 1530s, and by 1550 the bulk of the transit trade was destined for the Spanish Caribbean. Thereafter, the trade to the Americas predominated until the decline of São Thomé at the end of the sixteenth century.[38]

The Kongo–São Thomé axis collapsed in the last third of the sixteenth century. In 1568, invaders from the interior penetrated the kingdom, even occupying São Salvador until a combined Portuguese–Kongolese expedition relieved the capital. This weakened Kongo temporarily, which worked to the advantage of the private traders. In 1576, the Portuguese crown, interested in containing the interlopers itself but relying less on the Kongo monarchy than previously, established a base at Luanda Bay, which had become the main avenue into the interior south of Kongo.[39] Now slaves were shipped directly to the Americas from Luanda, as well as from São Thomé. Official Portuguese efforts appear to have impeded the interlopers somewhat; before the establishment of Luanda, this southern trade from Ndongo was estimated at 10,000 slaves in peak years; after 1576, exports declined, although the government share increased. The private traders were forced to bypass the Portuguese stations, just as they had previously bypassed the Kongolese capital at the height of Kongolese control. As a result, the trade as a whole probably remained at about the same level, that is, several thousand slaves per year.

From 1451 to 1600, 345,000–391,000 slaves were exported from Africa via

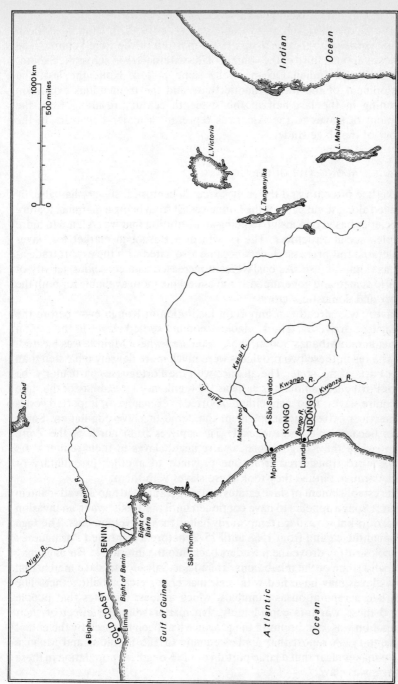

2 The Kingdom of Kongo and the Gulf of Guinea in the sixteenth century

the Atlantic basin, including those ending up on São Thomé and other islands off the African coast. Those slaves destined for internal African markets gradually became a smaller proportion of the total volume. The trade was about a third of the volume of the external trade across the Sahara, Red Sea, and Indian Ocean in the same period. None the less, the development of the trans-Atlantic trade and the tremendous expansion beginning in the last half of the sixteenth century resulting from the shipment of slaves to the Americas represent a major departure in the history of the slave trade.

SLAVERY ALONG THE GUINEA COAST

By the late fifteenth and the early sixteenth centuries, slavery had already changed along some parts of the Guinea coast from being a marginal feature of societies based on kinship to being an institution that was related to more complex social structures. The growth of a European market for slaves accelerated this process: slavery became associated with the export trade as well as domestic use. As enslavement increased as a conscious activity of ambitious men and governments, slaves became more available for both the export and domestic sectors.

Slavery was already an important institution in Kongo even before the Portuguese arrived.[40] The Kongolese nobility settled slaves in the capital district and in Mbanza Sonyo, the coastal area where Mpinda was located, and as a result these two provinces were much more densely inhabited than other parts of the state. The alliance with the Portuguese, particularly the use of Portuguese soldiers as early as 1514, enhanced the ability of the state to acquire slaves, who were either exported in exchange for imported goods and services or used to supplement the domestic slave-population. Some slaves became soldiers, especially Tio captives from north of the Zaire River, while the Kongo nobles also retained slaves in their retinues. As nobles were transferred from one province to another for military or administrative duties, they took these slaves with them.

The establishment of slave estates and villages around São Salvador and in Mbanza Sonyo appears to have continued until the 1560s, when an invasion of warriors known as Jaga temporarily halted these developments. The Jaga occupied the capital from 1568 until 1572, before a combined Portuguese–Kongolese army drove the intruders back into the interior.[41] The Jaga may have sold some of the inhabitants around São Salvador to slave merchants; many slaves may have fled with their masters or escaped altogether. The Jaga had a reputation as cannibals, which at least indicates that people feared these warriors considerably. No matter what the effect of their occupation was, conditions in the province had been restored by the end of the century. A report that applies equally to São Salvador and Mbanza Sonyo makes clear that a large portion of the Kongolese population in these districts was slave:

There are no [free] men who cultivate the ground, nor men who work by the day, nor anyone who is willing to work for a wage. Only slaves labour and serve. Men who are powerful have a great number of slaves whom they have captured in war or whom they have purchased. They conduct business through these slaves by sending them to markets where they buy and sell according to the master's orders.[42]

This report suggests that slavery was no longer a simple case of dependency in a society based on kinship. While a complete transformation of the social order on the scale of Muslim areas probably had not occurred, slave holdings were still large enough to indicate that a transformation was under way.

Kongolese nobles even invested in plantations on São Thomé, which may indicate that slave labour in Kongo itself was sometimes organized on a plantation model. A Portuguese description of São Thomé in 1550 makes it clear that there were a number of black planters who were rich and whose daughters married the Portuguese residents.[43] By this time, the largest plantations ranged in size from 100 to 400 slaves. Slaves not only worked in the sugar fields but also grew their own provisions. They usually lived in huts with their families, although later in the century slaves were sometimes housed in barracks.[44] These conditions were probably not very different from those on the estates in Kongo, except that it is unlikely that barracks were ever a feature of slavery in Kongo. The real difference between slavery on São Thomé and slavery in Kongo was in the intentions of the slave owners; São Thomé planters raised sugar for export to Portugal,[45] while Kongolese slave masters wanted food crops, particularly millet, which was consumed by the large establishments of the nobility and was not destined for export.

The demand for slaves on the Gold Coast, which the Portuguese satisfied by importing slaves from Benin and Kongo via São Thomé, reveals that slavery was an important institution in Benin and the small Akan states on the Gold Coast, as well as in Kongo. It may be that slaves were used in gold mining and panning at this time, as they were in the early seventeenth century. Local merchants on the Gold Coast used slaves as porters, which establishes their importance as common workers. Around 1600, de Marees reported: 'Here there are no labourers to be found to serve people for hire and reward, but only slaves and captives who must wear out their lives in slavery.'[46] At this time, and probably indicative of practice for sometime into the past, debtors could be seized – de Marees says that they could be enslaved. This indicates that local mechanisms were also responsible for establishing servile relationships.[47] Debtors may well have become slaves, although de Marees appears to have confused pawns with slaves, or at best he learned of the illegal enslavement of pawns, who were theoretically protected from sale.

Slavery in the Sierra Leone hinterland was related to war. In the sixteenth century, a series of invasions from the interior displaced many people, some of whom were enslaved. In the 1560s, at least some of these captives were used in the fields. The English slave merchant and pirate, John Hawkins, who was there at the time, learned about the importance of slavery first hand; from an island base, Hawkins led raiding parties to the mainland in order to seize slaves, which helps to establish that the trade had not yet become firmly part of the slave supply-mechanism that later characterized the trans-Atlantic trade from Sierra Leone. Otherwise, European merchants would simply have bought slaves, which usually took less time and involved fewer risks than capturing slaves.

> In this Island we stayed certaine daies, going every day on shore to take the Inhabitants, with burning and spoiling their townes, who before were Sapies, and were conquered by the Samboses, Inhabitants beyond Sierre Leona ... These inhabitants have diverse of the Sapies, which they tooke in the warres as their slaves, whome onely they kept to till the ground, in that they neither have the knowledge thereof, nor yet will worke themselves, of whome wee tooke many in that place, but of the Samboses none at all, for they fled into the maine.[48]

Hawkins' description suggests that the slave population was large enough for many of the productive activities of society to be performed by slave labour. This exploitation of slaves may well have been confined to those captured in war; there is no evidence on the fate of slave children, who, none the less, probably would have been incorporated into lineages. Significantly, Hawkins' party seized the 'Sapi' slaves, not the 'Sambose' masters; this appears to have been a common practice in many places. Slaves were often re-enslaved, thereby preventing the assimilation and amelioration of status that was their due according to custom. Slavery was changing, but a full transformation had not occurred. The presence of Europeans on the coast and the growth in market demand probably encouraged this change. Now captives could be sold as well as used domestically. Whereas the size of the slave population may have fluctuated in the past in accordance with war and peace, now a steady demand for slaves drained victims from the area. The extent to which this was internalized into local society is not yet clear, but the number of slaves available for export soon became sufficient for European demand, so that it was no longer necessary for pirates like Hawkins to seize people. It is likely that the size of the local slave population also increased.[49]

Father Baltasar Barreira, a Jesuit priest who visited the Cape Verde Islands and Sierra Leone in 1605, enquired into the methods of enslavement on the upper Guinea coast, and, since he was concerned with justifying the institution of slavery and Portuguese involvement in the slave trade, he collected useful information on the origins of slaves. While his tract, 'Concerning the Slaves ... that come from the Parts of Guinea which are called Cape Verde', contains a distorted view of African society and hence does not represent an African perspective on enslavement, Barreira did rely on information from slave owners and traders, as well as earlier Portuguese sources, which does establish the range of methods involved in the enslavement of people.[50] Barreira lists captivity in war as common; he was even under the impression that local wars were sometimes fought to obtain slaves for export. Whether or not this was true, slaves were certainly readily available, and Europeans no longer had to raid for slaves, as Hawkins had done.

Convicted criminals were also enslaved. Barreira provides a list of offences that were punishable through enslavement, although it is unclear how old such punishments were or how often they were enforced.

> There are other ways of enslaving in a legal way, as when it is proved that one black is a witch, or he confesses it himself; or that he has killed another with poison; or that he is intimate with any of the king's wives; or that he is inciting war against the king; or that he asks the *chinas* – so they call their idols – to kill the king, in which case if the king happens to fall ill, not only do they kill the delinquent or sell him outside the kingdom, and confiscate all his possessions, but they also enslave and sell all his relatives, for fear that any of them, in revenge, also asks the *chinas* to kill him. This is also done by subjects who are not kings.[51]

In this description, 'kings' referred to powerful men in general, for there were no large states in the interior at this time. Barreira also provides information on the means of determining guilt through poison ordeals and spirit possession. Besides these 'legal' means, people were kidnapped, and since neither local merchants nor the Portuguese enquired into the methods of enslavement at the time of purchase, these practices probably became more common as the export trade expanded.

The relationship between the European slave trade and developments in local African societies helps clarify the process of historical change related to the development of slavery as an institution.[52] In its indigenous form, slavery functioned on the edge of society. There were some slaves who had failed to pay debts, been convicted of crimes, charged with sorcery, seized in war, or transferred as compensation for damages. None the less, the basic structure of society was the kinship unit. Slaves emerged almost as incidental products of the interaction between groups of kin. Slaves could be sold to outsiders, and here lay the possibility for regular trade, although one that could vary in importance. The presence of merchants provided an incentive for developing a sustained trade, not a haphazard one that fluctuated depending upon the problems of kinship. Once merchants organized the collection of slaves, the exchange was transformed. Whereas slaves continued to move back and forth between groups of kin, with little if any discrepancy in the balance of this flow, now slaves were funnelled towards the export market too. The net effect was the loss of these slaves to Africa and the substitution of imported commodities for humans.

3

The export trade in slaves, 1600–1800

By 1600 an important structural change in the political economy of some parts of Africa was well under way. Islam continued to be an agent of change in the northern savanna and along the shores of the Red Sea and Indian Ocean. Slaves were exported on a sustained level, and enslavement and slavery were still interpreted largely in terms of Islamic law and tradition. The growth of the trans-Atlantic slave trade had already exposed west-central Africa to a radically new influence. In the next two centuries, this influence was to have an even greater effect on much of the Guinea coast than the earlier trade in slaves had had anywhere in Africa, with the result that the people of the Atlantic basin experienced a major transformation in their social organization.[1] The dynamic changes along the Atlantic shores where the export trade became so substantial in the seventeenth and eighteenth centuries transformed slavery there in ways quite different from the earlier pattern in the Islamic belt, although structurally the impact was the same: where slaves had once been an incidental element in society, they now became common. The ability to supply slaves required adjustments in the methods of enslavement and the development of a commercial infrastructure. These changes in turn were accompanied by increased domestic use of slaves.

VOLUME OF THE EXPORT TRADE, 1600–1800

Despite the unevenness of the data available for a census of the export trade in slaves, it is possible to make some broad comparisons between its various sectors (see table 3.1). The trade increased steadily from the sixteenth to the eighteenth century. The total number of slaves exported, about 1,175,000 in the sixteenth century, includes 850,000 slaves allocated to the Islamic trade and 325,000 for the trans-Atlantic trade. The estimate for the Islamic trade could be significantly off the mark, but is unlikely to be less than 500,000 or more than 1,000,000. The estimate for the trans-Atlantic trade is far more accurate. Hence the sixteenth-century trade probably was in the order of 800,000 to 1,300,000. The seventeenth-century trade is subject to less error,

Table 3.1 Slave exports from Africa, 1500–1800

Export region	1500–1600	%	1600–1700	%	1700–1800	%	Total	%
Red Sea	200,000	17.0	200,000	7.0	200,000	2.7	600,000	5.2
Trans-Sahara	550,000	46.8	700,000	24.4	700,000	9.4	1,950,000	17.0
East Africa	100,000	8.5	100,000	3.5	400,000	5.4	600,000	5.2
Trans-Atlantic	325,000	27.7	1,868,000	65.1	6,133,000	82.5	8,326,000	72.6
TOTAL	1,175,000	100.0	2,868,000	100.0	7,433,000	100.0	11,476,000	100.0

Source: tables 2.3, 3.2, 3.3, 3.4, 3.5, 3.6.

and the eighteenth-century trade subject to less still, because the proportion of the trans-Atlantic trade – which can be estimated far more accurately than the Islamic trade – steadily increased, thereby reducing the relative size of the Islamic trade and correspondingly minimizing the error inherent in an assessment of its volume.

In the seventeenth century, the Islamic trade was probably on the same scale as in the sixteenth century – roughly 800,000 – although again perhaps as low as 500,000 or as high as 1,000,000, but the great increase in the Atlantic trade meant that the total export volume doubled from the sixteenth to the seventeenth century and more than doubled from the seventeenth to the eighteenth century (2,868,000 to 7,433,000), even though the Islamic trade expanded in the eighteenth century too (up perhaps 300,000, all in the Indian Ocean). The trans-Atlantic trade rose from about one fourth of the trade in the sixteenth century to more than four-fifths in the eighteenth century. Over the period as a whole, the trans-Atlantic trade accounted for about 72 per cent of all slave exports from Africa. The total number of slaves exported across the Atlantic between 1600 and 1800 was in the order of 8 million.[2] It is likely that scholars will be able to modify the conclusions reached in the pages that follow as new material is examined that will revise the export figures. The concern here, therefore, is to understand where *most* of the slaves that were shipped to the Americas came from, that is, the 1,868,000 who were sold from 1600 to 1700 (table 3.2) and the 6,133,000 who were sold in the eighteenth century (table 3.3).

The largest exporting region in the early seventeenth century was west-central Africa, which continued sending thousands of slaves a year to the Americas, thus consolidating a pattern that began a century earlier. Senegambia and Benin maintained their relatively modest share of the trade as well, each providing about a thousand slaves a year. Slaves came from elsewhere too. The really dramatic expansion of the Atlantic trade began after 1650, and from then slave exports affected ever larger parts of Africa, not just the Kongo region. In the last fifty years of the seventeenth century, more slaves were sold to Europeans on the Atlantic coast than in the previous two hundred years combined. This phenomenal growth was a response to the spread of plantation slavery in the Americas. From the 1640s through the 1660s, sugar spread from Brazil to the lesser Antilles – Barbados, Martinique, Guadeloupe, St Kitts, Antigua – and these new colonies acquired tens of thousands of slaves. The figure for the third quarter of the seventeenth century was double the previous twenty-five-year period, averaging 17,700 per year, while in the last quarter, almost 30,000 slaves were exported annually. By now sugar plantations were being established on Jamaica and Saint Domingue, which rapidly became the two largest producers of sugar. As a result, the dramatic surge in slave exports continued into the eighteenth century, reaching figures in the order of 61,000 slaves per year for the whole century. We must remember that these figures are primarily based on the known volume of slave imports into the

Table 3.2 *Atlantic slave trade, 1601–1700*

	Imports (Americas)	Exports (15% loss in transit)	Exports (20% loss in transit)	Exports (25% loss in transit)	Annual average (20% loss in transit)
1601–25	261,800	308,000	327,300	349,100	13,100
1626–50	242,600	285,400	303,300	323,500	12,100
1651–75	371,200	436,700	464,000	494,900	18,600
1676–1700	618,900	728,100	773,600	825,200	30,900
TOTAL	1,494,500	1,758,200	1,868,200	1,992,700	

Sources: Curtin 1969, p. 119; Vila Vilar 1977b, pp. 206–9; and Fogel and Engerman 1974, p. 30. The mortality figure of 20 per cent is based on the following: Davies (1957, p. 292) reports that the Royal African Company experienced losses at sea in the order of 23.5 per cent between 1680 and 1688. Van den Boogaart and Emmer (1979, p. 367) calculate an average loss of 17.9 per cent on Dutch ships between 1637 and 1645 (sample of 27,477 slaves). The loss in the trade to Brazil was in the order of 15–20 per cent in the sixteenth and seventeenth centuries (see Goulart 1950, p. 278, as discussed in Curtin 1969, p. 277).

Table 3.3 *Atlantic slave trade, 1701–1800*

Carrier	Total
English	2,532,300
Portuguese	1,796,300
French	1,180,300
Dutch	350,900
North American	194,200
Danish	73,900
Other (Swedish, Brandenburger)	5,000
TOTAL	6,132,900

Sources: English trade: for 1701–50: Curtin 1969, p. 151; for 1751–1800: Anstey 1976, p. 607. I have adjusted for Anstey's total by allowing a figure of 245,000 for 1801–7; see Drescher 1977, p. 28. Also see Anstey 1975c, p. 13. Portuguese trade: H. S. Klein 1978, p. 27, for Angola, 1701–60; Curtin 1969, p. 207 for West Africa, 1701–60; Anstey 1977, p. 261 for 1761–1800. French trade: Curtin 1969, p. 211 for 1701–10; and Stein 1978, p. 519. I have also added 10,000 to the total for the French trade in order to allow for unrecorded vessels between 1713 and 1728 (Stein, personal communication). Dutch trade: Postma 1975b, p. 49. I have preferred this estimate to the one in 1975a, p. 237. North American trade: Anstey 1975b, p. 201, for 1733–60, and Anstey 1977, p. 267, for 1761–1800. Danish trade: for 1733–60, Green-Pedersen 1957, p. 201; for 1761–1800, Anstey 1977, p. 267.

Americas and not on the actual number of slaves who were exported from Africa, which undoubtedly was higher because some slaves, perhaps in the order of 15–20 per cent, died on the Atlantic crossing. Hence the estimates of exports during each quarter are subject to considerable error.

The first major source of slaves for the Americas, the area of Angola and Kongo, remained a substantial exporter far into the nineteenth century. The second region to become a big supplier was the Slave Coast (Bight of Benin), which entered a period of particularly rapid expansion in the late seventeenth century, continuing into the eighteenth century until the end of the trade in the nineteenth. The third area to experience a profound rise in slave exports was the Gold Coast, whose exports rose sharply in the early eighteenth century, but fell off by 1800. The fourth area was the Bight of Biafra, centred on the Niger delta and the Cross River, which suddenly became a major exporter in the 1740s and continued to be so for a century. Other parts of West Africa had temporary spurts in their export figures. Thus the Bandama River was important before 1750, the coast near the Futa Jallon highlands was busy in the 1750s and 1760s, and ports near where Monrovia and Freetown now stand handled some traffic at different times. Finally, the Senegambia, with its connections to the Muslim interior, always supplied some slaves, although never on the scale of the four major exporting regions.

These regions are discussed in terms of the estimated volume of slave exports by quarter in the seventeenth century and by decade in the eighteenth century. These figures are presented in several forms. Firstly, the trade before the last third of the sixteenth century most profoundly affected west-central Africa, although the lack of data does not allow a closer examination of the relative proportion of that trade to the total trade (table 3.2). Secondly, data from the Bight of Benin (Slave Coast) for the last half of the seventeenth century are used to supplement the quarterly returns for the trade as a whole. This allows a consideration of the relative importance of west-central Africa and the Bight of Benin, which together accounted for the vast majority of exports in this half-century. Thirdly, the regional composition of the trade is examined for each decade in the eighteenth century (table 3.4), but only for that portion of the trade dominated by the four largest carriers, England, France, the Netherlands, and Portugal. Even the figures for the big four are lower than the estimate for their contribution to the trade as a whole. This discrepancy between the regional estimates and the total trade is in the order of 619,600 slaves for the eighteenth century as a whole (tables 3.3 and 3.4), a significant proportion of the volume, representing about 10 per cent fewer slaves in the regional estimates than in the figures for the total trade. Part of this difference relates to the exclusion of North American, Danish, and smaller carriers from the regional totals, and the other major part of the difference relates to a better estimate for the French trade, which does not include a coastal breakdown and hence cannot be used for a regional assessment of the trade. There is no reason to suppose that the regional breakdown for this additional 619,600 slaves was significantly different than for the rest, but the regional analysis here is limited to the 5,513,300 slaves whose coastal origins are reasonably clear. Since the intention is to demonstrate the impact of the slave market on local society and the institution of slavery, a higher figure for the export trade would only strengthen the argument.

For the eighteenth century as a whole, the trade was very complicated. Not only were the figures for west-central Africa (2,057,700) and the Bight of Benin (1,278,600) very large, but other parts of the coast contributed significant numbers of slaves. Based on the Portuguese, Dutch, French, and British accounts, the Gold Coast exported 677,400 slaves; the Bight of Biafra 814,400; Sierre Leone (here defined as modern Guinea, Sierra Leone, and Western Liberia) 483,900 slaves, and the Senegambia region 201,400. Because these figures do not include all countries transporting slaves to the Americas, the actual volume of exports was probably 10 per cent higher than these figures. The major omissions are the North American trade after 1760 and a substantial number of slaves carried by French merchants who do not show up in the regional returns.

The price structure of the Atlantic slave market over these two centuries suggests, moreover, that prices rose in the order of fourfold or fivefold, while supply increased in the order of two-and-one-half times. The data on slave prices are most complete for the last third of the seventeenth century and the eighteenth century (see table 3.5). Although iron bars, cowrie

Table 3.4 Regional origins of slaves in the eighteenth-century Atlantic trade (000s)

Region	(Dutch, British, French and Portuguese)										
	1701–10	1711–20	1721–30	1731–40	1741–50	1751–60	1761–70	1771–80	1781–90	1791–1800	Totals
Senegambia	18.4	30.9	22.5	26.2	25.0	22.5	14.4	12.4	22.1	7.0	201.4
Sierra Leone	17.4	20.6	22.5	33.3	49.4	45.2	108.1	82.2	47.2	58.0	483.9
Gold Coast	25.0	46.6	72.7	85.6	91.4	66.3	63.4	56.0	93.7	76.7	577.4
Bight of Benin	161.3	169.3	160.3	154.8	109.9	98.7	102.7	90.7	159.8	71.1	1,278.6
Bight of Biafra	10.0	10.0	4.5	45.1	71.3	100.7	126.3	127.3	133.8	185.4	814.4
West-central Africa	80.1	72.0	115.5	177.3	189.2	195.6	220.2	211.4	431.1	365.3	2,057.7
TOTALS	312.2	349.4	398.0	522.3	536.2	529.0	635.1	580.0	887.7	763.5	5,513.4

Sources: For all figures in the period 1711–1800 for West African regions, see Curtin 1975b, p. 112; for central African figures, 1711–1800: H. S. Klein 1978, p. 27; a regional breakdown for the decade 1701–10 is not available but has been reconstructed on the basis of the following sources: Postma 1975b, pp. 42, 49; Curtin 1969, p. 207; Daaku 1970, p. 46; Manning 1979, p. 117; and Davies 1957, p. 226. A figure of 10.0 has also been assigned to the Bight of Biafra, on the assumption that the trade was in the order of 1,000 slaves per year in this decade. Curtin has no estimate for this period, and it is likely that his estimate for the 1720s is low; see Northrup 1978, p. 54, although the figures used here are considerably more conservative than those suggested by Northrup. Following the analysis of Jones and Johnson 1980, pp. 17–34, the slaves previously attributed to the Windward Coast have been reassigned to the Sierra Leone and Guinea coasts for British exports and to the Slave Coast for French exports. There is room for considerable error in this assessment, since some slaves did come from the western Ivory Coast and Liberia, in the case of the British, and some of the French trade probably included purchases on the Gold Coast and in the Bight of Biafra. None the less, the majority of slaves in both cases almost certainly came from the areas to which they have been assigned. Hopefully the forthcoming work of Jones and Johnson will help clarify this matter. Curtin's figures for 1761–80 (1975b, p. 112) include the revisions of Anstey 1975c, p. 13; and Postma 1975b, pp. 42–9. I have also used Anstey 1977, p. 261. For 1781–90, I have accepted J. E. Inikori's tabulation of the number of British ships involved in the slave trade but have employed a slave/ship ratio from Anstey and assigned these slaves to different regions following Curtin's formula; see Lovejoy, 1982c. For the 1790s, I have substituted the total for the British trade derived by Drescher 1977, p. 28, following Anstey's distributional formula.

Table 3.5 *West African slave prices: semi-decadal averages, 1663–1775*

Year	Price in £ sterling of 1601	Number of observations
1663–67	3.29	1
1668–72	3.00	2
1673–77	1.76	3
1678–82	3.67	12
1683–87	3.74	9
1688–92	3.22	3
1693–97	4.24	4
1698–02	5.43	12
1703–07	10.24	10
1708–12	11.21	9
1713–17	11.75	13
1718–22	12.77	13
1723–27	11.89	13
1728–32	13.37	9
1733–37	17.65	9
1738–42	18.92	5
1743–47	11.13	6
1748–52	14.26	19
1753–57	12.52	16
1758–62	14.07	9
1763–67	16.54	15
1768–72	17.76	15
1773–75	15.96	9

Source: Bean 1975, p. 72. Bean's prices are calculated as the prime cost in Britain of goods used to purchase slaves rather than the actual price of slaves on the African coast.

shells, lengths of cloth, and other items were actually the currencies used by African merchants in calculating the price of slaves, the sterling value of goods exported to Africa can be used as a guide to the price structure of the slave trade. The cost of goods purchased in Europe that were used to buy slaves remained fairly steady at £3 to £4 sterling between the 1660s and the early 1690s, whereupon the price doubled within a few years. The prime cost of goods in Britain levelled off at £10 to £13 from the middle of the first decade of the eighteenth century until the early 1730s, when it rose again to about £18 to £19, before falling back to a lower level during the 1740s. For the rest of the century, the prime cost of goods gradually rose again, ranging from £13 to £18. During this period, supply rose from 30,900 slaves per year in the last quarter of the seventeenth century to 78,000 per year in the last two decades of the eighteenth century; hence it is clear that prices increased with the supply of slaves (see table 3.4). Various scholars have measured the elasticity of the supply of slaves with respect to price changes: Bean has calculated a figure of 0.75 and 0.83 for two different periods within a century; Manning has reached a figure of 1.5 for the Slave Coast alone; LeVeen has estimated a figure of 0.81.[3] LeVeen's calculation, for example, means that a 10-per-cent increase in prices corresponded to an 8.1-per-cent increase in exports. While these calculations do not deny that non-economic motives were important in the rising supply of slaves, these comparisons of volume and price do indicate that economic factors were major determinants of the response of African suppliers to rising demand.

The question of price is important in determining the extent to which African suppliers responded to market forces in catering to the export trade. This issue has concerned historians who are interested in establishing the cause of the expansion in slave exports. Was the increase in volume related to the conscious decisions of slavers who were responding to higher prices, or was the increase in supply a relatively incidental feature of the extension of enslavement that resulted from the spread of warfare and other politically-motivated actions?[4] LeVeen's analysis of prices clearly demonstrates that market factors did influence the supply mechanism; at least he has been able to show a correlation between rising prices and expanding supply.[5] Market forces alone, however, are not the only influence on the supply of slaves. A response to changing economic conditions reflects the attitudes of the enslavers, and their acceptance of the slave trade as a legitimate activity. Further, the costs of investment in equipment and the organization of slave gathering and marketing became an influence on the available supply of slaves. The sale of war prisoners, even if prices were low, was desirable to those government officials wanting to rid themselves of enemies; if some compensation could be gained through their disposal, so much the better. In short, market conditions aside, the maintenance of a steady demand for slaves influenced attitudes; when combined with rising demand, the supply of slaves could and did increase dramatically.

THE DOMINANCE OF WEST-CENTRAL AFRICA

West-central Africa, including the coast from Cabinda and Loango to Angola, accounted for the majority of slaves exported to the Americas until the last quarter of the seventeenth century and a major share of the total thereafter.[6] From 1600 to 1800, perhaps 2.5 million slaves were shipped from this region alone, which represented about a quarter of all slaves exported from Africa in these two centuries, including the trans-Atlantic trade and the established Islamic trade. The portion of the Atlantic trade that can be attributed to west-central Africa is correspondingly larger than a quarter. At the height of the trade in the eighteenth century, this region was the largest single exporter, except for the first three decades, when it was the second largest source. In the last several decades of the century, the peak years of the trans-Atlantic trade, west-central Africa contributed a third of all exports, with the figure sometimes rising to 40 per cent.

The Kingdom of Kongo was no longer an important source of slaves in the region. Instead, other states on the periphery of Kongo assumed the major role in transferring slaves to the Europeans on the coast. These included the Vili to the North of the Zaire River and several Mbundu states to the south and east. Secondly, European rivalries on the coast resulted in direct intervention in local politics, especially in Angola, where the Portuguese maintained bases for raiding and trading. The extent of European involvement on the mainland was more pronounced here than anywhere else on the Guinea coast. The Portuguese used Luanda as a base for raids into the interior, except for a few years in the 1640s when the Dutch expelled the Portuguese. Otherwise, the Portuguese dominated Angola, and the Dutch and English traded at Cabinda and Loango, north of the Zaire River, or at the mouth of the Bengo River, north of Luanda. Thirdly, a series of commercial corridors tapped the interior, so that the supply area was gradually pushed further inland as slave demand increased. These routes included overland trails and rivers that channelled slaves towards two points, Malebo Pool (Stanley Pool) on the Zaire River in the north and Luanda in the south. Rapids on the river prevented boats passing from Malebo Pool to the coast, and hence slaves were marched overland to one of several ports on the Loango coast and Cabinda. In the south, river transport was not used, for the tributaries of the Zaire flowed northward, while slaves had to march westward to reach the coast. Fourthly, during the eighteenth century several remote inland states became the principal suppliers, the most important of which were Lunda and Kazembe, whose provinces paid tribute in slaves who could then be exported. The population of the region lived in widely scattered kinship groups that provided the slaves, either through direct taxation or raids or both.

Already by 1600, several thousand slaves per year were being exported from this stretch of coast, with a particularly dramatic expansion taking place in the last quarter of the sixteenth century. In the first quarter of the seventeenth century, exports rose to as many as 7,500 per year for all of Africa, but most of the total was a result of the trade along the central African coast. This average was maintained through the second quarter of the seventeenth century. After 1650, annual exports averaged 4,000 to 5,000. While Portuguese expeditions into Kongo and other parts of the interior continued to supply slaves, areas deeper in the interior became more important. Two Mbundu states, Kasanje and Matamba, dominated the trade routes from Luanda inland.

The trade was maintained on a level of 7,000 to 8,000 slaves per year from 1700 to 1720, when exports increased once again, rising to 12,000 per year in the 1720s, to 20,000 from the 1730s through the 1750s and exploding to astronomical heights in the last four decades: over 21,000 per year in the 1760s and 1770s, and 35,000 to 37,000 annually during the 1780s and 1790s. In the course of the eighteenth century, the trade increased more than fourfold, and this increase was from a base that was already considerable in the history of slave exports. The structural changes that accompanied this growth were extremely important to the local political economy. The scale of the trade required major adjustments in the ability to enslave people and to ship them to points of export (see chapter 4). These changes in turn affected a larger and larger geographical area, beginning with Kongo and the Portuguese stronghold at Luanda but ultimately reaching the far interior of the Zaire River basin.

THE BIGHT OF BENIN, 1640–1800

The Bight of Benin, or the 'Slave Coast', as the Europeans knew it, was the only exporting region that temporarily displaced west-central Africa as the largest single supplier.[7] The modest trade of early Portuguese contact continued into the early seventeenth century. Estimates from the 1640s suggest a trade in the order of 1,200 slaves per year, primarily from Benin and its neighbours. Restrictions on the trade there prevented the steady growth in slave volume, and it was not until new states and different routes were developed in the second half of the seventeenth century that the trade entered a period of expansion that was to justify the European epithet. The trade rose from about 1,000 per year in the 1650s to 1,700 per year in the 1660s, 3,200 per year in the 1670s, 5,500 per year in the 1680s and 10,500 per year in the 1690s (table 3.6). For this fifty-year period, total exports were in the order of 218,000 slaves, about 20 per cent of all slave shipments to the Americas. By the first decade of the eighteenth century, the scale of trade had increased to over 17,000 slaves per year, a figure that was more than twice the volume of trade from west-central Africa. The Bight of Benin retained this position until the 1730s, whereafter the volume continued to be large but none the less did not match the expansion in slave exports that once again placed west-central Africa in the lead as the largest supplier. The trade from the Bight of Benin fell to a level of 9,000 to 11,000 per year in the 1750s, 1760s, and 1770s. A modest recovery in the 1780s checked but did not stop the gradual decline. None the less, over 1.3 million slaves were shipped from the 'Slave Coast' in the eighteenth century.

Table 3.6 *Bight of Benin slave trade, 1641–1700*

Decade	Total	Annual average
1641–50	12,000	1,200
1651–60	9,000	900
1661–70	17,000	1,700
1671–80	32,000	3,200
1681–90	55,200	5,500
1691–1700	104,900	10,500
TOTAL	230,100	

Source: Manning 1979, p. 117.

The surge in exports from the Slave Coast had no connection with the kingdom of Benin, which had once supplied a thousand or more slaves to European merchants. In fact, the export of slaves from Benin actually declined as a result of government restrictions on the sale of male slaves. Instead, three new factors account for the astronomical expansion in exports. Firstly, the Yoruba Kingdom of Oyo initiated a series of wars in the interior that resulted in the enslavement of many people. Oyo was a savanna state; its capital was located only 50 km from the Niger and 300 km inland from the coast. Its strength lay in its cavalry, based on horses imported from farther north, which enabled the state to dominate trade to the coast. Secondly, the towns along the coast – Ardrah, Whydah, Porto Novo, Badagry, and Lagos – fought to control Oyo's trade with the Europeans, and in the process themselves seized many slaves who were also exported. Thirdly, Dahomey, centered 100 km inland, intervened in coastal politics and raided its northern neighbours, thereby adding to the export volume too. Oyo forced Dahomey to pay tribute, but this prevented neither occasional raids on the coastal ports nor continued rivalry in the export trade.[8]

There were a number of important differences in the development of the export trade on the 'Slave Coast' from the pattern that prevailed in west-central Africa. Firstly, there was no European military presence like that of the Portuguese at Luanda, and Europeans did not raid for slaves. Instead Portuguese, French, British, and other traders were confined to coastal ports where they were compelled to trade on terms established by port officials. Secondly, Muslim traders provided links between slave-exporting states and the far interior, so that some slaves and other goods were acquired through a network of inter-regional trade. The export trade in slaves was only one sector in a complex internal, African trade. Thirdly, the growth of the slave trade was closely associated with political developments, as was the case in west-central Africa, too, but in the interior of the Bight of Benin the emerging states were more centralized, in part because of the commercial links with other states to their north and in part because of the profits gained from the European trade. The difference was one of degree, but the presence of an Islamic factor, the confinement of Europeans to mercantile activities, and the more developed commercial sector contributed to a setting that was distinct.

THE GOLD COAST

In the late seventeenth and eighteenth centuries, the West African slave trade expanded westwards from the Bight of Benin to neighbouring parts of the coast. Since European merchants were already stationed on the Gold Coast, it is perhaps logical that the quest for slaves spilled over to this area and indeed to places further west, including the Comoe and Bandama River valleys in eastern Ivory Coast. The Gold Coast – a term used here to include eastern Ivory Coast too – was closer to the Americas; ships could stop at the various European establishments on their way to the better stocked markets of the 'Slave Coast', and they could return via the Gold Coast if their holds were still not filled. All that was necessary was a sufficient supply of slaves. By the early seventeenth century, the Gold Coast was no longer a net importer of slaves; occasionally a few slaves were exported. None the less, slave sales did not become significant until the last three decades of the century. Even then supplies fluctuated wildly, from 2,000 or more slaves in some years during the 1670s to 408 slaves exported between June 1687 and November 1688, a seventeen-month period.[9]

These variations hardly made the Gold Coast a reliable source, but the market for gold sustained European interest and kept ships available for any increase in slave supply. By the first decade of the eighteenth century, moreover, political rivalries on the Gold Coast had provoked a number of wars, and the resulting turbulence accomplished what market demand had failed to achieve: a steady stream of slaves ready for export. Between 1701 and 1710, perhaps 25,000 slaves were sold, an average of 2,500 per year. This volume rose to 4,700 per year in the next decade, jumping to 7,300 in the 1720s, reaching 8,600 per year in the 1730s, and peaking at 9,100 per year in the 1740s. This volume was smaller than that of the adjacent Slave Coast or distant west-central Africa, but considering the proximity to the Bight of Benin – the Gold Coast and the Slave Coast in fact formed a continuous stretch of territory that was shorter than the coast of west-central Africa – a phenomenal expansion in slave exports had taken place. The trade fell by more than a quarter in the 1750s and continued to decline through the 1770s, before a temporary recovery in the 1780s.

The political situation responsible for slave exports was the struggle among the Akan for mastery of the interior, including a region from the Bandama River and its port at Grand Lahu, through the Comoe River and its port at Grand Bassam, as well as the Gold Coast itself. The victor was Asante, which ultimately conquered much of the forest area and several states in the savanna as well.[10] Something in the order of 150,000 slaves came from the Grand Lahu and Grand Bassam in the last half of the eighteenth century as the Baule, Akan refugees fleeing the successful Asante armies, displaced the Guro and Senufo who had been living there.[11] The trade-route north from Grand Lahu to the savanna towns of Boron and Kong, a route that had been opened by Muslim merchants in the seventeenth century but was now cut temporarily by the Baule, may have supplied some slaves from the Muslim traders of the savanna, but most slaves probably were a product of the Baule wars. When the Akan region is treated as a unit, approximately 665,000 slaves were exported in the eighteenth century, not including Danish, North American, and other carriers. Thus we see that the initial expansion in the Bight of Benin spread westward, forming a continuous string of ports where slaves were readily available.

The similarities between the Gold Coast interior and the Bight of Benin are readily apparent. Slave exports were closely associated with the emergence of centralized states, as was also the case on the Slave Coast. Europeans were confined to coastal establishments and had little direct involvement in the enslavement of people. The Muslim factor was strong, providing commercial connections with the far interior, so that the Akan states were involved in continental trade on a scale that was at least equal to Oyo, Dahomey, and Benin and was perhaps even greater. None the less, there were important differences that set the Gold Coast apart. Firstly, Akan society was matrilineal, while the people of the Slave Coast recognized patrilineal principles of social organization. This difference affected both the political structure of the state and the institution of slavery. Secondly, the Akan region had major sources of gold – hence the name for the coast – that were absent further east, and the forest area here also had extensive groves of kola-nut trees that produced an essential item of trade with the north. A similar industry did not exist in the interior of the Bight of Benin.

THE BIGHT OF BIAFRA

A similar process of commercial expansion happened to the east of the Bight of Benin, where the Niger delta and the Cross River valley – often referred to as the Bight of Biafra (Bonny) – also experienced a surge in slave sales.[12] Some slaves were purchased in the Niger delta in the early sixteenth century, but most of these came from the western delta and more properly belong to a discussion of the Bight of Benin. Slaves apparently came from 'Gaboe', which has been identified as Aboh on the Niger River. By the late 1670s and early 1680s, two other towns, Bonny and Elem Kalabari, supplied 'a vast number of slaves, of all sexes and ages'.[13] Unfortunately, more specific estimates are lacking.

The real expansion for the Bight of Biafra occurred in the eighteenth century; between 1700 and 1800, the French, British, and Portuguese exported at least 832,000 slaves, and it is likely that the total approached 1 million. The region became especially important in the trans-Atlantic trade after the 1730s, when the trade expanded from about 1,000 slaves per year to 17,000 per year in the 1790s. The remarkable feature of this portion of Africa is that it experienced a spectacular increase in slave exports relatively late in the trade. By the middle of the eighteenth century, this region responded so positively to the demand for slaves that it quickly became a major exporter at a time when the trade as a whole was at its peak. Here is ample proof that the economic pull of the American market could force a fundamental change within Africa. It can be expected, as will be shown below, that such an impact would have serious repercussions on the institution of slavery in the hinterland.

In the 1730s, the Niger delta and Cross River exports rose to at least 4,500 per year, and this spectacular increase continued into the 1740s (7,100 per year) and 1750s (10,000 per year), levelling off in the 1760s and 1770s at over 12,500 per year. The peak of the trade was reached in the 1790s, with an average export of over 17,000 slaves a year. These slaves were brought to the coast through the maze of creeks and lagoons that formed the delta of the Niger River and included the mouth of the Cross River. Much of the coastal area was mangrove swamp, very different from other stretches of coast that we have already examined. Large river-boats were used here to transport both slaves and food from the interior, which included some of the most densely populated parts of Africa. Because of the swamps and their unhealthy environment, Europeans did not maintain coastal depots, as was the case on the Gold Coast, in the Bight of Benin, and in west-central Africa, nor was there direct military intervention comparable to Portuguese adventures in Angola and Kongo. The political structure in the heavily populated forests behind the mangrove swamps was segmented. There were no centralized states on the scale of the other regions, although a loose confederation based on commercial and religious ties and reinforced through the use of mercenaries provided some unity. The political element in enslavement, including wars, tribute payments, and punitive raids, was relatively less significant here, in contrast to the other areas. Instead, slaves were obtained in small-scale raids by one village on another, through extensive kidnapping, and as a result of legal proceedings and religious rites. The degree of decentralization, the relatively late entry into the export trade on a large scale, and the lack of European residence on the coast mark this area off from the rest. Finally, the Islamic factor was also minimal here, although it was not completely absent as it was in west-central Africa. People along the Niger River traded north, thereby having some links, at least through intermediaries, with Muslim merchants, but this trade never became a factor in the region itself, as it did in the interior of the Slave and Gold Coasts.

THE UPPER GUINEA COAST AND SENEGAMBIA

The routes that supplied slaves to far western coasts of the Gulf of Guinea, including the area of modern Sierra Leone, Guinea, and the Senegambia basin, were linked with the trade of the interior where Muslims were the main traders. None the less, the coastal people along much of this coast were not Muslims, and many slave exports were unconnected with developments in the interior. The Senegambia basin, where the Islamic factor was strongest, sustained exports in the order of 1,000 to 3,000 slaves per year in the late seventeenth and throughout the eighteenth century;[14] trade from the Futa Jallon highlands where Islam was equally pervasive fluctuated, depending upon political developments there, while some slaves reached the coast via routes from the Sierra Leone–Liberia and Ivory Coast interior where the Islamic influence was least developed.[15] The supply areas for the western coast were the Senegal and Gambia valleys, the Futa Jallon highlands, the kola forests, and the savanna country beyond. One factor in the export figures here was a series of Muslim holy wars that began in the late seventeenth century and continued into the eighteenth.

The Senegambia trade averaged about 2,000 slaves per year in the eighteenth century, with slightly higher figures in the period 1711–50 and the 1780s. The rise of exports from the Sierra Leone–Guinea coast in the eighteenth century was related to the founding of Futa Jallon in a holy war that was pursued from the 1720s through the 1740s, with the consequence of a gradual rise in exports into the 1740s. The second and most violent phase of war lasted from the 1760s through the 1780s, when exports more than doubled to almost 11,000 per year. Sierre Leone and the neighbouring coast probably exported over 500,000 slaves in the eighteenth century.

The Atlantic trade affected the far interior of West Africa more in the eighteenth century than ever before. Now the pull of the trans-Saharan trade and the Atlantic trade overlapped to a considerable extent. Only in the valleys of the Senegal and Gambia Rivers had the savanna regions supplied both parts of the external trade before the eighteenth century. With the increased volume of the Atlantic trade, exports came not only from the interior of Senegambia but also from areas to the north of the Bights of Benin and Biafra. These slaves are often identifiable because they were Muslims. Some were shipped down the Niger River to the delta; others went through Oyo and Asante; and still others travelled along the routes through the kola forests to ports on the western coast. Muslim and other slaves from the interior became particularly noticeable on the trade registers of the late eighteenth century, although they appear to have amounted to only a few percentage points of the total volume of slave exports in the last decades of the eighteenth century.[16]

THE VOLUME OF THE TRADE ACROSS THE SAHARA, RED SEA, AND INDIAN OCEAN

Approximately 1.3 million slaves were sent across the Sahara, the Red Sea and the Indian Ocean in the seventeenth and eighteenth centuries.[17] The trans-Saharan traffic was about 700,000 per century, which allows 7,000 per year, but which may well be too high. A figure of 100,000 for the Red Sea, reflecting an annual average of 1,000 per year, is allowed for the seventeenth century, and 200,000 is assessed for the eighteenth-century (table 3.7). The figures are based on very limited data, but trade across the Red Sea did seem to increase in the eighteenth century. Data are most complete for Egypt in the last decades of the eighteenth century, when an estimated 3,000 to 6,000 slaves were imported each year, but other markets in North Africa also consumed slaves – when the Moroccan sultans wanted slave soldiers in the late seventeenth and early eighteenth centuries, they looked to sub-Saharan Africa as one source of recruits.[18] Furthermore, the demand for children, young females, and eunuchs appears to have been steady throughout the two centuries.

The East African trade was somewhat more complex. In the seventeenth

Table 3.7 *Slave exports across the Sahara, Red Sea, and Indian Ocean, 1600–1800*

	1600–1700	1700–1800
Saharan trade	700,000	700,000
Red Sea	100,000	200,000
East Africa	100,000	400,000
TOTALS	900,000	1,300,000

Sources: Austen 1977*b*, 1979*b*, and 1979*a*, p. 68; Filliot 1974, pp. 54, 69; Martin and Ryan 1977, p. 82; Alpers 1970. It should be noted that the more conservative estimates of Austen's various calculations have been used here.

and early eighteen centuries, slave exports were essentially an extension of the trade across the Red Sea and Sahara. Slaves were destined for harems, domestic service, and government employment. They were exported in small numbers, perhaps in the order of 1,000 per year for the whole coast, or 100,000 from 1600 to 1700. In the eighteenth century, however, new currents affected this maritime trade. Slaves were taken to the Dutch settlement at Cape Town, and the French established plantations in the Mascarene islands in the Indian Ocean. Dwarfed by trans-Atlantic exports of the time, this trade was related to developments in the Americas, since some slaves were taken to Brazil, and since Europeans were trying to establish a plantation economy on the American model in the Indian Ocean. About 115,000 slaves went to the Mascarene islands to grow coffee, indigo, and sugar-cane. Over half came from Madagascar, while the rest were from the mainland. The trade reached its height in the last three decades of the century. At this time, the volume of the Islamic sector was in the order of 4,000 to 5,000 per year, while the trade from Kilwa to the Mascarenes averaged 2,500 per year between 1786 and 1794. Finally, Mozambique increased its share of the trade to the Americas; exports expanded from almost nothing in the 1770s to an average of 5,400 per year between 1786 and 1794.[19] The East African trade as a whole amounted to about 400,000 slaves in the eighteenth century. About two-thirds of this total went to traditional markets in the Muslim world, and the remaining third went to the Mascarenes or the Americas.

DEMOGRAPHIC IMPLICATIONS OF THE EXPORT TRADE

The export figures can be used as one indication of the scale of slavery within Africa. Over 7.85 million people were exported across the Atlantic from 1600 to 1800, and another 2.3 million were probably exported to the Muslim world across the Sahara, Red Sea, and Indian Ocean in the same period – a total figure that exceeds 10.1 million people. Perhaps as many more did not leave, because many slaves died in Africa and others were incorporated into local societies.

Losses from deaths in Africa can be estimated at 6–10 per cent at the port of departure and 10–14 per cent or more *en route* to the coast in the last decades of the seventeenth century and throughout the eighteenth century, when most slaves were exported. These estimates suggest that the volume of the trade was about 20 per cent higher than the export figures alone – that is, 9.8 million slaves for the trans-Atlantic trade and its supply network. It is likely that the rate of loss for the trade to the Muslim world was roughly comparable, suggesting a total volume for that supply system of 2.9 million. Others who were not enslaved in raids and wars were none the less casualties of slaving wars, although they cannot be classified as slaves. Deaths at the point of enslavement had a significant impact on the demography of the trade, but there is little information on the scale of such deaths, and consequently these are not included in the discussion here. Instead the discussion concentrates on the number of people actually enslaved.

Estimates of losses are based on admittedly scattered and incomplete material. Losses at port of departure, for example, can be derived from reports on the Gold Coast in 1678 and the first decade of the eighteenth century and from census data from Angola in the late eighteenth century. Other places and other periods may have been significantly different. The Gold Coast data suggest, none the less, that approximately 6–7 per cent of slaves brought to the Dutch castle at Cape Coast died or escaped. Between April and December 1678, 1,854 slaves were brought to account at Cape Castle; 1,146 were exported; 587 were not sold; and 121 died or escaped. Losses amounted to 6.5 per cent of imports. In a 32-month period from September 1701 to April 1704, almost 3,000 slaves were brought to account: 2,320 were shipped off or employed as castle slaves; while 217 slaves died or escaped.[20] The remainder awaited shipment. In this case, losses were 7.2 per cent of imports. It is not possible to estimate the relative importance of losses from death and escape, although deaths were probably greater. For Angola, losses were as high as 10–12 per cent of those brought to the coast.[21]

Deaths were also common on the march to the embarkation points. Since journeys varied considerably and the number of deaths increased with distance, an allowance of 10 per cent is entirely a guess, although the study of losses at sea lends support to this guess. Miller has shown that many of the slave deaths on the Atlantic crossing occurred during the first part of the ocean journey, which indicates that nutritional factors and diseases contracted on land were probably a more significant cause of ship-board deaths than conditions on the ships themselves.[22] This hypothesis accords well with epidemiological studies that show that the incidence of death increases dramatically when people move from one disease environment to another. Those slaves transferred to the coast for export had already experienced this movement between disease environments, and the weakened condition of slaves after long marches – and probably inadequate nourishment in many cases – only intensified the health hazards for the slaves. European merchants took care to purchase the healthiest and strongest slaves; rejects were presumably sold off in local markets at reduced prices, so that deaths among this segment of the slave-trade population are lost to the record. Even though the strongest slaves were purchased, ship-board deaths that can be attributed to diseases acquired on land were still a significant proportion of total deaths – perhaps an overwhelming proportion. Since these rates varied from 9 to 15 per cent, it seems reasonable to assign a comparable figure for deaths on land that occurred as a result of similar causes. It should be noted, however, that Miller estimates that 40 per cent of the slaves purchased in the interior of Angola died before reaching the coast in the six months between initial purchase and delivery.[23]

The age and sex ratios of the exported slave-population were also variables in the trade, and these ratios were different for the Islamic and trans-Atlantic trades.[24] In the trade across the Sahara, Red Sea, and Indian Ocean, there was a much higher proportion of females and children, while in the trans-Atlantic trade many more slaves were male than female (table 3.8). Very few slaves in either trade appear to have been older than thirty. This demographic difference affected the supply areas profoundly. In the areas catering to the Islamic trade, where there was also a strong domestic preference for women and children, the structure of the market consistently reflected a price differential based on age and sex. Males, unless they were castrated, were usually cheaper. The competition between domestic and

Table 3.8 *Sex and age distribution of exported slaves* (%)

Category	Sample A	Sample B	Sample C	Sample D	Weighted averages
Children	13	25	7	21	14
Women	35	28	36	17	30
Men	51	47	58	62	56
Women as % of Adults	41	37	38	21	35
Men as % of Adults	59	63	62	79	65

Sample A: 60,000 slaves delivered by the Royal African Company, 1673–1711.
Sample B: 12,697 slaves exported from Dahomey, 1713–20.
Sample C: 49,884 slaves arriving on English ships in Jamaica, 1791–8.
Sample D: 47,851 slaves arriving in Havana, 1790–9.

Sources: Sample A: Davies 1957, p. 299; sample B: Mettas 1978; sample C: H. S. Klein 1978, p. 149; sample D: H. S. Klein 1978, p. 223 (I have considered those slaves listed as teenagers to be adults). Samples B, C, and D are also discussed in Manning 1981, p. 517.

foreign markets for females and children raised their prices to levels that were often twice that of males. This market situation had two profound effects on the development of slavery in the domestic economy. Firstly, the depressed prices for males made slave labour an attractive investment for slave owners, and consequently male slaves were used extensively in production. Secondly, the drain on the population hit frontier areas most severely. The withdrawal of women and children had a disproportionate impact on small-scale societies, for it limited their ability to maintain themselves demographically. It kept politically weak people in a difficult position, always in danger of extinction. The centres of political power mobilized male slaves in production and maintained themselves demographically through the incorporation of new slaves into a population that often had more men that women.

The age and sex distribution of the exported population is useful in calculating who the slaves were that remained in Africa.[25] The major exporting regions – west-central Africa and the area of the Gold Coast and the Bights of Benin and Biafra – had the highest concentrations of slaves outside Muslim Africa, and a disproportionate number of slaves retained in these areas were women and children. This dimension of the slave trade contributed to the type of slavery prevalent in west-central Africa and along the West African coast, and helps to account for some differences between slavery there and slavery in Muslim areas.

The percentage of newly enslaved people who were not exported but retained in Africa can be assessed by reversing the age and sex ratios of exported slaves, although this is attempted here only for the trans-Atlantic sector. Manning has estimated that equal numbers of males and females were enslaved and that the percentage of children (aged 13 and under), young adults (aged 14–30) and older people (over 30) in the enslaved population was 30 per cent, 50 per cent, and 20 per cent respectively.[26] If Manning's assumptions are accepted as a likely indication of the enslaved population, then the export figures only account for 44.6 per cent of the total enslaved population. The other 55.4 per cent stayed in Africa, although at least 10 per cent of these slaves probably died for disease-related causes similar to the deaths of those exported. None the less, Manning's model suggests that approximately 8 million slaves whose enslavement was associated with the export trade remained in Africa. It is obvious, however, that this model is inaccurate in determining the size of the slave population in Africa, for not all males were exported and some slaves over thirty were exported. Since it is not possible to estimate the number of these slaves, no figures are offered. The calculations on the size of the female, child, and elderly categories would change proportionally. This rough estimate, therefore, demonstrates that a significant number of slaves must have been kept in Africa but does not represent the total slave population.

If Manning's model is applied to the export trade data, then about 18 million people, with a normal age and sex distribution, would have had to

Table 3.9 *Estimated population of trade slaves, 1600–1800 (millions)*

Category	Exported	Retained	Total
Young females (14–30)	2.40	2.08	4.48
Young Males (14–30)	4.48	0	4.48
Children (under 14)	1.12	4.26	5.38
Mature adults	0	3.58	3.58
TOTAL	8.00	9.92	17.92

Sources: tables 3.1 and 3.8, based on an estimated sex ratio of 1:1, 30% children, 20% adults over age 30, and 50% young adults, aged 14–30, in the enslaved population.

have been enslaved to produce an export figure of 8 million slaves, with the age and sex distribution of the export sector (see table 3.9). It assumes that no captives over age 30 were exported and that all young males were exported. The retained population of almost 10 million young women, children, and mature adults would increase proportionally at a ratio of three to one, that is, for every 100,000 adult males retained, 100,000 women, 120,000 children, and 80,000 adults over 30 would also be retained, if the sex and age ratios remained the same. To the extent that males were enslaved in greater numbers because of warfare, or that people were deliberately killed as undesirable captives, these estimates varied. There were also regional variations; data from the Biafran area show a more balanced age and sex distribution, which suggests that fewer women and children were retained, and that a greater percentage of all captives were exported. For other regions, however, this model appears to have accorded well with local demographic conditions.

Thornton's analysis of the census data from Angola in the 1770s reveals a high proportion of women in the local slave population.[27] The censuses of 1777 and 1778 show that the female population of Angola at least, and possibly the neighbouring states of Matamba and Kasanje as well – which were heavily involved in the slave trade – outnumbered the male population by two to one. Since females tended to be undercounted, the ratio may have been even higher. Not only does Thornton's material confirm the data on the sex ratio of the export trade, but it indicates that the societies of west central Africa were affected significantly. Polygyny was certainly more prevalent than it could have been in earlier periods, before the scale of the export trade was as large as in the second half of the eighteenth century.

As Thornton rightly concludes, the relatively dense population of the Angola–Kasanje–Matamba region was a direct consequence of the slave trade; female slaves were incorporated into local society, while males were exported. It may well be that this increase in population – at the expense of devastated regions in the interior – also applied to the relatively heavily-populated areas of the West African coast. The Gold Coast, Bight of Benin and Bight of Biafra areas – where a majority of slaves came from – were also some of the most densely populated parts of Africa. If a disproportionate number of women and children were retained at the same time that males were exported, as was the case in Angola, then the population of the slave-exporting societies would have increased. Manning's model also suggests such a conclusion, although his study of the proportion of Aja and other slaves in the exporting population of the Slave Coast is based on the assumption that most slaves came from near the coast – this may be true, but if his model is accepted then other slaves had to be incorporated from further inland, especially the women.[28]

4

The enslavement of Africans, 1600–1800

The growth of the export market, particularly the spectacular surge of the late seventeenth and eighteenth centuries, could not have taken place without a corresponding increase in the ability to enslave people, and, consequently, an intensification of political violence.[1] While this adjustment implies disorder in the social framework wherever the external trade was important, the effective organization of slave supply required that political violence be contained within boundaries that would permit the sale of slaves abroad. The inherent contradiction in this situation was resolved through a separation of the commercial infrastructure from the institutions of enslavement. On the one hand, the disruption in the process of enslavement was associated with political fragmentation. On the other hand, the consolidation of an independent commercial network permitted the movement of slaves within Africa and beyond. Both dimensions were necessary features of the emerging system of slavery in this African context. The export of about 11.3 million slaves from 1500 to 1800, including the astronomical increase between 1650 and 1800 in the Atlantic sector, could not have occurred without the transformation of the African political economy. The articulation of the supply mechanism required the institutionalization of enslavement, which was disruptive (examined in this chapter), and the consolidation of a commercial infrastructure, which was integrative (examined in the next chapter).

A POLITICALLY FRAGMENTED CONTINENT

The most pervasive feature of African history in the period from 1600 to 1800 was the inability of military and political leaders to consolidate large areas into centralized states, despite the presence of many small polities. In the sixteenth century, only Songhay and Borno can truly be called empires. The other states of the period were much smaller than these, and large areas had no states at all. In 1800, there were no large empires, although the number of states as a whole had increased, and the area of stateless societies had been reduced. Political fragmentation accompanied by instability was characteristic of the period. This political environment was well suited for enslaving people.

The savanna region, where Muslim states had long been established, underwent a transformation in the sixteenth century that at first might seem to disprove this generalization. Songhay, for example, extended its boundaries over much of the West African savanna, and its influence reached even further. Undoubtedly it was the largest state in Africa before the nineteenth century, truly an empire on a grand scale. In the Lake Chad basin, Borno also consolidated a large sphere of influence, although not as large as Songhay's. In the upper Nile valley, the Funj Sultanate of Sennar almost achieved similar results, while a Muslim holy war threatened to destroy Christian Ethiopia, thereby consolidating the Ethiopian plateaux into a strong, Islamic state too. Finally, in the interior Zambezi basin, Muanamutapa had united the gold-producing region into a single state. It seemed as if political centralization was the order of the day, not fragmentation.

All of these achievements promised more than they produced. In 1591, a Moroccan army crossed the Sahara and attacked Songhay. Morocco was not able to consolidate its own rule; nor was Songhay able to expel the invaders. As a result, the vast area that had been controlled by Songhay was thrown into a state of confusion and political instability. Borno actively engaged in slave raiding, in order to finance trade with the Ottoman Empire in North Africa in the dubious hope that a political alliance would legitimize and extend Borno's hegemony south of the Sahara. Such a policy impressed some, but the costs of continuous slave raiding surely undermined Borno's influence in the affected areas and limited the spread of Islam. The Ethiopian *jihad* failed to generate a large state. Instead, a few Muslim principalities were all that were left after Christian Ethiopia regained parts of the highlands, while the Funj of Sennar only consolidated an area around the confluence of the Blue and White Nile. Once more, no empire appeared from the mirage of Dar es Salaam – the world of Islam. Nor did Muanamutapa survive; instead it disintegrated into several smaller states.

The general pattern of political disintegration and small-scale states prevailed along the whole Atlantic basin, in precisely those areas where the influence of European demand for slaves, gold, and other commodities was most profound. Kongo collapsed in civil war in the 1660s, after a century of gradual decline. Rivalries along the Guinea shores from the Gold Coast to the Niger delta resulted in the concentration of political power, but states remained small and belligerent. In the interior of the Niger delta and the Cross River, there were not even any states, despite a dense population, extensive trade, and strong cultural similarities. Between 1650 and 1750, two larger states emerged in this coastal zone: Oyo after 1650 and Asante after 1700, but they were never very large. They have often been called 'empires', but by comparison with the countries of Europe, the Middle East, and Asia, with their vast provinces and colonies, they appear small. Neither Asante nor Oyo even remotely paralleled the wealth and power of Ottoman

Turkey, Ming China, Moghul India, or the British, Dutch, French, and Spanish empires.

In this situation of political fragmentation, the characteristic figure was the soldier, who lived as a parasite off the turmoil of the continent. The record of warfare that fills the accounts of past states and rulers may not seem very different from the history of contemporary Europe or Asia, except that here the enslavement of people was the result, and no large states emerged that could provide some semblance of unity and safety. Even the economic and technological developments of the period promoted this political environment. The major technological improvements were in military organization, new food crops, and commercial organization. Guns and breeding horses facilitated the emergence of the soldier as the dominant historical figure. The introduction of new crops from the Americas increased food production and thereby helped to maintain population levels despite the export of slaves. Advances in commercial institutions, including credit facilities, currency, bulking, and regularized transportation, assisted in the movement of slaves. Africa remained the poor cousin in the world community, despite its partial incorporation into the world political-economy. The continent could deliver its people to the plantations and mines of the Americas and to the harems and armies of North Africa and Arabia. The most accurate depiction would characterize this period of African dependency as one of war-lord-ism. Who were the war-lords? How did they operate? Why were they successful in their perpetuation of rivalries that effectively maintained Africa in a retarded state of economic and political development?

THE MUSLIM TRADITION OF WAR AND STATE

Between 1500 and 1800, something like 3 million slaves were exported across the Sahara, the Red Sea, and the Indian Ocean, which represented approximately 30 per cent of the total exports from Africa. Another million or so were sent to the Americas from Muslim areas in the interior of the Senegambia and the upper Guinea coast, which represented an additional 10 per cent of the trade. Hence the Muslim trade accounts for probably 40 per cent of the slaves exported from Africa between 1500 and 1800. The volume of exports during the sixteenth century can largely be attributed to wars of political expansion, while the volume of exports for the next two centuries primarily resulted from the wars of political fragmentation.

At the beginning of the seventeenth century, the glorious tradition of Islamic empire had been checked; instead, the many small states struggled amongst themselves to acquire slaves and land. None was successful in creating a new empire, but many slaves changed hands. The three patterns that prevailed in these two centuries included, firstly, wars between Muslim states and non-Muslim people; secondly, wars among nominally Muslim governments; and thirdly, Islamic holy wars against established authorities of all kinds. Whether Christian, Muslim, or pagan, all the states of this period contributed to the slave population through their military actions, and these states had substantial slave populations themselves. Despite variations, the conception of slavery conformed more or less to the Islamic norm, even in Christian states – most of whose markets and most of whose merchants were in any case Muslim.

Local warfare and periodic drought combined to create a cyclical pattern of history that was closely related to the institution of slavery. War and drought, while impeding political and economic expansion, provided a solution to the inherent problem of finding new sources of slaves. The war-lords of the savanna seized captives, settling them around their capitals or selling them to merchants. Although some captives were exported from the savanna, the general movement resulted in the concentration of population, at least temporarily. During periods of drought, however, people had to move to save themselves, whether they were slave or free; defeat in war could also lead to a similar flight. This demographic shift replenished lands stripped of people by slave raids and war and made it possible for later war-lords to enslave or re-enslave people once climatic and political conditions stabilized.

Droughts were common in the seventeenth and eighteenth centuries, although, ironically, the period as a whole was relatively wet. As a climatic epoch, however, these two centuries experienced drastic shifts in rainfall conditions that reinforced the cyclical pattern.[2] The wetter era is apparent in the level of Lake Chad, which was at record highs, and in the vegetation patterns along rivers and lakes, whose remains demonstrate a lush period. The first serious drought struck from 1639 to 1642–3. It was reported in the Senegambia and Niger bend regions and may have coincided with a period of famine remembered in Borno as *dala dama*. There were other bad years: 1669–70 in Senegambia; 1676, 1681, and 1685 in the Niger bend; and sometime in the 1690s, perhaps simultaneously with the drought in the Niger bend, at Agades and possibly in Borno. Drought probably caused a famine of seven years' duration in Borno, in the second half of the century. While the drought of 1639–43 was the worst, it cannot be identified in the central Sudan nor in the Nile valley and Ethiopia.[3]

The eighteenth century was more dramatic for all regions, there being two and perhaps three major droughts and many localized ones. The first appears to have occurred in the middle Niger valley from 1711 to 1716 and was also reported in Borno, where it lasted seven years. The second drought struck in the early 1720s: 1721–2 in the middle Niger valley and 1723 in the Senegal basin. The most severe drought of the eighteenth century, and indeed probably the longest and most disastrous one in recorded history, took place in the middle of the eighteenth century. It lasted from 1738 to 1756 in the middle Niger valley; in Senegambia it was most serious from 1747 to 1758; it hit Borno in the 1740s and 1750s. Famine was recorded as far south as the middle Volta basin, most seriously in 1745–6. The remainder of the century included more droughts: 1770–1 in the Timbuktu area, 1786 in the Gambia, and the 1790s for the central Sudan. None of these appears to have been as disastrous as the Great Drought of 1738–56.[4]

The population displacement accompanying these droughts was severe. As in periods of political instability, there was opportunity for slaves to escape; sometimes they had to flee. Because most slaves were at the bottom of society, moreover, they were often the first to suffer when food became scarce. Furthermore, many people, not just slaves, found themselves in a desperate condition, as traditions from the Senegal River valley demonstrate for the middle of the eighteenth century when the number of slaves apparently increased as a result of this suffering. Similarly, half the population of Timbuktu reportedly died during the famine accompanying the same drought. Self-enslavement to avoid starvation and the sale of children were both possible at such times.

Wars between Muslims and non-Muslims continued the tradition of militant Islam, which held that enslavement and military action were proper methods of conversion. The political reality of the seventeenth and eighteenth centuries conflicted with this ambition, for Islamic governments did not possess the power to subject much non-Muslim territory. Consequently, enslavement was conceived as a necessary means of pursuing the same goal. In this period, Borno presented itself as a caliphate, allied to the Ottoman Empire; Sennar pictured itself as the advance guard of Islam, having smashed through the vestiges of Christianity in the upper Nile valley where Christian Nubia and Ethiopia had checked the spread of Islam. Adal continued to harbour the hope that its abortive holy war of the previous century could be revived. New states, including Dar Fur and Wadai in the region between the Nile valley and Lake Chad, pushed forward the frontiers of Islam against pagan populations, and again Islam was used as a rationale for war.

These Muslim states organized official slaves raids, known as *ghazwa* or *salatiya* in Dar Fur and Sennar.[5] The Sultan of Sennar appointed an officer to oversee the expeditions there. Each noble organized his own contingent, usually comprising his private slave-army. The Dar Fur sultan issued certificates· that designated where raiding parties were allowed, so that competition between units could be minimized. He also placed the expedition under an official, and specific units here included volunteers as well as slave soldiers. The Borno armies pillaged the lands to the south of Lake Chad, some raiding into the hill country of Mandara and others sweeping into the plains of the Benue, Shari, and Logone River valleys. These sultans claimed half the booty, which they were then free to dispose of as they saw fit. Some women were placed in harems; some men were drafted into the army; still others were settled on plantations; and the rest were sold. Such organized slave raiding reflected the dependence of the political economy on slavery. Slave catching was a business. For the Sultan of Sennar it was his second largest source of revenue, after direct taxation of the peasantry.

Christian Ethiopia accepted Portuguese military support to counter this Muslim danger, but the Portuguese alliance proved to be a mixed blessing.[6] The Portuguese neutralized Ottoman influence on the Red Sea, thereby isolating Adal and other Muslim sultanates on Ethiopia's flank. By the early seventeenth century, Ethiopian independence was assured, but it was necessary to expel the Portuguese, too. Jesuit missionaries were intolerant of local Christianity and were forced to leave. Ethiopia then found itself in an unenviable position. With Muslim states on the east and west and the Red Sea trade severely depressed, the Christian monarchy became weaker and weaker. The nobility fought amongst itself, employing immigrant Galla nomads in its private armies. The nobles raided for slaves, sometimes against the Muslims and at other times into the pagan lands to the south. When necessary, the monarchy could secure cooperation to check Muslim inroads. None the less, political instability was so pronounced by the last half of the eighteenth century and continuing into the first several decades of the nineteenth century that this period is remembered as the 'era of princes' in recognition of the absence of strong central government. Moreover, the economic situation continued to be unfavourable. Some gold, perfume, and other luxuries were exported, but slaves were the most important commodity. And these depended upon Muslim markets.

The most serious enemy of Borno was Jukun, a pagan confederation in the Benue River valley. Jukun periodically marched on Borno and the tributary Hausa cities of Katsina and Kano. These counter-attacks were so feared that the defeat of one Jukun force by Borno was celebrated in verse by the seventeenth-century Katsina scholar and poet, Dan Marina:

'Ali has triumphed over the heathen, a matchless
triumph in the path of God.
Has he not brought us succour? Verily, but for him
Our hearts had never ceased from dread of the unbelievers.
Narrow had become to us the earth pressed by the foe,
Till 'Ali saved our children and their children yet unborn.
He drove back to their furthest borders the army of the Jukun,
And God scattered their host disheartened . . .
Give thanks again for what our Mai 'Ali has wrought;
For he has ransomed the whole Sudan from strife.[7]

Jukun stormed Kano, sacking the city, in the seventeenth century, although the walled towns of Borno and Hausaland were usually strong enough to prevent such severe incursions. Slaves were taken, however, no matter whether Muslims or non-Muslims were the aggressors.

Muslim slave raids and pagan counter-raids account for many slaves in the central Sudan, but by no means all. The Muslim states were often at war with each other, despite the concern in Islamic legal circles over such abuses.

Ahmad Bābā, in his 1614 treatise on slavery, specifically condemned the Hausa states for conducting such wars:

> Sometimes there is disharmony among the chiefs of these lands and one *sultān* might march against another, and invade his country and capture whatever he can from the other's followers, who are Muslims, and he sells the prisoners although they are free Muslims. Alas! This is much practised among them. The people of Katsina invade Kano and others do the same although their tongue is one and their language is one their conditions are approximate.[8]

Between 1600 and 1800, the five small Hausa states of Gobir, Zamfara, Kano, Katsina, and Zazzau fought dozens of wars, sometimes forming alliances and at other times fighting each other directly.[9] Furthermore, Borno maintained nominal sovereignty over several of these states, collecting tribute or marching its own armies through Hausaland whenever such payments were in arrears. Only at the very end of the eighteenth century were slaves sent from this area to the Guinea coast for shipment to the Americas, and then in relatively small numbers. In general, slaves were marched north across the Sahara or redistributed locally. None the less, the political turmoil of the period and the inability of Borno to transform its hegemony into a strong imperial system once again reflect the general insecurity of the era.

Further west, where the upper Niger and Senegambia basins supplied both the trans-Saharan and trans-Atlantic slave markets, the pattern of enslavement was different in two respects. Firstly, the division between Muslim and non-Muslim had become institutionalized. The commercial and religious community was Muslim, while many governments were either pagan or only nominally Muslim. Even when some aristocracies were recognized as Muslim, their armies tended not to be. Secondly, Islamic holy war (*jihad*) overthrew some of these states, establishing in their place theocracies in which the association betwen political power and paganism was broken. In both situations, slave raiding was an important function of the state; only the rationale for enslavement changed. The *jihads* were significant as an inspiration for a new political order, but in the eighteenth century they only perpetuated the general insecurity that prevailed almost everywhere.

One pagan state that was a major supplier of slaves was the Bambara state of Segu, located on the banks of the Niger River and founded in the early seventeenth century in the wake of Songhay's disintegration.[10] Its first ruler, Kalajan Kulubali, attracted a following of young men who ravaged the countryside, sometimes as mercenaries in the employment of petty rulers and at other times as enslavers interested in the profits and glory to be gained from military action. This tradition of raiding was pursued over the generations because local society allowed young men to form hunting associations that were easily adaptable to illegitimate ends. Bands of men would waylay caravans, or kidnap children and the occasional farmer in his field. This tradition was carried to its logical extension under the grandson of Kalajan, the more notorious Mamari Kulubali, whose military career led from raiding to organized warfare. Mamari Kulubali attracted escaped slaves, debtors, criminals, as well as his own age-mates, whose quest for adventure had provided the nucleus of his army. Before Mamari Kulubali died in the mid-1750s, Segu had raided north to Timbuktu, occupied briefly in 1727, and south to Kong, near the forest edge. So many slaves were taken in these campaigns that Segu became a major source of slaves for the European slave-ships in the Senegambia basin. Incorporated slaves became the largest contingent in the army and the real power behind the throne, so much so that when Mamari's son and successor proved unacceptable to the army, he was assassinated and replaced by a series of more tractable men.

Royal power in such states in Senegambia as Kajoor, Kaymor, and Saalum depended upon slave soldiers (*tyeddo*) whose antipathy towards Islam was pronounced. Those soldiers collected taxes and were responsible for many administrative tasks, as well as the fighting. Their heavy drinking, long hair, bright clothing, and arrogance earned the deep hatred of Muslims.[11] In these ways, the *tyeddo* of Senegambia were similar to the Bambara warriors of Segu and other states further inland. Indiscriminate enslavement and the export of free Muslims to the Americas and across the Sahara frustrated many Muslims. In the course of the seventeenth and eighteenth centuries, this discontent crystallized, as Muslim reformers gathered a following that hoped to establish more orthodox, Islamic states. Neither slave raiding as such nor trade with Christian Europe was criticised, only the sale of free Muslims and the lax practices of political authorities in enforcing Muslim law and tradition.

The new theocracies, Futa Bondu, Futa Toro, and Futa Jallon, eliminated some anti-Muslim regimes, but only in the Futa Jallon highlands and along the interior stretch of the Senegal River. Futa Bondu, the first and smallest of these states, produced some slaves, while the holy war in the highlands resulted in the enslavement of many people, particularly in the 1740s and again in the 1780s. The pattern repeated itself. Enemies of the new regime were enslaved and sold, unless they were free Muslims. None the less, these Islamic governments, despite their intention of initiating a new political and religious order, contributed to the insecurity of the western Sudan. Enslavement continued to be a function of the state.[12]

WAR-LORDS OF WEST-CENTRAL AFRICA

During the sixteenth and seventeenth centuries, the main source of slaves for sale to Europeans was west-central Africa, especially the Mbundu lands to the south of Kongo, and the area around Malebo Pool on the Zaire River. Of the more than 1.7 million slaves shipped from Africa to the Americas between 1500 and 1700, probably three-quarters came from the region. In the eighteenth century, almost 2 million slaves were exported from west-central Africa alone; so that the total trade from 1500 to 1800 probably exceeded 3,200,000 slaves.

Where did the slaves come from? How were people enslaved? The analysis of the export figures in the preceding chapter demonstrated that three phenomena made these exports possible. The first was the disintegration of the Kongo kingdom, which experienced civil war in the last half of the seventeenth century. Kongo was then a major source of slaves. The second involved Portuguese expeditions into the interior in an attempt to expand the colony and capture slaves. The third was the rise of Imbangala war-bands that operated in the area where the Mbundu lived to the south of Kongo. The trend was towards political instability. Where once the kingdom of Kongo had dominated the area, now no central authority could enforce law and order. Instead, the period was one for the war-lords, whether they were Kongo nobles, Imbangala chiefs, Portuguese commanders, or new warrior princes further inland. The common element was the emphasis on war and plunder, and the consequence was enslavement on a massive scale. Without doubt the majority, perhaps the vast majority, of the million or so slaves exported from west-central Africa between 1500 and 1700 were a product of the interaction between these Imbangala, Kongo, and Portuguese war-lords. The eighteenth century required the inclusion of areas further inland in order to maintain the level of exports, but this meant that other war-lords were added to the list of participants in the campaigns to supply slaves for export.

Although Kongo continued to participate in the slave trade in the first half of the seventeenth century, the state was not the major source of slaves that it once had been. In part this resulted from the collapse of the Mpinda–São Thomé trade and the shift to Luanda and the direct export of slaves to the Americas.[13] But the decline also resulted from the inability of the Kongo nobility to re-assert state trading, as Afonso I had once done. The Kongolese aristocracy was more interested in incorporating slaves into the retinues and agricultural estates of the capital district and Mbanza Sonyo than it was in capturing slaves for export. Occasionally, nobles raided the peasantry in order to collect taxes, and these captives were likely to be exported. This was especially so in the 1650s, when such raids appear to have been quite common. This internal conflict reflected deeper cleavages in Kongolese society, which intensified to the point of civil war in the 1660s. The coastal province of Mbanza Sonyo invaded São Salvador, and the entire nobility of the capital district then deserted the city, together with its slaves and followers. Those slaves who did not escape were seized and taken to Sonyo. The disintegration of Kongo, with the exception of the victorious province, continued after the desertion of São Salvador, as is evident from the increase in pawning, even in Mbanza Sonyo in the 1680s. The nobility also continued to harass – and enslave – the peasantry. Both pawning and raids on the peasantry demonstrate that nobles and peasants alike were hard pressed in these decades.[14]

The new commercial system, which had developed with the founding of the Portuguese colony of Luanda in 1576, was largely confined to the commercial corridor that followed the Kwanza River valley into the interior.[15] In this region, a series of Imbangala war-lords roamed the countryside living off what they could plunder. By 1601, some Imbangala had come into contact with the Portuguese, forming temporary alliances to capture slaves in exchange for imports. By the second decade of the seventeenth century, these arrangements had become permanent, and the Imbangala in effect were transformed into mercenaries for the Portuguese. Some Imbangala remained in southern Kongo and elsewhere near the coast; others founded states in the interior.[16] These included Kalandula, Kabuku ka Ndonga, and Kasanje.

The Imbangala operated from fortified camps and recruited members through enslavement. Initiates were restricted to uncircumcized males, which effectively meant that only boys were incorporated and trained in the rituals and military techniques of the organization. Circumcized males and women were usually sold to the Portuguese or Dutch, except for those women taken as wives and other captives who were killed. The practices of the Imbangala were designed to terrorize the general population and to encourage the martial skills – valour in war, total loyalty to the leader of the camp, and a denial of kinship relations. These practices included the killing of slaves before battle, cannibalism, and infanticide. The Imbangala based their military superiority on a psychological advantage over the peasantry. They perpetuated customs that were abhorred by most Mbundu farmers. They had no kin. Symbolically and ritually, they renounced human reproduction and kinship, which in the lineage-based societies of the Mbundu and Kongo were at the heart of society.

Kasanje and Matamba, the most important of these small interior states, maintained a monopoly of the export–import business. That their officials were more than state merchants is revealed in the importance they placed on war and organized slave raids. These activities demonstrate that war-lordism remained dominant. Kidnapping, raids beyond the borders of the state, and periodic wars indicate a political order that relied on violence and lawlessness. The peasantry was not exempt from this affliction. Periodic levies that had to be paid in slaves were imposed on the lineages. The Matamba and Kasanje war-lords wanted to ensure that no challenge to their supremacy could develop. Failure to pay tribute was punished by raids, while compliance reduced the number of people in each lineage.[17]

Slavery in Kasanje, therefore, was essential to the political and economic structure of the state. Since slaves were regularly sold to Portuguese firms for export to the Americas, all slaves in the state faced the real possibility that they were next on the list. The lineage, knowing that they were subject to tribute payments, kidnapped strangers and organized raids to acquire slaves. When possible, they purchased slaves, for slaves represented an investment against future exactions from the government. The Kasanje rulers maintained the most respected oracle in west-central Africa, so famous that the surrounding Mbundu chiefs sent troublesome rivals and other undesirables to suffer judgement before the Kasanje 'great *ndua*'. Guilty defendants, sometimes with their families, were sold into slavery. The Kasanje rulers also weakened rivals within the state by requisitioning slaves from among them – a special tribute that had to be paid in order to prevent a punitive raid.[18]

The turbulence of west-central Africa spread inland further still, ultimately affecting the inner basin of the Zambezi too. From the last decade of the seventeenth century onwards, a series of wars erupted and so fed the slave routes to the coast. These wars were associated with the consolidation of several states, the most important being Luba, Lunda, Kazembe, and Lozi.[19] Luba was probably the first to institute changes that resulted in the emergence of a class of war-lords. It was located in the Lomami and Lualaba valleys, from where splinter-groups of aristocrats spread to the west and south. One of these imposed itself in the area that became Lunda, centred between Luba and Kasanje and hence well situated to profit from the slave trade to the coast. The ruler of this state, the *mwant yaav*, founded a capital district (*mussumba*) from where Lunda armies raided outwards, capturing slaves. In due course, a number of provinces and other small states were established under Lunda war-lords, who channelled slaves to the *mussumba*. These dependencies were located throughout the valleys of the Kasai, Kwango, and Luapula and hence dominated most of modern eastern Angola, southern Zaire, and northern Zambia. Two of these states became important in their own right. Kazembe, located in the Luapula valley south of Luba and south-east of Lunda, was founded in the 1740s and expanded eastward. By the end of the century, Kazembe was trading with Portuguese and other merchants from the Zambezi valley, as well as sending slaves to Lunda for trans-shipment to Angola. Hence by this time the interior supply-system of the Lunda and Luba states provided slaves to both the east and west coasts, and probably for the first time a continuous network stretched across this part of Africa. The last state of note, Lozi, was located in the interior flood-plains of the Zambezi valley, south of Lunda. Here, too, slaves were available for export to both coasts, although Lozi was more conveniently situated as a supply area for Benguela, rather than Luanda.

The Zambezi corridor to the Indian Ocean was an old route, dating back to the medieval period when gold was the principal export from the interior of south-eastern Africa. In the eighteenth century, gold was still exported, along with some ivory, but slaves commanded an increasingly important share in the value of trade. Slaves brought from Kazembe and Lozi, while demonstrating the links that crossed the continent by the last decades of the eighteenth century, were never a major portion of the Indian Ocean trade; most slaves from Kazembe and Lozi went west. The catchment area for the Indian Ocean was in the Zambezi valley itself and the area around Lake

Malawi. Two routes connected the interior with the coast: one down the Zambezi valley to Quelimane or branching overland to Mozambique Island; the other stretching from Lake Malawi to Kilwa. These two routes became a major source of slaves in the 1770s, principally for the French sugar islands in the Indian Ocean.[20]

The pattern of enslavement in the south-eastern portion of central Africa was similar to that in west-central Africa: war-lords operated on a relatively small scale, collecting slaves from exploited populations and shipping these slaves to the coast. As in Angola, the Portuguese were actively involved in enslavement. Portuguese war-lords, whom Isaacman has called *prazeros*, operated as far inland as the commercial centre of Zumbo.[21] Their landed estates, won from the local population and sanctified by the Portuguese crown, served as bases for slave raiding in the interior. Further north, along the Lake Malawi–Kilwa axis, local African war-lords fulfilled the same function as the *prazeros*. Various Yao warriors in particular emerged as strong men who raided their less well-organized neighbours, although, nearer the coast, wars among the Makonde and others accounted for some slaves for export.[22] In none of these cases did a large centralized state evolve; the Yao were divided among war-lords who rose to prominence for brief periods, while the tenuous links between the *prazeros* and the Portuguese crown hardly qualified as a strong political bond that could provide the basis of a colonial state. South-eastern Africa remained a frontier region in which enslavement was a product of frontier instability.

While Zambezia and the Lake Malawi region provided many of the slaves for the Mascarenes, Madagascar was the source of virtually all the rest. Once again, the development of Madagascar as an exporting region represented a further extension of the slaving frontier. This island, and the Comoro archipelago – located between Madagascar and the mainland – had been involved in the commercial patterns of the Indian Ocean since the medieval period, but the developments of the late eighteenth century were different from the earlier trade.

Various Muslim sultanates controlled the Comoro Islands, and these catered to passing ships in the Indian Ocean until the late eighteenth century, when invasions from Madagascar upset their commercial prosperity.[23] The raids were directed from Sakalava, which, together with Betsimisaraka and Imerina, was locked in a power struggle for control of Madagascar. Until the end of the eighteenth century, Sakalava and Betsimisaraka had succeeded in aportioning most of the island between them; the rise of Imerina in the central highlands upset this balance of power. Sakalava raided the Comoros, as well as its own frontier on Madagascar, in search of slaves and other booty. The slaves were sold to the French for use in the Mascarenes, and the proceeds were used to buy firearms. The Sakalava even raided the East African coast, including Kilwa. Imerina's rise was based on land-based military expansion and an attempt to capture the French slave-market. Already by the 1790s, Imerina had become the main source of Madagascan slaves in the Mascarenes. Again, the importation of firearms enabled the Imerina aristocracy to continue its imperialist drive to control the island, although Sakalava still maintained its independence in 1800. The Betsimisaraka League had largely lost its autonomy by this time, however.[24]

POLITICS OF SLAVE TRADING ON THE WEST AFRICAN COAST

Perhaps as many as 4,500,000 slaves were exported from the West African coast in the seventeenth and eighteenth centuries, although estimates by regional origin only account for 4,000,000 between 1640 and 1800 (table 4.1). As discussed above, the difference between these two figures relates to the lack of data for a regional breakdown for the seventeenth century and the inability to calculate the departure points for North American vessels, some French ships, and the vessels of the minor carriers. Of the 4,000,000 slaves whose coastal origin is known, 38 per cent, or about 1.51 million, came from the Bight of Benin – the Slave Coast; 18 per cent, or about 730,000, came from the Akan area along the Gold Coast (including probable exports as a result of the Baule wars to the west); and another 21 per cent, or about 850,000, from the interior of the Bight of Biafra. The remainder, perhaps another 910,000, came from the western coast as far north as the Senegambia basin. These last exports have been discussed in the section on enslavement in Muslim areas. The stretch of territory where the Akan, Aja, and Yoruba states were the dominant powers, including the areas that experienced wars caused by refugees or other enemies of Oyo and Asante, supplied over two million slaves, over half of all exports from West Africa. The vast majority of these slaves were taken in wars. Those slaves who came from the Niger delta and the Cross River – the Bight of Biafra – had a more varied background, and it seems likely that the majority of these slaves were not enslaved in war. Raiding, kidnapping, judicial conviction, and religiously-sanctioned enslavement were the main sources.

The expansion of Oyo began in the middle of the seventeenth century and is reflected in the export figures for slaves.[25] The Oyo aristocracy, composed of the king and a council of nobles, had learned the secret of military success in the savanna the hard way. The horse had to be the basis of the military. Oyo had suffered defeat at the hands of Nupe, which controlled the Niger River valley in central Nigeria in the early seventeenth century. Forced into exile in the neighbouring Bariba states, the Oyo leadership slowly reconstituted its army. Once Oyo reoccupied the district near the Niger, where a fortified capital was built, the king and nobles pursued policies to guarantee access to horses for the cavalry. Oyo established commercial relations with the coastal ports in order to sell slaves and import cowries, textiles, and other goods. These in turn were used to purchase horses from the north.

Oyo's conquests were along the savanna corridor that stretched from the Niger to the coast. The Yoruba and other people who lived within striking

Table 4.1 *West African slave exports, c. 1640–1800 (approximate totals)*

Region	Total	Approximate percentage
Western coast	910,000	23
Gold Coast and Akan interior	730,000	18
Bight of Benin	1,510,000	38
Bight of Biafra	850,000	21
West Africa	4,000,000	100

Sources: table 3.4; Manning 1979, p. 117; Postma 1975*b*, p. 49. These projections do not include slaves whose regional origins are unknown, which probably affects the eighteenth-century estimates by 9 per cent.

distance of this route were raided, and the prisoners were sold to Europeans. By the last half of the seventeenth century, Oyo controlled much of the territory south of the Moshi River, which was the border with the Bariba states to the north, and east to Igbomina, along the forest–savanna divide through Yoruba country. The whole of the upper Ogun River valley was under Oyo control, as was the region westward to the Opara River, which separated Oyo from Sabe. In the south-west, Oyo had direct control of the northern Egbado and Anago areas. It may well be that parts of southern Bariba and Nupe country were tributary, while Oyo raided south-westward into Allada, Dahomey, and Weme, perhaps receiving tribute from these states too. By the early eighteenth century, Oyo dominated the interior of the Slave Coast.[26]

Early reports indicate that most of the slaves exported from the Bight of Benin before the middle of the eighteenth century came from a region that stretched from the coast a distance of no more than 200 to 300 km inland, and the ethnic origins of the slaves was largely Aja and Yoruba.[27] One reason for this preponderance of coastal people was the struggle for power among the Aja, who vied for position in the trade with Oyo and the north and who attempted unsuccessfully to assert some order in Aja society itself. There were many ports on the coast here: Allada, with its ports of Offra and Jakin, and Hueda, with its port at Whydah, were the most important from the end of the seventeenth century until the 1720s; Akwamu, which dominated the coast from Winneba through Accra on the Gold Coast after 1681, and as far east as Whydah by 1700. Hueda and Allada were well placed to tap the trade north along the natural corridor of savanna country that reached the coast at this point and thereby facilitated travel between the coast and the interior. Akwamu dominated the routes north along the Volta River and also had access to gold supplies, and, because of its expansion eastward, was a factor in the politics of the Slave Coast.[28]

The emergence of Dahomey inland from Whydah and Allada and adjacent to Akwamu was both a product of the power struggle on the Slave

Coast and contributed to the further export of slaves.[29] The area had been subject to raids from the coast, but an enterprising war-lord, Agaja, organized a tight military machine, based on firearms, and attacked Allada in 1724 and Hueda in 1727. The immediate cause of the invasions was the efforts of the two coastal states to tighten their administrative control of the export trade in slaves, thereby reducing the benefits to such inland contributors as Dahomey. By resorting to arms, Dahomey secured control of the ports of Jakin and Whydah and now, along with Akwamu, dominated the coast.

To maintain its own coastal interests, Oyo intervened in Dahomey between 1726 and 1730, forcing Dahomey to pay tribute as a guarantee that the trade routes would remain open. In 1727, Oyo was still trading at Jakin, but in 1732, Dahomey once again moved on the port, destroying it and thereby endangering its own relationship with Oyo. Despite the tributary status of Dahomey, the Oyo government and principal traders began to develop alternative outlets to the sea. In the 1720s, Epe was one alternative; by the early 1730s, Apa temporarily became a major port, replaced in 1736 by Badagry, which thereafter remained a principal port. In the 1750s, another port emerged at Porto Novo, and after the 1760s, Lagos also emerged as an outlet, although then it was only a minor port.[30]

Because of this political jockeying, it is no wonder that many of the slave exports in the late seventeenth and first half of the eighteenth centuries came from the immediate interior of the coast. In the peak decades of slave exports from 1690 to 1740, perhaps 80 to 90 per cent of those slaves sold on the coast were Aja captives or imported slaves from further north who had been at least partially acculturated.[31] Virtually all the rest of the slaves were Yoruba. Without doubt these estimates of ethnic origins are distorted; they probably disguise a higher percentage of Yoruba in particular, and it is likely that some slaves, at least, were brought from further north.

After the middle of the eighteenth century, the origins of slave exports changed. While Aja and Yoruba still predominated, reflecting the same likelihood as in the earlier period that Aja, Yoruba, and imported slaves who were at least partially acculturated were the majority of exports, now slaves from further north appear regularly in the registers of slave ships. Those speaking Eastern Voltaic (from the Bariba states and Atakora Mountains), Nupe, and Hausa emerged as identifiable categories of slaves, although their numbers remained small by comparison with the total volume of exports, amounting to about 183,000 slaves for the last half of the eighteenth century. These ethnic labels also implied a more varied background for the slave population, but the presence of these categories suggests that now a significant percentage of exports did not experience a period of acculturation before being sold to Europeans.[32] The frontier of enslavement had moved inland, therefore. This expansion of the catchment area was a logical feature of the large-scale, sustained export of slaves.

This expansion was also directed westward to the Gold Coast, where

Akwamu had already participated in the early growth of slave exports through its involvement in the politics of the Slave Coast.[33] Although Akwamu was an Akan state, with its capital, Nyanaoase, located west of the Akwapim Ridge, its expansion had been directed eastward. Its closest access to the coast was at Winneba, but between 1677 and 1681 several Akwamu armies invaded Accra, whereafter the European trade-castles there became the major outlets for its gold, ivory, and slave exports. By 1700, as noted above, Akwamu controlled the whole coast as far east as Whydah. During the next decade or so, as many as 50 to 60 ships stopped at Accra each year, while others stopped at lesser points to the east. Since slaves were also transported along the coastal lagoon to Whydah, the number of slaves dispatched from Akwamu was probably a considerable portion of total exports from the Bight of Benin–Gold Coast region between 1700 and 1730.

Akwamu also faced west, where there was a power struggle equal in intensity to the struggle in the interior of the Slave Coast. After 1650, Akwamu shared power with many Akan states, the most important of which were Akyem and Denkyira. The main economic goal was control of gold, not slaves.[34] Intermittent warfare between these states ended in a stalemate, until a new state, Asante, gradually emerged as the dominant power after 1700. Denkyira and Akyem formed an alliance against Akwamu and Asante, but the destruction of Denkyira in 1701 left Asante free to expand. Other wars followed, now that Asante, Akyem, and Akwamu were the dominant powers, and these accounted for the export of slaves. This power struggle for control of the gold, kola, and slave resources of the region was narrowed further when Akyem defeated Akwamu in 1730.[35]

Asante's principal campaigns in the north included the conquest of Bono-Mansu, the early Akan state where the old Muslim town of Bighu was located, in 1724, and the invasion of the trans-Volta, resulting in the occupation of eastern Gonja in 1744–5. These thrusts increased the power of Asante considerably, since slave exports could be used to purchase firearms in preparation for the final defeat of Akyem in 1742. Once Asante had consolidated its position in the south and the north-east, all that remained was the extinction of the remaining independent states, the most important of which was Gyaman in the north-west, defeated in 1746–7.[36] Thus by mid-century, the Akan wars had devastated the region, thereby accounting for most, if not all, of the 321,000 slaves exported from the Gold Coast between 1700 and 1750. The volume of exports was maintained at about this level for the rest of the century, with a notable expansion in the 1780s and 1790s, when Asante attempted to occupy the Fanti coast.

In the interior of the Bight of Biafra, the pattern of enslavement was remarkably different from that on the Gold and Slave Coasts. Here, no strong state comparable to Oyo and Asante emerged. The possibility of political consolidation was there. Like the ports of the Slave Coast and the towns of the Gold Coast, the Bight of Biafra had its commercial centres,

Calabar on the Cross River, Bonny and Elem Kalabari in the Niger delta and Aboh on the lower Niger. But none of these centres was able to transform commercial supremacy into territorial rule, nor did any interior polity try to control the ports. While war-lords were present, they usually acted as agents for the merchants. Neither the merchants nor the warriors created a centralized state.[37]

The earliest known example of war-lord-ism involves the origins of the Aro, who were an amalgamation of Ibibio and Igbo settlers on the escarpment overlooking the Cross River valley.[38] The Aro are significant because they began as mercenaries and became merchants without consolidating their position politically. The first Aro were mercenaries for the merchants of Calabar, and they are remembered as the ones who introduced firearms into the interior of the Bight of Biafra. They established a base at Aro Chukwu, subduing the local residents and settling war captives there. This original band of soldiers – called Akpa – remained a recognizable section of the Aro, but other sections emerged. Elsewhere, the initial Aro settlements in Afikpo, Ndizuogu, and Ndikelionwu were for slave-raiding parties and only later became centres of trade.

In the absence of a centralized state, the Aro turned to the manipulation of religious institutions in order to secure slaves. Their oracle (Ibinukpabi) at Aro Chukwu was directly or indirectly responsible for the transfer of thousands of slaves to European ships waiting at the coastal ports.[39] This shrine was respected throughout much of the hinterland as a particularly powerful agent of the supernatural. In fact, the Aro carefully coordinated the oracle with military and commercial institutions that they controlled, and thereby monopolized the markets and fairs of the populous Igbo and Ibibio countryside. There was no need for a centralized state with its war-lords, tribute payments, and courts, Instead, groups of villages, closely connected through kinship, formed alliances, marital and commercial, with other sets of villages. This local orientation required close cooperation, but friction between communities could erupt in warfare when disputes over marriage, sorcery, or crime were not settled. Tensions were relieved through mediation as well as violence, and it was the role of the oracles and other intermediaries to placate communities and so reduce the level of potential disruption.

The Aro clans inserted themselves into the vacuum that a centralized state could have filled. They negotiated alliances with various sets of villages that allowed them to monopolize trade and establish market-places and fairs, and they promoted their oracle as a supreme court of appeal in judicial and religious matters. The oracle itself was widely recognized to speak for the supreme god of the religious pantheon, and as such was respected among the three dominant ethnic groups of the region, the Ijaw of the Niger delta, the Ibibio of the Cross River valley, and the Igbo of the densely populated country astride the lower Niger River. The religious oracle and the commercial network both filled a structural need in the region. The oracle

82

settled disputes and legitimized agreements, in part through divine interpretation of the social order and in part through secular deals based on
information supplied by the commercial network of the Aro traders. The
force needed to impose decisions and protect the merchants in their travels
was furnished through alliances with other sets of villagers who acted as
mercenaries. This loosely structured federation dominated one of the
heaviest concentrations of population in Africa.

Slavery was fundamental to the successful operation of this federation.
Firstly, slaves were a major item of trade, and the prosperity of the Aro
depended upon the sale of slaves to European merchants on the coast.
Secondly, slaves were used as porters in the trade of the interior, and they
farmed the lands of the merchants at Aro Chukwu. Thirdly, enslavement
was the ultimate sanction of the oracle, payment often being in slaves. The
oracle was even known to seize parties who had humbled themselves before
it. Fourthly, failure to respect the decisions of the oracle and physical abuse
of Aro merchants and their property were sufficient grounds to expect a
lightning raid from the mercenaries. Indeed, these warrior bands enslaved
people whenever called upon, and the slaves were turned over to the
merchants via the oracle.

The manipulation of religious institutions is now obvious. There were
many shrines, but only that at Aro Chukwu achieved such renown. Its
location at the bottom of a steep hill in the thick jungle of a stream that
flowed down the escarpment from Aro Chukwu to the Cross River
strategically marked the transfer-point from the plateau of Igbo country to
the valley of the Ibibio. This stream cut the high terrain where the Aro
villages were located, so its secrets were well understood locally but must
have seemed awesome to strangers. Plaintiffs who had travelled to Aro
Chukwu to face the oracle were housed in one of the Aro villages, paying
lodging fees and being filled with stories of the horrible sight that awaited
them. Once the visitors descended the slippery hillside, they faced a tall cave
on the bank of the stream where the oracle spoke. The opening had been
hollowed out to allow for a lining of human skulls, a sufficient warning that
the required sacrifices could well include slaves as their victims. The priests
informed the terrified delegations why they were there. It was not necessary
to plead a case, thanks to the intelligence relayed from Aro merchants, and
it certainly was not widely known, if it was known at all, that the slaves
'eaten' by the oracle in recognition of the services rendered were easily
passed along a path that followed the stream to the Cross River and the
waiting ships of the Europeans.

THE DYNAMICS OF SLAVE SUPPLY

During the seventeenth and eighteenth centuries, there were four patterns
in the development of a slave-supply mechanism. Firstly, wars and
large-scale slave raiding by centralized states stripped surrounding areas of

their population; these states expanded, but in doing so reduced the possibility of acquiring slaves as the enslavement frontier was pushed back. Secondly, wars between neighbouring states in which no single state established its ascendancy resulted in the enslavement of people without the necessity of expanding the enslavement frontier. Thirdly, the spread of lawlessness, as demonstrated in kidnapping and small-scale raiding, led to the random enslavement of people without the creation of depopulated zones. Fourthly, the spread of enslavement as a punishment for convicted criminals, witches, and other miscreants became a means of supplying slaves from within a society, again without affecting the population density in a dramatic way. The sanctions of religious oracles fitted into this category. Structurally, these methods of enslavement affected the demographic profile of particular areas differently.

Individual states could not expand their frontier for enslavement indefinitely. Either the state had to turn to other methods of providing slaves, such as through criminal prosecutions, or it had to abandon its function of enslaving people. This function could be passed on to tribute-paying provinces or to merchants who brought slaves from elsewhere. In west-central Africa, the Imbangala war-lords raided for slaves for the first few decades of the seventeenth century; thereafter, the slaving frontier moved inland, until in the eighteenth century the Lunda aristocracy filled the role once occupied by the Imbangala. In the interior of the Slave Coast, Oyo collected slaves through its own raids and political expansion, and this involved the extension of the catchment area for slaves. By the end of the eighteenth century, however, Oyo had shifted from enslaving people to trading for them.

When wars raged between neighbouring states over a prolonged period, as they did along the Slave and Gold Coasts during the late seventeenth and first half of the eighteenth centuries, then eventually new slaves had to be imported in order to restore the demographic balance, or else there was a net loss of population. The internecine wars between the many coastal states on the Slave and Gold Coasts provided a continuous stream of slaves for about five decades; this strife resulted in the enslavement of many people without pushing back the enslavement frontier. None the less, by 1800 the region as a whole was relatively densely populated, in part because Oyo and Asante emerged as the dominant states, checking the population drain, and in part because the exported population was replaced by new slaves brought from further inland.

The erosion of custom through the spread of kidnapping, raiding, and the sentencing of convicted criminals to slavery was another means of solving the slave-supply problem. Organized slave raiding – as distinct from war – and kidnapping both became more prevalent along the West African coast and in west-central Africa in the seventeenth and eighteenth centuries than in earlier periods. Kidnapping is a small-scale activity, often lost to history, while slave raiding is sometimes hard to distinguish from punitive expeditions against recalcitrant subjects or for the harassment of enemies. None the less, both activities are general indicators of a prevailing lawlessness, which the absence of central government made possible.

This political fragmentation had its impact on all walks of life. The times were insecure. The enslavement of people was easy. Without centralized authority that could safeguard personal liberties and property over large areas, individuals had to face the risks of travel if they wanted to pursue a commercial undertaking, and communities always feared the dangers of war, kidnapping, and raids. In many cases, it is difficult to separate the desire to capture prisoners for slavery from economic and political rivalries not directly related to enslavement.[40] None the less, warfare was by far the most important source of slaves. The three centuries from the sixteenth through the eighteenth are filled with the rise and fall of states. Some of these have been chronicled above in order to demonstrate their contribution to the slave population.

The problem was not simply one of legality. State violence, either through war or raiding, was usually justified on religious or political grounds. The punishment of criminals, sorcerers, and political opponents was also perceived as a legitimate method of protecting society. Kidnapping was often illegal, but attempts to stop it often failed. Social pressure also prevented many abuses, including the sale of pawns.

Olaudah Equiano, an Igbo slave who was kidnapped in 1756 and was ultimately sold to European slavers, provides a clear picture of the efforts of local people, his father included, to protect people from illegal seizure and sale. The account is particularly important because Equiano's father owned slaves himself and was involved in the enslavement of criminals. Hence this is not the account of an innocent bystander but of an active participant in a society that accepted slavery within clearly defined limits. Equiano came from the west bank of the Niger River, perhaps not too many kilometres from Aboh, the major slave-trading port on the Niger. He remembered that merchants frequently passed through his village:

> They always carry slaves through our land; but the strictest account is exacted of their manner of procuring them before they are suffered to pass. Sometimes indeed we sold slaves to them, but they were only prisoners of war, or such among us as had been convicted of kidnapping, or adultery, and some other crime, which we esteemed heinous. This practice of kidnapping induces me to think, that notwithstanding all our strictness, their principal business among us was to trepan [ensnare] our people. I remember too they carried great sacks along with them, which not long after I had an opportunity of fatally seeing applied to that infamous purpose.[41]

In this case, of course, Equiano's father was not involved in an investigation of his son's status, and since poor Equiano was traded to a blacksmith and subsequently to Europeans, it is clear that not everyone accepted the responsibility of determining the legality of a slave's status. None the less, the attempt to examine the origins of slaves is instructive. It reflects an attitude that was concerned about the abuses of the slave trade.

There were similar concerns elsewhere. In sixteenth century Kongo, King Afonso established courts of enquiry designed to investigate illegal enslavement.[42] He wanted to protect the rights of aristocrats, not enemies of the state or convicted criminals. He knew well that most slave traders were only too ready to buy anyone and ship them to São Thomé as quickly as possible. Afonso attempted to regulate the trade in order to control it. The king was not against the trade in principle, and his efforts at monopoly failed because it was easy for local officials and Portuguese merchants to violate the directives of the king. The consequence was not the elimination of illegal enslavement but the greater disintegration of central authority and an increase in slave exports.

The debate over legitimate enslavement also involved Muslims, who traced their right to enslave people back to the Qur'ān and other early legal and religious texts. Only Muslims and members of subject groups paying a special tax were exempt from enslavement. Violation of this code was a major preoccupation of such scholars as Ahmad Bābā of Timbuktu. Ahmad Bābā's treatise on legitimate enslavement is an important indication that the question of slavery was a difficult one, but one that involved the attention of the most learned scholars of Muslim society.[43] For Ahmad Bābā, neither Muslims nor the subjects of those states that he recognized as Muslim could be enslaved: 'The cause of slavery is non-belief', he wrote in 1614.[44]

The basic concern of Ahmad Bābā was shared by other thoughtful Muslims of his day both north and south of the Sahara, and sometimes abuses were corrected. For example, Medicon, a slave from Borno, one of the Islamic lands that Ahmad Bābā specifically mentioned, was freed in North Africa only a few decades after Ahmad Bābā wrote his treatise. The slave, a nephew of the Borno ruler, had been enslaved during civil strife in Borno and was subsequently sold in North Africa. Once he was identified, as a result of his uncle's efforts, he was redeemed from bondage. Despite his illegal enslavement, merchants were unwilling to accept his previous status until forced to do so through royal intervention. Medicon was either redeemed or given his freedom outright, probably in return for some compensation to the master.[45] South of the Sahara, free-born captives could be ransomed. This became a lucrative business, so that once again the effort to protect people from the abuses of slavery was undermined.

These attempts to check abuses reveal a strong tradition that tried to limit the worst effects of slavery. Here was a heritage, both Muslim and non-Muslim, that came close to considering the inherent evils of slavery. The questions people were asking related to the efforts to stop the practices of unscrupulous merchants and the activities of thugs. In general, however, these efforts failed. Individual wrongs were rectified, but the debate over enslavement continued. Slavery had become pervasive and morally destructive of many institutions.

This moral battle affected legal procedures, as can be seen in the shift of punishments towards enslavement and away from communal penalties, material compensation to wronged parties, and death to murderers and others convicted of particularly serious crimes. Enslavement increasingly became the most commonly imposed penalty. Francis Moore observed the consequences of this tendency in the Senegambia, where he bought slaves in the 1730s:

> Since this Slave Trade has been us'd, all Punishments are changed into Slavery; there being an advantage on such condemnations, they strain for Crimes very hard, in order to get the Benefit of selling the Criminal. Not only Murder, Theft and Adultery, are punished by selling the Criminal for Slave, but every trifling case is punished in the same manner.[46]

Moore had no moral difficulty in participating in such subversion of custom; like other merchants, it was not in his interest to question slaves about their origins. Similar observations to those of Moore were made elsewhere. Criminals, debtors, and sorcerers were condemned to slavery. This general erosion of society must be understood within its political context. The lack of strong governments that could impose a system of law over a wide area was a serious obstacle in preventing the steady increase in the number of slaves.

5

The organization of slave marketing, 1600–1800

In contrast to the disunity reflected in the political fragmentation of the continent, the commercial infrastructure that relayed 10,130,000 slaves to the Americas and the Islamic lands between 1600 and 1800 served to integrate the various parts of Africa with each other and with the external market.[1] This infrastructure did not handle all African slaves by any means, for many slaves never entered the market system. Captives seized in wars and raids were often redistributed among the armies responsible for capturing them. They were occasionally presented as gifts to religious shrines or Muslim scholars; girls and women were parcelled out as concubines and wives; young boys were pressed into military training. Nonetheless, merchants bought and sold the millions of slaves who were exported and millions of others who stayed in Africa.

Slaves were a major item of trade almost everywhere that commerce was well developed, particularly in regions where Muslim merchants operated and where European demand was high. Slaves increased in value as they were moved further from their home country, for the possibility of escape into familiar territory diminished with distance. At the point of capture, slaves were inexpensive, and consequently merchants often lingered around army camps in the hope of buying cheaply and subseqeuently driving their chattel to distant markets and selling at a better price. The export trade was especially effective in separating slaves from their homes. Captives seized near shipping-points were usually exported for this reason, since these slaves could be the most difficult to manage because of their local origin. Sale to foreign merchants, whether they came from North Africa, Europe, or a distant place within Africa, offered a profitable exchange, even when prices were relatively low. It was better to sell people who knew too much about the area and to replace them with other slaves purchased from the interior.[2]

MUSLIM NETWORKS

The Muslim trade can be divided into three interrelated sectors: government agencies, foreign merchants, and local Muslims. Firstly, government

88

officials had access to the large number of slaves seized in wars and raids and collected as tribute. The state acted as a bulking agency and on occasion could turn this position to advantage. The movements of private traders could be restricted, and official caravans could be organized to export slaves. Secondly, foreign merchants, particularly from North Africa, Egypt, Arabia, and India, came to African markets to purchase slaves, usually along with other commodities. They often dealt directly with government suppliers, advancing goods on credit to be repaid upon the successful completion of military expeditions. Foreign merchants either maintained houses locally, or they acted through brokers. In both cases, they were a source of credit for other merchants. Thirdly, native Muslims operated throughout the northern savanna, Ethiopia, and the East African coast, sometimes dealing with officials and foreign merchants and sometimes handling the bulking and exporting of slaves on their own. These merchants always invested in a variety of goods, not just slaves, and they could just as well sell slaves within Africa as export them.

The Funj Sultanate of Sennar, in the upper Nile valley, was one government that attempted to monopolize the export trade.[3] The Funj organized annual slave caravans to Egypt. This was done most effectively in the seventeenth century, but the practice continued into the next century. These caravans could export as many as a thousand or more slaves in a single year. Private traders also dealt in slaves, but not on the scale of the state. Nor could they coordinate slave raiding with the export business. Once the royal expeditions to seize captives in the south and west returned to Sennar, the slaves were segregated into lots for distribution to the military, settlement on plantations, or export to Egypt. This pattern of state management was also pursued in Dar Fur, Borno, and elsewhere.

In these cases, Muslim merchants had to adjust to the restrictions on marketing. They competed when possible, but usually were more involved with trade in goods other than slaves, at least until state monopolies weakened or collapsed. Hence in Borno, which successfully maintained a system of administered trade until the early nineteenth century, foreign merchants were allowed to buy slaves from the government, but the biggest exporters remained state officials who traded both on behalf of the government and on their own account.[4] Private merchants were relegated to the traffic in salt, textiles, livestock, and foodstuffs. They also imported some slaves, and these could be re-exported to North Africa or settled on the estates of the merchants, but such activities were relatively unimportant in comparison with the activities of the state officials.

The foreign merchants seeking slaves were mostly Muslims, but not entirely. Those who came from the northern desert oases, such as Ghadames, Tuat, Murzuk, and Kufra, often acted as middlemen for still other merchants at Tunis, Tripoli, and Cairo. Those from Yemen, Oman, and Egypt might travel directly to Sennar, Ethiopia, or East Africa, and they in turn distributed their slaves throughout Arabia, the Ottoman Empire, or the Indian Ocean basin. The non-Muslims included Jews, who were scattered throughout the Muslim world, and Venetians, Ragusians, Maltese, and other Christians who penetrated the Islamic barrier in small numbers.[5] There always remained this foreign element, both Muslim and non-Muslim, in the commercial life of the Islamic states of black Africa. Some merchants immigrated permanently, married local women, and founded businesses that were passed on to sons. One group of immigrants that deserves special mention because of its long importance and wide dispersion is the *shurfa*, consisting of Muslims who claimed direct descent from the Prophet Muhammad.[6] They used this claim to forge extensive commercial associations. These immigrants, and others who identified more generally as Arabs, were part of this regular influx of foreigners who proved useful in reinforcing the links between black Africa and the outside world.

The native Muslim merchants were known locally under a variety of names – Juula (Dyula), Jellaba, Swahili, Beriberi, Jabarti – but they shared a common religion, and this association brought with it a legal and commercial heritage that had profound consequences both for the conduct of trade and for the institution of slavery. The commercial legacy included a legal code that carefully explained acceptable practice, provided a system of weights and measures, and recognized that Muslim scholars could arbitrate in cases of commercial disputes. Islamic law forbade interest on loans, which meant that business terms could not directly involve the collection of interest. Hence, goods were advanced on credit, in lieu of future payment, and interest was carefully disguised through differential prices and the manipulation of weights and measures. Clearly, such practices could stretch the intent of the law, but the commercial tradition set limits on behaviour, and in so doing, established a common pattern of trade over a very extensive part of Africa.

Juula was the general term for the Muslim trading-community that was scattered over much of the western Sudan.[7] Their identity was based on common origins, mostly Soninke from the sahel country where ancient Ghana had flourished, but the requirements of regional markets had resulted in their dispersal and had promoted the emergence of sub-communities. Thus the Jahanke dominated the Senegambia basin and Futa Jallon, the Maraka controlled the commerce of the Bambara states, and the Yarse did the same for the Mossi states. Common surnames such as Ture, Cisse, and others helped maintain the social basis for cooperation throughout these different ethnic communities. Whenever a merchant found himself in a distant market that was not part of his regular network, he usually found someone with the same surname or other connection through whom he could conduct his affairs.

The Juula network could supply the trans-Atlantic market and maintain its share in the trans-Saharan trade. Consequently, this portion of the far-reaching Muslim system expanded during the seventeenth and eighteenth centuries. Juula had plied the routes of the Senegambia for a long time before 1600 and were already operating in the interior of the Gold Coast, and they continued to do so. They also opened new roads through the forests to ports in Sierra Leone, Liberia, and Ivory Coast. These routes extended the existing links between the savanna and the northern forest where kola nuts were grown. Now the commerce of this region included the sale of slaves on the coast and the transport of European imports inland.

The operations of the Juula can be glimpsed from the accounts of Mungo Park, who travelled with a slave merchant from Bambara country via the Gambia River valley to the coast. The merchant had purchased thirteen slaves; his consignment was all that was left of a much larger number taken in slave raids by the Bambara army of Segu. They had been kept at Segu in irons for three years, before being sold to various merchants from Nyamina, Bamako, and Kangaba. These destinations indicate that slaves were exported in all directions. Some may well have remained in the general area, perhaps sold to nomads from the Sahara, while others were exported west to the coast. Eventually, other merchants with an additional twenty-two slaves joined Park's small caravan. As Park observed, these thirty-five slaves:

> are commonly secured, by putting the right leg of one, and the left of another, into the same pair of fetters. By supporting the fetters with a string, they can walk, though very slowly. Every four slaves are likewise fastened together by the necks, with a strong rope of twisted thongs; and in the night, an additional pair of fetters is put on their hands, and sometimes a light iron chain passed round their necks.[8]

The central savanna had a commercial structure similar to the Juula system.[9] Merchants from the Bariba states called themselves Wangara, which demonstrated an earlier association with Songhay and ultimately with the gold trade of the Juula. Hausa merchants identified with their city of residence or place of origin or both. Those who came from Borno called themselves Beriberi; while Katsinawa (from Katsina), Kanawa (from Kano), Gobirawa (from Gobir), and similar designations were also common. Wangarawa was a local adaptation for immigrants from the west, including people connected with the old Songhay network, the Wangara of the Bariba towns, and the more distant Juula. And like the Juula, these traders also supplied both the trans-Saharan and the trans-Atlantic slave markets, although European demand for slaves began to affect the central savanna later than was the case further west. Muslim merchants, present in Oyo and at the confluence of the Niger and Benue Rivers in the seventeenth century, apparently reached Whydah and other ports on the Guinea coast only in the early eighteenth century. Usually, moreover, Muslim traders were confined to the northern markets of Oyo, Asante, and Dahomey, where they sold slaves and other merchandise and bought European imports, in the case of Oyo and Dahomey, and kola nuts, in the case of Asante. That some Muslims were occasionally seen on the coast confirms the importance of their established commercial network in supplying slaves for the trans-Atlantic market and the domestic market of the coastal states.

Muslim merchants dominated the trade routes in the Nile valley and Ethiopia, even where Christian governments were the territorial masters. Jellaba were the Muslim merchants who originally came from Sennar and other centres along the Nile River.[10] In the seventeenth and eighteenth centuries they pushed westward into Dar Fur and Wadai and operated to the copper-mines south of Dar Fur. They also traded to the Red Sea and to the frontier markets with Ethiopia, and they took slaves to Egypt, where they maintained special quarters for their business. Jabarti traders controlled most of the trade of Ethiopia.[11] Christian merchants were legally barred from selling slaves, although it seems that Muslims had a distinct advantage anyway. Jabarti could more easily deal with other Muslims, both at the Red Sea ports and in the neighbouring Muslim sultanates south and east of the Christian kingdom. The Jabarti also sold slaves to the Jellaba for re-export to Egypt. Neither the Jellaba nor the Jabarti appear to have expanded their commercial frontiers significantly in this period. Sufficient numbers of slaves could be obtained within the same region that had been tapped for centuries.

Along the East African coast, Swahili and visiting Omani Arabs controlled most of the trade, including slave exports.[12] They operated from a series of ports including Mogadishu on the Somali coast to Mombasa, Pate, Lamu, and Kilwa further south. Only in the last decades of the eighteenth century did this trade begin to expand, and then non-Muslim merchants in the interior, including Yao and Nyamwezi, provided the impetus for this modest growth. As a result of the interaction between these interior people and the coastal Muslims, some Yao and Nyamwezi eventually converted to Islam.

ADMINISTERED TRADE IN WEST-CENTRAL AFRICA

The principal characteristic of trade in west-central Africa during the seventeenth and eighteenth centuries was the attempt by local states, including the Portuguese colony at Luanda, to administer trade and the activities of interlopers who periodically upset these efforts. The long-term effect of these rivalries and attempts at commercial domination was a relatively competitive market. Between 1600 and 1800, there developed a complex network of routes and towns that enabled west-central Africa to export an astonishing number of slaves.

In the early seventeenth century, Portuguese and their agents (*pombeiros*) dominated the trade of the Angolan coast between Luanda, several lesser ports, and the inland markets about 300 km behind the coast.[13] These merchants continued to travel to Malebo Pool, and they purchased slaves from the Imbangala war-lords operating to the south of Kongo. The Portuguese position was temporarily undermined in 1641, when a Dutch expedition occupied Luanda, but when the Dutch were expelled in 1648 the Portuguese re-asserted their position. Thereafter the Dutch moved their operations further north. They established a trade network from Mbanza Sonyo through São Salvador to Ngongo Mbata by the 1650s, and by the same time the Vili of Loango Bay had contacts through Kongo to Matamba.[14] After 1648, the Portuguese and *pombeiros* controlled the southern routes, extending credit inland. Massangano and Cambambe (Dondo) were interior river ports on the Kwanza, from where caravans left for the interior. In the eighteenth century, other centres were established further inland, most notably at Ambaca.[15]

Matamba and Kasanje were the most important states in the interior of Luanda in the seventeenth century. The Dutch relied on Matamba in the 1640s for their slave supplies, but with the return of the Portuguese and the defeat of Matamba, Kasanje became the principal state; Matamba – reorganized as Ginga – continued to participate in the trade, only on a reduced scale. Kasanje had been founded in 1618, when Imbangala warriors took advantage of the relatively fertile area at a time when the region as a whole suffered a severe drought. Initially, the Imbangala were primarily interested in raiding for slaves, but after 1650 they profited from the growing trade into the far interior. Kasanje maintained a particularly effective fair (*feira* in Portuguese), organized by the government to restrict the movement of Portuguese merchants. From 1650 to 1800, the Kasanje *feira* remained an important source of slaves. There were other centres too. Slaves came to Luanda from Kongo via Encoje and other areas, and in the eighteenth century, the Ovimbundu plateau was important. In the 1740s and 1750s, Mbailundo was the major slaving power, while Bihé coalesced as another source of slaves in the 1760s or 1770s and achieved dominance on the plateau in the 1790s.

The northern coast, which the Portuguese could not control, became the principal market for the Dutch, French, and English, especially after the 1670s.[16] European merchants lacked their own port facilities here, although the Portuguese tried unsuccessfully to establish a permanent base at Cabinda around 1720 and again in 1783. Rather, ship captains were required to deal with local officials at Loango Bay, Malemba, and Cabinda, the three most important harbours. Europeans were allowed to build temporary slave accommodations on shore. Slave prices, duties, and brokerage fees were negotiated with these officials, who also supervised royal brokers who served as intermediaries between Vili merchants and the Europeans. The king also organized royal caravans to Malebo Pool and other places in the interior. Armed guards escorted these caravans to protect them against bandits, to prevent excessive tolls at river-crossings, and to forestall slave escapes. These caravans dealt in turn with the Tio merchants who controlled the market at Malebo Pool. This market was the meeting-point for merchants travelling down the Zaire River, who began to bring slaves to the Pool by at least the middle of the eighteenth century, and for traders from Matamba and Lunda in the south and east, who sold slaves to Vili merchants travelling overland through Kongo.

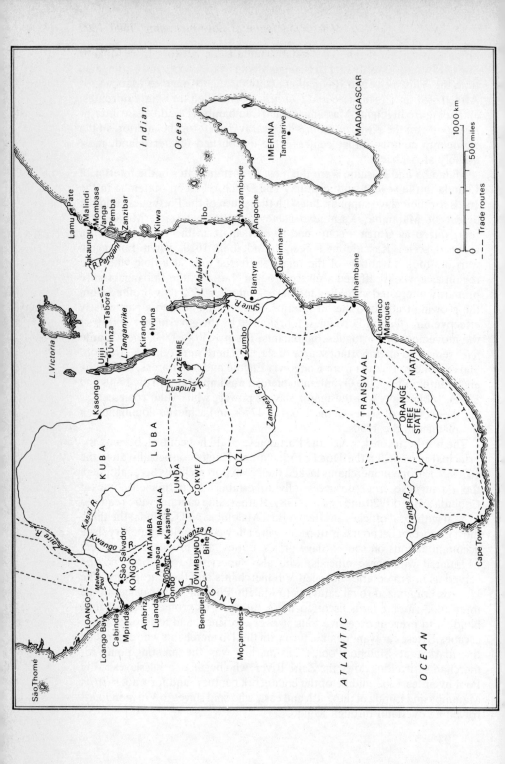

In the far interior, Lunda, Luba, and Kazembe each developed in turn as a major source of slaves. The rulers of these states perpetrated a myth of common allegiance that facilitated the exchange of commodities. Trade was not openly competitive; the various states negotiated bilateral agreements with one another. In this way, slaves, salt, textiles, copper, and other goods changed hands, and ultimately many slaves found their way to the Imbangala fairs and the European ships at Luanda and other ports along the coast. Salt was a crucial item in this exchange, for major sources were found in Imbangala territory or elsewhere near the coast. European imports were also a major item, and again the source was the Imbangala fair.

The centre of Lunda trade was the royal district, *mussumba*, where the king (*mwant yaav*) organized slave exports. The trade was tightly administered. Some slaves arrived at the *mussumba* as a result of tribute obligations from outlying districts. More slaves came from other Lunda states that recognized the *mwant yaav* as the senior official of the Lunda state-system. The movement of goods, including slaves, textiles, salt, and copper, was arranged through officials. Since these officials pretended that they were kin, the trade was seen as reciprocal gift-giving. In theory there was no 'market' for slaves or other goods, but in fact this system was comparable to market exchange.[17] In many ways Lunda and its dependencies were similar to Kasanje and Matamba: they all relied on slave raiding and state-controlled trade. The system of the coastal zone had moved inland. As Kasanje and Matamba had become important as intermediaries, Lunda too came to provide slaves through its own administered fairs.

COASTAL WEST AFRICA: STATE TRADE, RIVER-BOATS, AND ORACLES

The commerce of the West African coast resembled the trade of west-central Africa in two respects: firstly, states attempted to dominate the trade in slaves, and secondly, private merchants broke through the government monopolies and established their own marketing arrangements. In both regions, therefore, there was a tendency towards monopoly or oligopoly. Along the West African coast, however, the competition between private merchants and government traders had an additional dimension: on the Gold and Slave Coasts, state traders were more successful in restricting the marketing of slaves than they were elsewhere, although still not without competition from private traders, while on the Bight of Biafra coast, private cartels emerged as the dominant factor, there being no large, centralized states.

Akwamu, Hueda, Allada, Dahomey, and Oyo – the major states exporting slaves on the Slave Coast and eastern Gold Coast between 1680 and 1730 – were all interested in administering trade on behalf of the state. After Akwamu conquered Accra in 1681, for example, Accra merchants were not permitted to reside in the interior; their function was restricted to that of brokerage near the trade-castles of the English, Danes, and Dutch.[18]

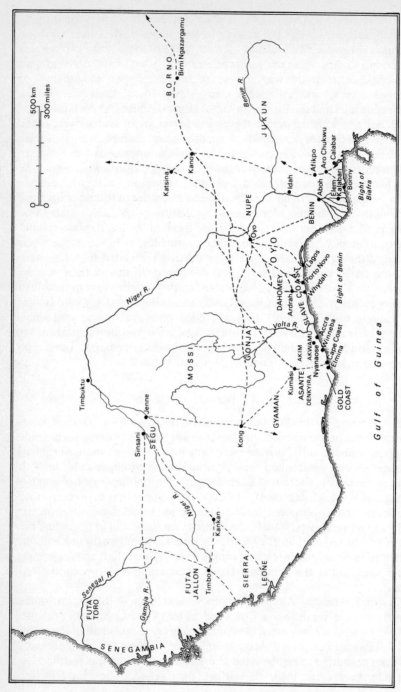

4 The West African slave trade in the eighteenth century

These brokers provided lodging and storage facilities to Akwamu official traders and wealthy merchants from Nyanaoase. Similarly, Hueda and Allada restricted the activities of private merchants; royal attempts to control the trade by forcing inland merchants to deal with officials were a major factor in the Dahomey invasion of both these states in the 1720s. Oyo too intervened to protect its interests; early invasions of Allada and Dahomey guaranteed Oyo access to the ports, but most particularly Oyo's conquest of Dahomey was a measure aimed at state control of the trade routes to the coast.[19] These efforts at state control resulted in the rise and fall of particular ports, as each competed for the export market. Offra and Jakin, the ports of Allada, and Ghehwe (Whydah), the port of Hueda, gave way to a new order in the second decade of the eighteenth century. Dahomey now controlled the coast, but Apa and Epe to the east were the rivals of Whydah. By 1736, Badagry was the principal competitor of Whydah, while after the 1750s, Porto Novo was also important.[20]

Once Asante established its hegemony over the interior of the Gold Coast, these efforts at state management were promoted further, but again never without significant competition from private traders. While in the first half of the eighteenth century most slaves exported from the Gold Coast were shipped from Akwamu and the Fanti coast, that is, eastward from Cape Coast to the Volta River, after mid-century the trade was concentrated on the Fanti coast. Asante operated through two principal outlets on the Fanti coast, the English castle of Anambo and the Dutch post at Kormantin. The Asante dominated the interior trade beyond the market town of Assin Manso, a distance of one day's march from the coast. The Fanti handled the trade between there and the European castles, importing firearms and other goods that were sold at Assin Manso for slaves.[21] The medium of exchange was gold, which also continued to be an important export. Another Asante route passed to the coast further west at Grand Bassam, which was under direct Asante political control and hence was a better outlet as far as state management was concerned. Some slaves also were exported further west still at Grand Lahu. Unfortunately for Asante, the Fanti coast was commercially more significant because of the availability of gold in greater quantities than at Cape Lahu and Grand Bassam. The value of gold and slave exports has been estimated at roughly the same levels during the last half of the eighteenth century, in the other of 10,000 to 40,000 oz. gold and slaves valued at as much as 36,000 oz. gold per year.[22] Because of the importance of the Fanti position, Asante attempted to establish tighter control over the route between Assin Manso and the coast; hence several invasions of the Fanti coast in the 1780s and 1790s were aimed at direct administration of the coast itself.

Oyo also intervened more openly on the Slave Coast in the second half of the eighteenth century. Dahomey was kept tributary, forwarding slaves, cowries, and other goods to Oyo, but otherwise retaining a competing influence at Whydah. The Oyo regime of Basorun Gaha (1754–74), while relying on Whydah, much as Asante allowed the coastal Fanti to handle the last stretch of the Gold Coast trade, began to develop alternative routes to Porto Novo and Badagry. With the restoration of the monarchy under Alafin Abiodun (1774–89), Oyo policy shifted to even tighter administration. Abiodun colonized a new route to the coast that bypassed Dahomey. A string of towns were settled in the province of Egbado, which enabled caravans to travel to the east of the Kumi Swamp, rather than to the west and into the Dahomey sphere.[23] The new port, Porto Novo, expanded rapidly as the outlet to the Egbado route, and while Whydah continued as a major port, the eastward movement of the slave trade towards Badagry, Porto Novo, and ultimately Lagos demonstrates that Abiodun and Gaha were successful in promoting Oyo's trade. The relative importance of these ports can be gleaned from the list of Portuguese ships visiting the coast between 1760 and 1770: 29 stopped at Whydah, 13 at Epe, 12 at Porto Novo, 14 at Badagry, and 2 at Lagos.[24] Eventually Dahomey destroyed Epe (in 1782), Badagry (in 1784), and the inland market of Weme (in 1786), which connected with several of the ports that rivalled Whydah.[25]

Coastal governments regulated the sale of slaves to Europeans whenever they could. In doing so they took advantage of the desire of ship captains to set sail as fast as possible. Coastal factors determined prices and negotiated assortments of commodities to be exchanged for slaves. Because the trade along the coast was heavily dependent upon credit, often extended in the form of goods that were taken inland to acquire slaves, numerous payments, ranging from custom fees to anchorage duties, transport services, and outright bribes were required and had to be added to the sale price for slaves in the accounts of European merchants. These payments, sanctioned by tradition, demonstrate the success of local merchant-princes and strong governments in regulating the export business.

Although states had an advantage in the slave trade as a consequence of their ability to amass large numbers of captives, private traders also dealt in slaves, and their share of the market often exceeded that of the government and its agents. In Akwamu, for example, private traders supplemented the supply mechanism of the government sector, despite restrictions placed on the merchants of Accra who were confined to an intermediary role. Other merchants, residents of Nyanaoase but not involved in the sale of the captives seized in Akwamu's wars and raids, 'are wholesale traders [who] sell slaves to the Europeans for cowries and other goods, and with these buy slaves far in the interior'.[26]

Ship records from two vessels trading at Whydah late in the eighteenth century provide a breakdown of the ratio of public to private trading in Dahomey. Of the 660 slaves purchased, only 10 per cent were sold by the state, 20–30 per cent were sold by large merchants dealing in more than 10 slaves each, 30–50 per cent were sold by merchants in lots of 3 to 10 slaves each, while 20 per cent were sold by individuals, one or two slaves at a time. When the state's share is adjusted to allow for income derived from taxes and other revenue connected with the trade, the state received about 20 per cent of the receipts from the trade.[27] It is likely that the government sector was more important than these figures indicate, for private merchants may well have bought slaves from the state prior to the transactions with the European ships. Other slaves still were redistributed in payment for services to the state, and these too could be among the slaves sold at Whydah. In short, the state sector did not always involve direct sales to Europeans, but even when this is taken into consideration, the share of the private sector was exceedingly large, especially when it is recognized that Dahomey is often used as an example of an economy dominated by the state.

The ethnic origins of slaves from the Bight of Benin also indicate the importance of the private sector. Many, if not most, of the slaves identified as eastern Voltaic, Nupe and Hausa, who numbered at least 183,000, probably came south as trade slaves.[28] These groups do not appear in the ledgers in appreciable numbers until the last third of the eighteenth century, although it is likely that other slaves, classified as Aja and Yoruba, were of northern origin too. Even so, the entry of Voltaic, Nupe, and Hausa as visible categories suggests a through trade from the northern savanna to the coast that may not have been as important earlier in the eighteenth century as it was in the last decades of the century.

The interior of the Bight of Biafra was different from other parts of the West African coastal zone. In the interior, there were no centralized states of any consequence and here no government trading at all. Even the ports were different, for they were run by the merchants, and commerce remained completely in private hands. The function of local governments in the ports was to regulate trade, not attempt to control it. Both politics and the economy were dominated by a merchant oligopoly.[29]

Merchants on the rivers and in the Niger delta, particularly from the towns of Bonny, Elem Kalabari, and Calabar, travelled into the interior in large river-boats, some of which were manned by crews of 50 paddlers and could carry as many as 120 people.[30] These vessels were heavily armed, since expeditions had to be prepared for conflict with rival firms as well as for trade. Europeans extended credit to the owners of these vessels, who then waited while slaves were purchased and brought to the ports:

> The Black Traders of Bonny and Calabar ... come down about once a Fortnight with Slaves; Thursday or Friday is generally their Trading Day. Twenty or Thirty Canoes, sometimes more and sometimes less, come down at a Time. In each Canoe may be Twenty or Thirty Slaves. The Arms of some of them are tied behind their Backs with Twigs, Canes, Grass Rope, or other Ligaments of the Country; and if they happen to be stronger than common, they are pinioned above the Knee also. In this Situation they are thrown into the Bottom of the Canoe, where they lie in great Pain, and often almost covered with Water. On their landing, they are taken to the Traders Houses, where they are oiled, fed and made up for Sale .. No sickly Slave is ever purchased ... When the Bargain is made they are brought away ... They appear to be very dejected when brought on board. The Men are put into

Irons, in which Situation they remain during the whole of the Middle Passage, unless when they are sick.[31]

The delta traders journeyed to one of many riverside markets in the interior, where they were able to buy slaves from the Aro, whose commercial network covered much of Igbo and Ibibio country.[32] By the middle of the eighteenth century, the Aro had established control over a series of market-places, where they also purchased slaves and sold European imports. These markets were operated on a rotating basis, so that each one was open every four days. The hub of the marketing system was two fairs that lasted four days each and were held twenty-four days apart. The southern one, Bende, connected with the ports on the coast, particularly Bonny, Elem Kalabari, and Calabar. The northern one, Uburu, was located at a major inland source of salt and was the focal point of many routes that stretched further inland and ultimately reached the Benue River valley. Different sections of Aro conroled their own routes and markets. Merchants made arrangements with local people to house visitors and store goods, but the Aro retained a monopoly on certain goods, including slaves, and they regulated the markets.

The Aro network was tied to the ports. Credit tended to flow inland from the coast, and the coastal merchants and the Aro recognized the same regulatory bodies. The most important agency was the Ekpe secret society, or its counterpart in the interior, Okonko, to which all these merchants, and even a few European ship captains, belonged.[33] This society had the power to enforce its decisions, including the administration of death penalties, and its principal concern was to regulate commerce and guarantee the payment of debts.

The other route into the interior of the Bight of Biafra was the Niger River, and here the river ports of Aboh and Idah dominated trade.[34] Like the coastal ports, these towns were run by merchants, so that the private activities of merchants could be coordinated to maintain the monopoly of the port. Aboh was situated on the lower stretch of the Niger, just above the point where the delta creeks made it possible for merchants to choose alternative outlets to the sea. Idah was located just to the south of the Niger–Benue confluence and therefore could benefit from trade that was funnelled into the lower Niger from both waterways.

PATTERNS IN RESTRICTIVE PRACTICES

In general, politics and slave trading were closely associated. Asante, Oyo, Dahomey, the Funj Sultanate, Kasanje, Lunda, and a host of other states tried to manage the slave trade, allowing few if any private traders to operate within their domains. There was good reason why governments tried to monopolize slave exporting, since the states themselves were often the main suppliers of slaves, either through wars, raids, or tribute collection. Consequently, a royal factor managed slave marketing.

The restrictive practices of merchants at strategic commercial centres fitted into this tendency towards monopoly in the slave trade, except that, in the case of market towns and seaports, merchants often dominated local government.[35] Hence official policies promoted the economic interests of the trading community. Again trade and politics were intertwined in a manner to reduce competition, although the primacy of merchants and officials was reversed. Rather than the state controlling trade, the merchants dominated the government. Seen from this perspective, the network of commercial alliances in the interior of the Bight of Biafra – including the towns of Aboh and Idah on the Niger River, Bonny and Calabar on the coast, and the Aro communities inland – served to monopolize the slave trade as effectively as Oyo and Asante did. Indeed, the similarity with the Imbangala, Lunda, and their coastal connections is equally striking.

The attempt at monopoly was invariably short-lived for the period from 1600 to 1800 as a whole. Merchants and states tried to confine the trade in slaves and other valuable products to themselves, and they were often successful for a decade or two, sometimes for longer. Queen Nzinga maintained a monopoly in Angola during the 1640s, when the Dutch temporarily occupied Luanda, but when the Portuguese returned, her position collapsed. Kasanje held its royal fair from the 1650s onward, but Portuguese and other merchants repeatedly tried to bypass it. Such examples could be cited almost endlessly.

The tendency towards monopoly, whether through government trading or through merchant arrangements, was matched by a counter-tendency towards open competition and the rise of interlopers. The same pattern effected the European trading firms. The big chartered companies – the Company of Royal Adventurers, the Royal African Company and others – or government-sanctioned cartels – such as the merchants who controlled the Portuguese contracts on slave duties – were attempts to limit the activities of private merchants and the traders of competing nations. These efforts at mercantilism were not startling successes. The Portuguese could usually keep foreign ships away from Luanda, but the Dutch and English traded elsewhere on the Angolan coast and to the north on the Loango coast. Slaves often came from the same interior markets for all these shipping-points. The external trade of Oyo followed a similar pattern. The ports serving as the main export-points for slaves changed almost every twenty years during the eighteenth century.

The pattern was one of short-term monopolies for relatively small portions of the total export trade in slaves. These either collapsed or merged with larger networks that demonstrated similar oligopolistic tendencies. Profits could be quite high during periods of restricted competition, but alternative sources of slaves usually guaranteed that long-term trends did not result in a sellers' cartel. For this reason, the general picture was one of a relatively unrestricted market situation. There were plenty of slaves available for sale, no matter how rapidly demand increased.

SLAVES AND OTHER COMMODITIES

Slaves were always an important item of trade within Africa, for they were an easy commodity to move. They could even carry other goods and food for themselves. Because it was better to transfer slaves to areas with which they were not familiar, trade was an important feature of slavery. By moving them, their value increased. It is not possible to determine the exact number of slaves who were traded, although the export figures provide some guide to the scale of the internal trade. None the less, slaves were one of the half dozen or so major items of commerce. As such they were traded away from the coast and the major export markets as well as towards them. Slaves moved in all directions, although because of the scale of the export trade it is likely that the net flow was out of Africa in such places as west-central Africa, along the West African coast, and in the areas bordering the Sahara, Red Sea, and Indian Ocean.

While slaves were the leading export from Africa between 1600 and 1800, in some places, slaves were second to gold and other commodities.[36] The Zambezi River valley, Ethiopia, the upper Nile, the Gold Coast, and Senegambia were the most fortunate areas because gold was available. Spices, perfumes, ivory, hides and skins, beeswax, and gum arabic were sometimes important. For the Slave Coast, the Bight of Biafra, and west-central Africa, slaves were almost the only export. The other goods in which merchants dealt included salt, African textiles, tobacco, livestock, dried fish and other condiments, kola nuts, jewellery, and precious metals, particularly gold, copper, and tin. All these goods were luxuries. Indeed, most long-distance trade in the days of difficult transportation and communication was in luxury items.

Salt was perhaps the most important of these commodities.[37] Indeed, it served as money in Ethiopia and west-central Africa, among other places. Large caravans distributed salt from production sites in the Sahara Desert and the Lake Chad basin to areas far to the south, even into the forest. The salt of west-central Africa came from areas relatively close to the coast, so that the sale of salt into the interior followed the same routes that the slaves followed to the coast. The same was true for Ethiopia, for salt came from the coastal plains along the Red Sea, while slaves came from the south where the market for salt was located. Numerous salt-pans were found along the Guinea coast, from the Senegambia region through the Bights of Benin and Biafra, so that here, too, salt was shipped inland while slaves were brought to the sea.

The east–west route along the Kwanza valley in west-central Africa was important because salt deposits were located in Kisama, south of the river, which supplied the salt-deficient interior. Kisama salt was used as currency both in Angola and in the hinterland. A regular trade already existed by 1563. Other salt was made at the salt-drying village of Kakwako on the coast; and after 1617 Kasanje controlled the salt-pans on the Kwango River. These last pans had been operated by the Pende before the Imbangala took over.[38]

Kola, a stimulant chewed as a refreshment, also demonstrates the inter-connection between slave trading and general merchandising.[39] The kola traded over the greatest distances was grown only in the forest west of the Volta River. This type was sold to Muslim merchants who came south from the savanna, for Muslims in particular were attracted to this luxury because Islamic custom prohibited the consumption of many other stimulants, including alcohol. The presence of Muslim merchants in the kola markets made it possible for them to deal in slaves as well. They often brought salt from the north and purchased gold in markets on the route to the kola centres. Moreover, the operation of these merchants in the kola markets led to the expansion of trade to the coast, where Europeans were buying slaves. Muslims pushed south through the kola forests of Sierra Leone, Liberia, and the Ivory Coast to the coastal ports in the seventeenth century and continued to be active in the Gold Coast interior as they had been since the Portuguese arrived there in the late fifteenth century. Similar observations on the compatibility of trading in kola nuts and slaves could be made elsewhere, particularly in west-central Africa and the Bights of Benin and Biafra. Here other varieties of kola were consumed, and the distances over which kola was distributed were often considerably less than for the area west of the Volta River, but such commerce took place alongside the trade in slaves.

THE IMPORT TRADE

What was brought to Africa in order to buy slaves? It was once thought that liquor, beads, bangles, and similar cheap or economically useless items formed the bulk of imports, but the list of merchandise includes many goods which were relatively high in quality, thereby disproving the myth that Africa got virtually nothing for the export of its sons and daughters. Of course the range of commodities changed over the centuries, and our assessment of the trade as a whole is necessarily impressionistic. In the medieval period, the main imports for the trans-Saharan trade were textiles, copper, breeding horses, and cowries. Some firearms, silver coins, and paper were added to the ledgers in the seventeenth and eighteenth centuries. The Atlantic trade included cowries, silver coins, iron bars, textiles, copper and brass bars and wire, firearms, and glass beads. The types of textiles changed over time. From the sixteenth to the eighteenth centuries, at the height of the trade in slaves, most textiles came from India, and British and other manufacturers only began to command a share of this market towards the end of the eighteenth century. Silver coins were also a late-eighteenth-century import.

Goods can be broken down into several categories. The first is money: cowries, silver coins, iron bars, copper and brass wire, and some textiles, which accounted for a third to a half of all imports by value.[40] This may seem like a strange list, except for the coins, but the economy of Africa used a variety of currencies, and the imported goods contributed to the money supply, even when most of these goods were also used for non-monetary purposes too.

The most widespread currency zone was that of the cowrie shell, which was used in much of west Africa. Cowries were imported on the Gold Coast, along the Bight of Benin, in the Niger delta, and in the Senegambia basin, even though some of these coastal areas did not use this currency domestically.[41] The cowries that were imported on the Gold and Slave Coasts were not only used as currency in Akwamu, Dahomey, and Oyo, but the shells were transported inland in order to purchase slaves and other goods. In the early eighteenth century, cowrie imports on the Slave Coast approached one third the value of all goods; by the end of the century, the amount still constituted 20 to 25 per cent of imports. Manning has estimated that cowries were worth from £50,000 to £75,000 per year at this time; based on a constant inflow and an annual loss of 2 per cent of current cowrie stocks, the aggregate money-supply approached a value of £4 million. For a population of four million over a region that included Dahomey, Oyo, Nupe, the Bariba states, and the Hausa cities, the per capita money supply was probably in the order of one pound sterling or 8,000 cowries, a figure comparable to the per capita money supply of the early twentieth century.[42] Manning's calculation indicates a thoroughly monetized economy over this vast region, although it can be assumed that the actual supply of cowries varied within the region as a whole, and some places probably had few or no cowries.

Besides cowries, the Senegambia markets required textiles from India – the 'guinée' – that were used locally as money. Narrow strips of cloth circulated in many parts of the interior, sometimes alongside cowries but usually in areas where cowries were not accepted. Of course, the strips could also be made into clothing, but their function as money was essential to the operation of the local economy.[43] Iron bars were sometimes the source of iron money and sometimes not. In the interior of Guinea, Sierra Leone, Liberia, and the Ivory Coast, where kola nuts were grown, small iron implements that looked like hoes were used as money. Most of this iron money was brought from the savanna, to the immediate north of the kola forests, but some was made from the iron bars bought from Europeans.[44]

Copper and brass wire and bars – often in the shape of bracelets called manillas – were the medium of exchange in the interior of the Niger delta and Cross River.[45] These metals were used in local transactions in a region extending as far north as the Benue River, and their only source was from the Atlantic trade.

Even gold was sometimes imported, despite the fact that it was produced in Africa. Both Asante and Dahomey imported gold in the eighteenth century, even though Asante produced gold, and Dahomey used cowries. Gold could be stored or used in royal insignia, and since it was accepted by

Europeans as money, it continued to have a monetary function that could be tapped whenever necessary, especially to finance the purchase of firearms and other imports from Europe.

The importance of money objects demonstrates that the slave trade was part of a world-wide commercial exchange. Cowries and Indian textiles were shipped from India to Africa via Europe, and indeed many of the ships bringing goods from India came from Indonesia – even further afield. Cowries came from the Maldive Islands, 200 km off the west coast of Ceylon (Sri Lanka), and southern India, and they were taken to Bengal, for purchase by the Portuguese and later by the Dutch. The Dutch sold them to English and French firms in Amsterdam, whence they found their way to Africa on the ships that sailed out for slaves. Indian textiles followed a similar route, transported to Europe for re-export to Africa.

The import of money was expensive for the economies of Africa.[46] While the currencies themselves facilitated trade, as money is supposed to do in all economies, it cost valuable export earnings in order to obtain the money supply, and in the case of earnings derived from the sale of slaves, there was a double loss. On the one hand, slave exports represented a loss in the productive capacity of the exported people. On the other hand, the imported money was not accepted by Europeans as a general-purpose currency, and hence its circulation was limited to areas within Africa. The quantity of goods that could be used for productive purposes was restricted accordingly.

Africans could not use commodities that were close at hand and that would not have required the export of valuable commodities, particularly slaves, because some merchants and governments made considerable profits from importing money objects, and they found it in their interest to continue to deal in any commodity that had high profits. There was no centralized authority that could decide to establish some other monetary system, and there was no consciousness among Africans that importing money was undesirable. Consequently, straight economic laws operated. European and North African merchants sold those goods that commanded a high price relative to their cost. Since the demand for cowries, manillas and guinées was strong, European and North African merchants found it profitable to supply these goods.

A second major import was military wares, most especially firearms and ammunition, but also knives, swords, and breeding horses. As with money objects, the continuity in the trade reaches far back in time. Horses were an early item of the trans-Saharan trade, and they continued to be so long into the nineteenth century. Imports improved the breed of horses used in the cavalries of many states along the southern side of the Sahara, and these improvements in turn made it possible to breed and sell horses to armies further south.[47] Swords and knives, also early imports from North Africa, were often given handles and sheaths south of the Sahara and then sold further afield. The Atlantic trade also supplied military goods, and while some, perhaps many, knives and blades were used for agricultural and other purposes, many were used in the military. As with some of the items used as money, there was a double purpose for some of these commodities. Firearms could be used in hunting. Even horses had ceremonial functions that were only indirectly related to their military importance.

Firearms were a staple of trade along the West African coast by the early eighteenth century, with as many as 180,000 guns per year imported by 1730.[48] These guns, which included flintlocks and muskets, continued to be a major item of trade for the British in particular. Between 1750 and the first decade of the nineteenth century, annual shipments for the British alone averaged between 283,000 and 394,000 guns to West Africa. Another 50,000 per year were sent to the Loango coast, north of the Zaire River. The size of the trade for other European countries and the quantity of firearms imported into Angola are unknown, which makes a firm assessment of the volume of the gun trade impossible. None the less, at least 20 million guns, an astonishing figure, were sold to African merchants. Also, between 1750 and 1807, England sold over 22,000 metric tons of gunpowder, an average of 384,000 kg per year, and another 91,000 kg of lead annually.

A third category of imports was luxuries including textiles, mirrors, needles, liquor, beads, and a variety of other consumer items.[49] On the Slave Coast in the last decades of the eighteenth century, for example, such luxuries were the largest single category of imports. Textiles alone were about one third of all imports, and here textiles were not used as money. Other luxuries particularly important on the Slave Coast included alcohol and Brazilian tobacco. Although some imports competed with local manufacturers, in general textiles, beads, tobacco, and alcohol supplemented African production. Luxury commodities for the wealthy and powerful were a great stimulus to trade. Liquor consumption and expensive clothing were conspicuous examples, while the royal umbrellas of Asante chiefs were symbols of power and prestige that also show this connection.

This assessment of the commercial organization of Africa between 1600 and 1800 shows the close connection with slavery. The monetary sector, although limited, was closely tied to the imported money exchanged for slaves. Improvements in military technology were also closely connected to external trade. The import of breeding horses across the Sahara strengthened the savanna cavalry states. Chain mail and muskets strengthened them still further. Along the coast, firearms, swords, and knives had a comparable impact, with the effect that has sometimes been called the 'gun–slave cycle'. The simple formulation of this theory holds that guns were sold to Africans in order to encourage enslavement. While some Europeans may have understood the connection between gun sales and slaves, it would be wrong to attribute the slave trade to such manipulation.[50] The correlation between the quantity of imported guns and the volume of the slave trade more accurately reflected the economic and political choices of African rulers and merchants who acted in their own best interests.

Curtin's analysis of the import and export trade of Senegambia from the 1680s to the 1830s demonstrates that the net barter terms of trade shifted consistently in favour of Senegambia.[51] The cause of this shift was primarily related to a steady increase in the price of slaves; not until the end of the period did falling prices for European goods begin to affect the terms of trade. Although it is not possible to measure accurately the other indicators of economic change in the region, it is clear that it was to the advantage of merchants and political elites, at least, to engage in foreign trade during this era. Information comparable to that supplied by Curtin is not available for other regions along the Atlantic coast for the era of large-scale exports. None the less, it seems likely that Curtin's conclusions apply elsewhere. In Senegambia, slaves were seldom as important in the total volume of exports as they were in the Bights of Benin and Biafra or west-central Africa. Consequently, the net barter terms of trade moved in favour of African exporters to a greater extent than in Senegambia.

The African participants in the external trade included the wealthiest and most powerful merchants and princes. Merchants were found dealing in slaves everywhere that long-distance trade was established; indeed, it is impossible to separate slave marketing from other commodities, either for the internal trade or for the external trade. Government officials found many opportunities to enslave people, supplying captives and criminals to the merchants. These merchants and princes both owned slaves and marketed them – princes because they had access to them through the state apparatus, merchants because their function was to trade. Hence the African elite was committed to slavery; this elite owned the most slaves.

The external slave trade, the process of enslavement, and the use of slaves within Africa were inextricably connected. The economy was profoundly affected, both the monetarized sector, dependent on imported money-objects, and the non-market portions of the economy, based on slave and other dependent relationships. The political order was equally affected, often being mobilized to enslave people in war, through the legal process or through outright slave raiding.

6

Relationships of dependency, 1600–1800

In the seventeenth and eighteenth centuries, there were a variety of slave regimes in Africa. At one extreme, in many places in the far interior and in isolated spots between the major states and trade corridors, slaves were still marginal to society, forming one category of dependants in kinship systems but ultimately having little structural impact on the local economy or society. Other regions along the Atlantic coast had more slaves, although the outlook towards slavery was still in terms of dependency, even though the impact of the European market provided a situation in which slavery changed. From Sierra Leone in the west to Angola in the south, slavery was transformed as the interaction between enslavement, trade, and slave use began to influence the organization of society. In some places, slavery was the basis of a mode of production; in a few areas, this productive system dominated the social formation. Two broad zones emerged: one strongly Islamic in the savanna belt, where there was a continuation and consolidation of earlier patterns of slave use and supply, and a second that was rooted in the tradition of kin-based societies that were now experiencing the transformation to slave societies. A final feature of this continuum of slave regimes was the foundation of European settlements where slave use shared some of the features of slavery in the Americas. These settlements were one bridge between the European-controlled productive regime in the Americas and the African-controlled system of slave supply.

THE EXPANSION OF SLAVERY

The external demand for slaves and the rivalry between African states directly affected the spread of slavery, for both caused tensions that led to the enslavement of people. The economy became dependent upon exports to satisfy the personal desires of merchants and rulers and to provide many parts of Africa with a money supply, textiles, firearms, and other goods that were essential to the economy and political rule. The fragmented political structure, reinforced by military purchases and the need to acquire slaves to finance imports, was related to a general state of insecurity that facilitated enslavement. These two conditions, the slave market and institutionalized enslavement, set the stage for the extension of slavery in Africa.

During the seventeenth and eighteenth centuries, the number of slaves increased, with the result that many societies experienced a social transformation. This transformation differed in the northern savanna, along the West African coast, and in west-central Africa because the nature of the export trade and other economic factors differed. In the northern savanna, where older patterns of economy and society continued, the transformation had already occurred, and slavery continued to be an important element in production. Women and children were exported in greater numbers than men, even though the domestic market for women and children was greater than for men. This market preference in both the export and domestic spheres meant that the cost of male labour was relatively low, which guaranteed the maintenance of a labour supply for agriculture.

Along the West African coast and in west-central Africa (and in scattered spots elsewhere), by contrast, the export market favoured young males, so that the domestic preference for women and children and the foreign trade complemented each other. As the rough calculations in chapter 3 (table 3.9) demonstrate, the sex and age distribution of the trans-Atlantic trade suggests that a large population of slaves was retained in those African societies associated with the export trade. Furthermore, these estimates suggest that a large proportion of the slave population available for domestic use consisted of mature adults over age 30, children under age 15, and young women, aged 15 to 30. Indeed, if the assumptions of these calculations are correct (that the newly enslaved population of the interior had a balanced sex and age profile), then the retained population of new slaves was larger than the exported population. Hence the 7.85 million slaves shipped across the Atlantic between 1600 and 1800 provide a rough indication of the scale of slavery within the exporting regions. While these calculations permit neither an estimate of the size of the domestic slave population nor a comparison of the relative size of slave and free populations, the figures do indicate a steady and substantial influx of slaves into the local societies of the Guinea coast and its hinterland, probably on a scale that exceeded the inflow of slaves into the societies of the northern savanna. As Thornton has observed for Angola, this demographic shift resulted in the expansion of population in the coastal enclaves and the commercial centres of the immediate interior where political power was concentrated.[1] The same pattern of population growth also occurred in West Africa. Losses were confined to the regions from which slaves came, a process of demographic adjustment examined by Manning.[2]

The influx of servile women, children, and older people reinforced social relationships based on dependency, including those deriving from kinship, marriage, pawnship, and clientship, but allowing for greater numbers of slaves. Increased stratification meant that the relative importance of these dependent categories shifted. Strong men, government officials, wealthy merchants, and military leaders controlled large followings of slaves, junior kinsmen, pawns, women, and clients. This group of powerful men formed the nucleus of a class society in which a relatively few people dominated the instruments of warfare, commercial credit, and the means of production. The war-lords who enslaved people, whether in political conflicts or slave raids, were committed to the institution of slavery as a means of acquiring people for use in government, the military, and production. These war-lords – aristocracies when they consolidated their rule – formed one part of a slave-owning class. The other part was made up of the merchants who traded in many goods but who also performed the vital function of transferring the newly enslaved to their final destinations. As a result of their access to slaves and credit, they too amassed large numbers of servile dependants. Like the war-lords, they shared a commitment to slavery, participated in the slave trade, and exploited slave labour. Sometimes the merchants suffered from particular actions of the war-lords, including raids on caravans or unstable political conditions that adversely affected trade. Sometimes it was difficult to distinguish between merchant-princes and war-lords, for merchants could participate in slave raids or fight each other for control of markets and trade routes, and war-lords could become actively involved in commerce or production. Furthermore, there were tensions between war-lords, not only because of succession disputes but also because of the fragmented political order itself. None the less, there was an identifiable class of slave owners who were those largely responsible for enslaving people, trading them as one more commodity on the market, and employing slaves on their own land for productive purposes.

While these class relationships altered kinship structures, there were still places with less social differentiation where elders coordinated labour, defence, marriage arrangements, credit, and other activities. The basis of social cohesion continued to centre on a core of people related through kinship. In these social settings, slavery still functioned in the context of dependency. Slaves were non-kin, but they were absorbed into corporate groups in order to supplement the number of people in a lineage, thereby circumventing the biological limitations of reproduction. When lineage members could afford to do so, they could augment their numbers by purchase or the extension of credit for pawns. Slavery in this situation was very different from that in the emerging class societies based on slavery. Here a person, slave or free, owed his allegiance to a cooperative group in which mediation and direct involvement in decisions were characteristic, while the dependants of war-lords and merchants followed the dictates of a lord or trader who gave them orders, no matter what their actual social status.

Despite the polarity of these two modes of production, one based on slavery and the other on kinship, the trend in the two centuries was toward the spread of slavery, especially in the Muslim savanna, along the West African coast, and in west-central Africa. In some places, such as the

Zambezi valley or the 'middle belt' between the northern savanna and the forest, these two modes of production existed side by side in relative isolation from each other, except for the warfare and slave raids that brought both into temporary contact. In those places with the greatest concentration of slaves, separate peasant communities maintained social structures based on kinship, even though the dominant relationships in such regions relied on slavery. In large parts of the far interior, including the forest regions of the Zaire River basin, the *sudd* region of the upper Nile, and the interlacustrine zone, slavery remained marginal to society. These areas were relatively unaffected by the spread of slavery in this period.

THE NORTHERN SAVANNA

Slavery was widespread in the Muslim states and near Muslim centres in the seventeenth century. Slaves continued to be used in armies, harems, and government administration, where loyalty could be closely developed within institutions that were centuries old.[3] Slaves were also employed on plantations wherever merchants and aristocrats had access to large numbers of slaves. In some places, there may have been fewer slaves in 1600 than in 1500, but new developments probably had the net effect of maintaining the number of slaves at about the same level as there had been. As in the medieval period, slavery was associated with the export trade, which has been estimated at 700,000 per century, but the volume of this trade was relatively small – usually no more than a thousand slaves per year for each route. Regional factors, including political rivalries and climatic conditions, generally had a greater influence on slavery than external demand. Only in the far west, where the trans-Atlantic trade and the trans-Saharan trade overlapped, was the external market strong. Even then, total exports from this wide region – Senegambia, inland to Bambara country – probably never exceeded 3,000 to 4,000 per year for both trades.

In theory, the conditions of slavery were supposed to improve over time. The ideological framework, based on adherence to Islam, emphasized the conversion and acculturation of slaves, not only for the many concubines and their free-born children but also for children brought up in the family, who might well aspire to freedom themselves. Second-generation slaves fared better than the newly-enslaved and normally could expect protection from sale; at least this is what the slave trader Francis Moore found along the Gambia River in the 1730s:

> And tho' in some parts of Africa they sell their slaves born in the Family, yet in the River Gambia they think it a very wicked thing, and I never heard of but one that ever sold a Family-Slave, except for such crimes as would have made them to be sold had they been free. If there are many Family Slaves and one of them commits a Crime, the master cannot sell him without the joint consent of the rest, for if he does, they will all run away, and be protected by the next kingdom to which they fly.[4]

111

Of course, masters could not guarantee that slaves would not be sold, and it is significant that Moore's account confirms the right of masters to sell slaves, just as his report establishes that public opinion and the expectations of slaves limited the ability to exercise these proprietory rights.

Furthermore, masters could not always protect slaves against re-enslavement, which appears to have been a frequent occurrence. The ideological framework continued to protect free men, particularly nobles and devout Muslims, from enslavement, as had been the case since at least the fourteenth century; by implication, this allowed the seizure of slaves, as well as non-Muslims, so that slaves could find that any improvement in their status through acculturation or birth was cancelled. Once captured, no matter what their previous status, they were reduced to the level of trade slave, filled with terror of an unknown fate. The importance of re-enslavement can be gleaned from the experiences of Mungo Park, who travelled through the western Sudan in the late eighteenth century. In Bambara country, he interviewed thirteen slaves purchased by a Muslim merchant. Eleven of these people had already been slaves at the time they were seized in a Bambara raid.[5] While this sample is small, it demonstrates one of the dangers of slavery in the western Sudan – renewed capture and the risks of death then and later on the road.

The prevalence of slave raiding, warfare, and re-enslavement indicates that the proportion of slaves in the population of the northern savanna was high, but there is a lack of detail on slave use during the seventeenth and eighteenth centuries. Still, it is likely that slaves were used extensively in production, particularly in agriculture. Ahmad Bābā's treatise of 1614 is typical of this problem of documentation; he made it clear that enslavement was common, but he reported nothing on the use of slaves.[6] The warrior class of Senegambia and the Bambara states incorporated slaves, and merchants had access to slaves, who were almost certainly employed as porters, stockboys, and labourers in the fields everywhere that long-distance trade was important.

In the Senegambia, scattered reports suggest that slaves were common in the commercial towns. For example, Richard Jobson, an English slave-trader on the Gambia in 1620–1, found that slaves formed a considerable portion of the population of Sutukho, whose Muslim clerics and merchants travelled throughout the Senegambia region, from the kola forests in the south to the gold deposits of Buré and Bambuhu and probably to the desert-edge in the north. Sutukho was probably typical of many towns along the trade routes of the savanna. Jobson learned that in this Muslim town:

> no common people [non-Muslims] have dwelling, except such as are their slaves, that work and labour for them, which slaves they suffer to marry and cherish the race that comes of them, which race remaines to them, and their heirs or posterity as perpetuall bond-men, they marry likewise in their owne tribe or kindred, taking no wives but the daughters of mary-buckes [i.e., Muslims], and all the children they have, are nourished and bred up, unto the ceremonies of their fathers.[7]

Jobson clearly identifies slavery as an inherited status, and while he provides little information on the organization of slave labour, it is likely that slaves worked in the fields. The availability of slaves for export across the Sahara and on the upper Guinea coast helps confirm this possibility.

Similarly, the traditions of the Borno kings contain numerous references to raids on the pagan region to the south of Lake Chad, and despite the trade across the Sahara many of these captives, too, stayed in Borno. Mai Ali, who ruled in the middle of the seventeenth century, engaged in massive campaigns, according to a *mahram* written in 1658, seizing as many as 4,000 slaves in a single expedition. Ali distributed slaves to the learned Muslims of his court; how many and for what purpose is not known, but even if the actual figure cannot be accepted as anything more than an indication of large-scale, organized plunder, the implication is clear that enough slaves were available for use in productive activities.[8] Certainly a few were used in administration; others were pressed into military service; while women were placed in harems. It is likely that others were settled in villages.

The Kano *sarki*, Kutumbi (*c.* 1623–48), is remembered as a great slaver; his military officials were responsible for wars and raids that netted thousands of slaves. Some of these were settled around Kano, including those at one place where the spoils of a single raid – reputedly 500 slaves – were concentrated. One of Kutumbi's generals apparently settled other captives at his headquarters at Ganjuwa, at least if his ability to forward to Kano some 2,000 slaves, whom he had seized in raids to the south-east, perhaps attacking Jukun, is any indication of his capacity to amass slaves. In building the town of Ganjuwa, he almost certainly relied on these captives.[9]

In the Funj Sultanate of Sennar, Badi II (1644–81) established a defensive network around his capital, where slaves were settled to farm the land and act as militia in case of invasion.[10] The original population of these settlements was supplemented by purchased slaves and new captives in the course of the next 150 years; by 1773, the slave population numbered 14,000 people. Their military importance was in fact marginal, because the men only had short javelins and shields, virtually no match for heavily armed cavalry, which was the basis of Sennar's power, as it was of most savanna states. The settlements were far more important as a source of agricultural produce than for defence.

The neighbouring state of Dar Fur instituted similar policies during its period of imperial expansion in the eighteenth century. Sultans Tayrāb (1752–85) and 'Abd al-Rahmān (1785–1801) settled slaves on agricultural estates near their capitals, at Dar Fongoro, and on Jabal Marra and its foothills. Tayrāb brought many slaves to his first capital, Shoba, and later settled more slaves at Ril. Many of these slaves were Turuj Nuba who were seized in the Daju Hills of Kordofan; those settled at Ril joined other Daju already living there. 'Abd al-Rahmān also relied on Nuba slaves from Kordofan for his agricultural enterprises. These slaves, known collectively as *'abīdiyya*, were scattered in communities of various sizes throughout Dar Fur. The sultan appointed officials to administer these holdings, which produced food used by the army and the palace. Some communities had special functions other than agricultural work, including the manufacture of padded horse-armour. Others were the homes of specialist military units. Some nobles may have had as many as 500 to 600 slaves on their estates.[11]

The link between enslavement, trade, and the use of slaves in production is clearly established for Futa Jallon in the eighteenth century. The establishment of this theocracy in the 1720s revolutionized the economy of this highland region. Tens of thousands of slaves were settled on plantations to supply the army and facilitate caravan traffic between the coast and the interior. These plantations belonged to merchants and the new Fulbe aristocracy. Although the largest of these belonged to the Fulbe, some idea of their importance can be gleaned from the account of Muhammad Kaba, whose father, a merchant, had a plantation at Bouka, a short distance from Timbo, the capital of Futa Jallon. Kaba's father was 'a substantial yeoman, possessing 140 slaves, several [herds of] cows and horses, and grounds producing quantities of cotton, rice and provisions, which he exchanged for European and other commodities brought from the coast by the Higglers merchants'.[12] Kaba was seized by highwaymen in about 1778 and sold to the Americas. His account makes it clear that plantations of considerable size were owned by commoners in Futa Jallon, for his 'mandingo parentage' set him apart from the Fulbe aristocracy that controlled Futa Jallon and owned most of the slaves. These holdings were so substantial and were amassed in such a relatively short time that there were several slave revolts in the last two decades of the eighteenth century. Even after these uprisings were crushed, tension remained high. When this situation is considered in the context of the export trade to the Americas, which Kaba had experienced along with tens of thousands of other people, then it becomes clear that the effort to pacify the highlands and resettle the countryside with plantation slaves had indeed transformed the social formation of the highlands.[13]

The *jihad* of Futa Jallon reflected economic and social pressures mounting elsewhere in West Africa, probably as a consequence of the periodic droughts. Fulbe cattle herders became more common than ever before, founding villages that served as bases for their seasonal migrations in search of pasture and water. The establishment of Fulbe government in the Futa Jallon highlands successfully repeated the earlier revolt in Futa Bondu (1690s); other Fulbe did the same in Futa Toro in the 1770s.[14] Fulbe pastoralists also appear to have become more numerous in Masina, south of the Niger bend, in the eighteenth century too, although they did not stage a revolution there. None the less, their migratory patterns made them less susceptible to the mid-eighteenth century drought; they could move their herds far to the south during bad times, and upon their return they often found whole areas deserted of population. In the central Sudan, which suffered less from these droughts than other parts of the savanna, Fulbe immigrants inserted themselves into peasant society, moving about the countryside supplying cattle and goats to local markets in return for grain and manufactures. During the dry season, they could graze their herds on the fields; farmers often paid the Fulbe because of the manure left behind.[15]

This type of livestock management proved to be tremendously successful. The relative proportion of Fulbe in the population appears to have increased everywhere across the West African savanna, while other pastoralists, including various Arab tribes, moved westward into the Lake Chad basin and the border areas of Sennar and Dar Fur. Some herders bought slaves, and, near the Hausa towns of the central Sudan, Fulbe masters established whole villages of slaves.[16] Such settlements served as wet-season camps for the nomads, and some of the biggest slave-owners and clan chiefs established relatively fixed transhumant patterns for their herds. These slave masters had different interests from those of the merchant class and aristocracies. Ethnic tensions and occupational specialization prevented the consolidation of a unified slave-owning class, and these divisive factors were often more important than class conflict between slaves and masters.

The information on a slave mode of production is scattered and often circumstantial for the savanna in the seventeenth and eighteenth centuries. Court eunuchs, slave officials, and concubines are more visible in the historical record than field slaves, salt-workers and gold-miners. Consequently, it is not possible to determine the relative importance of slave production, tribute collection, raiding, and trade to the incomes of the dominant classes. The effect of slavery is clear, however. Enslavement was a major function of government. This meant that individuals were safer when they were attached to nobles than when they were not. Enslavement was a form of social control; it was a highly exploitative method of population redistribution. Slavery permeated society, promoting other types of dependency as a means of security. Clientage was perhaps most important in the states and commercial towns of the savanna and southern Sahara. People attached themselves to a patron, working for him or fighting for him. Such quasi-feudal relationships were a by-product of slavery, since failure to participate in such dependent relationships involved great risk.

THE WEST AFRICAN COAST AND ITS INTERIOR

It stands to reason that an area capable of exporting at least 4.5 million slaves from the early seventeenth century to the end of the eighteenth century must have had a significant proportion of slaves in the local population. There were already many slaves in the interior of the Gold Coast by 1600; there were many more there and elsewhere along the Guinea coast soon after. By the middle of the seventeenth century, slavery was common on the Sierra Leone coast and in the Yoruba and Dahomey region of the Slave Coast as well. Several decades later, and especially by the middle of the eighteenth century, the interior country behind the Niger delta and Cross River estuary experienced the same trend. There were major differences between these areas that affected slavery. Firstly, the Akan area was matrilineal, while the other regions were patrilineal; hence inheritance rights and marital customs varied. Secondly, centralized states amassed large numbers of slaves in the Gold and Slave Coast areas, while in the Bight of Biafra interior and Sierra Leone the absence of centralized states prevented the emergence of this sector (except Futa Jallon in the northern interior of Sierra Leone after the 1720s). Thirdly, there were major economic differences related to the availability of local resources. None the less, the similarities in the institution of slavery over this area were strong: slaves were killed at funerals, and they were sacrificed at religious occasions or state functions. Slaves were also seen as kinless dependants who could be incorporated into domestic groups, and they were a valuable asset that could be sold if circumstances warranted such action.

In the coastal region west of the Gold Coast, slavery was more important as a means of acquiring dependants than as the basis of a productive system, except at relatively isolated port settlements. At Grand Bassam and Grand Lahu, for example, the volume of trade probably enabled some local merchants to employ slaves in agriculture and as porters and canoemen.[17] Along the rivers of Sierra Leone, where there were no centralized states of any size, individual merchants also increased the size of their slave holdings in accordance with their success in business. Among the Vai, for example, Dapper found that slaves were inherited in the 1620s, but even during the height of the slave trade from this stretch of coast, European merchants could never obtain more than ten to fifteen slaves at any place on the coast, which suggests that holdings were relatively small.[18] Still slaves were common among the Vai. The same was true for the Sherbro; for example, slaves probably did most of the heavy farming for those families involved in hunting, fishing, salt-making, and commerce. The salt-region of Tasso had numerous slave villages in the early nineteenth century, although it is unclear how old these settlements were and when the concentration of slaves in them began. Almost certainly, however, the main development of these plantations occurred in the eighteenth century or the second half of the seventeenth century. Such trading families as the Caulkers, descended from the English agent Thomas Corker of the Royal African Company, stationed on the Sherbro coast in 1684, were important merchants in the eighteenth century, and their access to slaves made it possible to employ many in agriculture.[19]

In the interior of the Gold Coast, one of the principal functions of slaves was working the gold deposits.[20] As early as the 1620s, Samuel Brun observed that the coastal Akan 'have numerous slaves looking for gold in the sand near our fortress . . . On one occasion, I found a good fifty slaves at the sea side looking for gold in the sand.'[21] In the 1670s in the area near the future capital of Asante:

> The Accasseers, assuming many difficulties and risks, have the veins of gold in the mines explored to a considerable depth. They use all manner of

instruments: huge iron hoes, baskets and strong ropes, not just to dig steps and galleries in the ground, but also to retrieve the gold found there. They tell as well how very often a large number of slaves disappear in the mine shafts because of cavein.[22]

In the 1690s, Tilleman reported that:

> The gold is dug out of the soil by the slaves of these Acaniers [Akan] ... When digging for it no notice is taken of any visible gold in the dug-up soil, but this soil is taken by the slaves in large wooden dishes and made into large heaps by the nearest water [for panning].
>
> In the dominions of Petu, Sabu and Commendo, several hundreds of slaves are often to be seen seeking for gold ... on the beach.[23]

The practice of using slaves in gold production continued under Asante. The risk of death in the pits was considerable because of the environment and relatively low level of technology. The rainy season left the ground damp for months, thereby increasing the danger of cave-in. This risk was perhaps a major reason why custom forbade the Akan from mining gold themselves. Custom sanctified the exploitation of slave labour, and because the gold industry was so important to the local economy, both before the rise of Asante and after, the use of slaves in production marked a fundamental shift in the organization of the social formation.

Slaves were used in other productive activities too, sometimes on a large scale comparable to that occasionally found in gold mining. In Akwamu, for example, the 'great caboceers' – which included government officials, nobility, and merchants – owned many slaves. When Tilleman visited the capital, Nyanaoase, in 1695, he found that plantations surrounded the city, and most of the workers on these plantations were slaves and pawns. These 'caboceers' – *abirempon* in Akwamu – were an urban class; they had armed retainers who were used to enforce tribute collection in the provinces and who sometimes engaged in raids and war for their masters. Individuals might have hundreds of such retainers and other dependants, relatives, clients, servants, and slaves as well. The plantation slaves and pawns were settled outside the capital and almost nowhere else in the state, in part because they were needed to provision the large establishments in Nyanaoase and in part because the *abirempon* preferred to live at the capital. The plantations also raised crops that were sent to the coast to buy fish and salt; some produce was sold to European forts and slave ships.[24]

Asante too developed a slave-based plantation sector, again concentrated around the capital, Kumasi. Information on the origins of this sector is lacking, but accounts from the second decade of the nineteenth century suggest that the settlement of slaves in the vicinity of Kumasi had begun in the middle of the eighteenth century, if not a few decades earlier.[25] Slaves lived in their own villages away from Kumasi, and their labour provided most of the foodstuffs needed to supply the army and large households of the aristocracy. It seems likely that similar concentrations of slaves were found around the capitals of other Akan states, including Denkyira, before it was destroyed in *c.* 1701, and Akyem before it fell in 1742. Similarly, the commercial towns of the forest–savanna frontier probably had a plantation sector as well. Muslim merchants were located at Bighu (destroyed in the 1720s), Nkoranza, Gbuipe, and Kafaba, among other places, and if the nineteenth-century successors to these commercial centres are any indication of past practice, then slave-based agriculture was vital to the provisioning of the caravan trade.[26] As Asante conquered these towns, this commercial network was reorganized. Individual plantations and towns were eliminated, but the continued importance of the Muslim sector suggests that the relationship between slavery and trade was maintained.

At the towns on the Gold Coast itself, slavery was also widespread, and the functions slaves fulfilled were similar to those of the interior. The coastal merchants used male slaves as armed retainers, porters in the trade with the interior, crew on boats, and agricultural workers. Many slave women were taken as wives, and they also laboured in the fields. Indeed, wealthy men on the Gold Coast conceived of their status in terms of the number of their slaves and children, as the Dutch merchant L. F. Romer observed in 1740: 'A Negro only has his children and slaves, that is what riches consist of . . . His children and slaves are really his wealth, his power and protection; the more he possesses, the more he is esteemed.'[27] Slaves were bought or seized outright. Children were the product of polygynous marriages that were arranged through the manipulation of legal pawnship or the purchase of slave women. Their children were recognized as legally free – that is, they were not supposed to be sold – but they lacked kinship affiliation with their master–father's kin for at least another generation until time and intermarriage blurred slave origins. Slavery enabled merchants to acquire dependants who could be incorporated into their establishments, but unless they were loyal and trustworthy, they could be sold, sacrificed, or exported.

The rationale for slavery differed between matrilineal and patrilineal societies, but the results were the same. It is easy to see why men wanted slaves in patrilineal societies: slaves were the personal property of the owner, with no responsibilities to his kin. In matrilineal societies, slavery was also a means of bypassing kinship obligations. Among the Akan, whose society was structured through the female side of the family, kinship was a powerful organizing principle that tied men to their sisters and maternal uncles.[28] They did not pass their wealth on to their own children, if those children were the offspring of a free woman who had lineage connections. Indeed, a man's children by a free wife had stronger economic and social ties to the wife's family. Slaves bypassed these restrictions and enabled wealthy men to establish large households that were dependent upon them and not some larger kinship unit. Slave women in particular were valuable, for they lacked kin, and the children they bore had only a loyalty to their father's family. Other slaves had the same relationship. There were no obligations

118

that existed outside those for the master. Hence a man could depend upon their labour and cooperation, because they had nowhere else to turn.

Except for the metropolitan districts of Akwamu, Asante, and other states and the commercial towns of the coast and far interior, slavery was relatively unimportant; slaves supplemented existing labour in small holdings based primarily on kinship obligations. This peasant sector paid tax to the state and was subject to harassment from officials and their slave retainers. Occasionally, individuals emerged as small merchants, gold producers, or kola exporters, but inheritence customs and death taxes usually prevented the consolidation of a prosperous rural elite. Either entrepreneurs moved to the commercial and political centres, or their activities remained relatively small-scale.

Oyo used slaves extensively in administrative and military capacities, and well this state could afford to, considering the role it played in the export of slaves to the Americas. The king (*alafin*) had a large staff of slaves who resided in the palace and adjacent compounds. These probably numbered several thousand in the first half of the eighteenth century and consisted of three categories. Eunuchs were one. Some guarded the king's wives and children, while there were three senior eunuchs who were responsible for judicial, religious, and administrative matters respectively. A second category of royal slaves was the *ilari*, designated as such because their heads were shaven and they were given special face and body scars. They served as the king's bodyguard, royal messengers, and tax collectors. There were several hundred of both sexes and they had their own officers. Still a third category of royal slaves included large numbers of individuals with administrative and ritual functions. This system appears to have developed gradually, reaching its zenith before 1754, and the *coup d'état* of Basorun Gaha. Gaha dismantled the royal administration and substituted one of his own, probably relying on his own slaves. After he was assassinated in 1774, Alafin Abiodun (d. 1789), re-established the royal slave-system.[29]

This administrative structure relied on provincial slave officials, known as *ajele*, who were appointed to administer specific towns and were responsible directly to the king. These officials in turn required the services of numerous slave subordinates, including tax collectors, customs officials, and messengers. The *ajele* system was particularly important in governing the province of Egbado, through which the main route to the coast passed after 1770. Slaves were also a central feature of the military. Besides the personal bodyguard of the king, slaves dominated the cavalry, which was the backbone of Oyo power. Hausa and Nupe slaves tended the horses and staffed much of the cavalry force. Because of environmental factors, the breeding of large and strong mounts for the military was not possible in Oyo country. Horses had to come from the north, just as the experts in horse care did. In addition, many retainers of the military officials were slaves, who often came from the north.[30]

Oyo's military slaves received special privileges because of their position –

they had the responsibility for the enslavement of other people. But they were not assimilated; they remained apart as Muslims and non-natives. Indeed, their allegiance to Islam was indirectly promoted, for religion gave them a status in a society based on the kinship ties they lacked. For many slaves, therefore, an identification with Islam became a feature of slavery. This did not imply exploitation, but it enhanced recognition as dependants.

Slave owners in the interior of the Bight of Benin also used slaves in productive activities, at least in Dahomey, which was a province of Oyo after 1726. William Snelgrave, a slave trader familiar with Dahomey in 1726–7, provides one of the few glimpses of the economic exploitation of slaves, which he associates with other aspects of Dahomean slavery:

> It has been the Custom among the Negroes, time out of Mind, and is so to this day, for them to make Slaves of all Captives they take in War. Now, before they had an Opportunity of selling them to white People, they were often obliged to kill great Multitudes, when they had taken more than they could well employ in their own Plantations, for fear they should rebel, and endanger their Masters safety.[31]

Snelgrave's account establishes the connection between three dimensions of slavery in Dahomey, including the execution of slaves, criminals, and prisoners at state functions, the sale of slaves to Europeans for export to the Americas, and the employment of slaves in agriculture in the domestic economy. The state executions and the export trade were effective methods of controlling the domestic slave-population.

Unfortunately, the earliest substantial knowledge of the slave population at the Oyo capital comes from 1830, only a few years before the final collapse of the Oyo state. At that time, it was estimated that two-thirds of the people in the city were slaves, and it is highly likely that many of these were farmers and craftsmen. This situation probably dated from the eighteenth century, if not earlier still.[32]

In the interior of the Bight of Biafra, from where 830,000 slaves came in the period from 1700 to 1800, many families had slaves, as Olaudah Equiano's account from the middle of the eighteenth century makes clear. Equiano's father had slaves in his household, and Equiano's generalizations about slavery suggest that slaves were common. Equiano himself, after he had the misfortune of being kidnapped, worked as a blacksmith's apprentice. Then he was sold to European merchants and eventually became a plantation slave in the Americas. His comparison of his experiences is instructive:

> Those prisoners which were not sold or redeemed we kept as slaves: but how different was their condition from that of the slaves in the West-Indies? With us they do no more work than other members of the community, even their master. Their food, clothing, and lodging, were nearly the same as theirs, except that they were not permitted to eat with those who were free born; and there were scarce any other difference between them than a superior degree of importance which the head of a family possesses in our state, and that

authority which, as such, he exercises over every part of his household. Some of these slaves have even slaves under them as their own property and for their own use.[33]

Equiano was aware, however, that justice was not always served in his native land, not only because he had been kidnapped, but also because his father had been involved in legal cases that indicate that illegal enslavement had become a serious problem. Indeed, slave merchants were customarily questioned in order to determine the legality of their merchandise. Only prisoners of war and criminals convicted of kidnapping, adultery, and murder were considered legitimate slaves, but merchants often carried large sacks to hide their wares, a heinous practice that Equiano experienced when he found himself inside one.

Equiano's comparison of Igbo and American slavery presents the obvious contrasts between small-scale domestic slavery and plantation slavery; inadvertently, Equiano attests to the contribution of slaves to production in his homeland. Slaves did the same work as 'other members of the community, even their masters', which would involve agricultural labour, crafts, trade, and domestic chores. That this work was 'no more' than what free people did cannot be accepted without qualification, however. Equiano left his country at the age of ten; his memory may well have been clouded by a romantic image of Africa and the influence of the British abolitionists who were his patrons. None the less, the details of slavery – the possibility that slaves could own slaves and the social distance maintained between free persons and slaves – indicate a social formation in which slavery was common.

Other than Equiano's brief account on the employment of slaves in production, there is simply little information to examine. The Aro settlements at Ikelionwu (Ndieni cluster) and Ndizuogu were founded by slaves.[34] Aro traditions do not reveal the functions of slavery; they suggest that the founders were commercial agents, but it is likely that slaves were employed in menial tasks and that tradition has emphasized the possibility of social mobility and commercial success rather than agricultural work and head porterage, in which most slaves were probably employed. In the Niger delta, slaves were involved in economic activities too. They were needed to man the large river-boats that were already operating between Bonny, Elem Kalabari, and Calabar and the riverside markets of the interior. The Igala, Aboh, and Ossamari traders on the Niger River also had large boats, and they too probably used some slaves at least.[35]

The types of slaves that were common in Equiano's time included funeral victims, cult devotees (*osu*), and other persons dedicated to non-productive and non-commercial uses. Secret societies and titled societies, which wealthy and influential men (and sometimes women) joined, probably required the sacrifice of slaves; at least, this was the practice in the nineteenth century, and there is no reason to suppose that conditions were not the same in the eighteenth century, if not earlier still. *Osu* were slaves dedicated to shrines who subsequently could not be sold, since they no longer had a human master. Funerals were considered a time to display wealth through sacrifice; the killing of slaves was later a particularly conspicuous display, although horses imported from the savanna were also used, along with less valuable objects. Other non-productive uses of slaves included the sacrifice of slaves to deities, such as to the salt-making gods at Uburu, the most important inland source of salt and the site of one major Aro fair.[36]

Despite the gaps in the documentation for the Biafran interior – and indeed for other places too – the historical trend is clear. A mode of production based on slavery emerged on some parts of the West African coast. Among the Akan, this mode of production antedated the development of the trans-Atlantic slave trade; gold production, head porterage, and agricultural employment for slaves long preceded the boom in slave exports in the late seventeenth and the eighteenth centuries. The external trade reinforced and encouraged the expansion of a slave mode of production, but the American market did not cause it. Along the Sierra Leone and Slave Coasts, there appears to have been a direct correspondence between the trans-Atlantic slave trade and the consolidation of a slave mode of production. Oyo, Dahomey, Allada, and other states struggled to exploit the possibilities of the export trade, and in the process slave masters employed their slaves in domestic production, apparently on an increasing scale. Along the Sierra Leone and upper Guinea coast, local merchant-princes emerged who used slave labour to advantage too, while the rise of Futa Jallon was closely associated with slavery. By contrast, in the Bight of Biafra, the interaction between enslavement, trade, and production only began to achieve a level of integration that can be equated with a mode of production based on slavery, and then only in the second half of the eighteenth century.

SLAVERY IN WEST-CENTRAL AFRICA

Although slaves were used in agriculture, commerce, and other economic activities in west-central Africa during the seventeenth and eighteenth centuries, the social formation there was different from that of the northern savanna and the West African coast. A mode of production based on slavery can be identified, but the size of the export trade – hundreds of thousands of slaves in the seventeenth century and almost two million slaves in the eighteenth century – demonstrates that west-central Africa remained primarily a supplier of slaves for export. In general the export trade drained population from the productive sectors, except in a few places where slaves became an important component in production. The supply mechanism thereby limited the expansion of a slave mode of production. Far too many slaves were exported, in comparison with the domestic slave-population, for slavery to assume the importance that it did in West Africa and the northern savanna.

Slavery was closely associated with the export sector and its supply network. Slaves were most numerous along the routes into the interior – Mbanza Sonyo to São Salvador in Kongo, Luanda to Kasanje and Matamba, the Loango coast to Malebo Pool on the Zaire River, and Benguela to Bihé (in the eighteenth century). While these routes and the various routes that intersected with these points prospered, the size of the slave population increased; when political and economic conditions deteriorated, the slave population stabilized or declined. Wherever slaves formed a substantial proportion of the population, their labour was an important component in production.

The concentration of slaves around São Salvador and Mbanza Sonyo in Kongo continued for the first two-thirds of the seventeenth century, even though the slave trade through the Kongo port of Mpinda declined with the collapse of the Kongo–São Thomé commercial axis. A belt of slave estates extended outward for a radius of 35 km around these two centres; the population of the capital district was between 60,000 and 70,000 people, most of whom were slaves whose agricultural labour supported the residents in São Salvador, which had about 9,000 to 12,000 people, comprised of nobles and their slave retainers. The population of the coastal district of Mbanza Sonyo was somewhat less but still had a substantial proportion of slaves.[37] The 1648 report of Giovanni Francesco da Roma, a Capuchin priest, makes it clear that the nobles were preoccupied with managing a slave society. The slave population was sometimes difficult to control, and the hegemony of the large slave owners depended upon keeping their plantation slaves and armed retainers divided.[38] As in the sixteenth century, the two urban districts were not typical of the rest of Kongo, which was less densely populated by small peasant communities of related kin. None the less, one-third of the population lived near the two centres, and since the peasant lineages owned some slaves, it is possible that the total slave population of Kongo was more than 100,000, perhaps slightly less than the free population.[39] The peasant and slave sectors were linked, moreover, for the state used enslavement as a political weapon. While most slaves – both those exported from Kongo and those settled at São Salvador and Mbanza Sonyo – came from further inland, some slaves, at least, were Kongo peasants who had failed to pay taxes or who had committed some action used to justify enslavement, as the reports of Giacinto Brugiotti in the 1650s make clear.[40]

In the 1660s, civil war tore Kongo apart and effectively reversed the role slavery had been playing in the state, at least in the capital district. The Sonyo army sacked São Salvador in 1666, seizing many slaves. Between 1666 and 1678, the entire nobility of São Salvador left the city together with as many slaves and followers as it could control. It moved to the provinces, where its slaves continued to farm, but the great slave estates of the capital district were broken up. The winner in the civil wars was Mbanza Sonyo, whose population appears to have doubled during the last half of the seventeenth century, partly as a result of the slaves taken in the invasion of São Salvador.[41] Sonyo now had the sole concentration of slaves; its government granted uncultivated land to nobles and missionaries, which was then cleared by slaves. Masters divided the land into two parts; the slaves worked the master's fields, and the whole of that product went to the master. On smaller plots, the slaves were expected to farm for their own subsistence.[42] According to one Portuguese missionary, Cavazzi, who travelled through Kongo in 1657, slaves constituted half the population, although it is likely that Cavazzi based his estimate on Mbanza Sonyo alone. Those slaves in Sonyo, at least, he found poorly fed and frequently mistreated: 'they are exhausted by all manner of tasks; their lives are always very trying; the only payment they can hope for is a slight improvement in the treatment they receive.'[43]

The Sonyo nobility exploited its population through the institution of pawnship and the taxation of the peasantry, as well as slavery. In the 1680s, the servile population included many pawns; one Capuchin missionary, Giuseppe Maria da Busseto, spent much of his time redeeming pawns, thereby collecting information on the prevalence of pawnship.[44] Raids on the peasantry also continued. In 1701, for example, one noble seized 58 people in a Kongo village that apparently had not paid its taxes.[45]

With the decline of the commercial corridor through Mpinda to São Salvador (already underway in the early seventeenth century and finalized during the civil wars), the focus of slave concentration shifted to the south. This region – home of the Mbundu and location of Luanda – supplied many of Kongo's slaves, but other slaves were also settled there, particularly after the foundation of Kasanje and Matamba. These slaves served three main functions: males were incorporated into the slave-supply mechanism as warriors; women bore children for their husbands and masters; and both males and females were used in economic capacities, especially agriculture and head porterage. There were other functions too, including sacrifice, but the contribution of slaves to enslavement, reproduction, and the economy were most characteristic of the slave mode of production here. Even sacrifice was important on the ideological level.

Slavery in the Imbangala war-bands was a type of slavery that required rapid assimilation and extreme dependence.[46] Those slaves who became soldiers were boys; only uncircumcised youths were taken into the Imbangala ranks, and this meant that the oldest boys were often only seven or eight. The Imbangala also wanted women, and older people as long as they could work. Some slaves had a less desirable fate: they were sacrificed before battle. Each Imbangala war-lord killed from one to five slaves before a raid, and these were fed to the warriors in a concoction that included sacrificed animals. This cannibalism had the military effect discussed in chapter 5: it was one among many tactics that terrified people and helped give the Imbangala the military advantage through psychological warfare. The killing of slaves also had an important effect on the slave population, for it demonstrated the power that masters had over their slaves. Imbangala captives faced two extremes: they could be assimilated into the war-band, with the expectation of full membership as soldiers or wives, or they could be killed or sold to Europeans. The prospect of death had the desirous effect of promoting assimilation among those slaves who were singled out from the trade.[47]

Once the Imbangala became less interested in raiding for slaves and established more permanent commercial ties with the interior – a process examined in some detail in chapters 4 and 5 – it was necessary to stabilize the interaction between the kinless Imbangala and the Mbundu lineages. This stabilization was advantageous, and indeed necessary, for the lineages, because the Imbangala had a monopoly on trade and military power. Now the lineages accepted a tributary position to the Imbangala: they sent slaves and women to the *kilombo* centres. If they did not do this, they were raided. If they met Imbangala exactions, they could achieve a level of safety and might receive some of the imported goods obtained from the Portuguese. They could at least expect the freedom to buy salt and other necessary items. This consolidation of a more peaceful transfer of people from the lineages to the Imbangala *kilombo* indicates that slaves were common in the lineages by the last part of the seventeenth century.[48]

The lineage slaves appear largely to have been convicted criminals, sorcerers, and people purchased from other lineages. It may be that some were victims of kidnapping and local quarrels. The relative importance of these sources is unclear, but it is certain that many of these slaves were not incorporated into the lineages. They could not be, for to do so would prevent their use as tribute. It was essential that each lineage should maintain slaves as a reserve for the Imbangala. Otherwise, full lineage members would have to fill the tribute quotas. The nature of slavery, therefore, reinforced kinship; slaves were held in common. They worked for the good of the lineage, and they could be sent to the Imbangala war-lords when necessary. Slavery, therefore, had more of a political nature than an economic one. It developed to safeguard people who were related genetically. Slavery was a means of segregating people who were not part of the lineage and who could be exploited because of their lack of kinship affiliation.

At the height of the slave trade in the second half of the eighteenth century. Matamba (Ginga), Kasanje, and Portuguese Angola incorporated large numbers of slaves. Again, the relationship with the export trade is clear. According to Thornton's analysis of census data for 1777 and 1778, female slaves outnumbered male slaves by more than two to one – the exact inverse of the sex ratio in the trans-Atlantic trade from Luanda.[49] Since females were often undercounted, the disparity was perhaps even greater. By this time, polygyny was widespread, probably on a greater scale than ever before. While the retention of women helped minimize the impact of the slave trade on the demography of west-central Africa, female slaves were concentrated along the trade routes and at political centres. Birth-rates were probably still lower than among demographically-balanced populations; at least, studies of comparable situations in other periods would suggest as much. None the less, the social formation was altered in a unique way. Some men controlled large numbers of female slaves and their offspring, while huge tracts of countryside were devoid of people.

These women were used in production. They wove rafia cloth, a craft that traditionally belonged to males elsewhere in the interior. Apparently the shift from a male to a female occupation occurred because of the availability of women. Most agricultural labourers were also women who farmed their own plots allotted to them by their husbands–masters. Plantation conditions appear to have existed only with the Portuguese and other merchants, although it is possible that some other slave owners had enough workers to organize field work in a regimented fashion. Marriage effectively protected women from this fate; instead, labour was obtained through a combination of the institutions of marriage and slavery.

Developments on the coast near Loango, a port frequented by European slave ships during the late seventeenth and the eighteenth centuries, demonstrate the kind of changes that occurred under the impetus of the demand for slaves in the Americas.[50] The methods of enslavement became more common over time, so that conviction for murder, robbery, adultery, and debt were punishable through enslavement, and this punishment reveals that foreign trade subverted local Vili society and economy. Severe punishment for theft and murder protected the operations of merchants and provided slaves for the merchants. Enslavement for debt helped guarantee credit arrangements. Previously, if the example of neighbouring people is any indication of the traditional practice, debts could be settled through pawning. A change in the penalty for debt, therefore, reflected the greater commercialization of Vili society. The seriousness with which adultery was treated, however, reveals that dependency was still characteristic. The institution of marriage continued to be sacrosanct because custom required that marriage arrangements do more than unite two people in matrimony. Marriage tied kin groups together in carefully managed contracts that involved commercial partnerships, exchange of property, and reciprocal pacts for defence.

The manipulation of the legal system evident among the Vili becomes clearer when it is realized that the judges in cases resulting in enslavement were the largest slave-owners and wealthiest merchants. The incidence of slavery increased from the seventeenth to the eighteenth century.[51] At the height of the external slave trade, the number of slaves owned by a man was a sure sign of his wealth, for the size of a man's following was an important indication of his commercial activities. Slaves were used as porters to carry ivory, copper, and other goods from the interior. The number of slaves is a good indication of wealth in any society, but among the Vili, as among many African societies, dependency was crucial. Slaves were not only commodities. They were also people, and their loyalty was assured by granting them concessions as they participated more fully in the affairs of the master. These acquired rights can best be seen with the Vili through the types of employment open to them. As porters in the caravan trade to the interior, they were allowed some freedom to act on their own account. Otherwise there was danger of escape and theft. As dependants of merchants, they were given certain safeguards for their future, and particularly for the future of their children. The inhabitants of the Loango ports were exempted from judicial enslavement. Anyone born there could not be sold into slavery, no matter what the crime. Other distinctions, perhaps less serious but none the less instructive of the ways in which Vili slavery conformed to similar patterns of dependency, were also recognized. When an important man displayed himself officially, slaves carried goods behind him, while other dependants fanned him.

The Lunda and Luba war-lords participated in the slave trade because they could mobilize the population of the interior for enslavement, production, and trade. Slaves were channelled towards the Imbangala fairs, but many were settled around the Lunda centres, as the case of the capital territory of the *mwant yaav* (king) most clearly demonstrates. This district, the *mussumba*, was located in the fertile valleys of the Kalanyi and Luiza Rivers, two tributaries of the Lulua River. The actual capital was moved when a new *mwant yaav* came to power, but throughout this district were plantations, worked by slaves and poor women. The origin of this plantation system is closely associated with the rise of slave trading.[52] It may well be that Luba was also drawn into the orbit of the slave trade in the eighteenth century and that patterns of slavery in Luba were similar to those in Lunda. Luba was centred in the area around Lake Boya and the Upemba Depression, further into the interior than Lunda, but political and commercial expansion are associated with the eighteenth century. While there is no direct evidence for a firm link with slave exporting, the Luba kings established slave villages and slave lineages as a result of raids and expansive wars.[53]

Most of the inland states incorporated slaves in ways not unlike other matrilineal societies, in which men wanted slave wives in order to negate the legal rights of in-laws. For slave women, there were no relatives. Hence many women found themselves in servile relationships that were substituted for other types of dependency based on kinship. Slave children, moreover, were probably assimilated as adopted kin, as they were in the nineteenth century. The status of slavery became less onerous over time, and children born into slavery – perhaps only a small portion of the total slave population – could expect to grow up as members of their master's lineage.

In west-central Africa, the social formation combined modes of production based on matrilineal kinship, slavery, and tributary relationships. The region was more directed towards the export trade than the West African coast or the northern savanna; the 2,500,000 to 3,000,000 slaves exported to the Americas between 1600 and 1800 appear to have come from a smaller population base than was true in West Africa and the northern savanna. The social formation was distorted accordingly. Kinship structures encouraged the incorporation of slave women, even though lineage society was rooted in matrilineal customs and thereby tied together through free women. This contradiction between the pull of matrilineages and the power of men who accumulated slaves and pawns found a resolution in tributary relationships. War-lords exacted tribute, often in the form of slaves, from the lineages; when regular payments were not forthcoming, slave raids accomplished similar results. The preponderance of female slaves in the lineages and among the commercial and tributary sectors was achieved through the export of disproportionately large numbers of men. The articulation of slavery with tributary and lineage structures demonstrates that the social formation of west-central Africa was first and foremost a supplier of slaves for export. The connection with the Americas was essential to this formation; the productive sphere was really concentrated there, despite some development on the periphery of west-central Africa itself (see below).

EUROPEAN SLAVERY IN AFRICA

The slave populations in the European enclaves along the Guinea coast, in Angola, at Cape Town, and in Zambezia were generally associated with trade, including the slave-supply mechanism; these slaves manned commercial establishments, performing menial tasks, loading and unloading ships, and transporting goods into the interior. Some slaves also worked on farms to supply ships and the European outposts. Other slaves served as soldiers, capturing people for export or guarding trade slaves. These slaves – owned by Europeans and Euro-Africans – are almost never discussed in the context of slavery in the Americas or slavery in Africa, although their existence was directly related to the expansion of the European economy that included the development of the plantation and mining economies of the Americas, the evolution of the slave-supply mechanism in Africa, and the growth of trade with Asia. By the end of the eighteenth century, the slaves in the European enclaves may have totalled 60,000 to 100,000.

By the eighteenth century, there were perhaps 5,000 or more slaves at the European outposts along the West African coast; many of these were owned by chartered companies, although the number belonging to Euro-Africans appears to have increased. At James Fort on the Gambia, there were 32 company slaves in 1730 and 43 in 1763, and, since the population of the fort was usually not greater than a hundred or so, slaves formed a large proportion of the inhabitants. At the larger French posts at Saint Louis and Gorée, the percentage of slaves was even greater, reaching as much as 86 per cent of the population. In 1755, for example, Saint Louis had 648 slaves, 98 owned by the French company and 550 by residents. The number of slaves was reported to be 3,108 in 1776, 1,858 in 1779, 2,000 in 1785, and 2,400 in 1786. At Gorée, there were 768 slaves in 1767, 1,200 in 1776, and 1,044 in 1785.[54]

Along the estuaries of the Sierra Leone and Guinea coasts, the number of company slaves was usually several hundred at the major shipping points. Except for convicted criminals, these slaves were not exported; instead, they were trained to operate the local stations. On the Gold Coast, the Dutch and English trade-castles kept slaves as domestics, agricultural workers, craftsmen, and common labourers. Most Europeans took concubines as well. These slaves and their descendants who had the skills needed by the European factors sometimes were successful in investing on their own. Along the upper Guinea coast, such Afro-Europeans occasionally owned plantations near the major commercial centres, supplying rice and other foodstuffs for the local market and the slave ships.[55]

The largest concentration of slaves at the European enclaves associated with the slave trade was in Angola, where Portuguese missionaries, traders, and officials had owned slaves since the sixteenth century. While the southward shift of Portuguese activities from the Kongo–São Thomé axis to Luanda reflected a decline in the importance of both Kongo and São Thomé, there continued to be European-owned slaves in both places. The plantations on São Thomé – greatly reduced in importance as plantation colonies – none the less still relied on slave labour, although on a relatively small scale by comparison with the Americas. In Kongo, missionaries and merchants employed slave labour from the early seventeenth century on; one man – Gaspar Alvarès – reportedly owned 'one hundred plantations or *arimos* [small farms] in Kongo and Angola, and thousands of slaves', which he amassed before 1632, the year he gave his holdings to the Jesuits.[56] All the missionaries used slaves extensively, both in agriculture and as porters.

By the middle of the eighteenth century, the greatest concentration of Portuguese-owned slaves developed in the area centred around Luanda between the Dande River in the north and the Kwanza River in the south, inland as far as the Lukala River. There was a second region further south around Benguela inland to the edge of the central plateau. These areas became centres of plantation agriculture operated by Portuguese and Afro-Portuguese who were involved in the slave trade with the interior.[57] Some estimate of the size of the slave population can be gained from the Portuguese census of 1777 and 1778, which establishes that slaves formed a considerable portion of the population in the core areas of Portuguese control. Women outnumbered men in this population – far greater percentages of male slaves being exported – but since women performed much of the agricultural labour in the region anyway, the demographic structure of the slave population reinforced existing patterns of labour organization.[58] Portuguese slave-owners relied on female labour in the

129

production of foodstuffs needed to feed the trade slaves and to stock the slave ships. The use of slave labour was a logical extension of the export trade, since some slaves could easily be put to work in the business of sending the majority to Brazil.

The accumulation of slaves at Cape Town and in its hinterland was also a by-product of European commercial expansion, although the connection with the trans-Atlantic slave trade was more indirect than slave use along the Guinea coast and in Angola. Founded in 1652 as a way-station in the Dutch trade to the orient, the Cape settlement catered to ships passing to and from India and Indonesia, whose cargoes included cowries and textiles for the slave trade as well as spices and other goods for European consumption. Even the cowries and textiles were first imported into the Netherlands before being re-exported back to Africa. A few slave ships from south-east Africa and Madagascar stopped at the Cape for provisions, but this trade was very small until the very end of the eighteenth century. The flow of trade brought slaves, however; most came from Madagascar; some came from south-eastern Africa, and a few came from Asia.[59]

In the early years of the colony, the Dutch East India Company owned most of the slaves at the Cape, who were used to maintain the port facilities, and the Company always remained the largest single owner of slaves. By the first two decades of the eighteenth century, the Company owned over 400 slaves; thereafter its holdings remained relatively fixed in size, averaging several hundred until after mid-century and attaining a peak of 946 in 1789. Many of these slaves were kept in company-owned barracks, first built in 1679 and expanded in later years. The occupations of the Company slaves included the range of activities needed in the port: carpenters, masons, coopers, smiths, stevedores, and general labourers, although some were also gardeners and shepherds. As is evident in these occupations, the Company had a major influence in determining the nature of slavery; commercial operations were foremost in the treatment of slaves and in the governing of virtually all aspects of the colony.[60]

As the number of Dutch immigrants increased in the late seventeenth and the eighteenth centuries, slavery became an essential part of the expanding colony; free whites considered manual labour fit for slaves or Khoikhoi, who were reduced to servile status as tenants or dependent shepherds. The white population expanded from only 125 in 1670 to 1,695 in 1711. Thereafter, population continued to grow slowly, reaching 4,511 in 1750, 7,736 in 1770, and attaining a high of about 20,000 by 1798. While many of these settlers were also associated with the transit trade around the Cape, some whites moved into the interior, where they opened farms or raised stock. By the early eighteenth century, the slave population was already equal to the number of free whites – approximately 2,000 slaves by the second decade of the century. The Company decided in 1717 to discourage the immigration of more Dutch in favour of importing more slaves;

thereafter, the slave population grew even more rapidly, eventually reaching a total of 25,000 in the 1790s.[61]

The size of slave holdings varied considerably, although in general holdings were not as large as on the plantations of the Americas. In the early eighteenth century, several settlers owned considerable numbers of slaves, but most settlers owned only a few, if any. One governor had over 200 slaves settled on his estate at Vergelegen, and other colonists had from 10 to 20 slaves each.[62] By the middle of the century, this range of holdings was well consolidated; there were relatively few large slave holdings; only seven owners had more than 51 slaves, with the largest having 94 slaves. None the less, these 7 masters had 24 per cent of all the colony's slaves. Another 25 masters held between 26 and 50 slaves, and 117 owners had between 11 and 25 slaves. These figures are significant because they demonstrate that a relatively few individuals owned most of the slaves at the Cape, and these same individuals dominated the agricultural economy. The Company satisfied its requirements for basic provisions by issuing supply contracts to the highest bidder, who then enjoyed a monopoly of the Company's business. None the less, the overwhelming majority of slave owners had only a few slaves, so that in the white population as a whole there was a high incidence of slave holding. In 1750, almost half the male population owned at least one slave.[63]

In many ways, slavery at the Cape was a cross between the slavery of the Americas and the castle slavery of the European commercial establishments along the West African coast.[64] Because the Company was the largest single slave-owner and many town-folk worked in commercially-related activities that depended upon the transit trade between Europe and the Indian Ocean, slaves were shielded from the harshest forms of slave management. Furthermore, the size of slave holdings also meant that many slaves had the opportunity to acquire skills that allowed for the possibility of some improvement in well-being. None the less, race was a significant factor in the control of the slave population, just as it was in the Americas. The pattern of conversion to Christianity, miscegenation, manumission, and cultural change are more similar to the history of slavery in tropical America than to other European enclaves in Africa.[65] The farmers in the hinterland used slaves as field hands, raising crops that could be sold at the port to provision ships and to maintain the town's inhabitants. The wheat farms and vineyards of the interior averaged 60 hectares in the early eighteenth century; these were large farms, not plantations. The cattle ranges beyond the farms and vineyards were much bigger, but slave holdings were not large. The trekboers on these frontier estates relied primarily on dependent Khoikhoi and only a few slaves.[66]

The Dutch community at the Cape prided itself on the differences between its treatment of slaves and the plantation slavery of the Americas. The comparison is instructive, even though the contemporary assessment needs considerable qualification, because the comparison is implicit recognition that slavery at the Cape and slavery in the Americas were similar. As Commissary General J. A. de Mist, who was sent to the Cape in 1802, reported:

> There is a great difference between the treatment of these slaves and [that] meted to those who are yearly shipped to America from the Congo and Angola. At the Cape they are, in the majority of cases at least, looked upon as permanent family servants . . . The abundance of the necessaries of life and the comparatively easy work of fetching and carrying wood, herding cattle, tilling the fields, labouring in the vineyards or attending to the daily housework makes their lot in life quite tolerable, and if, at times, some inhuman wretch is found who ill-treats his slaves, nowhere is there a better opportunity of obstructing and altogether preventing this ill-treatment by means of good laws than at the Cape.[67]

This account clearly establishes that slaves performed most of the work at the Cape. While de Mist was probably correct in suggesting that the lot of most slaves in the Americas was worse than the majority here, the reasons for this were not because of a superior legal system in the Dutch colony. Rather, it was usually the case that slaves in small holdings, particularly at commercial centres, fared better than plantation slaves. In this sense, the Cape slaves benefited, but when allowance is made for a distinction between the town slaves and the agricultural workers of the countryside, which de Mist does not do in his portrait, then the Dutch settlement must be considered to be similar to the Americas.

Slave holdings among the Portuguese settlers in the Zambezi valley were also considerable, originating in the sixteenth century but becoming particularly important in the seventeenth. Here slavery was really determined by the military functions that the Portuguese had traditionally filled in the Zambezi region. Their earliest contacts were as mercenaries, and they acquired slaves to fill the ranks of their private armies.[68] These soldiers, called *achikunda*, sometimes farmed, but only to feed themselves, and more often they lived off the tribute provided by African peasants on the lands claimed by the Portuguese war-lords. These vast tracts of territory, nominally granted by the Portuguese crown as landed estates that were supposed to revert back to the crown after three generations or some other specified period, in reality constituted a political order that received local recognition only because of the armed might of the slave soldiers. Ties of dependency characterized the relationship between lord and *achikunda* warrior. They lived off the tribute extracted from the peasantry in the same way that Bambara regiments did in the western Sudan. Some slaves were employed in mining gold in the Zambezi basin; a few Portuguese settlers had as many as 300 slaves in gold production. None the less, the dominant pattern was the use of slaves as soldiers.

Fernando de Jesus Maria described the corporate identity that prevailed among slaves on the *prazos* in 1762, revealing their essentially military function. It was not possible to order these slaves around as if they were mere chattels. As soldiers they knew that the strength of the *prazo* was dependent upon their support, and despite their slave origins they secured for themselves a status above that of the free peasantry. Fernando's account reveals this feature of slavery on the *prazo*:

> The slaves which are kept in each household as though part of the entail are called the *botaca*. These slaves have a leader who is called a *mocasambo* and another second to him called *sachicunda* who is the same as the treasurer in these *botacas* who does all the business. The *senhor* [master] cannot give a single negro of the *botaca* away without the others all mutinying . . . to the *mocasambo* the negroes have such a blind obedience that if it is necessary to execute any one of them he will briefly consult with the eldest of the slaves and the execution will be carried out at once without any demur.[69]

Fernando was referring to the able-bodied men who were organized into military units of ten or twelve men under a *tsachikunda*, and together formed regiments under the command of a *mukazambo*. Production was left to the women, who formed a considerable portion of the slave population. In 1759, the family of Dona Ines Pessoa de Almeida Castellobranco had an estimated 6,000 slaves, and contemporary Jesuit records provide inventories that confirm a total of 1,837 slaves on her two largest estates at Cheringoma and Gorongosa, exclusive of women and children. Ten *prazo*-holders had holdings of over 1,000 slaves in 1759; eleven had holdings of 500 to 1,000 slaves; and there were many holdings with less than 500 slaves. Altogether there were some 33,500 slaves reported. Other holdings included those of Nicolau Pascoal da Cruz, who claimed to own 340 slaves in this same period. In 1788, the slave holdings of João Fernandes do Rozario consisted of 25 adult male slaves and 8 females on one *prazo*; at another, he had 20 men and 60 women; while at a third, he had 15 males and 30 female slaves. On a fourth *prazo*, the sexual division of its 60 slaves is not reported. In his household were 50 boys and 30 girls, as well as 42 slaves with special skills, but whose sex is unknown. Altogether João Fernandes de Rozario had over 500 slaves.[70]

Slavery in the Zambezi valley came closest to duplicating the kind of developments that resulted in the emergence of Islamic slavery in Africa. The Zambezi model of slavery shared some features of local African ideas of slavery as a form of dependency, but Europeans and Afro-Europeans were the masters. The resulting adaptation of European slavery to the African setting helped transform the social formation so that it became connected with the slave trade. The *prazo*-holders increasingly relied on the export of slaves for a major portion of their income, especially in the last decades of the eighteenth century. Tribute from the subject peasantry was associated with slavery through the threat of violence which the *achikunda* slave armies could inflict on recalcitrant people. European forms of slavery were not directly imposed on Africans; rather the Portuguese became another group of war-lords. The partial assimilation of the Portuguese into the local political economy merged the Portuguese need for slave labour in the Americas with African conceptions of slavery.

African slave owners did not generally exploit slaves in the same ways as Europeans because the possibilities of productive agriculture and mining based on slavery were largely absent, except in a relatively few places. This confinement of productive slavery reveals a crucial feature of the seventeenth and eighteenth centuries. The exploitation of slaves for purely economic motives was found in the European enclaves and in some places like Asante and Dahomey, but the association of slavery with the economy was more characteristic of the European sector than the African, except when the African sector was strongly associated with exports. The existence of *prazos* with large numbers of slaves in a region where lineages had only a few slaves is typical of this pattern. In effect, two modes of production existed side by side; estate-holders, with their *achikunda* armies and slave villages, were tied into a system of slavery, while the small peasant communities scattered throughout the Zambezi valley were only marginally affected by slavery and instead were organized on the basis of kinship.[71]

While slavery underwent a transformation in response to the expansion of the slave trade, the nature of this transformation was unique in different parts of the Atlantic coastal basin. The interaction between indigenous patterns of dependency and the foreign trade resulted in major social changes. These were closely associated with centralized states on the Gold Coast and in the Bight of Benin, with a decentralized commercial confederation in the Bight of Biafra, and with a system of administered trade in west-central Africa. What linked all three tendencies was the legacy of an ideology based on kinship structures. Whether slaves were employed in production, as retainers, in the military, or as bearers of children, slavery strengthened kinship groups. The primacy of kinship remained secure even as the political economy became interwoven with the intercontinental network of slavery. Kinship helped define who could be exported and who would benefit from this exchange. Increasingly, slavery became the basis of social differentiation.

By 1800, Africa was divided into three zones, whereas in 1500 it had been divided in half. The Islamic frontier still existed; indeed it had expanded somewhat in the intervening centuries. Along the Guinea coast and in the Zambezi valley, the European slave trade had affected changes so that slave societies had emerged where previously there had been none. These were the two externally-orientated regions where slavery was most pronounced. In between these two spheres was a zone in which slavery remained marginal to society.

7

The nineteenth-century slave trade

By the beginning of the nineteenth century, the slave trade from Africa had assumed gigantic proportions. The largest human migration before the movement of Europeans overseas in the middle of the nineteenth century was well underway. The peculiar nature of this migration, based as it was on slavery, made its organization complex, for the infrastructure necessary to move such large numbers of people against their will required the mobilization of resources on several continents. After the temporary decline caused by war in Europe during the 1790s and the first decade of the nineteenth century, the trans-Atlantic slave trade from the Guinea coast resumed its previous level, and the export trade now affected East Africa considerably. Slaves became more common wherever the export trade was important, and the transformation of the political economy that resulted in the more systematic enslavement of people and the organization of the domestic slave trade pushed the African societies toward the more intensified exploitation of slave labour. Indeed, the productive dimension of slavery became more important than ever before.

A new factor in the history of slavery in Africa emerged in the midst of this situation. This factor was the movement to abolish the slave trade.[1] Reformers began to attack the trade in the last decades of the eighteenth century; the first United States laws were enacted in 1791 and 1794; Denmark instituted abolition in 1802; in 1807 Great Britain, the largest carrier of slaves to the Americas, made it illegal for her merchants to participate in the trade. The United States embarked on the same path in 1808, the same year that British laws actually became effective. From then on, despite many set-backs, half-hearted enforcement, and extensive smuggling, the days of slavery were numbered. The British government subsequently pressured other European and New World countries to follow its lead, a diplomatic effort that took most of the nineteenth century before the trans-Atlantic trade really came to an end. Besides its diplomatic assault, Great Britain stationed part of its navy off the African shore in order to enforce abolition. France, the United States, and other countries joined this military effort. This blockade, which was relatively ineffective early in the nineteenth century, had an increasingly severe impact on the trade, making it difficult for European ships to buy slaves in many places. The full effects of these measures, however, were not really felt until the 1840s.

Once the trans-Atlantic slave trade became the subject of attack, it took many decades for all the countries of the Americas and Europe to reach a common commitment to abolition. The same was true for the emancipation of slaves in the Americas, begun first in the French Revolution and pursued in due course by England, the United States, Spain, Brazil, and other countries. As this attack proceeded, the anti-slave trade forces directed their attention against the Islamic world, forcing the Ottoman Empire and other states into diplomatic positions where abolition was necessary. The attack on the slave trade within Africa, not to mention slavery itself, proceeded more slowly. European countries were unwilling to intervene in African affairs, except when European rivalries required some action. Consequently, it was often argued that slavery in Africa was different from slavery in the Americas and therefore could be left alone. None the less, the logic of abolition pushed European countries into untenable positions which, despite vacillation and contradictory behaviour, steadily led to greater intervention and ultimately to the abolition of both the slave trade and slavery.

One example of such a contradiction was the pursuit of 'legitimate trade', a term used at the time and by scholars ever since to distinguish between the slave trade that increasingly was recognized as illegal and commerce in 'legitimate' goods, particularly ivory, peanuts, palm oil, gold, rubber, cloves, hides and skins, ostrich feathers, beeswax, and gum arabic.[2] Many of these goods were already exported alongside slaves, but their share of total exports gradually increased. For abolitionists, moreover, this shift in exports had an especially significant meaning. They argued that the abolition of the slave trade and the development of legitimate trade would bring slavery itself to an end. With respect to Africa, however, they could not have been more wrong. Many of the 'legitimate' goods destined for world markets were grown or transported by slaves, for slavery had become an integral part of the African economy. The end of the external slave trade did not mean collapse of the internal slave trade. Despite the aims of the abolitionists, the transition from exporting slaves to exporting other commodities resulted in the increased use of slaves in Africa.

The dynamics of slavery in the nineteenth century involved the interaction between the forces of abolition and the pervasiveness of slavery in Africa. On the one hand, the ability to enslave people was at its height, and the domestic use of slaves was most intensive. On the other hand, the abolitionists exerted increasing pressure on African societies, leading to a series of clashes that were intimately connected with the imposition of colonialism. These two dynamic forces, one internal and one external, set

136

Table 7.1 *Slave exports from Africa in the nineteenth century*

Exporting sector	Number of slaves	%
Trans-Atlantic	3,330,000	61.4
Trans-Sahara	1,200,000	22.1
Red Sea	450,000	8.3
Indian Ocean	442,000	8.2
TOTAL	5,442,000	100.0

Sources: Trans-Atlantic: table 7.5 for the period from 1801 to 1867; for the trade in *libertos* between 1876 and 1900 (55,889 people), see Duffy 1967, p. 98. Trans-Sahara: Austen 1979a, p. 66. Red Sea: Pankhurst 1964. Pankhurst's estimate is revised downward in order to avoid double counting via the overland trade to the Nile valley. Indian Ocean: Martin and Ryan 1977, p. 79. For imports into Persia, Arabia, and India, a mortality rate of 9 per cent has been used to calculate exports. Another 95,000 slaves were exported to the Mascarene Islands in the first decade of the nineteenth century; see Table 7.7.

the framework for the full transformation of slavery within the African context. Ironically, this transformation was achieved precisely at the moment in history when abolition was inevitable.

Slave exports for all parts of the continent reached 5,422,000 (see table 7.1), about 2 million fewer than the total for the eighteenth century. There were 3,330,000 slaves sold across the Atlantic, representing 62 per cent of all exports. The Atlantic trade was down 46 per cent from the volume of the trans-Atlantic trade in the eighteenth century (6,133,000). Meanwhile, however, the other sectors of the nineteenth-century trade expanded. Some 442,000 slaves were traded from East Africa within the Indian Ocean basin; while if the 276,000 slaves shipped from south-eastern Africa to the Americas are included, 648,000 slaves left East Africa, a figure much larger than the volume of any earlier century. Between 450,000 and 500,000 slaves crossed the Red Sea from Ethiopia and the area to its south, and again the number surpassed earlier trade.[3] This general increase also applied to the trans-Saharan trade, which accounted for another 1,200,000 slaves, many of whom came from the upper Nile valley. While the figures for the Red Sea, East African, and trans-Saharan trades are still not as reliable as the other estimates, they are more accurate than the comparable figures for earlier centuries. None the less, the total for these sectors could be several hundred thousand slaves lower or higher.

The aggregate totals for the export trade suggest some general hypotheses that are similar to those explored for the period from 1600 to 1800. Firstly, the volume of the trade was so large that the incidence of slavery in the exporting regions probably increased. The age and sex distribution of the trans-Atlantic trade demonstrates that this conclusion is likely (table 7.2). The distribution of the exported population continued to be skewed, although the greater number of children in the sample populations suggests

Table 7.2 *Age and sex distribution of exported slaves, nineteenth century*

Category	Sample A		Sample B	
	Number	Percentage	Number	Percentage
Children	34,863	26.0	9,618	39.3
Women	28,847	21.5	3,713	15.2
Men	70,348	52.5	11,171	45.6
TOTAL	134,058	100.0	24,502	100.1
Women as % Adults		29.1		24.9
Men as % Adults		70.9		75.1

Sample A: Slaves arriving in Havana, 1800–20.
Sample B: Slaves from the Bight of Biafra captured by the British Navy and liberated in Sierra Leone, 1821–1839.

Sources: H. S. Klein 1978, p. 223. Slaves classified as teenagers in Klein's table are treated as adults here. Northrup 1978, pp. 235–9.

Table 7.3 *Slave prices, Bight of Benin (1790s–1860s) (based on £ sterling, 1913)*

Period	Price	% change
1790s	22	—
1800s	17	− 23
1810s	14	− 18
1820s	16	+ 15
1830s	14	− 13
1840s	14	—
1850s	12	− 14
1860s	11	− 8

Source: Manning 1982.

that the American market may have changed slightly, perhaps in anticipation of the ending of the trade. The percentage of females in the adult population declined, moreover, down from approximately 32 per cent in the eighteenth century to 20–30 per cent in the first few decades of the nineteenth century. The preference in the trans-Atlantic trade was clearly for males and children, which meant that an even greater proportion of female slaves was retained in Africa than in the eighteenth century.

Secondly, the price of slaves at the export points dropped substantially as a result of abolitionist efforts to end the trade. On the Gold Coast, for example, the price of a male slave dropped from 12 ounces 4 ackies (£45.0) in May 1789 to 9 ounces (£32.4) in about 1803 to 7 ounces (£25.2) in about 1807 to 3 ounces (£10.8) in 1815.[4] LeVeen has recorded this decline in terms of dollars: prices were close to $100 (£20.8) along the West African coast from 1790 to 1810, but decline set in by the 1820s, falling from about $80 (£16.7) in 1820 to $50 (£10.4) by 1860, even though the price in the Americas continued to rise during this period.[5] The decline in the Bight of Benin followed this trend, as Manning has shown (table 7.3). The value of a prime male slave was £22.0 in the 1790s, but dropped to £17.0 in the first decade of the nineteenth century and to £14.0 in the 1810s. By the 1860s, the price was £11.0, half the value of the 1790s.[6]

The decline in price meant that slaves were more readily available for African buyers, since there does not appear to have been any decrease in the number of newly enslaved people. Certainly the price of slaves was cheap; at least data from the Sokoto Caliphate, Zanzibar, and elsewhere indicate as much. For the Sokoto Caliphate, Tambo has shown that the average mean price for young females was Maria Theresa thalers (MT$) 26 (£5.4) before 1850 and MT$35 (£7.3) afterwards; while for young men the comparable figures were MT$14 (£2.8) and MT$19 (£3.9).[7] When monetary inflation is taken into consideration, the real price of slaves declined, since monetary values fell by over 50 per cent during the course of the century. A similar trend is evident for Zanzibar. The mean price of male slaves appears to have dropped from MT$22.5 (£4.7) in 1844 to a low of MT$11 (£2.3) in 1863, and only rebounded in the 1880s when abolitionist pressures interupted slave supplies. By 1885, the mean price was MT$34.5 (£7.2), and in 1888 it was MT$36 (£7.5). Scattered reports from the 1880s for the interior of East Africa, however, indicate that prices at Ujiji, Tabora, and other centres was lower; in the order of MT$31.5 (£6.6) at Tabora in 1880 and MT$18 (£3.8) at Ujiji in 1883.[8]

Indeed, the enslavement frontier seems to have been pushed further into the interior than ever before, so that it is likely that the number of captives and other new slaves increased. The decline in price – which also reflected the increased cost of exporting slaves – suggests that slave labour became one of the most attractive investments for those with capital to invest. The trend was a continued high level of slaves in the areas traditionally supplying the Americas and increased numbers of slaves in many places where the slave trade had not been particularly important.

THE TRANS-ATLANTIC TRADE: THE LAST SURGE

The areas most affected by the continuation of the slave trade were west-central Africa, the Bights of Benin and Biafra, and south-east Africa (see table 7.4). Together, these areas probably accounted for 90 per cent of the 2,608,100 slaves exported from 1801 to 1843, and west-central Africa alone accounted for most of the slaves exported after 1843 (at least 381,000 out of 634,000). The trade slumped in the first decade of the nineteenth century (585,500), down 150,000 slaves over the previous decade, a drop of 20 per cent, because Europe was at war. The slump had little, if anything, to do with the abolition of the slave trade by Great Britain, which did not take effect until 1808, near the end of the decade. The slump continued until the peace of 1815; the trade was 536,500 for the second decade. Thereafter, the trade rebounded, with levels close to 650,000 for the 1820s and 1830s and almost as many for the 1840s. The trans-Atlantic trade dropped off rapidly after 1849, with only a couple of hundred thousand slaves exported during the rest of the century, almost all of these registered before the late 1850s. About 95 per cent of the nineteenth-century trade took place before 1850.[9] The volume for the far western shores from the Gold Coast through the Senegambia declined sharply during the first decade of the nineteenth century. As recently as the 1760s, the various parts of this coast had exported over 18,500 slaves per year; this figure dropped to 6,100 after 1800, a level that was maintained until the early 1840s. Hence abolition only maintained a pattern of decline that had already occurred before 1807.

The slaves exported from the Bight of Benin, 450,000 before 1844, representing 18 per cent of the trade, and perhaps 102,000 afterwards, were primarily Yoruba. In the 1820s and 1830s, Oyo, which had been so closely associated with the export of slaves in the eighteenth century, collapsed, and throughout the nineteenth century Dahomey and various Yoruba war-lords fought among themselves in an effort to re-establish a centralized state in the region.[10] The Oyo nobility had relied on Muslim slaves in the military, and these Muslims became involved in Oyo politics, first as supporters of one group of war-lords and then as an independent factor. The crucial split occurred in 1817, when the Muslims, who dominated the cavalry, were called into action on behalf of the Oyo military. The autonomy gained in this uprising weakened Oyo, which suffered reversals at the hands of its subject provinces, while the defeat and collapse of Owu, long a loyal ally of Oyo in the south, poured many more slaves on to the market between 1818 and 1823. The Muslim faction in Oyo allied itself to other Muslims further to the north, and, from a stronghold at Ilorin, destroyed the Oyo capital in the early 1830s. By this time, Ilorin recognized the religious and political authority of Sokoto and Gwandu, the twin capitals of a new Islamic empire

Table 7.4 *Trans-Atlantic slave trade, 1801–67*

Region	1801–10	%	1811–20	%	1821–43	%	1844–67	%	Total	%
Western Africa (Senegambia to Gold Coast)	66,000	12.8	52,000	9.7	161,000	10.8	47,000	7.5	326,000	10.3
Bight of Benin	82,800	16.1	99,300	18.5	268,000	18.0	102,400	16.3	552,500	17.5
Bight of Biafra	100,100	19.5	68,200	12.7	227,000	15.3	12,200	1.9	407,500	12.9
West-central Africa	255,500	49.7	256,600	47.9	624,000	42.0	381,200	60.8	1,517,300	48.0
South-east Africa	10,000	1.9	60,000	11.2	206,000	13.9	84,300	13.4	360,300	11.4
TOTAL	514,400	100.0	536,100	100.0	1,486,000	100.0	627,100	99.9	3,163,600	100.1
Adjusted Total	617,200						634,700		3,274,000	

Sources: Curtin 1975b, p. 112, and 1969, pp. 234, 261; Eltis 1977, p. 429; Miller 1975, p. 161; Manning 1979, p. 117; Anstey 1977, pp. 261, 265, and 1975b, p. 65, which accounts for 100,470 slaves in the adjusted total for 1801–1810. The adjusted total also includes 6,800 slaves carried on Portuguese ships and 110 slaves on French ships (Anstey 1977, pp. 261, 265), and the figure allows for 2,000 slaves on Danish ships for 1801–1802 (Green-Pederson 1957, p. 201). The calculations on the trade from south-east Africa between 1801 and 1820 are examined in Lovejoy 1982c. It should be noted that figures for 1811–1820 are otherwise derived from the calculations of David Eltis, who kindly shared his findings with me. For the period 1844–67, see Eltis 1981. The adjusted total for these years includes 7,600 slaves of unknown origin. Eltis's figures have been rounded off to the nearest hundred. P. C. Emmer also provided information on 2,000 slaves exported from the Gold Coast between 1836 and 1842 and 500 slaves exported from the Gold Coast between 1858 and 1862 (personal communication).

in the savannah. Although the ruling officials of Ilorin were not Yoruba, the subject populations of this new emirate were, and Ilorin continued to be actively involved in the wars that occurred with the collapse of Oyo. The development of new centres (including Ibadan and Abeokuta) and the independence of Dahomey reflected a new era of war-lord-ism.[11]

It might be argued that the Yoruba wars were fought only for political reasons. Indeed, the struggle for political supremacy was paramount in the minds of the war-lords, but the political dimension also included enslavement as an effective weapon in destroying the independence of rival factions and in acquiring the human resources that could be exploited domestically or sold on the market. There is not better testimony to the consciousness of the enslavement process than the account of Samuel Crowther, who was seized, along with his family, during one of the many battles that ravaged the Yoruba country. The women and children had attempted to flee into the bush, but:

> While they were endeavouring to disentangle themselves from the ropy shrubs, they were overtaken and caught by the enemies with a noose of rope thrown over the neck of every individual, to be led in the manner of goats tied together, under the drove of one man. In many cases a family was violently divided between three or four enemies, who each led his away, to see one another no more. Your humble servant was thus caught – with his mother, two sisters (one an infant about ten months old), and a cousin – while endeavouring to escape in the manner above described.[12]

Joseph Wright, another Yoruba slave who has also left his account, reported a similar deliberateness on the part of the enslaving army: 'The enemies satisfied themselves with little children, little girls, young men, and young women; and so they did not care about the aged and old people. They killed them without mercy ... Abundant heaps of dead bodies were in the streets, and there were none to bury them.'[13]

In the 1830s and 1840s, almost 190,000 slaves were exported from the Bight of Benin, but the trade there fell off, too. In the 1850s, the total was down to 48,000, while in the 1860s it dropped to 24,000. Some slaves were exported after that, but the trade was only a fraction of its earlier volume. The effective ending of the trade related to the abolition of exports to Brazil and the British occupation of Lagos, both occurring in 1851. The French seizure of neighbouring Porto Novo in the 1860s contributed to the blockade. Inland, however, enslavement and trade continued at their previous levels.[14] The Yoruba wars accounted for many new slaves, and some came from the savanna to the north. The situation in the interior became increasingly complex. Slavery was an expansive institution from the 1850s through the early 1890s.

The Bight of Biafra supplied 15.6 per cent of trans-Atlantic slave shipments between 1800 and 1843. The decentralized system of trade extending inland from the Niger delta was able to maintain levels of exports slightly below those of the last half of the eighteenth century. In part this was possible because the lagoons and creeks of the delta made it difficult for naval patrols, even when stationed at Fernando Po in the Bight itself, to detect the presence of European slave ships. Furthermore, some slaves exported from the Bight of Biafra came from greater distances inland than had previously been the case. Some were shipped down the Niger River; others reached the Cross River from the savanna country to the north.

The Aro commercial system, examined in chapter 5, reached its fullest development in this period. Approximately three-quarters of the exported slaves still came from the Igbo–Ibibio area, but now the Aro relayed slaves from further inland too.[15] There was the odd foray by a coastal merchant-firm, as one river-boat surprised that of a rival company in the delta, but most slaves appear to have been taken in raids and wars in the central and northern Igbo areas. Young men hired themselves out to help settle disputes, and enslavement was a common tactic. Even more serious, Abiriba, Abam, Ohafia, and Edda warriors continued to serve as mercenaries for the Aro and others, sometimes attacking villages more than once. Of the 25 villages they are known to have raided, 20 were located in central and northern Igbo country.[16] In the northern frontier areas, new settlers carved out huge tracts of land, which usually involved wars with the Igala. In this way, the Nike and the north-eastern Igbo captured slaves for sale and their own use, although counter-raids also resulted in the enslavement of these Igbo.[17]

In the southern and central Igbo districts, most newly enslaved people were pawns, victims of kidnapping, or captives for oracles. Parents sold their own children because of debts, laziness, and insubordination; the distinction between slave and pawn disappeared in some places, such as Nguru, where both were called *ohu*, the usual term for slave. In Enugwu-Ukwu and elsewhere, domestic slaves could be sold, despite a traditional prohibition against selling those born into slavery. Kidnapping was so common that in many places parents did not let their children play outside their walled compounds; the oral traditions collected by Elizabeth Isichei, which convey information on the last decades of the nineteenth century but appear to characterize most of the century, contain numerous stories of kidnapping.[18] The oracles, despite their religious and legal functions that helped stabilize the segmentary political order, also contributed to the number of new slaves. The oracles required slaves as payments for misdemeanours and services rendered; the Ibinukpabi oracle of the Aro was the most important of these, but the Kamalu oracle at Ozuzu on the Otamiri River and other oracles of the Nri also enslaved people.[19]

Slave exports from the Niger delta fell off rapidly in the late 1830s, in part because the British were increasingly effective in their interception of slave ships and in part because of significant increases in the sale of palm oil to European merchants. In the 1830s, the British navy liberated 17,622 slaves from the Bight of Biafra. This was only a portion of the slave traffic, but it served as a deterrent that ultimately helped end the trade. Palm oil exports rose spectacularly, rising from about 3,000 tons in 1819 to almost 8,000 tons in 1829 to 12,800 tons in 1839. By the mid-1850s, the volume topped 24,000 tons per year and reached 41,000 tons annually in the 1860s.[20] The impact of this adjustment in the export sector was profound. Until the late 1830s, the economy expanded rapidly as a result of trade in both commodities. Thereafter, the palm oil trade attracted the attention of merchants and farmers, while the slave trade languished, except in so much as the local economy could absorb slaves domestically. But enslavement and slavery continued in a different setting, and the institutions that had facilitated the export of over one million slaves in the previous century still functioned. In the second half of the century, the scale of the slave trade along the Niger River and overland from the Benue River valley and Bamenda plateau in the north indicates a considerable volume of slave imports.[21] This portion of the trade had only amounted to a fraction of total exports in the period 1800–35, but its continuation demonstrates the ability of the Biafran hinterland to absorb a steady stream of new slaves. Kidnapping, inter-village raiding, and enslavement through oracles and other legal–religious means also persisted. There is no reason to believe that the general level of enslavement declined significantly. The only difference was that slaves were not exported but used domestically.[22]

Between 1801 and 1867, west-central African exports were 1,517,300 slaves which accounted for 48 per cent of the slaves shipped to the Americas. In the half-century from 1800 to 1850, west-central Africa exported as many slaves as in the last half of the eighteenth century (1,335,000), when the region was the largest single supplier of the export trade.

The explosion in exports during the first half of the nineteenth century required changes in the interior that were as significant as the developments associated with the earlier phases of export growth.[23] The expanded volume of trade taxed the capabilities of the existing networks. The Lunda and Luba war-lords siphoned off people from further inland. In these decades Kazembe, the most important of the Lunda states in the far interior, reached its height. Lunda, too, acquired wealth on an unprecedented scale. The new developments included the expansion of trade along the Zaire River and its tributaries to the north. Previously, most slaves came from the savanna to the south of the Zaire. Even slaves exported from Loango Bay and Cabinda came from Malebo Pool and ultimately from the savanna to the south and east. At this time of greater demand for slaves, however, Bobangi fishermen and merchants to the north-east of the Pool began to bring slaves down the river. The spread of cassava cultivation was related to this commercial growth, just as it had been in the earlier consolidation of trade between Lunda and the coast. Cassava could be transported easily on river-boats, and this enabled the merchants to feed themselves and their slaves *en route*. The organization of Bobangi trade was similar to the trade of the Niger River and its delta. The Bobangi were not connected with a strong state but

144

turned their control of river transport to advantage. This required a willingness to fight as well as trade.

The other major change in the commercial organization of west-central Africa involved the emergence of the Cokwe as a factor in politics and trade.[24] The Cokwe were hunters whose knowledge of the forests in the country between Kasanje and Lunda placed them in a favourable position to benefit from the rise in demand for ivory and beeswax, which became important exports from Angola in the 1830s. The Cokwe also raided for slaves, as they bought more guns from the proceeds of ivory and wax sales. The Cokwe sold their services to rival factions in succession disputes of the Imbangala, Ovimbundu, and Lunda, and they sometimes seized captives for no reason at all, other than the inability of anyone to stop them and their own avarice.

At the time the Cokwe became a significant factor in the enslavement process, however, the export trade from west-central Africa was in its final stages of decline. Indeed, the Cokwe were instrumental in destroying Lunda hegemony and hence played a major role in the collapse of the supply mechanism that had been responsible for the export of so many slaves. It is likely that the internal troubles in Lunda were related to the decline in the demand for slaves; civil war apparently reflected a struggle over increasingly scarce resources. Cokwe slave raiding supplied new markets within central Africa. Now slaves might be sold north to Kuba or other markets, or they could be directed along the old routes to the coast. The reluctance of the Portuguese to enforce anti-slave trade provisions helped maintain slave demand, although on a reduced scale, late into the century. Even when slave shipments across the Atlantic declined abruptly after 1850, slave raiding, warfare, and other means of enslavement did not cease.[25] Indeed, the level of enslavement remained at record highs throughout the nineteenth century.

South-eastern Africa also shared in the continued demand for slaves in the nineteenth century, and because the British blockade was first concentrated along the West African coast, the trade from south-eastern Africa expanded to record levels. While slaves were sent to the Mascarenes in the eighteenth century, only a few slaves found their way to Brazil and other parts of the Americas before 1815. Thereafter, exports boomed, accounting for approximately 350,000 slaves between 1815 and 1870, when trans-Atlantic shipments effectively came to an end. Many of these slave exports came from relatively near the coast, particularly from the Zambezi valley. Where once *prazo*-holders had been content to trade into the interior for ivory, gold, and other goods, leaving the free people on their land alone, as long as they paid tribute, the *prazo*-holders now responded to the export demand and raided their subjects. Between 1818 and 1835, new men – many from Goa – assumed title to the Zambezi *prazos* and acquired quick fortunes through slave raiding. Other slaves came from further inland – the Shire

145

valley and the region west of Lake Malawi. The net effect was to turn Quelimane into a major slave port.[26]

THE VOLUME OF THE NON-SLAVE TRADE

As the abolitionist movement succeeded in curtailing the export of slaves to the Americas, some European countries attempted to circumvent the anti-slave trade conventions through various legalisms. The French and the Portuguese were the most serious offenders; the French labelled contract labourers, who were in fact slaves purchased in Africa, *engagés à temps*.[27] Their legal status allowed for their freedom after a specific period of 14 years servitude, but they left Africa as slaves and consequently, from an African perspective, must be included in the volume of slave exports in the nineteenth century. The Portuguese terms were more varied, *libertos*, *serviçaes*, *livres*, and *ingénuos*, but they too were slaves. Technically, the contracts for these slaves ranged from 5 to 7, and even 10, years, but contracts could be bought and sold and lengthened without the consent of the *libertos*. The Dutch and British were more clever still, since both considered themselves leaders in the fight against slavery. None the less, both countries found it convenient to recruit soldiers for the West Indies among the slave populations of Africa. The number of these recruits was small, a total of only a few thousand, but again they were originally slaves, no matter what their status as British and Dutch soldiers (see table 7.5).

The French initiated their disguised trade in slaves under the second empire of Louis Bonaparte, after 1848. The trade consisted of two sectors: a West African sector, largely from Senegal and Gabon, to the West Indies. This trade accounted for the export of 20,426 slaves between 1854 and 1862 alone. The other sector was the trade from south-east Africa to Nossi Bé, the

Table 7.5 *The volume of the non-slave trade: contract and other forms of servile labour*

Carrier	Period	Volume	Origin
Dutch	1836–62	2,500	Asante
French	1854–62	20,400	West Africa
French	1848–99	50,000	south-east Africa
Portuguese	1860–99	80,000	west-central Africa
TOTAL		152,900	

Sources: Dutch: La Torre 1978, p. 415, accounts for 1,170 slaves, P. C. Emmer (personal communication) has accounted for 2,490 slaves in his examination of the archives of the Dutch recruitment agency at Kumasi. I wish to thank Dr Emmer for sharing this information with me. French: Renault 1976, pp. 158, 204–5. Portuguese: Duffy 1967, pp. 11–13, 27, 35, 98.

Comoros and Réunion (Bourbon). Between 1848 and 1861, 33,958 slaves were brought into these islands in the Indian Ocean as *engagés*. Allowing for a mortality rate of 2 per cent, probably 35,000 slaves left south-east Africa and Madagascar. These two periods are the best documented; perhaps 70,000 slaves were involved for the whole of the *engagé* period.[28]

The Portuguese system of contract labour was centred on São Thomé and Principé, which benefited from a boom in coffee production in the late 1850s and later from the expansion of cocoa production too. In the 1850s, the legal trade in slaves from Luanda was virtually over, although some slaves were still exported from the mouth of the Zaire River and at scattered places elsewhere on the west-central coast. Instead, Portuguese merchants began to ship slaves disguised as *libertos* to São Thomé and Principé, a few hundred at a time and sometimes under a decree that limited the legal number of such labourers to 10 per ship. Under the watchful eyes and the repeated protests of the British, who had consular agents stationed in Luanda, this system gradually expanded until the mid 1860s, when upwards of 1,000 *libertos* per year were probably being exported, virtually none of whom returned to the mainland after their terms of service were technically finished. Official Portuguese statistics were compiled for the last 25 years of this trade, from 1876 to 1900, when 55,889 *libertos* are recorded. Exports varied from lows of 1,400 per year to as many as 8,000 per year. It is likely that the total trade from the late 1850s to 1900 was at least 80,000 *libertos*.[29]

The Dutch portion of this emigration of slaves under other labels was small by comparison with the French and Portuguese sectors; its purpose was different too. The Dutch recruited slaves in Asante between 1836 and 1842. They purchased 2,035 young men: 1985 were then sent to the East Indies, and 50 were sent to the West Indies. Another 455 slaves were bought between 1858 and 1862 for the East Indies.[30]

THE TRANS-SAHARAN AND RED SEA TRADE

The export trade to the Islamic lands of North Africa and the Middle East involved the movement of about two million slaves. The largest portion of this trade was from the upper Nile valley basin and Ethiopia, which together probably accounted for one million slaves. About 650,000 slaves travelled across the Sahara from the savanna country to the west of the Nile valley, including the central and western Sudan. Another 347,000 slaves came from East Africa, and will be discussed in the next section.

Ethiopia and the Nile valley fitted into the general pattern of increased slave raiding and trade that prevailed in Africa, although the market was different. Routes fed the ports of the Red Sea and the desert caravans destined for Egypt. Perhaps more than half of the one million slaves from the region crossed the desert to Egypt, while the rest came from Ethiopia and were shipped to the Arabian peninsula. The origin of this trade, as was the case for East Africa, can be traced to the eighteenth century. Dar Fur was capable of exporting several thousand slaves per year at the end of the century and continued to be a major exporter in the first few decades of the nineteenth century, although no caravan left Dar Fur between 1810 and 1817. Sennar, however, exported about 1,500 slaves per year during this period.[31] The most important change occurred in the 1820s, when Egypt, which was nominally part of the Ottoman Empire but was in fact largely independent under the dynamic leadership of Muhammad Ali, invaded Sennar, fashioning an empire in the upper valley of the Nile.[32] Egypt also seized ports along the Red Sea, so that Christian Ethiopia once more found itself surrounded by an expansive Islamic power. Muhammad Ali and his successors were after gold, slaves, and other goods. The level of slave raiding rose considerably until 1880, when British pressure to abolish the slave trade undermined Egypt's strategy.

Muhammad Ali and his successors in Cairo wanted slave troops for the Egyptian army. In 1820, a training camp was established at Isna for officers of the slave regiments that were to be recruited through the conquest of the Nilotic Sudan. In the following year, a large depot was set up at Aswan to receive slaves, where they were vaccinated, clothed, and instructed in the rudiments of Islam. Muhammad Ali ordered 20,000 recruits, but the high rate of mortality during the desert crossing and in the recruitment camps from fever and dysentery sabotaged efforts to supply these numbers.[33] In 1822 and 1823, the figure was supposed to approach 30,000. Muhammad Ali spurred his troops on, reminding them in a special despatch sent in 1823, 'You are aware that the end of all our effort and this expense is to procure negroes. Please show zeal in carrying out our wishes in this capital matter.'[34] The army subsequently organized raids outward from the northern Sudan in the quest for more and more slaves. Troops attacked the Shilluk and Dinka in the Nile flood plains to the south. They seized Kordofan in the west, and from there launched raids into the Nuba mountains. In the 1830s, an effort was made to reduce death on the desert crossing. The commander at Dongola constructed boats, with timber and nails sent from Egypt. This facilitated the movement of provisions for the slave convoys and allowed the transport of slaves along some stretches of the river. In the 1830s, the occupation forces were increased from one regiment to three, both to consolidate Egyptian rule and to expand slave-raiding operations. Muhammad Ali needed as many slaves as possible to assist in the conquest of Syria and Arabia. By 1838, an estimated 10,000 to 12,000 slaves were arriving in Egypt each year.[35]

Under British anti-slavery pressure, Egyptian tactics had to change in the course of the 1860s and 1870s, but by then the vast network of Muslim merchants and raiders was able to maintain slave supplies, despite 'official' opposition. In the 1860s, the Bahr el Jebel and Bahr el Ghazal regions were exporting 1,000 to 2,000 and 4,000 to 6,000 slaves per year respectively, figures that are partially confirmed by the activities of the anti-slavery river patrols, which seized over 3,500 slaves between June 1864 and February

1866. Estimates for 1867 placed the total export trade from the Sudan at between 10,000 and 30,000 per year, with half travelling overland down the Nile valley and the rest being sent to ports on the Red Sea. Merchants at Jedda on the Red Sea had agents at Shendi, Khartoum, Sennar, El Obeid, and at ports elsewhere on the Red Sea and the Somali coast, and thousands of slaves marched out of the Sudan and southern Ethiopia each year. From June 1878 to March 1879, 63 caravans with 2,000 slaves were seized at various places, and a government raid freed 1,000 at Kalaka, as the Egyptians, through British officials, retreated from the earlier policy of military recruitment. As late as 1876, the volume of exports was thought to number tens of thousands per year, only now more were sent via the ports along the Red Sea than overland down the Nile valley and across the Sahara.[36]

The efforts to reverse this slave trade unleashed an Islamic revival that was anti-Egyptian and pro-slavery. A dynamic leader, Muhammad Ahmad, emerged as the focal point of resistance, when in 1881 he proclaimed himself the Mahdi, a messianic figure who was to purge the world of unbelief and, in this context, to end colonialism. The wars that followed did expel Egypt, along with its British and Ottoman supporters, from the Nilotic Sudan until 1896.[37]

In Ethiopia, the Egyptian presence was also strong. Egyptian forces raided peripheral areas of the highlands and dominated the Red Sea, but most slaves here were seized in the south. The ports of Massawa, Tajura, Berbera, and Zeila supplied thousands of slaves each year for Egypt and the Muslim holy lands in Arabia,[38] while caravans left the town of Metemma for the Nilotic Sudan. The Ethiopian slave trade was largely a trade in children, especially girls. Females outnumbered males by at least two to one, and the great majority of all slaves were under twenty years of age. These children came from areas to the south and south-west of Christian Ethiopia; the Galla and Sidama principalities obtained many of these children in slave raids on their weaker neighbours or in disputes between themselves. Many children were also kidnapped, and some undoubtedly were purchased in times of famine. A distinction was made between 'red' slaves and 'black' slaves, a difference relating to physical characteristics associated with various ethnic groups. In general 'red' slave girls were worth more in the export trade, while the 'black' slaves, *shanqalla*, were often retained in Christian Ethiopia, the Galla principalities, or the Muslim towns as menial labourers.[39] The peak period in the Ethiopian trade was during the second quarter of the nineteenth century, when as many as 6,000 to 7,000 slaves were exported each year through the various ports. For these 25 years, 150,000 to 175,000 slaves were exported.

Efforts to end the slave trade in North Africa and Arabia came much later than in the Atlantic basin. The Ottoman state outlawed the trade in the mid-1850s, and at about the same time Emperor Teodros of Ethiopia decreed a similar measure.[40] Neither had much effect. Only the direct intervention of the British in Egypt, with a corresponding presence in the Red Sea, resulted in pressure on the trade. The trade declined, particularly after the Mahdist revolt isolated the Sudan from the external world. Thereafter slaves were still smuggled across the Red Sea, but the scale was greatly reduced.

Various *jihads* in West Africa, particularly the one that led to the foundation of the Sokoto Caliphate after 1804, also resulted in the shipment of slaves across the Sahara. Perhaps a half-million or more slaves were involved in this traffic.[41] The Sokoto Caliphate and neighbouring Borno exported between 3,000 and 6,000 slaves per year from 1810 to 1870; in the 1870s, the trade dropped to a level of 1,000 to 2,000 per year, while the volume declined further in the 1880s and 1890s. Other slaves were exported northward from Timbuktu, perhaps in the order of 1,000 to 2,000 per year for most of the century. Although trade from Wadai and areas further west was only a small proportion of the total export trade of the nineteenth century – in the order of 9 per cent – in fact it represented far more significant developments in West Africa, which resulted in the enslavement of people on a scale comparable to other areas.

THE EAST AFRICAN TRADE

The East African trade consisted of three sectors: a northern trade to Arabia, Persia, and India, a southern trade to the Americas, and a coastal trade that terminated at Zanzibar, Pemba, and several places on the mainland opposite these islands. Together these sectors involved the sale of slaves; 718,000 slaves (48.3 per cent) were exported, while 769,000 (51.7 per cent) were retained on the coast (tables 7.6 and 7.7). As these figures demonstrate, the slave trade boomed in the nineteenth century. Even though the export trade exceeded anything this region had ever experienced, the truly great expansion was related to developments on the coast itself.

Table 7.6 *East African slave exports to Arabia, Persia, and India, 1801–96*

Period	Imports	Exports (9% mortality)
1801–29	72,500	81,000
1830–39	35,000	39,000
1840–49	40,000	44,000
1850–73	156,000	173,000
1874–96	9,200	10,000
TOTAL	312,700	347,000

Source: Martin and Ryan 1977, p. 79.

Table 7.7 *The slave trade of East Africa in the nineteenth century*

Sector	Volume	%
Arabia, Persia, India	347,000	23.3
South-east Africa	276,000	18.6
Mascarenes	95,000	6.4
East African coast	769,000	51.7
TOTAL	1,487,000	100.0

Sources: Arabia, Persia, and India: table 7.6. South-east Africa: Isaacman 1972a, p. 92; Alpers 1975, pp. 187–9 (pp. 213, 216 for 1801–20); Eltis 1977, p. 429. I have derived a figure of 10,000 slaves for 1801–10, based on Isaacman and Alpers, and a figure of 60,000 for 1811–20, based on projections from the known exports during 1816–20 of 31,139. Mascarenes: Filliot 1974, p. 54; Table 7.5; p. 221 below. East African coast: Martin and Ryan 1977, p. 82.

The trade was in the order of 80,000 slaves in the first decade of the nineteenth century. At this time about 30,000 slaves were retained on the coast; approximately 25,000 slaves were shipped north to Arabia, Persia, and India; another 25,000 went to the Mascarenes; and the rest (10,000) were taken to the Americas. Thereafter the Mascarene trade declined, but the American trade absorbed most of the slack, rising to 60,000 in the second decade and much higher in the third and fourth decades (100,000 per decade), before falling off to insignificant numbers in the late 1840s. The export trade to the north grew more modestly; rising to 35,000 in the 1830s, 40,000 in the 1840s, to 65,000 in both the 1850s and 1860s, before declining drastically after 1873. The retention of slaves on the coast increased from about 35,000 slaves in the 1810s to 40,000 in the 1820s, to 60,000 in the 1830s, to 147,000 in the 1840s, to 111,000 in the 1850s, to 142,000 in the 1860s, to a high of 188,000 in the 1870s. Thereafter this trade fell too, back to a level of 28,000 in the 1880s and 16,000 from 1890–6.

The expansion of the slave trade on the coast was a result of the development of plantations at Zanzibar, Pemba, Malindi, Mombasa, and other places.[42] Omani and Swahili planters invested in agriculture, growing cloves, coconuts, and grain for the international market. The staple export crop was cloves, grown on the islands and mostly exported to India. Previously, the Omani Arabs had been interested in the commercial prospects of the East African coast, including the slave trade, but the enterprising Sultan Sayyid Sa'id promoted a variety of crops of which cloves proved to be the most successful. This plantation development had many similarities with the slave plantation economies of the Americas and the Mascarene Islands. The emphasis was on the export crop, although grain production on the mainland became a subsidiary industry related to the clove and slave trade. The peak period in the growth of clove production was from the 1840s to the 1870s, which is reflected in the slave trade. The slave figures represent a tremendous increase in the use of slaves on the coast and hence are part of the growth in the employment of slaves within Africa, even though in this case many of the slave owners were aliens from Oman.

This rapid growth of the East African slave trade involved considerable change in the interior.[43] Previously, the major route inland was via the Zambezi valley. Portuguese adventurers and their slaves were based on landed estates that were nominally granted by the Portuguese crown but in fact were recognized locally because the Portuguese often acted as mercenaries in African wars. Further north, there had been few direct commercial links inland, but by the first decade of the nineteenth century two groups of merchants from the interior were operating to the coast, bringing slaves and ivory. These were the Nyamwezi in the interior of Tanzania and the Yao who traded between the coast and Lake Malawi.

Most slaves who ended up in Zanzibar and Pemba came from Kilwa, which was the main receiving-point for caravans from the Lake Malawi interior and for other ports further down the coast. Slaves from the Kilwa hinterland formed a significant portion of the trade as early as 1811. By the 1840s, the importance of this source had increased even more; in 1860, 75 per cent of Zanzibar's slaves came through Kilwa; by 1866, the percentage had risen to 95 per cent.[44] Even after the trade to Zanzibar and its dependencies declined in the 1880s, the number of slaves travelling from the interior towards the coast continued unabated; only now they were destined for other plantations on the mainland. In the 1870s, thousands of slaves were reported crossing Lake Malawi on their way coastward. This pattern of internal trade continued until the end of the century.

There was also an internal slave trade in the region immediately inland from Mombasa, Malindi, and Zanzibar, but only a quarter of the slaves on the plantations of Zanzibar and adjacent areas came from the northern interior. Most slaves in the region of Lake Tanganyika and Lake Victoria never reached the coast. Instead, ivory was by far the most important export here. The trade in salt, copper, and imports from the coast reflects commercial patterns that were only distantly connected with the coastal plantation-economy.

By the third and fourth decades of the nineteenth century, Swahili and Arab merchants also traded along these commercial corridors, and increasingly they extended credit to Nyamwezi and Yao traders too. The intensification of trade resulted in fierce competition inland, so that slave trading and slave raiding often went together. Merchants were heavily armed, and it proved impossible to check their aggression. The Nyamwezi responded by establishing centralized states under particularly dynamic war-lords, but the efforts of such men as Msiri and Tippu Tip (who was half Arab and half Nyamwezi) only redefined the commercial arrangements between the various commercial factions. Ultimately, the Nyamwezi, Yao, Swahili, and Arabs needed each other, since the enslavement of people, their movement to the coast, and their sale on the international slave market were all connected. The Portuguese and their warrior slaves, known as *achikunda*, provided the same functions in the south.[45]

The slave raiding of the Nyamwezi, Yao, Portuguese, Swahili, Arabs, and *achikunda* was one major source of insecurity in the nineteenth century, but it was not the only one. By the 1820s, bands of armed men using short spears and well-disciplined tactics moved northward from southern Africa.[46] These regiments, part of the *dificane*, the 'crushing', traced their origin to the rise of the Zulu in South Africa. As people were defeated by Zulu, they adopted Zulu military techniques and conquered new lands. These regiments moved north, destroying every established state they encountered and enslaving people in the Zambezi valley, the Rhodesian plateau, and parts of Tanzania. Between the combined impact of the *dificane* and the slave raiders from the coast, many captives were seized. War-lord-ism had become the dominant feature of the East African interior from Tanzania to South Africa.

Even the decline in the export trade did not immediately reduce the insecurity in the interior. British measures to force an end to the slave trade were relatively ineffective until the 1880s. Various diplomatic efforts had legally limited the coastal trade in stages that began with an agreement by Zanzibar in 1822 to prohibit the re-export of slaves north. Not until after the abolition law of 1873 was there any real chance for success, and then not until the next decade did the trade actually fall off.[47]

THE INTERNAL TRADE

A recurrent theme in my discussion of the vicissitudes of the export trade has been the growth of an internal market for slaves – most notably the plantation sector on the East African coast, but elsewhere too. The volume of this domestic market was probably as large, if not larger, than the volume of the export trade. Together, the slave trade was larger than it had ever been, although it will never be possible to estimate the internal trade as accurately as the external. None the less, the size of the slave trade indicates that the supply of slaves was maintained. Since people born into slavery were seldom sold, this ability to supply slaves on a large scale required new solutions to the eternal problem of the slave mode of production – how to find new sources of slaves.

For the export trade, the problem of slave supply was solved by shifting the geographical focus from the Atlantic basin to the Nile basin, Ethiopia, and East Africa. The far-western coast of Africa became less important than previously; its exports declined considerably as early as the first decade of the nineteenth century. The Bight of Biafra dropped out of the export trade in the late 1830s; the Slave Coast continued for another two decades, but virtually all of the Guinea coast above the equator was out of the trade by the middle of the century. West-central Africa lasted longer, although after the 1850s the trade in contract labour was only a fraction of the earlier volume.

By contrast, the East African trade grew rapidly in the 1820s and continued on a large scale through the 1870s. This trade primarily affected the Lake Malawi area and the Zambezi basin. Finally, the explosion in slave exports from the Nile valley and across the Red Sea took place from the 1820s through the 1870s. Thereafter, some slaves and contract workers continued to leave Africa, but only on a greatly reduced scale. By the 1880s, the export trade had lost its momentum in all sectors.

To some extent, the internal demand was related to the collapse in the export market; this is evident along the West African coast. While slaves were numerous before the decline of exports, slaves became more numerous afterwards. The growth of the plantation economy on the East African coast that accounted for the majority of slaves traded there was another example of the connection between the difficulties of exporting slaves and the possibility of using them closer to the source of enslavement. One reason that plantation agriculture became profitable was because of the rising costs of exporting slaves in the face of the anti-slave trade blockade.

In many places, however, there was a growth in the internal market without any strong links with the external market and its collapse. The *jihad* states of the northern savanna had little direct association with the foreign trade in slaves, although some slaves were in fact exported from these states. The growth of slavery there was more related to internal factors. This expansion in the number of slaves can be followed with reference to the consolidation of each of the major *jihad* states – the Sokoto Caliphate after 1804, which incorporated much of the central Sudan; the caliphate of Hamdullahi (Masina) in the 1820s; Segu Tukulor under al-Hajj 'Umar in the 1840s through the 1860s in the region between the Niger and the Senegambia; the Samorian state in the 1870s and 1880s to the south of Segu Tukulor; the Mahdist state in the 1880s; and Rabeh's state in the 1890s in the Chad basin. This continuous string of *jihads* reverberated from the central Sudan westward and then eastward, doubling back toward the central Sudan at the end of the century. While some slaves were exported (examined above), the vast majority of new slaves were retained within these states or exported to neighbouring countries for use there.

These *jihads* created a new slaving frontier on the basis of rejuvenated Islam. To a great extent, the Muslim reformers seized slaves from the masters of their enemies, thereby re-enslaving many people and in the process reversing the process of slow acculturation and assimilation that had been a characteristic of slavery in the northern savanna. Many free people who resisted *jihad* were also enslaved, while the political and military mobilization based on religion enabled the expansion of the slaving frontier. Pagan populations that had been too distant from the centres of political power to suffer more than an occasional raid were now within the orbit of enslavement. The Sokoto Caliphate raided far to the south, eventually reaching the northern limits of the Zaire River basin. The caliphate also intervened in the Yoruba wars through the intermediary of Ilorin, a

154

dependent emirate under Gwandu.[48] Al-Hajj 'Umar directed his wars against the pagan Bambara, although he was not adverse to destroying Muslim commercial centres – such as Sinsani – when necessary, and he even defeated the caliphate of Hamdullahi, despite its own claim to legitimacy in terms of Islamic reform.[49] Samori and Rabeh, in their own regions, attacked Muslim and pagan populations alike; they both centred their movements in the southern parts of the savanna where strong Muslim states had previously not existed. None the less, both destroyed Muslim regimes; for Samori the most notable Muslim state in his path was Kong, while Rabeh seized Bagirmi and Borno.[50] In all these cases, the problem of the enslavement frontier was solved. The call to reform was licence for raiding Muslims and non-Muslims who did not heed the warning. In effect, *jihad* enabled both the raiding of people on an external frontier defined on the basis of religion and the seizing of people on an internal frontier who resisted the revolutionary movements.

This pattern of enslavement was institutionalized, as the case of the Sokoto Caliphate demonstrates.[51] Once the caliphate was consolidated, dozens of emirates and sub-emirates recognized the authority of the twin capitals of Sokoto and Gwandu, but there were centres of independent rule scattered between these emirates. Some autonomous towns, such as Maradi, Abuja, and Argungu, were located within a very short distance of major caliphate cities – respectively, Katsina, Bida, and Sokoto itself. Elsewhere, pockets of resistance offered other problems; the Ningi maintained an independent base between Kano and Bauchi and within striking distance of Zaria and several smaller emirates (Jema'are and Katagum). Despite the quest for the development of a pure theocracy, the Sokoto regime found it expedient to establish treaties with these enemies so that prisoners of war could be exchanged. A neutral market was maintained between Maradi and Katsina, for example, and another town between Zaria and Ningi, to the south of Kano, served the same purpose there. People could be ransomed at these towns, unless they were already slaves, but if no one came forward on behalf of a free person quickly, then enslavement was the result.

The various political regimes along the West African coast solved the problem of slave supply in equally ingenious ways, so that again new slaves came from a combination of an expanded catchment region and an internal supply-mechanism. Asante, for example, attempted to maintain slave supplies through a combination of tribute and trade with the north. Tribute payments alone were in the order of 2,000 slaves per year around 1820; Gonja and Dagomba sent 500 each; Aduapem paid 300; while Takyiman, Wankyi, Atebubu, Abease, Kwawu, Akwamu, Fanti, Ewe, and lesser dependencies contributed 700 in all.[52] The trade with the north, through the market at Salaga principally, also brought in hundreds of slaves each year, perhaps more. While the exact volume cannot be assessed, data collected between 1837 and 1842 (see table 7.8) allow some comparison of the origins

Table 7.8 *Origins of imported male slaves in Asante, 1837–42*

Origin	Number	%
Akan and Ewe	5	0.8
Northern Asante	142	21.6
Mossi states	358	54.5
North-west	5	0.8
Gurma area	51	7.7
Sokoto Caliphate	96	14.6
TOTAL	657	100.0

Sources: La Torre 1978, pp. 417–18, 420. It should be noted that La Torre's ethnic classification has been adjusted. I have accepted an identification of 'Marabu' with Hausa; Borno, Adamawa, Songhay, and Yoruba slaves are credited to the Sokoto Caliphate, since the main route for all these slaves would have been the same and therefore these distinctions, while important, probably reflect the caliphate export trade. Northern Asante includes slaves who identified with Dagomba, Mamprussi, Gonja, and Wa. Gurma includes 48 slaves who identified as Gurma and 3 slaves from 'northern Togo'. Akan and Ewe are grouped together as representing southern Asante; four slaves were Akan and one was Ewe.

of these slaves imports.[53] In a sample of 657 slaves purchased by Dutch agents seeking army recruits, only 5 (0.8 per cent) came from southern Asante, while 142 (21.6 per cent) came from the northern provinces (probably including slaves seized in raids by these provinces as well as people ethnically identified as Dagomba, Mamprussi, etc.). The Mossi states were the biggest supplier, with 358 slaves (54.5 per cent), while slaves who appear to have come from the Sokoto Caliphate (96 slaves, or 14.6 per cent) were a distant second from external sources. Only 5 slaves (0.8 per cent) came from the Juula commercial network to the north-west, a surprisingly small number considering the age-old links. The rest of the slaves came from the Gurma area, which was between the Mossi states and the Sokoto Caliphate.

These figures, despite the fact that they represent male imports only, are probably a good indication of the importance of northern slaves. Although the Sokoto Caliphate was far away, a significant percentage of slaves came from there and hence can be identified with the *jihad* of the central Sudan. None the less, Asante temporarily solved the problem of slave recruits largely within the upper Volta basin, not from more distant places. At the end of the century, too, the northern region was the major supply area; at that time Gurunsi country south of the Mossi states and west of Mamprussi was the chief supplier.[54] These figures demonstrate that Asante had successfully transferred the burden of enslavement to its northern provinces and adjacent countries.

The movement of slaves through trade and as tribute was considerable throughout the savanna and remained so until the last few years of the nineteenth century. This movement can be seen in the scattered reports of contemporary observers. In the 1850s, for example, Yola despatched 1,000 slaves per year as tribute to Sokoto and received in turn an estimated 5,000 slaves from its own dependencies of Rai-Buba, Ngaundere, Bibemi, Tibati, Banyo, Koncha, Marua, and Madagali. This flow of new slaves does not account for many others – an unknown volume – who were purchased by slave merchants. Undoubtedly some of these slaves were exported across the Sahara, but many trade slaves were sold down the Benue and Niger or retained within the Sokoto Caliphate.[55] The wars of Samori and Babemba in the western Sudan involved the movement of slaves on a similar scale and at a time when the trans-Saharan trade no longer consumed as large a portion as in the Sokoto Caliphate in the 1850s. The French counted 1,183 slaves (776 women and 407 men) in caravans passing through Bamako in a seven-month period in 1885.[56] Four years later, some 2,000 slaves were sold at Médine in the course of several months. Both figures attest to the continued transfer of slaves on a massive scale.[57]

The Yoruba response to slave supply was dependent upon internal sources and imports from the north. The Yoruba civil wars, already discussed above, were the major source of slaves for the various Yoruba states, but imports were also significant, as the proportion of slaves at Abeokuta and other towns who identified as Muslims or Hausa makes clear. The wars had the effect, comparable to that of the *jihads*, of creating an internal frontier of enslavement, while the northern trade, connected to the Sokoto Caliphate, permitted the importation of slaves from an external frontier. Especially in the last decades of the nineteenth century, Yoruba merchants travelled to Ilorin to buy slaves.[58] The political difficulties between Ibadan, Abeokuta, Dahomey, and other powers upset this import trade in some years, but the net effect was the concentration of northern slaves in the heart of the palm-oil belt.

The principal mechanism for enslavement among the Igbo was internal; raids, kidnapping, and religiously-sanctioned enslavement.[59] There were routes to the north and along the Niger River that accounted for the import of slaves; there are reports of Hausa and Muslim slaves along the Niger, for example. None the less, the Igbo frontier was largely internal, as the reports of kidnapping from late in the century make amply clear. The lack of political centralization prevented a coordinated effort to limit local enslavement; rather some raids and other acts of enslavement for criminal offences were a necessary consequence of a political order that relied on methods of political adjudication other than state structures. These practices appear to have been common during the peak of the export trade; the relative importance of these politically sanctioned methods and kidnapping, which most people condemned but which nobody could stop, is more difficult to assess.

The common theme in west-central and eastern Africa was the maintenance of slave supplies through the activities of marauding war-lords; in short, the enslavement frontier was constantly pushed outward as new waves of invaders devastated whole regions, sometimes following in the tracks of earlier war-lords.[60] The Cokwe destroyed Lunda; the Arabs and Swahili pushed into the lakes region and beyond; the *dificane* hordes moved north from South Africa; the Jellaba raided southward from the Nile valley; and the *achikunda* attacked up the Zambezi. Unlike the other areas, there was no viable internal mechanism of slave supply; the customs of kin-based societies permitted people to define all non-kin as outsiders and hence potentially slaves. Small groups of marauders could act on their own account, treating everyone as enemies. In this way, a steady stream of slaves was available for export to the coast and for distribution within the sub-continent itself. These bands could also incorporate captives too.

The problem of slave supply in a continent that had already suffered from the massive export of slaves for several centuries was thus solved through a combination of internal mechanisms and the redefinition of frontiers across which it was acceptable to seize captives. This adjustment was necessary so long as slavery continued to be important. Frontiers were created in various ways: the movement of slavers into new areas, the redefinition of people as enemies within regions where slaves had long been common, the increase in political insecurity or illegal activities such as kidnapping, and the invasion of marauders who had no local identity and hence did not care about injustice. These aspects of enslavement and the related slave trade were essential to the further transformation of slavery in the nineteenth century. In those areas where a slave mode of production already existed, a continual influx of slaves was necessary to sustain the slave population; in other areas, a slave mode of production developed where previously there had only been a few slaves.

8

Slavery and 'legitimate trade' on the West African coast

The collision between a Europe that was increasingly, if sometimes reluctantly, committed to the end of slavery and an African political economy rooted in slavery was most pronounced along the coast of West Africa in the nineteenth century. Here slavery had been transformed into an institution affecting the very structure of society, at least in Sierra Leone, along the Gold Coast, and in the Bights of Benin and Biafra. There continued to be areas in Liberia and western Ivory Coast where slavery was relatively marginal, but for the most part the social formation included a mode of production based on slavery, despite great variations between particular slave systems. Occasionally, slave regimes modified specific practices to assuage the principles of missionaries and European diplomats, but more often the anti-slavery forces themselves compromised. Europeans had to tolerate and sometimes openly support slavery in order to achieve aims other than the abolition of slavery and the slave trade, unless European public opinion was a factor.

As we have seen in the previous chapter, the export trade in slaves from West Africa continued well into the nineteenth century, with the volume being particularly high until the 1840s. By 1867, 1,286,000 slaves had been exported from the whole of West Africa, including the Bights of Benin and Biafra and the long stretch of coast from the mouth of the Volta River to the Senegambia. The Bights alone accounted for 960,000 slaves, or 75 per cent of the total. This trade indicates one feature of slavery in coastal West Africa during the nineteenth century: the export trade continued to have an important influence on the region, so that domestic slavery was still under the umbrella of external demand. This meant that institutions of enslavement and slave trading continued to function, despite British efforts to interfere in ocean shipping.

SLAVERY AND 'LEGITIMATE TRADE'

None the less, there were changes in the export trade that reflected a fundamental re-orientation in the economy of the West African coast, for

159

here the shift to agricultural exports, particularly palm oil and palm kernels – two products of 'legitimate trade' – resulted in the use of many slaves in the local economy.[1] Slaves became the largest component in the agricultural labour force, and they served as porters and canoemen to transport 'legitimate' goods to market. This more intensive use of slaves in trade and production occurred despite the location of the British navy off the coast. Established patterns of slave trading had to be altered, but the proximity of the area to Europe also meant that this region could benefit from the demand for agricultural goods. The fight against the slave trade, the shift to 'legitimate' commodities, and the consolidation of European outposts in Sierra Leone, on the Gold Coast, at Lagos, in the Niger delta, and at Fernando Po were elements of the shift from exporting slaves to exporting other commodities, but the transition from slave exports to other commodities did not result in the decline of slave trading and slavery within the coastal zone.

The export trade in 'legitimate' commodities accounts for many of the slaves used in production and commerce in the West African coastal region in the nineteenth century but not all. Internal commercial patterns included the export of kola nuts to the savanna, the production of food-stuffs for local consumption and regional distribution, and the mining of gold. Slaves were needed as porters in caravans and as crews on river-boats in these sectors, because transportation was so labour intensive.

Slaves became increasingly more important in production, sometimes in large concentrations and other times in small holdings. Slaves lived in their own villages and on plantations to produce agricultural goods, including palm oil and kernels, rice, yams, and other crops. These plantations were found near the coast and along the rivers of Sierra Leone, in Asante, Dahomey and the Yoruba states, and at scattered locations in the Biafran interior. Small holdings were found almost everywhere. Sometimes slaves were owned jointly by lineages as a result of inheritance or cooperative purchase, and other times individuals bought one or two slaves to assist on their farms. This pattern had existed previously, only now, more than ever before, slave-produced commodities were sold on the market. The greater commercialization associated with 'legitimate' trade and with the growth of the domestic economy more generally was part of the final stage in the consolidation of a slave mode of production. Ironically, this transformation occurred at a time when the agents of abolition hovered on the edges of the political economy. The system of slavery would be dismantled, but the characteristic feature of the nineteenth century was the full development of slavery as a productive and social institution.

The use of slaves in non-productive capacities (military, government, marriage) continued unabated, even as productive employment increased in scale. Slaves were still used as soldiers throughout this region, so that slave recruits were crucial in the control of the plantation sector and the peasantry at large, as well as in the enslavement of foreign enemies. Deliberately or not, the employment of slaves in the army prevented the consolidation of slave consciousness, while continued military action made flight more difficult by reducing the areas where it was safe to be. The assimilation of female slaves and children also did not change significantly. Women swelled the households of the wealthy for the same reasons as before. Without the safeguards of kinship, they were more dependent than free wives. As before, the status of slave wives and their children was allowed to improve, despite occasional limitations on access to land, credit, and other rights derived from lineage membership.

The myth for all slaves, whether they were actually incorporated into households or confined to plantations, was that individuals were assimilated. Culturally, they had to adopt the master's language and respect his mores. Failure to adapt could result in punishment, sale, even death at the funeral of a wealthy man looking for victims to accompany him into the next world. None the less, the scale of slavery in most areas was so great that real assimilation was impossible for many slaves. In parts of Asante, Dahomey, the Yoruba states, and the Biafran interior, slaves formed a majority of the population and were classified as separate from free society. Kinship terms could be used to govern slave–master relations, but slaves were not kin. Kinship operated to protect the free and to regulate the status of slaves and pawns. It provided access to land, labour, religious shrines and ceremonies, and hence governed virtually every aspect of society. Those who traced their descent through a free father in patrilineal societies or through a free mother in matrilineal ones belonged to the class of free men. This class was subdivided into the wealthy and politically powerful men (and a few women) on the one hand, and the majority of free commoners on the other.

Some slaves who attained military and government positions accumulated slaves of their own, but they acquired these slaves as dependants themselves. These elevated slaves almost formed a caste of high-ranking slave officials in some places. This exception to the general subordination of slaves to the free population indicates that in unstable political conditions and periods of economic transition, enterprising individuals who were protected by the wealthiest and strongest political leaders could take advantage of a personal opportunity to change their status. In no way did the existence of large slave-owners among people of slave origin endanger the operation of these societies. In some situations, kinship rules were adjusted to incorporate a particular person, and his descendants joined the ranks of the master class. None the less, there were two clearly defined classes, slave and free, with the free subdivided into a commercial–political elite and commoners.

THE WESTERN COAST AND ASANTE

The sharp drop in slave exports from the stretch of coast westward of the Volta River to Sierra Leone meant that many slaves who otherwise would have been exported added to the local population. This demographic shift required a serious adjustment in the coastal economy, as the rapid expansion of the servile population, particularly along the Sierra Leone coast and the Gold Coast, encouraged the expansion of productive activities. This economic adjustment did not result in depression, however. The availability of slave labour enabled merchants and political leaders to find employment for new slaves; their success largely accounts for the continued prosperity of Sierra Leone and Asante.

The Sierra Leone region offered no coordinated response to European pressure against the slave trade. The only major state in the area was Futa Jallon, centred in the highlands in the interior, and despite the slave revolts of the late eighteenth century there, the Futa Jallon economy continued to be based on slavery. On the coast itself, the decentralized political structure was one reason that the British and the Americans could found colonies for freed slaves at Freetown and Monrovia. The location of these settlements and the use of Freetown by the British anti-slave trade squadron transformed this stretch of coast into a potential bridgehead in the struggle against slavery. The slaves seized on the high seas were liberated at Freetown, and many converted to Christianity and eventually returned to their homelands to assume an active role in local changes that helped undermine slavery. Similarly, the ex-slaves who came to Liberia from the United States were Christians with a commitment to freedom, even if they proceeded to establish a political order that discriminated against local people.[2]

Along this stretch of coast, which had once accounted for the export of many thousands of slaves per year, therefore, one might expect to find that slavery was a marginal institution. In fact the opposite was true. Instead, local conditions that included the extensive use of slaves in trade and production prevented the spread of anti-slavery sentiments until late in the century. Rather than press the issue of abolition, the British and the freed slaves accommodated themselves to the slave societies of the coast. Freetown, as its name suggests, was a bridgehead against slavery, but there was no victory there. Indeed, it was not until 1928 that slaves were freed in Sierra Leone, despite the presence of the British for 130 years.[3] Nor did Liberia, despite its name, stand for the liberty of slaves, other than those from the United States. There were fewer slaves in Liberia than elsewhere along the coast, but this lower proportion had little, if anything, to do with the presence of freed slaves.

Among the Sherbro, slaves were employed on plantations to grow foodstuffs and to produce palm oil. The Ya Kumba clan, for example, owned land along the Kagboro River, south of Freetown, where they had developed a salt industry. The salt was shipped inland in order to purchase slaves from Susu merchants, and these slaves were then employed in the cultivation of cassava. The mulatto offspring of Portuguese and English merchants also owned considerable numbers of slaves, who were settled on plantations along the coast. The Caulkers were one such family, descended from Thomas Corker, an agent of the Royal African Company who was stationed on the coast in 1684, and a ranking woman of the Ya Kumba clan, which owned land on the coast.[4]

A similar concentration of slaves existed in neighbouring areas, but not everywhere. The crucial variable appears to have been the extent of trade with the interior. Along the Sierra Leone–Guinea coastal region, there was regular trade inland, with salt, rice, and imported European merchandise sent inland, and slaves, kola, and palm produce brought to the coast. Hence among the Mende, who participated in this exchange, perhaps half the population at the end of the nineteenth century was slave, many of whom were settled on plantations, where they grew food and gathered palm products for transport to the coast.[5] Along the Mellacouri and other rivers, where the Susu and Temne lived, a similar concentration of slaves existed, and again slaves were often on plantations, in this case collecting kola for sale to the coast or growing rice for export inland.[6] Further down the coast, the Vai, who numbered only 15,000 or so, were largely a slave society; estimates indicate that three-quarters of the population was slave.[7] By contrast, among the Kru of the Liberia coast, there was far less contact with the interior, and consequently there was less opportunity to acquire the wealth that could be invested in slaves. On this stretch of coast, there was a relatively low proportion of slaves in the population; there do not appear to have been any plantations like those on the Sierra Leone coast. This same pattern characterized most of the Ivory Coast too, except for areas at the mouths of the Bandama and Comoe Rivers, where again there were routes inland.[8]

Asante and its dependencies on the Gold Coast also experienced the economic adjustment required by the shift from slave exports to the sale of other products early in the century. Here the system of trade centred on European trade-castles at Cape Coast, Elmina, and other places made it difficult to smuggle slaves past these establishments.[9] Some slaves were taken further west, but Asante was forced to abandon the slave export business. The crisis of adjustment was profound. Some slaves were added to the population around the capital at Kumasi, but the concentration of slaves became so great that many were executed as war prisoners, there being no export market for them. By 1820, at a time when exports from the Bights of Benin and Biafra were at an all-time high, Asante was diverting its slave population into kola production and gold mining. The response is instructive, moreover, because it reveals a pattern that was to characterize much of Africa, not only other parts of the West African coast. Slaves were available in such numbers that their employment in the domestic economy was logical, indeed a necessity.

Asante is not usually mentioned as an example of an African country that responded to the pull of 'legitimate trade'. Usually the designation 'legitimate trade' is reserved for palm oil and peanuts, not gold and kola nuts. Gold had long been exported from Africa and hence did not represent a new departure in the export economy, while kola nuts were sold within Africa and not to Europe. None the less, both goods were similar to palm oil, peanuts, rubber, and other goods. Despite local consumption, both gold and kola commanded an international market and provided alternatives to the export of slaves. Furthermore, gold and kola nuts, like palm oil and peanuts, were closely related to the increase of slavery within the domestic African economy. The requirements for slave labour varied with each product and between different producing areas, but slavery and the economy were intimately connected.

Slavery in Asante and the adjacent areas on the Gold Coast was a complicated institution, with many variations in the treatment of slaves and the scale of slave concentration. On the one hand, the matrilineal Akan were divided between those who were subjects of Asante and those who were not. On the other hand, in parts of Asante the subjects were not even Akan or matrilineal. The northern provinces in particular had a large population of Muslims, and practices among these people were very different from those of the Akan. In effect, Asante had two sets of laws relating to slaves. One pertained to Akan owners and the other to Muslims. Both groups of slave owners cooperated in maintaining the strength of the Asante state and their supremacy over the slave population.

From their commercial towns along the edge of the forest and in the savanna further north, the Muslims continued to export kola nuts, gold, and other goods with which Asante was able to finance the import of textiles, livestock, salt, slaves, leather goods, and many other products. Muslims employed slaves in their commercial establishments. Slaves were also needed to carry firewood and fetch water because at some towns, particularly Salaga, the water supply was inadequate during the peak season of caravan trade. They gathered fodder for the livestock of visiting merchants and ran errands for itinerant merchants as well as their masters. Many slaves lived on plantations around the towns, where they grew the crops that fed the large caravans of merchants. Since slave masters, in their capacity as commercial brokers, housed and fed visiting traders free of charge, plantation output was a necessary feature of the successful business activities of the Muslim commercial population. For much of the nineteenth century, Muslims were also resident to the south-west of the Volta River, in the area bordering on the forests where kola nuts were harvested. The largest plantations around Salaga and Bonduku had several hundred slaves each.

The French reconnaissance officer, L.–G. Binger, passed through Salaga in 1888, fourteen years after the province of Gonja had asserted its independence from Asante but still soon enough afterward to demonstrate the pattern of plantation development that characterized this important commercial centre. Binger first reached the slave plantation of Dokonkade, to the north of Salaga:

> Dokonkade is a village of between 400 and 500 inhabitants and is a place of agricultural importance. Many people from Salaga are settled there with their

164

captives during the winter months. A small market is set up there where one can buy foodstuffs: naturally, potatoes are the most popular, as in the whole region. Sorghum is not sold at market, but one has simply to approach an inhabitant to get some easily and cheaply ... Going from Masaka to Salaga, one does not go through any villages but passes near Belimpe or Bourompe, Abd-er-Rahman-iri, Gourounsi-iri and other small farming communities dependent upon Salaga – villages of captives engaged in farming under the surveillance of a member of the master's family. These assume the name of their owner, adding *iri*, *sou*, *pe* or *kade*, depending on whether they speak Dagomsa, Mande or Gonja; the suffix in each of the three languages means 'villages, habitation'.[10]

Another French officer, Benquey, reported on Bonduku in 1904, some thirty years after Gyaman had asserted its independence from Asante, that many slaves worked in the fields alongside their master:

For the Abron and above all for the Kulango agriculturalist, a slave is an assistant who enables him to increase the area he cultivates or who lessens the burden of heavy field work. The master himself works alongside his captives. A sort of intimacy which lessens the distinctions between them and renders the captive a servant rather than a slave grows out of their daily contact.[11]

These conditions indicate relatively small-scale production by peasants and their slaves. Among the Muslim merchants, however, Benquey found that the situation was very different; again plantations were common:

Among the Dioula [Juula, i.e., Muslim merchants], on the contrary, there is no contact between masters and captives. The latter, dispatched to cultivator villages, have but little to do with their masters. The Dioula man is above all else a merchant eager to gain, seeking to draw the greatest possible profit from everything that can be bought or sold. Now the slave is ... an easy investment and the source of considerable profit. Therefore, to the Dioula merchant, the slave is a piece of merchandise to which he gives the same consideration he would an ox or sheep.[12]

The two agricultural sectors at Bonduku and elsewhere in Gyaman consisted of one in which farmers had few slaves and another comprising plantations with much larger slave-holdings.

Further south, in the central Akan areas of Asante, slavery was cast in a different mould. The matrilineal Akan were organized into eight great clans that dominated the Asante government. Muslim contingents were organized for the army, and Muslim advisers were usually important in government circles, but the real political battles in Asante were between the different clans. The issue of slavery was an important aspect of this political rivalry. Different clans tried to bolster their position by acquiring the two most important capital resources in Asante: gold and slaves. The king, in a perpetual struggle to assert and maintain the primacy of the state, confiscated gold through inheritance taxes, but slaves remained in the hands of the lineages that comprised each clan and could not be touched. Hence slaves were a particularly valuable investment, more especially since slaves were employed in mining or panning gold. J. Dupuis, the British ambassador to Asante in 1820 learned:

> On the banks of the Barra [Ba], a river whose source is near the great Muslim city of Kherabi and which flows south to join the Tando or Assinia river [actually the Comoe], the Gyaman also practice gold-washing, and my informants relate that during the rainy season there is work for eight to ten thousand slaves for two months.[13]

Slaves could assist in the harvesting of kola nuts, and they could be used as porters in the transport of kola to the north or other goods to the coast. R. La T. Lonsdale, a British intelligence officer, who travelled extensively in Asante and its former province in the early 1880s, reported that 'The traders in all the regions of the interior mostly use slaves as porters.'[14] Wealthy traders and officials, as well as corporate groups, owned slaves, but despite the ability of individuals to acquire large numbers, the tendency was towards corporate ownership by lineages. This was so for two reasons. Firstly, lineages inherited the slaves of wealthy individuals, whereupon the slaves then belonged corporately to the person's maternal relatives. Secondly, different sections of lineages, often maternal brothers, banded together to buy a slave or two at a time. Since access to the kola groves was related to lineage membership, the kola was treated as a virtually free good by lineage members. All that was needed was to pick the kola, sort and package it, and carry it to market. Women and slaves did much of this work, except in the major harvest, when everyone participated. Through inheritance and this kind of corporate activity, lineages acquired dependent lineages of slave origins that were liable to work for the corporate group.

In the early nineteenth century, the slave population of central Asante, particularly in the area around the capital, Kumasi, had become so large that the government feared a slave revolt. Whole villages of slaves had been established to populate this district and to supply food for the army. Thomas Bowdich, who visited Kumasi in 1817, learned that:

> The higher class could not support their numerous followers, or the lower their large families, in the city and therefore employed them in plantations (in which small crooms [villages] were situated), generally within 2 or 3 miles of the capital, where their labours not only feed themselves but supply the wants of the chief, his family and the more immediate suite. The middling orders station their slaves for the same purpose and also to collect fruit and vegetables for sale, and when their children become more numerous, a part are generally sent to be supported by these slaves in the bush.[15]

John Beecham, another British commentator on the Asante scene, also mentions the existence of a plantation sector using slave labour:

> The large towns of Ashantee (As-hánti) contain a considerable population . . . The towns of this part of Africa are surrounded by a number of plantations belonging to the inhabitants; and the natives always include the slaves on those plantations in their estimates of population of the towns to which they are attached.[16]

Beecham based his information on the reports of a Methodist missionary who visited Kumasi in 1839. It is clear that at this date plantations continued to be a feature of the rural economy.

This policy was related to the collapse in the export trade for Asante. In the period from 1790 to 1810, slave exports fell sharply, although the acquisition of slaves through tribute and war had not reduced the number of slaves flowing into the country. The agricultural development of the central district was one solution to the redeployment of slaves who otherwise would have been exported. The Kumasi district was not an area where kola nuts were produced; hence it appears that the government policy was partially makeshift. Slaves may have been settled there first in anticipation that they would be exported when the trade revived, but subsequently many were settled in the provinces. Bowdich thought that this policy

> was particularly consolatory and beneficial to those slaves who, to prevent famine and insurrection, had been selected (from that fettered multitude which could no longer be driven off to the coast directly they arrived at the capital) to create plantations in the more remote and stubborn tracts; from which their labour was first to produce a proportionate supply to the household of their chief, and afterwards an existence for themselves.[17]

By 1820, however, when several diplomatic missions from England made it clear to the Asante government that the trade would not resume, the decision was made to disperse this slave population throughout the country, particularly to areas where gold was produced and kola harvested. The Asante government achieved the redistribution of slaves in two ways. Firstly, it openly encouraged the acquisition of slaves through implementation of commercial policies, inheritance taxes, and other measures that favoured small producers, particularly lineage segments. Secondly, it protected rules governing matrilineal inheritance so that the slave holdings of wealthy officials and merchants were dispersed among kin rather than retained in a single bloc close to the capital or other places where merchants and officials had located their holdings. Hence it appears that Asante pursued a conscious policy that was designed to adjust to the end of the export trade in slaves. Instead, gold and kola resources were developed, using slave labour through the medium of the clans and their subordinate lineages, as an alternative to slave exports.[18]

Estimates on the servile population of Asante are understandably impressionistic, but scattered reports indicate that a substantial portion of the population was slave or pawn. Most observers visited the major centres and followed the principal routes from the coast into the interior; hence the reports are most accurate on these places. Estimates ranging from 60 to 90 per cent of the population are likely to be too high, but in the early 1870s, the population of the Kumasi area was thought to be about equally slave and free. On the coast, the ratio of slave to free was at least as high. This assessment for late in the century is probably roughly accurate for the early decades of the nineteenth century too. This is partially confirmed by the policy of the Asante government in dispersing slaves throughout the countryside after 1820 in order to check the growth of the slave population there. But this policy did not eliminate large concentrations of slaves, either there or elsewhere.[19] If the estimates on the size of the slave population are even roughly accurate, then some wealthy merchants and government officials had large holdings involving many hundreds and perhaps thousands of slaves. Gold mining continued to be work for slaves, and this sector of the economy was so important to the central government that conditions in the mines were probably strictly controlled. It was not an easy job, since pits caved in frequently and had to be dug anew after each rainy season. Deaths were common among the thousands of slaves involved in this vital sector of the economy.

None the less, Asante attempted to plan its economy through the deployment of slaves in agriculture and mining to cushion the country from the effects of the abolition of the export trade in slaves and to accommodate the large-scale import of slaves through tribute, trade, and war. This policy involved making slaves available to the lineages, so that the common people had a stake in the perpetuation of the state in a period of economic transition. Lineages acquired slaves through trade, particularly in kola nuts. In order to safeguard the opportunity to buy slaves, the government restricted the movement of foreign merchants, confining them principally to Salaga, north-east of the Volta River. Kola producers, usually a few related kin, and their slaves, transported kola to Salaga, where they obtained better prices for their kola than would have been the case if merchants were allowed to travel into the production zone. Higher profits from kola sales were matched by lower prices for slaves at the Salaga market.[20] This policy assured a steady influx of slaves that would benefit the lineages. It also guaranteed the prosperity of the Muslim sector in the north, with merchants and local government officials there able to acquire many slaves of their own for use on plantations and in other capacities.

The corollary to this economic policy was the perpetuation of customs that encouraged the cultural assimilation of slaves into Akan society. Slaves who had been purchased in the north could not themselves experience full integration into Akan society. They seldom lost their accent, and they usually were marked with facial and body scars that set them off from free Akan who had no such markings. Legally, these slaves could not inherit land or other property because they had no kinship link with a matrilineage. Nor could they perform religious rites that were associated with the ancestors. These disabilities did not disappear in the course of a lifetime, but the myth of Asante slavery, supported by custom and government action, held out the possibility of assimilation to the descendants of slaves. The truth was that full assimilation took several generations and was fraught with great difficulties. Matrilineal rules required that a person's mother be free and have brothers or other relatives whose property and access to land could eventually be inherited. The children of slave women, whether the husband was slave or free, had no such connection, and throughout their lives they remained second-class citizens at the sufferance of the lineage that owned them. They normally would not be sold, but they could be pawned if the family fell into debt. Culturally, they were indistinguishable from free men, and it was both impolite and illegal to refer to their slave ancestry. None the less, they lacked many legal and property rights, and their children often fared no better. The result was that many villages were inhabited by both free and slave, but only those who traced their ancestry through a line of free women controlled land distribution, made decisions over pawning, or managed joint investments in trade. The policy of cultural assimilation effectively prevented the consolidation of class consciousness among the servile population, but it did not result in the full integration of slaves into society.[21]

To the west of Asante, among the Baule refugees who had fled after the fall of Denkyira and other Akan states in the eighteenth century, slavery was on a much smaller scale.[22] The Baule seized people in raids, and they bought slaves from Muslim merchants in the north as well as from their Guro, Senufo, and Dida neighbours, but rarely were slave holdings very large. Like other Akan, the matrilineal Baule wanted slaves to work in the fields, to serve as porters, and to bear children. Since there were usually only a few slaves in each family, it was relatively easy to incorporate them. Slaves worked alongside free people, and they were openly encouraged to identify with Baule culture. The bands of refugees who moved westward in the eighteenth century successfully displaced the Dida, Senufo, and Guro, incorporating many of these earlier inhabitants into Baule society through the institution of slavery. Indeed, these non-Akan were particularly attractive candidates for purchase and capture because they came from patrilineal societies. In this case, the matrilineal rules of the Baule provided a convenient justification for captivity. The Guro, Dida, and Senufo lacked the legitimate matrilineal links to the original refugee groups. They could become Baule, but they remained dependants for generations, until time had erased memories of slave ancestry and cultural distinctions that might endanger Baule domination. The Baule had to be concerned about their survival. They had lost out to Asante in the struggle for control of their homelands. Through the institution of slavery, they increased their numbers and guaranteed that they would not lose their newly acquired lands in the east.

On the periphery of the Baule country, along the coast between the Comoe and Bandama Rivers, were fishing villages and salt-making camps that supplied the interior with salt and fish in exchange for foodstuffs, cloth, and slaves.[23] These communities had sold some slaves to Europeans during the eighteenth century. In the nineteenth century, the people at the mouth of the Bandama River shifted to the palm-oil trade in response to the rise in demand. The relative prosperity from this trade made it possible for these merchants – the Alladian – to buy many slaves, so that there were larger concentrations than among the Baule or other people of the interior. The Alladian traded up the Bandama River to the town of Tiassale, which was the major staging-point for trade with the Baule and with Muslim merchants from the savanna. The Alladian needed porters and field hands, and some merchants had as many as 60 or 70 slaves. By comparison with slavery elsewhere along the West African coast, these holdings were relatively small. None the less, the scale of slavery here was still significant and suggests that the possibility of incorporation, which characterized slavery among the Baule and many Akan, was more difficult.

DAHOMEY AND THE YORUBA STATES

Slavery was as important in Dahomey and the Yoruba states to the east as it was in Asante.[24] These states continued to export large numbers of slaves through the 1840s, and the volume of the trade, while greatly reduced after mid-century, continued at a level of several thousand per year until the 1870s. More significantly, slaves were used in the domestic economy on an unprecedented scale. Here the shift to 'legitimate trade' involved the production of palm oil and its transport to the coast. Both the production and the transport were almost exclusively the work of slaves, and this required thousands of field hands and porters. Hence one aspect of slavery in this area was the concentration of slaves in the hands of a relatively few owners. The plantation economy and the movement of freight by slave porters required the restructuring of the domestic economy. Slave owners emerged not only among the ranks of government officials and the state itself but also among merchants, both native and foreign.

As in the Akan provinces of Asante, the legal setting for slavery emphasized kinship structures. Marriage contracts, access to land, cooperation in defence, and religious beliefs were conceived of in terms of genetic relationships. Unlike Asante, however, kinship rules were governed patrilineally, not matrilineally, and this difference affected the basic ideology. Practices varied because the male line was the important connection, and these distinctions required an emphasis on paternity that affected the institution of slavery. Children of slave women were technically free, as long as the father was free. The emphasis on owning domestic slaves, including newly acquired slave women and slave children, was on their incorporation into the family unit as they became acculturated and proved their loyalty. The trend, as in Asante, was towards the assimilation of these slaves, and the social myth about slavery held that assimilation was proper and inevitable, as long as slaves, particularly their descendants, complied with the cultural expectations of society. Once slaves or the children of slaves had become culturally assimilated, they could expect to be treated as full members of the family.

This was the way slavery was supposed to function. The actual practice was quite different. Slave holdings in Dahomey and the Yoruba states of

170

Ibadan, Ijebu, Abeokuta, and Lagos were so large that free people constituted only a minority of the population, particularly by the middle of the nineteenth century. Individual war-lords and wealthy merchants, including a few women also, amassed hundreds, even thousands of slaves, far too many to assimilate into their kinship groups. Because slave masters were primarily concerned with success in war and the functioning of the market, they largely ignored traditions and laws that encouraged the incorporation of slaves and their gradual emancipation. A few individuals could be rewarded through the extension of kinship rights, and children of slave women by free fathers could expect better treatment than children of slave unions. Full assimilation was also difficult because of divisions within the slave-owning class. Some masters were Muslim; others were Christian; while others still were animist. Slaves also had different cultural and religious traditions that hindered their incorporation, especially for those from the Muslim north. The most significant distinctions were political anyway. People were identified as citizens of Abeokuta, Ijebu, Ibadan, Ilorin, or Dahomey and not as Yoruba or Fon, the two major linguistic and cultural divisions.

Dahomey, the notorious slave-raiding and slave-trading state where regiments of Amazons captured the imagination of abolitionists in Europe, was particularly prosperous in the nineteenth century, and this prosperity rested on slavery, as the critics of the slave trade charged. Not only were many slaves exported, even after mid-century, but slaves were successfully employed in the domestic economy to produce palm oil and other goods for local exchange and export. The king did indeed have thousands of women in his army and harem, and these women also traded on his behalf. None the less, the most important development in the nineteenth century was the king's investment in plantation slavery.

By the time the palm-oil trade became important in the 1840s, there were many plantations around the port towns of Whydah and Porto Novo and near the Dahomey capital of Abomey.[25] The owners of these plantations included the king, local merchants and officials, and Brazilian traders. One Dahomey businessman, Kwenun, the son of a local merchant, owned thousands of slaves by the 1860s. Domingo Martinez, a Brazilian, had plantations near Porto Novo, while the king confiscated some palm groves, establishing plantations in the area between his capital and the coast. Freed slaves, returning from Sierra Leone and Brazil, bought slaves for their farms on the coast, too. Some of these were Muslims whose origins were much further north, and a few became quite wealthy.

F. E. Forbes visited Abomey in 1851 and learned that slaves constituted a third of the population, an estimated 10,000 out of the capital's 30,000 inhabitants. He also found slave plantations on the outskirts of the capital: 'Near Abomey is a royal plantation of palms, corn etc., called Leffle-foo. It is inhabited by people from the province of Anagoo, prisoners of war, and is under the direction of a Dahomean caboceer [official]. The gifts of nature

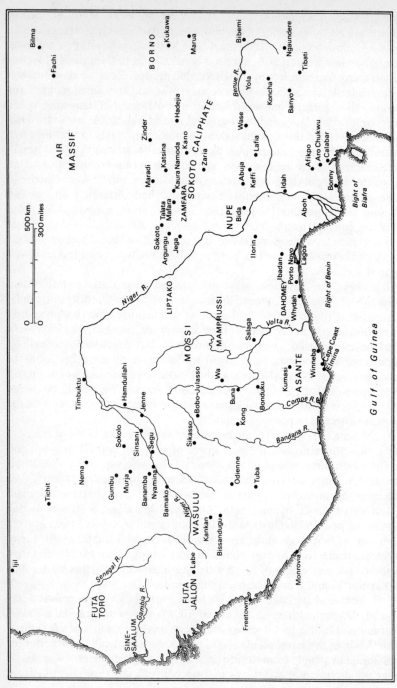

5 Major concentrations of slaves in nineteenth-century West Africa

are all bountifully bestowed, and the soil rich and capable of producing every vegetable production.'[26] Forbes learned that wealthy merchants had thousands of slaves, including one trader at Whydah, whose 'very extensive palm-oil plantations ... [required] very little labour in procuring this valuable and lucrative article of trade. On the estate are many establishments, slave villages, for the manufacture, which is very simple.'[27] Forbes underestimated the labour needed to prepare palm oil for export. The oil had to be extracted and then transported to the coast; both activities were labour intensive, but his observations on the scale of slavery reveals the extent to which Dahomey was now based on slave labour.

A similar pattern of extensive investment in slave-based trade and agriculture characterized the economies of the various Yoruba states.[28] These small states, based on well-fortified cities of considerable size, used slaves as the basis of their armies, usually organized as private militia units belonging to individual war-lords, but slaves also occupied extensive plantations outside the walls of the cities. One war-lord, Kurumi, can serve as an example. This man marched his private army into the town of Ijaye in 1829 and seized the government. By 1859, Kurumi had 300 wives and a slave army 1,000 strong. One slave subordinate – who was servile in origin but no longer in status – had 300 slaves of his own. Kurumi also owned farmland, and he had many other slaves for agricultural work. Yoruba war-lords like Kurumi were found at Ibadan, Abeokuta, Ijebu-Ode, Ogbomoso, Ife, and Ketu.[29]

Ibadan had one of the largest slave societies on the Slave Coast. The city was founded as a war-camp in 1829 and subsequently rose to prominence as a place of refuge for many people forced to evacuate their homes during the Yoruba wars that followed the disintegration of Oyo. Until the 1840s, the Ibadan war-lords exported many of the slaves they captured, and they continued to sell some even as the trans-Atlantic trade entered its final decline. By the 1850s, however, most large slave-owners were organizing their slaves for agricultural production. Samuel Johnson, the renowned Yoruba historian who wrote about the history of his people in the late nineteenth century, recorded that the influx of slaves into Ibadan was often several thousand per year. The able-bodied male slaves were trained as soldiers; the old and infirm were sold for whatever price they could fetch; pretty female slaves were placed in harems or married. 'All the rest are sent into the farms, each to be be employed in his or her own line. The chiefs had large farms and farm houses containing a hundred to over a thousand souls. These extensive plantations not only support their huge establishments but also supply the markets.'[30] As palm oil became a major export to Europe, slaves were needed to produce the oil and carry it to the coast. Slaves were also used to grow okra, beans, maize, yams, and vegetables, which were marketed locally and also distributed to other Yoruba towns. Ibadan became militarily the strongest and demographically the largest of these towns, and consequently its agricultural output was important throughout the region.

By the 1860s and 1870s, there were 104 families who together owned over 50,000 slaves, an average of 500 per family. These slave owners included all the political leaders, among them the Basorun, the military ruler of the city, as well as the various war-lords.[31] Slave holdings included private armies, plantation workers, craftsmen, livestock herders, and porters. Oluyole, the Basorun from 1837 to 1847, for example, had thousands of slaves, most of whom were Hausa and Muslim. Many of these were soldiers, but his land holdings were extensive, including separate plantations for yams, okra, beans, maize, and vegetables. Ogunmola, a war-lord during the 1850s and early 1860s, had 1,800 slave soldiers alone, not including his plantation hands. Madam Efusetan, one of the few women with extensive slave holdings, had some 2,000 slaves on her plantations in the 1870s, and she owned more in her Ibadan home. These examples could be repeated for Ondo, Ijebu, and Abeokuta.[32]

Most of the slaves in Yorubaland were employed in the military, on plantations, as porters, and in harems. Thousands of slave soldiers were assembled on a permanent war-footing. There were many wars, numerous skirmishes and regular raiding into enemy territory. Neither Ibadan nor other strongholds gained supremacy in these struggles. Military slavery, therefore, was one response to political insecurity, but private armies made little if any contribution to the productive activities of their master's household; indeed, they lived off the labour of other slaves. They could be used as porters, but they were not usually involved in farm work. Slave soldiers were given part of the spoils, and they could advance in military rank if they proved themselves in battle. They were fed by the war-lord from the output of plantation slaves and often were given wives.

Plantation slaves worked under overseers, risked capture in raids, and lived in separate villages outside the cities. Labour requirements included the construction of yam mounds – following the experiments of Basorun Oluyole, who wanted to grow yams that were large enough to constitute a single load, e.g., upwards of 40 kg each. He achieved this by building large compost heaps of weeds, banana and plantain stalks, and earth. Yam seedlings were planted on the top, so that the roots would grow into the soil and fill the compost mound. The experiments proved successful, and this became the method of yam cultivation among all the large slave-owners.[33] The technique required extensive labour, of course, and careful management. Slaves worked from sunrise until early afternoon, and then were free to work their own plots, where they grew subsistence crops. Planters also owned groves of kola, palm, and other trees, although there were few economies of scale in sylvan production. Many small producers also competed, particularly in the palm-oil trade. Besides the large slave-owners, there were other farmers who owned fewer slaves, still sometimes as many as 20 or 30.

Concubinage also required thousands of slaves, and these were more likely to be incorporated into a kinship group. Marriage to a slave woman changed her status, so that she was no longer liable for sale. Virtually all influential men – prosperous farmers and war-lords – had more than one wife; some had hundreds.[34] This demonstrates an extremely uneven distribution of women in society. Many slave soldiers and plantation slaves had no wives or married relatively late in life. None the less, the incorporation of slave women through marriage and the granting of free status to their children demonstrates two features of Yoruba society in the nineteenth century. Firstly, the status of women was low, and access to women through enslavement undermined marriage customs. Secondly, this treatment of slave women reflected an assimilationist tendency. Control over the reproductive capacities of women remained as important as it had been when slavery was marginal to the functioning of kinship. Even the introduction of Christianity and Islam did not alter this practice. The Christians included repatriated individuals from Sierra Leone and the Americas who had been freed from slavery and resettled at Abeokuta and elsewhere. Many of these Christians acquired slaves and had more than one wife themselves. Muslims could have four, and as many concubines as they could afford.

On the one hand, there was a tendency towards assimilation, practised more in some places than in others. On the other hand, plantations and large military establishments were a countervailing force in which slavery was far different in practice than the ideal of the assimilated slave. Samuel Crowther, an ex-slave from the Yoruba country who later became Anglican bishop on the lower Niger River, reported that the nature of domestic slavery, as opposed to plantation slavery, was relatively benign in 1857. The main feature, true to the perception of slavery in those holdings that were small, was that slaves were treated as if they were members of the family. 'The slaves and masters in this country live together as a family; they eat out of the same bowl, use the same dress in common and in many instances are intimate companions, so much so that, entering a family circle, a slave can scarcely be distinguished from a free man unless one is told.'[35] In 1881, the Lagos merchant and slave owner, Braimah Apatira, provided a similar view of his relationship with his slave assistants:

> The boys [trader slaves] live with their masters in the house, receiving food, clothing, and being treated as one of the family. But no wages are paid. If they need money they are dashed [given] some. If they conduct themselves well the master gets them wives and gives them money to start for themselves. The boys work for their masters and go to market for them. If they don't behave they are sent away with nothing.[36]

Both Crowther's and Apatira's comments describe how slavery was supposed to function, as seen by pro-slavery apologists. In commercial establishments such as Apatira's, some slaves may well have been treated as if they were family members, but where slave holdings were substantial it simply was not possible to do so.

THE BIGHT OF BIAFRA

Slavery was almost as common in the Biafran interior as elsewhere on the West African coast. The concentration of slaves varied, with the highest ratios of slaves to free men near commercial centres, in the Niger delta, and along the northern frontier of Igboland. Slave to free ratios were lower in the densely populated central areas of the region, and here individual slave-holdings tended to be small too.[37] The region became the largest exporter of palm products, but unlike Dahomey and the Yoruba states, the palm trees remained primarily in the hands of small producers, particularly in the lineage-based villages of the densely populated central Igbo country and among the similar communities of Ibibio of the Cross River valley.

In this situation – when slave exports declined to insignificance in the 1830s and palm-oil exports were already substantial – there was no serious economic recession.[38] As elsewhere, the availability of slaves who earlier would have been exported made it possible for slave owners to redirect their labour into the domestic economy. The largest slave-holders among the Aro, the Efik of Calabar, Igbo of Aboh, and the Ijaw of the Niger delta continued to concentrate on commerce. They invested in more slaves because they were needed as porters and canoemen, and slaves were also used in agriculture near Calabar, Aboh, and the Aro settlements, where significant pockets of plantation development emerged. None the less, the bulk of the export crop was not produced on plantations but on family farms, and the oil was often carried to bulking-points by free people – usually women – as well. Central Igboland and the Ibibio country were densely covered with palm trees, and farmers could increase production merely by protecting young trees and allowing them to mature.[39] Slave labour was used in this expansion, but on a small scale and in small holdings. Slaves were indeed useful in agricultural tasks, either in processing palm oil, carrying it to market, or tilling the land for yams and other crops, for all these activities were limited by the labour available. Those peasants who could afford to supplement the labour of their wives and children could increase output only if they had access to slaves or pawns.

In the Ngwa region of the palm belt, adult males harvested the palm produce on the trees near their compounds, while their wives cracked the nuts and extracted the oil. On certain days, lineage members also could harvest produce on the communal land of the clan or village. This land, administered by the heads of the lineages (*okpara-ukwu*) or the villages (*eze-ala*), contained large numbers of palm trees, so that the fruit gathered there was an important supplement to the palm supplies of the small producers. Once the oil was extracted, the women – sometimes accompanied by a few males if the distance to market was great – carried the oil, and late in the century kernels too, to the riverside depots; for Ngwaland, the principal markets were Akwete, Ohambele, and Azumiri. Merchants in these towns bought the oil and kernels and then re-sold them to merchants from Bonny, and after 1869, from Opobo too. The women kept the proceeds from kernel sales, while the receipts from oil went to their men.[40]

The lineage and village heads were also major producers of oil and kernels, primarily because they controlled the ancestral lands and because they had more wives and dependants – including slaves – who could increase the scale of production. These lineage and village heads also received additional labour from the community as a form of tribute on each *orie* day of the four-day Igbo week. Such men as Egege Nwannenta, Nwagalasi Oguikpe, and Olujie Egbulefu became major producers at the end of the nineteenth century; profits from palm-produced sales strengthened the position of the lineage heads within Ngwa society. Similarly, the heads of Akwete, Ohambele, and Azumiri – the three major produce markets – were also large producers; their wives received credit from the Bonny and Opobo merchants, which enabled them to become influential intermediaries in the purchase of oil and kernels from the small producers. These women journeyed to such Ngwa towns as Obegu, Aba, and Abala, where oil and kernels were plentiful, to buy direct from the producers. At Obegu, Chief Ananaba dominated production and marketing; his share of the oil sold at Akwete has been estimated at one quarter of the volume shipped from Akwete to Bonny.[41]

Throughout the Biafran region, wealthy men (and some women) consolidated their position in society through the control of lineage land, trade, and the acquisition of slaves and pawns. Isichei has characterized these 'persons of property' (*ogaranya*) as a class, distinguished by the size of polygynous families and the number of slaves and clients. In Item, for example, 'a man's wealth depended on the number of slaves.' There were three important slave-owners in Item, each with an estimated 400 slaves. All three were local doctors who made and sold war charms. Some slave dealers at Arondizuogu had 20 to 40 wives and many slaves, and they too were part of the *ogaranya* class.[42] The Ngwa lineage and village heads were members of the *okonko* secret society, and membership in this and comparable societies seems to have been one of the criteria of the *ogaranya*. These societies – *okonko* among the Ngwa and Aro; *ekpe* at Calabar; the *ozo* titled societies at Asaba and elsewhere – promoted class interests.[43] The *okonko* society, for example, was a masked society, which terrorized offenders, burned their houses, and sold people into slavery. Its main functions were to guarantee credit and provide commercial links with other parts of the region, particularly with the Aro.

The heaviest concentration of slaves was at the commercial centres, including Aboh, Asaba, Onitsha, Ossomari, Ndoki, Akwete, Uzuakoli, Aro Chukwu, and the towns of the Niger delta (Brass, Akassa, Elem Kalabari, Bonny, and Opobo). The slave population of Ossomari numbered in the thousands, for example.[44] A report of 1902 estimated the population of the town at 6,000 to 8,000, many of whom were slaves, while the outlying districts had thousands of slaves, perhaps as many as 14,000. At Asaba, where slaves were also numerous, farms extended for thousands of hectares on the west side of the Niger, and while the number of slaves there is unknown, it is likely that much of this land was worked by slave labour.[45] The Aro communities, not surprisingly, also had many slaves, since the Aro were the major slave traders in the region. In the Afikpo area, for example, where the Aro formed almost 10 per cent of the population, they owned the most slaves. By 1900, one wealthy Aro merchant at Aro Chukwu, Okoroji, owned thousands of slaves, according to local tradition. These were settled on three plantations, two of which were 15 km from town. Yellow Duke of Calabar owned an estimated 3,000 slaves in the early 1880s, most of whom were settled on plantations, where the slaves worked under an overseer. Slaves farmed the fields of their master and carried palm oil into Calabar. Yellow Duke and other planters visited these plantations occasionally. The fact that Yellow Duke was formerly a slave demonstrates that there was a significant difference in status and opportunity between those slaves brought into the merchant firms of the town and those confined to plantations.[46] After 1869, some Bonny merchants followed the Calabar lead in diversifying the activities of their slaves; plantations were established adjacent to the creeks inland where palm produce and food could be raised. While the Bonny merchants still concentrated on trade, rather than production, it is unlikely that even a modest investment in agriculture would have been possible without slaves.[47]

The incidence of slavery also increased on the northern frontier of Igboland. The more extensive cultivation of palm trees in the densely populated areas of the Biafran interior required a corresponding decrease in the production of food crops, and the palm belt eventually needed to import foodstuffs from other areas, particularly the region further inland. Here slaves were employed in growing yams on plantations. Around Nike, for example, slaves lived in their own farm settlements.[48] There were also slaves in the central Nike villages with their masters. These slaves also farmed, for free men here did not engage in agricultural labour. Nor did free men marry slaves. Hence, this use of slaves in agriculture was indirectly related to 'legitimate' trade. Slaves were seldom settled on palm plantations, but were settled in their own villages or separate parts of their masters' compounds to grow yams for sale to the palm belt. All along the northern frontier of Igbo country, where land was readily available, adventuresome men secured large tracts of land and acquired slaves. It was necessary to conquer some of this land or protect it from invasion from the north, so that people relied on kinship in order to form militia units. Slaves were barred from the military here. Their task was to farm, sometimes in separate settlements that were more vulnerable to enemy raids. They could respond in self-defence, but their principal military function was to warn their master and his lineage of impending attack. Some of these northern centres, such as Nike, were allied to the Aro, supplying the Aro with slaves, yams, and other goods in exchange for firearms and manufactures.

178

An examination of the commercial organization of the Niger-delta trading-house is essential in order to understand how slavery functioned in this setting.[49] Some firms had hundreds of slaves, and since they were organized on a para-military basis, the opportunities for advancement in the firm could be great. Occasionally, enterprising young men became wealthy and influential enough to recruit a crew for their own river-boat. These new subsidiaries continued under the central direction of the parent firm, but they traded largely on their own account. A man, slave or free, had to have sufficient capital or credit – usually a combination of the two – to outfit a boat and buy trade goods. He needed permission to operate in the markets of the parent firm, and this was either readily given because it promoted the interests of the house in general or it was decided to expand operations into new areas in the hopes of eliminating a rival or acquiring new sources of palm oil. In either case, the new enterprise needed a crew, often 50 or more men, and these were invariably slaves that the investor owned himself or in combination with several other investors. It is clear from this example that individuals could become extremely wealthy and powerful, unless they were eliminated in the fierce competition of the trade. Slaves successfully rose to the highest positions in the trading firms of the Niger delta towns, particularly at Bonny and Elem Kalabari, but also at Brass. One slave, purchased in his youth at an inland market, even rose to head the most successful commercial establishment at Bonny, and when he was forced into a difficult political position there he moved his following to a new site at Opobo and became that town's ruler. This man, Jaja, accomplished in a single life-time a transformation in status from humble Igbo slave boy to powerful ruler, owning over a thousand slaves, including slave subordinates who had large holdings themselves.

Slavery in the Niger delta and at other commercial centres in the region, including Calabar, Aboh, and Duala, had more similarities to the military slavery of the Yoruba towns and Muslim countries than to domestic slavery or plantation slavery. Crowther observed that at all the commercial centres along the Niger, from the delta towns northward towards the confluence of the Niger and Benue Rivers, slave holdings were often quite large:

> Accumulation of slaves at Abo, Idda, and Gbegbe, to show how wealthy they are – because a man's worth is estimated by the number of his wives and slaves – is the prevailing ambition of the people. Olumene [of Idah] is said to hold about 200 slaves, with whom he lives in a separate group of huts at Idda. Akaia and his brother, who have inherited their father's property, are said to own about 400.[50]

At Aboh in the 1850s, where many firms owned large numbers of slaves, some of whom traded on the account of their master, Crowther learned that some trusted slaves had become wealthy on their own. 'Some of the old slaves have themselves become owners of a large property and many slaves; and thus become, in a great measure, independent of their masters, except waiting on them occasionally.'[51] That slaves could in fact acquire their own

179

slaves demonstrates that slave status could change. The designation 'slave' could be little more than a sign of origin and association with the commercial firm of the slave's original master. Once slaves had assumed an independence and an effective social freedom that placed them in the class of slave owners, emancipation had effectively taken place. Here was a system that promoted slaves as a means of securing strict loyalty and dependence.

Slaves were also sacrificed to religious deities, at funerals and on other occasions; these practices too promoted social control. At Uburu, for example, a slave was usually killed in deference to the supernatural protector of the salt lake and marked the opening of the salt season, while in the Niger delta, a slave could be offered to such river spirits as Duminea.[52] The taking of titles, especially *ozo* titles, required the death of slaves too. The 400 title-holders at Asaba in 1881, for example, had each sacrificed a slave on assuming their titles; two more slaves were to be killed at the funerals of each of these men.[53] At Calabar, the number of funeral victims was much larger; hundreds of slaves were killed at several important funerals in the nineteenth century. In most places, however, one or two deaths was usually sufficient. The cheapening of human life symbolized in these practices was perhaps most gruesomely displayed at the house of skulls in Bonny and the shrine of Ibinukpabi at Aro Chukwu, which was lined with the heads of slaves.[54]

Slaves hoped that successful apprenticeship in trade could lead to full assimilation and social mobility. Kinship terminology and structures were modified to allow for exactly that possibility. Newly purchased slaves, who were most grateful that they were not destined for an early grave or export across the Atlantic, learned their lessons quickly. They called their mistress 'mother'. They accepted a legal status that was likened to that of children, and they learned Ijaw, the Efik dialect, or Aboh Igbo because these languages were used to maintain a corporate distinctiveness that was useful in business and easily revealed the extent of assimilation. Strict discipline was required of these slaves. They learned the skill of the river trade and sudden military confrontation with rivals, where there could be no tolerance of insubordination. Those who would not conform suffered the consequences of sale or death, and such failures must have been far more numerous than the examples of slaves who rose to positions of power and influence. None the less, both extremes were possible, and it did not take long for newly purchased slaves to realize this.

The possibilities of social mobility represented one extreme in the practice of slavery in the delta. People used the terminology of kinship, but this was not a situation in which slaves were incorporated into kinship groups as they were where small domestic units prevailed. Slaves were far too numerous. They comprised the bulk of the population and could aspire to any position in society except for the kingship. And Jaja even challenged the restriction on royal succession by staging a *coup d'état* at Bonny and then withdrawing his supporters to Opobo in 1869.[55] Real relationships based on marriage between free people and genetic ties between generations were not the most important social bonds in Bonny society. Rank was acquired, and slavery was not a serious obstacle to improving one's status.

Elsewhere, such fluid social conditions did not exist. At Calabar, which shared many of the same features of commercial organization, slaves were barred from attaining the highest positions in firms.[56] Calabar traders also used river-boats to reach markets along the Cross River, but the descendants of free merchants prevented almost all slaves from acquiring positions of authority within *ekpe* – the secret society that established and enforced the laws necessary for commerce, including the protection of creditors. By denying access to slaves, *ekpe* guaranteed that slaves would not achieve the kind of mobility found at Bonny. Furthermore, Calabar merchants settled those slaves that they could not export or use in their commercial firms on plantations outside the town. These slaves grew foodstuffs for the firms, and until the middle of the century they had the dubious honour of serving as funeral victims as well.

Hope Waddell, a missionary at Calabar in the 1850s, contrasted the two kinds of slavery, domestic and plantation, that were most common in the commercial centres:

> Most of the slaves are employed in farming and trading. The former cultivate a portion of land, allotted by their masters for their own use, and generally supply the town markets with produce. Their labour is much less continuous and severe than that of West Indian slaves. If called into towns to work, they receive a small allowance. Those employed in canoes are fed, and are in crews of six to ten to each canoe, under a captain or supercargo. He has a commission on his trade and may trade on his own account a little, but not in palm oil, or so as to neglect his master's interests. The canoe people traffic in provisions, buying with English goods up country, and selling to the townspeople, ships, and mission houses.[57]

Until the 1850s, plantation slaves were also subject to seizure for sacrifice at funerals, which may well have been a poor consolation for the less strenuous labour conditions that they enjoyed over their Jamaican cousins. The amount of labour required on the plantations here and elsewhere in the Biafran interior did not render plantation conditions particularly enjoyable. Usually slaves worked for their master three out of every four days, with the other day reserved for their own fields and for market trading. These slaves had the possibilities of a more autonomous life from their master than plantation slaves in the Americas. At Calabar, slaves formed an association, tied by blood pacts, which struggled to end the sacrifice of slaves at funerals. Through a series of demonstrations and riots, they successfully challenged the right of their masters to take the lives of slaves, thereby forcing a redefinition of the status of slave. This struggle, none the less, hardly amounted to a fight for emancipation, nor did it seriously challenge the

181

institution of slavery.[58] It ameliorated the conditions of slaves, but it left the institution, with its division between plantation slaves on the one hand and the domestic slaves of the trading firms on the other, firmly intact.

In the central areas of Igbo country, where slave holdings were small, the treatment of slaves also varied. In some places, slaves were readily incorporated into lineages.[59] Free men took slave wives, and the children were treated as full members of the father's lineage. Slaves could also acquire land from the lineage and start their own homestead, sometimes with the requirement that social deference be shown to the truly free members of the lineage and sometimes with the expectation that first fruits be forwarded to the lineage head. But slaves in some places, even when holdings were small, were not allowed to participate in religious ceremonies, and some villages discouraged or prohibited marriage between slaves and free. The general picture for domestic slavery, therefore, must emphasize the variations in practice. The tendency was towards cultural assimilation for non-Igbo or outsiders from distant parts of the country. They could expect to learn the local dialect, honour the taboos and shrines of the community, and look to the lineage for access to land. They were usually the ones to handle the heaviest agricultural work, particularly the construction of yam mounds. They also carried water. It was possible, none the less, for many of these people to blend into the community, and if they could not accomplish full integration, their children or grandchildren often did.

Domestic slaves were the first to suffer when the family or village faced difficult times. If a sacrifice was needed for a shrine, a slave would be bought for the purpose, but if poverty prevented this, a domestic slave would have to be used. Slaves were held as hostage, too, and even after many years they were not allowed to join the community fully. Debt, too, could result in the transfer of a domestic slave, even one born into the community. Similarly, the loss of a legal case, a dispute with a neighbouring village, or cases of sorcery or crime could all lead to the removal of one or more slaves from a village. For a lineage, therefore, slaves were an investment and a source of insurance. A lineage could encourage integration, but only up to a point.

One peculiar feature of slavery in the central Igbo provinces – where plantations were rare, population was dense, and palm-oil production greatest – was the existence of cult 'slaves' (*osu*).[60] These *osu* belonged to a deity and were placed under the direction of a shrine priest. They were often pledged to a shrine during a time when individuals were experiencing personal difficulties, but sometimes families disposed of unwanted children by offering them to the deity. In other cases, family members who knew that they were about to be pawned or sold outright sought sanctuary at the shrine and in return became *osu*. The *osu* themselves performed religious duties. They acted as mediators in disputes and occasionally enforced decisions that were blessed by the shrine priest. The shrines were part of a religious system that included the more powerful oracle at Aro Chukwu. Indeed, the practice of attaching *osu* to shrines is sometimes attributed to the example of the Aro

Chukwu oracle, and shrine priests and the Aro often shared similar interests and supported each others' actions. The *osu*, because they belonged to the deity, really constituted a caste. Although they were despised, they were also feared. In the absence of a central authority in the Igbo country, they can be thought of as being comparable to government slaves in other situations.

The peculiar characteristics of *osu* demonstrate that slavery retained many local features along the West African coast during the nineteenth century. The continuation of earlier practices both in the Biafran interior and elsewhere reveals the strength of tradition in the face of economic and social change. Where once slavery had existed on the fringes of the social formation, now it had become a central institution. Older practices might persist, but the dynamic feature of slavery during the nineteenth century was the more intensive use of slaves in production. While slavery remained marginal in many places, and slaves supplemented peasant production in many other places, the dominant trend was towards a transformation of the economy by relying on slave labour. In this sense, there emerged a mode of production based on slavery. The stages in the transition to a slave mode of production had included the transformation of slavery from a type of dependency in societies based on kinship into a means of supplying the export slave trade. The consolidation of institutions of enslavement and commerce in turn had promoted a commercial and political elite that owned large numbers of slaves. These slaves were then available for productive purposes, and this economic exploitation was promoted through the collapse of the export trade and the simultaneous rise in market demand for locally produced commodities. In the space of four centuries, West African society had been transformed, and slavery and the slave trade were central to the transformation.

The transition in the social formation involved two internal transformations. Firstly, between 1800 and 1850, the slave mode of production still included the export sector for slaves; trade and enslavement were integrated with this export market, while slave-based production was largely a by-product of this external orientation. Pockets of slave-based production were clustered in areas most fully associated with the export trade. In the second half of the century, after the decline and collapse of slave exports, slaves were used more extensively in the domestic economy; slaves were now destined for internal markets, while the output of slave labour was directed for export and domestic use. In terms of European capitalism, this transition in the social formation involved a major structural adjustment that strenghtened the slave mode of production along the West African coast, thereby clearly separating the African economy from the capitalist world-system by maintaining slavery as a barrier. Slavery was the basis of the political economy in Africa; it no longer mattered in the European-controlled world.

9

Slavery in the savanna during the era of the *jihads*

The nineteenth century was a period of violent upheaval in the northern savanna and Ethiopia. From Senegambia in the west to the Red Sea in the east, the series of holy wars (*jihads*) that began in 1804 transformed most of this region, and slavery played a vital role in the transformation. The increased importance of slavery is evident in the export figures for slaves – 1,650,000 slaves sold north across the Sahara Desert and the Red Sea – but the *jihads* resulted in the enslavement of millions of other people who were settled within the new states. This led to the more intensive use of slaves in production, which further consolidated a slave mode of production.

Increased slave use was related to two factors. Firstly, some areas benefited from the export trade, which included not only slaves but steadily growing quantities of 'legitimate' commodities. This expanding market for other merchandise, especially ostrich feathers, ivory, tanned skins, and gum arabic, was connected with the general economic growth of Europe in the nineteenth century. These commodities were taken across the Sahara, although gum arabic and peanuts were shipped from the Senegambia coast, and ivory and sheabutter were exported via the Niger–Benue confluence. The second and most inportant factor was the expansion of the regional economies that were centred in the northern savanna itself. For the first time in centuries, there was no serious multi-year drought that undermined the economy, although drought still affected developments locally. Production in foodstuffs, livestock, textiles, and other manufactures expanded, especially in the new Islamic theocracies. A corresponding expansion occurred in commerce, with the result that the southern desert, the savanna, and the northern forest-zone were closely integrated, probably more so than ever before.[1]

THE SIZE OF THE SLAVE POPULATION IN THE SAVANNA

By the end of the nineteenth century, 30 to 50 per cent of the total population of the western Sudan was slave, and in some locations the percentage was higher, reaching 80 per cent near some commercial centres

184

(table 9.1). These estimates are based on French efforts to assess the importance of slavery in the 1890s and first decade of the twentieth century.[2] The estimate for 1904 accounts for at least 382,800 slaves. There is no way of judging the extent to which the incidence of slavery had increased in the course of the nineteenth century, and it may well be that the proportion of slaves in the population at the end of the century was greater than 50 per cent overall. Slave masters had many reasons to falsify the information given to French census-takers, and the censuses themselves were subject to tremendous error. None the less, these data are essential to the reconstruction of the history of slavery. The scale of slavery alone was so great that the productive employment of slaves was the most important aspect of the institution during the century.

In the central Sudan, the incidence of slavery was in the same order as in the western Sudan, although there are no census data comparable to the French records. The largest and most populous state in the central Sudan – the Sokoto Caliphate – had a substantial slave population, a conclusion reached from widely scattered information.[3] In the capital districts of Sokoto and Gwandu, the overwhelming majority of inhabitants were slaves, while in the populous emirates of Kano and Zaria, perhaps 50 per cent of the population was slave, at least by the end of the century. A similar pattern prevailed elsewhere; slaves came to form a considerable part of the population of Nupe and Yola after mid-century – they comprised the majority of people near the capitals of these emirates. Even smaller emirates, including Liptako in the far west and Hadejia on the border with Borno in the east, had large numbers of slaves. Throughout the Sokoto Caliphate, the slave population tended to be concentrated near the major towns and along trade routes, and as these developed in the course of the century, the slave population expanded too.

Concentrations of slaves were also found in the Nilotic Sudan and parts of the Ethiopian highlands. Again the nineteenth century witnessed an unprecedented growth in slavery. In the Nilotic Sudan, slaves – already numerous around Sennar – became common along the river north of the Nile confluence. In the southern slaving grounds, local societies were totally restructured as slave armies and slave settlements spread south and south-west. Eventually this trend affected the Zande country and other parts of the northern Zaire River basin, and events traceable to the Nilotic Sudan reverberated as far west as Borno, which fell to the army of Rabeh Fadlallah, a Jellaba by origin, in 1891. In Ethiopia too, slavery became more prevalent, especially in the southern Galla towns, which grew with the influx of new slaves. Even in the Christian highlands, slaves were numerous.[4]

The availability of slaves made possible the more extensive use of slaves in production, especially in agriculture but also in other activities. Slaves lived on plantations or in their own villages near all the major commercial centres. War captives were settled in defensible positions in order to provide the

Table 9.1 Demographic profile of slave populations in the western Sudan, 1904

Administrative district	Men	%	Women	%	Children	%	Total
Bafoulabe	4,825	32.6	6,540	44.1	3,455	23.3	14,820
Bandiagara	2,356	35.6	3,161	47.7	1,108	16.7	6,625
Bougouni	1,700	37.6	1,640	36.2	1,186	26.2	4,526
Buriya	2,000	25.0	2,500	31.3	3,500	43.8	8,000
Dinguiraye	3,114	28.5	4,388	40.2	3,415	31.3	10,917
Dori	15,300		24,565				39,865
Dunzu	3,000	37.5	3,800	47.5	1,200	15.0	8,000
Fernkodogo	2,000	13.3	4,000	26.7	9,000	60.0	15,000
Gao	Women and children are 2/3 of slaves (about 8,000)						12,000
Gumbu	Women and children outnumber men 3:1 (18,000 to 6,000)						24,000
Jenne	3,961	24.8	7,981	49.9	4,039	25.3	15,981
Kadé	5,000	38.5	6,000	46.2	2,000	15.4	13,000
Kaedi	10,000	27.8	8,000	22.2	18,000	50.0	36,000
Kolen	1,250	25.0	1,750	35.0	2,000	40.0	5,000
Koutiala	4,050	41.8	4,020	41.4	1,630	16.8	9,700
Kurussa	3,600	32.7	4,200	38.2	3,200	29.1	11,000
Lobi	2,000	25.0	4,000	50.0	2,000	25.0	8,000
Louga	2,696	30.2	3,629	40.6	2,615	29.3	8,940
Maasi	1,200	24.0	1,800	36.0	2,000	40.0	5,000
Medina Kouta	5,389	41.1	5,437	41.5	2,276	17.4	13,102
Médine	125	19.2	400	61.5	125	19.2	650
Raz el Ma	440	28.6	500	32.5	600	39.0	1,540
Satadugu	545	36.3	380	25.3	575	38.3	1,500
Segu	9,172	36.5	8,805	35.0	7,184	28.5	25,161
Siguiri	4,097	34.2	3,480	29.0	4,410	36.8	11,987

Sokolo	6,152	46.1	4,002	30.0	3,189	23.9	13,343
Sumpi	2,036	33.5	2,131	35.0	1,918	31.5	6,085
Tenkodogo	2,000	13.3	4,000	26.7	9,000	60.0	15,000
Timbi – Medina	1,300	17.3	4,000	53.3	2,200	29.3	7,500
Timbi – Tunni	1,500	37.5	1,100	27.5	1,400	35.0	4,000
Tivouane	2,951	25.4	4,236	36.4	4,447	38.2	11,634
Tuba	2,400	30.0	2,720	34.0	2,880	36.0	8,000
Yatenga	2,573	36.7	2,436	34.8	1,994	28.5	7,003
TOTAL	108,700*	30.9	135,600	39.3	102,500	29.8	346,800*

* Excludes Gao and Gumbu. Totals are rounded to the nearest hundred.
Source: M. Klein forthcoming.

agricultural and manufacturing foundation for economic development, with the result that the metropolitan districts of the major states imported slaves *en masse*. Merchants too participated in this expansion; they settled slaves at the towns along the established trade routes of the savanna and used labour to open new routes that stretched beyond the borders of the major states. In some cases, the output of slave labour was coordinated to supply armies and palace staffs, while in others, harvests were sold on the market or used to feed itinerant merchants.[5]

The expansion of the plantation sector, based on the regeneration of the centuries-old system dating back to the medieval era, began with the reorganization of the political economy in the northern savanna during the early decades of the nineteenth century. This first phase ended roughly at mid-century. During this phase, the relatively densely populated areas of the Senegambia, middle Niger valley, Hausaland, and the northern Nilotic Sudan experienced an increase in the slave population, although there were large areas between these regions where slavery remained marginal. During the second phase, from 1850 to 1900 (and in some places, lasting even later), new centres of slave concentration were opened, generally to the south of the earlier developments. In these decades, the upper Niger region, the Benue River valley and neighbouring parts of the Niger valley, and the southern basin of the Nile were incorporated into this expanded slave-based productive system. A subsidiary expansion also occurred along the desert-edge. In some places, it began in the early part of the century, but it experienced dramatic growth in the closing decades of the century, especially in the western Sudan.

THE WESTERN SUDAN

The legacy of *jihad* was an important factor in the history of the far western Sudan. The rivalry between Muslim reformers and the old warrior elite had already led to war in the eighteenth century. Futa Jallon and Futa Toro were the successful products of this struggle; but an outbreak along the Gambia in the 1790s failed, as did another revolt in Walo and Kayor in 1830. In the middle Niger region, however, the caliphate of Hamdullahi was established in 1818. An even more important uprising began under al-Hajj 'Umar in 1852 and spread throughout the region from the foothills of Futa Jallon to the middle Niger valley, while another movement under Ma Ba operated in Senegambia after 1861.[6] In the 1870s, Samori led another movement in the upper Niger basin, so that by the closing decades of the nineteenth century virtually the whole of the western Sudan was in the hands of Muslim reformers. Based on the results of these *jihads*, the western Sudan comprised three sub-regions: firstly, the Senegambia and Futa Jallon; secondly the area incorporated into Segu Tukulor as a consequence of the *jihad* of al-Hajj 'Umar; and thirdly, the upper Niger basin, which came largely within Samori's sphere of influence.

In 1806, the first ruler of Futa Toro, Abd el-Kader, was deposed. A conservative, land-owning aristocracy was determined to reap the rewards of the successful struggle of the 1770s; the expansive phase of *jihad* was terminated, thereby setting the stage for the exploitation of slaves and free peasants who worked the land along the river. Until 1860, most slave holdings appear to have been relatively small; farmers were considered wealthy if they owned a slave or two. Thereafter, the slave market was saturated with fresh imports from the interior, and average holdings increased. In the French census of 1904, slaves accounted for at least 20 per cent of the population; there were 38,600 slaves reported, although it is likely that this figure was an undercount. About 35 per cent of these slaves had been born in Futa Toro; many other people who were second- and third-generation slave could easily be disguised from the inquisitive French agents.[7]

Elsewhere in Senegambia, the struggle between the old *tyeddo* class of warriors and the Muslim reformers resulted in the extension of Muslim communities and the increase in the number of slaves. According to British reports in 1894, slaves outnumbered free men two to one among the Malinke communities along the Gambia. The French census of 1904, which came after long interaction between local societies and French colonialism, also showed large numbers of slaves, although the French were only able to account for a portion of the slave population of Senegambia in the census of 1904. Local knowledge of French anti-slavery sentiments had resulted in extensive concealment of the actual situation. One third the population of Sine-Saalum was identified as slave, none the less. The Kaymor area of southern Saalum was one area of relatively high slave concentration. The Muslim population there was largely involved in agriculture and used slave labour. An important trade route passed near the coast. Salt from the pans formed by an inlet from the Atlantic was sold south to the Gambia River and then inland; grain and cotton were grown extensively, and textile production fed the same trade route.[8]

The growth of peanut exports after mid-century encouraged the importation of slaves to be used in agriculture, although some of the expansion involved the movement of free, migrant farmers and escaped slaves into the region too. Peanuts were first exported from the Gambia River in the 1830s; by 1840, the Gambia exported 1,100 tons; the figure rose to 8,500 tons in 1848. By the 1850s, areas to the north also became significant producers; Senegal exported 5,400 tons in 1854, while Gambian exports were already 11,000 tons. This expansion continued, especially in Senegal, until the 1880s, when the world depression resulted in a fall in price and the temporary decline in the volume of the trade. In 1882, Senegal sold over 80,000 tons, and in 1884, Gambia sold almost 18,000 tons, although this peak of 98,000 tons was not attained again until the 1890s. By then the completion of the Saint Louis–Dakar railway (1885) and relief from the series of world depressions encouraged peanut cultivation once again. This last phase of expansion was directly related to the influx of slaves into the area along the railway in Kajoor and western Bawol.[9]

There were few economies of scale in the cultivation of peanuts, so that large slave-owners had no particular advantage over small producers. Consequently, the growth of the trade encouraged both the spread of peasant production and slave production. Free migrant farmers were travelling to the Gambia from the 1840s on, and they also moved into Kajoor a few decades later when the expansion spread there. In 1851, the British governor of the Gambia estimated that migrants produced one-third of the export crop, and while estimates for the role of peasants in the production of peanuts in other areas are not available, their contribution to total output was significant.[10] The origins of these migrants is not clear; some may have been of slave background, while others may have moved west in order to escape the wars of the interior. Despite the importance of the peasant sector, slave labour was also essential to the expansion of peanut production. The proportion of slaves in the population was high in precisely those areas that were most involved in the export trade: the Gambia River valley, Sine-Saalum, Kajoor, and the Senegal valley.

While peasant production and slave-based agriculture were both common in the Senegambia basin, plantations continued to dominate the economy of Futa Jallon, as they had in the last decades of the eighteenth century. In 1820, René Caillié reported numerous plantations, which he called *ouronde* (*runde*), in the parts of Futa Jallon he visited on his journey into the interior. For example, near Gneretemile was 'an ouronde, or slave village, surrounded by good plantations of bananas, cotton, cassavas and yams, [while after] Maraca ... we found ourselves in a sandy plain, containing several small slave villages.' Two days' journey from the capital of Timbo was the plantation of Popoco, 'containing between one hundred and fifty and two hundred slaves, who are employed in agriculture'.[11] These slaves grew cassava, yams, peanuts, rice, and millet. He passed many others as well, and spent some time at Cambaya, the village of the caravan leader Ibrahim, with whom he was travelling. He accompanied Ibrahim to his rice plantation:

> to see the slaves employed in preparing the ground for sowing. The poor slaves work entirely naked, exposed to the heat of the burning sun. The presence of the master intimidates them, and the fear of punishment expedites the work; but they make themselves amends in his absence. The women, who had very little clothing, had their children tied to their backs. They were employed in collecting dry grass, which, being burnt, forms a kind of manure, indeed, the only kind they use.[12]

These slaves had their own huts, where the older women prepared food for the field hands. Behind these huts were small gardens that belonged to the slaves and from which they were expected to feed themselves. The slaves were allowed two days per week to work in their own gardens. The only major distinction between Ibrahim's plantation and many others in Futa

Jallon was that he was a private merchant, not associated with the Fulbe aristocracy who owned the vast majority of slaves in the country.

Demographic data collected in Futa Jallon after slavery had been abolished and many slaves had fled provide a sufficiently large sample of plantations to give some idea of the size and number of slave holdings. Of the 34,600 people in the province of Labe in the 1940s, there were 11,300 people who still lived in villages that had once been plantations.[13] In the language of the colonial period, these inhabitants were no longer called slaves, but 'serfs'. These 11,300 'serfs' were settled on 121 'roundes', or plantations, an average of 93 people per plantation. In the past, the percentage of slaves in the total population had been much higher, perhaps reaching two-thirds. Furthermore, the size of individual plantations had certainly been greater. When these data are put together with earlier accounts, they confirm the existence of a highly developed plantation economy. The plantation slaves, moreover, were not assimilated in the full sense of that term. Otherwise, they would not be recognizable in distinct communities as late as the 1940s.

The Maraka and Juula towns of the middle Niger valley were also centres of plantation agriculture, with slave populations sometimes as high as 70 to 80 per cent of the total population in the immediate vicinity of the towns. Their prosperity was based on the ecologically-based trade that stretched from the Sahara Desert to the forests. Salt, livestock, and imports from North Africa came from the north, while kola nuts, gold, and European imports came from the south. Grain and textiles, produced locally by slaves, entered this regional commercial network. Another route westward to the Senegal and Gambia valleys was an alternative avenue to the coast and became particularly important in the nineteenth century as a result of, firstly, the *jihad* of al-Hajj 'Umar and, secondly, the military expansion of the French. These towns served as staging-points for caravans to the south and west, and they were the wholesale centres for imports from the north.[14]

In the first half of the nineteenth century, before al-Hajj 'Umar conquered Segu Bambara and transformed this pagan state into the reformed Muslim state of Segu Tukulor, Sinsani was the most important of several Maraka and Juula towns. The integration of its plantation sector and regional trade was typical of the commercial life of the region as a whole. Slave-produced grain was sold to visiting merchants from the sahel, who brought salt from Ijil, while cotton fed the local textile industry. Sinsani was destroyed in 1861, and its trade shifted to the new centre at Banamba.[15] None the less, even in its period of decline, the slave population was still substantial. In 1904, the French were able to count 6,436 slaves at Sinsani, which represented 31 per cent of the population. Popular tradition remembered the more glorious past, when some slave owners were credited with substantial holdings, upwards of 3,000 slaves in some cases.[16] While these figures cannot be verified, they probably are an accurate indication of the importance of the plantation sector in the period before 1861.

191

As the successor to Sinsani, Banamba grew rapidly because slaves were imported from the south. In 1864, the town already had 8,000 to 9,000 people and rapidly became the commercial centre of Segu Tukulor, just as Sinsani had been the commercial centre of Segu Bambara. The wars of Segu Tukulor accounted for many slaves brought into the region in the 1860s and 1870s. In the 1880s, Samori, Tièba, and Babemba enslaved people by the tens of thousands, and these captives were sold north, where many were added to the holdings of the merchants from Banamba and other towns. By the 1890s, plantations surrounded Banamba for a distance of 25–50 km, and the slave population outnumbered the free inhabitants by a ratio of two to one. While the number of slaves is not known, estimates in 1910 indicate that 20,000 slaves fled from the region of Banamba and Tuba, which may have been half the slave population of the area.[17] Tuba, a town of 3,000, had an estimated 6,000 to 7,000 slaves in its outlying plantations, so that the slave population of Banamba may have been in the order of 30,000 to 35,000. Other towns – at least those that the French officers tried to tabulate – show a similar pattern. Kiba, a town with 2,300 people, had a plantation sector of 5,000 slaves. The district of Segu, which was al-Hajj 'Umar's capital, had a population 53 per cent slave in 1894, which indicates that there were about 70,000 slaves in the Segu area.[18] Taken together, the slave population of the middle Niger Valley must have been well over 100,000.

The area to the immediate north, particularly around Gumbu and Sokolo, was not as densely populated, but the ratio of slave to free was about the same. Sokolo had more slaves than free people in 1894;[19] there were at least 13,300 slaves in 1904. Gumbu had about the same proportion of slaves and free. The area as a whole had some 24,000 slaves, while in Gumbu itself, thirty families owned 1,700 slaves between them. Some holdings were as large as 100 to 200, but there were many small holdings of 10 slaves or less.[20]

In 1818, Sheku Ahmadu and his supporters – many of whom were Fulbe – defeated the Bambara war-lords of the interior Niger delta and established an Islamic state, with its capital at Hamdullahi. The state lasted until 1862, when al-Hajj 'Umar destroyed Hamdullahi and incorporated much of Masina into Segu Tukulor, although a smaller successor state was founded to the east of Hamdullahi at Bandiagara. Masina controlled much of the interior delta as far north as Timbuktu and south to Jenne. The economic development of the state relied on the exploitation of slave labour, based on farming state lands, and the taxation of peasants, who were forced to work on fields set aside by the government. Slaves had varying obligations, depending upon the productivity of their location and the owner. Sometimes masters took a quantity of grain equivalent to a man's annual subsistence. Occasionally, slaves were expected to pay twice the subsistence amount. Usually slaves worked five days on the master's land and two days on land set aside for their own use. The output of those slaves who worked for the state went directly into the state treasury; private slaves were taxed indirectly through levies on their masters in lieu of military service and communal taxes. While the government was the largest owner of slaves, merchants still had a substantial number. In the Timbuktu area, particularly in the most northerly part of the delta, slave communities already existed before Ahmadu's *jihad*. Timbuktu slave owners depended upon these communities for part of their grain supplies, since Timbuktu itself was not able to support much agricultural production. At Jenne, to the south, there were also many slaves, if the 1904 estimates of slave populations are any indication. In 1904 there were 15,000 to 16,000 slaves in the Jenne area. The prosperity of Masina ended with its incorporation into Segu Tukulor, and many of the slaves fled or were seized for resettlement elsewhere. Bandiagara systematically devastated the western delta, thereby reducing the population further.[21]

An equally spectacular increase in the number of slaves took place further south, precisely in that region where there had been relatively few concentrations of slaves in the early nineteenth century. A number of Juula reformers in Wasulu, Konyan, Toron, Worodugu, and other areas in the upper Niger valley attempted to seize power. This Juula revolution culminated in the creation of the Samorian state in the 1870s and 1880s. In each case enslavement, slave trading, and the settlement of slaves for productive uses were essential policies of the Juula revolutionaries. Pre-existing towns and Muslim communities were generally absorbed into this movement for political consolidation, so that established centres of plantation agriculture expanded too.

Among those existing Muslim towns that survived the Juula revolution was Kankan, located inland from Futa Jallon and associated with the kola trade between the forest and northern savanna. The fertile plain around the town (population: 6,000 in 1820) was the location of slave settlements: 'In every direction there are small villages, or ourondes [*runde*], for the slaves. These villages are ornaments to the country, for they are surrounded by fine plantations, where yams, maize, rice, foigne [fonio], onions, pistachio-nuts [peanuts], and gombo are grown in abundance.'[22] The masters generally lived in Kankan, travelling to their plantations in order to supervise the work. Planters obtained their slaves in Kissi country in the south, in exchange for gunpowder, muskets, and textiles. The Kankan planters not only provisioned the caravan traffic in kola and other goods, they also sold some produce to the gold fields of Buré to the north – where slaves worked the gold, as they had for centuries.[23] Caillié was of the opinion that a man 'who possesses a dozen slaves may live at his ease without travelling, merely by taking the trouble to superintend them'.[24] The continued importance of Kankan as a commercial centre demonstrates that many slave holders in Kankan did more than merely manage their slaves; as late as 1904, the French still found a large slave population in the region, and in Kankan itself there were 6,000 slaves and 4,500 free men, or 57 per cent slave.[25] Unfortunately, there is no estimate of the size of the plantation sector around Kankan, although it must have included tens of thousands of slaves. Kankan was eventually absorbed into the Samorian state.

One of the more successful of the early reformers was Vakaba Toure, who was a craftsman by origin. In 1848, his armed following established the small state of Kabadugu, with its capital at Odienne, in north-western Ivory Coast. By the time Vakaba died in 1858, slavery had become the central pillar of Kabadugu society. Slaves lived in villages of their own or at temporary camps on the plantations of the aristocracy. Estimates from 1898 indicate that free men inhabited only eight of the 104 villages in the state; slaves numbered 12,000 in a total population of 19,000. The king alone reportedly owned 4,500 slaves, scattered in 34 villages owned exclusively by the royal family and another 26 villages in which other proprietors also had slaves.[26]

In the 1860s, the Juula revolution found a strong leader in Samori, whose wars soon engulfed Konyan and Wasulu.[27] By 1874, Samori controlled a large area south of Kankan, and by 1879 he dominated the whole of the upper Niger basin. Two years later, Kabadugu and Kankan were incorporated. The Samorian state now bordered Futa Jallon in the west and Segu Tukulor in the north. The Samorian economy relied on the proceeds from the sale of slaves north, which financed the importation of horses and other goods, while contacts with the coast enabled the purchase of firearms. Samori's armies enslaved so many people that it was possible to finance this foreign trade and also settle slaves on plantations. The slave populations of Kankan and Kabadugu were supplemented, and new centres of production were established. The most important was near Bissandugu, located south of Kankan, which became Samori's capital.[28] Because Samori came into conflict with the French in the 1880s, he was forced to evacuate the Bissandugu region, and consequently the plantation sector was dismantled and it was not possible to reassemble it in its entirety in the lands Samori conquered further east. None the less, it is clear that Samori tried to establish an economic base for his state that relied on slave labour. Political conditions made him rely on enslavement and the sale of slaves to an extent that maintained slave supplies for much of West Africa into the 1890s.

Sikasso and Kong, two rivals of the Samorian state, were also centres of slavery. Sikasso successfully maintained its independence, and under the dynamic leadership of Tièba, expanded its slave holdings. When the French examined Sikasso in 1904, they found that two-thirds of the population was slave, which indicates that plantations were as common there as elsewhere.[29] Kong was not as fortunate as Sikasso in maintaining its independence; during the eastward exodus, Samori levelled the town, just as al-Hajj 'Umar had had to destroy Sinsani because of local opposition. None the less, the remains of its slave economy were still evident in 1904. There were an estimated 180,000 slaves and 220,000 free men in the Kong region, or 45 per cent slave – for the region as a whole. In areas immediately around Kong and Bandama (the two main centres in the *cercle*), however, the percentage of slaves approached 80 per cent.[30]

In areas between Kong and the middle Niger valley – along the trade route

194

north from Asante to Jenne and Timbuktu – the same pattern of slavery prevailed, although this area was not consolidated into a state during the nineteenth century. At Bobo-Julasso, slaves formed two-thirds of the population,[31] while Wa, Buna and other towns had large numbers of slaves too. Information is most complete on Buna, a town that had 10,000 people in 1889. There were about 100 slave settlements (*djoso*) around Buna, all within a radius of 10–30 km from the town. The largest had populations ranging from 200 to 300 people, each under the management of a trusted slave or relative of the owner. The town, divided into different wards for the aristocracy, merchants, and indigenous commoners, had between 3,500 and 4,500 slaves; 2,000 of these slaves belonged to the aristocracy, while the merchants owned most of the others.[32] Although the total population of the plantation sector is not known, Holden has been able to estimate that 60 of the plantations in the area had a combined population of 2,700 an average of 45 per estate.[33] In his sample, plantations ranged in size from 20 to 100 slaves, which are smaller than the estates reported by Boutillier. It may well be that the total slave population in the Buna area approached 10,000. Besides their employment in agriculture, the slaves of Buna were also used in the production of gold.

THE CENTRAL SUDAN

The region between the middle Niger valley and the Lake Chad basin had many similarities with the area further west. Muslim holy war was again the dynamic political force, in this case the *jihad* led by Usuman dan Fodio and his family. There were many towns in the vast territory from Timbuktu in the west to the Cameroon highlands in the east. These towns usually had populations of only a few thousand, but a few were much larger. The heaviest concentration of these towns was in the Hausa country and included Sokoto, Gwandu, Birnin Kebbi, Katsina, Kano, Zaria, and many more – at least several hundred by the middle of the nineteenth century. Elsewhere, towns were more scattered, but an extensive network of trade routes connected them, so that there was a string of towns radiating outward from the centre of the caliphate and from secondary pockets of political and economic concentration elsewhere.

Heinrich Barth, the learned classical scholar and Arabist, spent several years in the Sokoto Caliphate in the early 1850s. During this time he learned several local languages, including Hausa, the principal tongue of the empire, and acquired a knowledge of local history, economy, and society that was unsurpassed by contemporary European observers of Africa. His observations tended to be conservative, and even his mild anti-slavery sentiments were subdued in his broader effort to portray African, Islamic civilization in a favourable light. Nevertheless, he estimated the percentage of slaves in the population of Kano, the largest and most prosperous province in the Sokoto Caliphate, as at least 50 per cent.[34] In other parts of the caliphate, similar proportions of slave to free were often found, and, as was the case in Kano, many of these slaves were located on plantations. Thus the Emir of Yola, a provincial capital to the south-east of Kano, had 'all his slaves settled in rumde or slave villages, where they cultivate grain for his use or profit.'[35] At Ngaundere, a district capital under Yola, population estimates taken during the colonial period still revealed this basic pattern of slave concentration. At Ngaundere itself, there were 6,400 free Fulbe and 6,700 slaves, while in the district as a whole there were 16,450 free Fulbe, 20,000 slaves, and 14,300 independent, free peasants.[36] These three cases, Kano, Yola, and Ngaundere, are taken here as examples of the dozens of provinces and districts in the Sokoto Caliphate where high concentrations of slaves were found. The figures from the 1850s and from the twentieth century demonstrate the scale of slavery and the persistence of servile traits that have made possible the reconstruction of the development of this slave society.

Some *jihad* leaders envisioned an economy based on commercial expansion, and commerce depended upon agricultural and craft production.[37] The aristocracy looked to the merchant class for entrepreneurial skills; therefore, the merchants were protected in their movements. They pushed south-eastward into and then beyond the Cameroon highlands; their operations to Asante and the Yoruba states increased in volume. Caliphate textiles and leather goods were exported over a wide area, while the importation of salt from the Sahara and neighbouring Borno brought areas that were nominally independent under the economic hegemony of the Caliphate. Under the policies of the Caliphate government, Hausa society became associated with the mercantile and craft community, which was identified as free and commoner. Even in those parts of the caliphate away from Hausaland, Hausa settlers dominated these occupations. Hausa commerce had been important before the nineteenth century, but supported by political consolidation, Hausa merchants became more numerous in much of the region bounded by the Benue River valley, the middle and Upper Volta region, and the Lake Chad basin.

Slaves provided much of the labour for the new Fulbe ruling class and the Hausa merchants and craftsmen.[38] Aristocrats employed slaves as messengers, retainers, and domestic servants, often in greater numbers than necessary. Male slaves were also drafted into the army, while females filled the harems of the wealthiest officials. Because palace establishments were often very large, many women were also needed to prepare and cook food. Merchants relied on slave agents, stock boys, and common labourers. Long and arduous caravan journeys required lots of work. At each caravan stop, animals had to be unloaded, fed, and watered; meals had to be cooked; and camp had to be prepared for the night. Slaves did these jobs in most cases. In town, merchants needed agents to sit in the market or hawk in the streets and countryside, and water, firewood, and fodder had to be carried. Although slaves also performed menial tasks for other craftsmen, slavery was particularly important in textile production. As in the western Sudan, female slaves carded and spun cotton, while male slaves wove. Slaves either worked for their masters or on their own account, often paying a weekly fee to their masters instead. Hence the craftsmen – including tailors, dyers, cloth beaters – owned relatively few slaves who were employed in textile production. Since there were approximately 50,000 dyers occupied at some 15,000 dye pits in the Kano area alone at the end of the nineteenth century, a large proportion of the slave population had to be engaged in spinning and weaving to supply this industry.[39]

Despite the use of slaves in aristocratic households, merchant firms, and craft production, the most important contribution of slaves was in agriculture. Millet, sorghum, indigo, and cotton were the main crops grown on lands watered by the annual rains; onions, tobacco, indigo, and vegetables were cultivated on irrigated plots during the dry season. As was the case in the western Sudan, plantations were common, although wealthy farmers owned slaves in small numbers too. Polly Hill is probably correct in stating that most slave owners in the central parts of the caliphate were small holders.[40] None the less, most agricultural slaves were almost certainly on the large estates of the aristocracy and merchant class.

The growth of the plantation sector occurred in two stages that corresponded with similar developments further west. In the first half of the century, most plantation development occurred in the northern parts of the savanna – near the core cities of Kano, Katsina, Sokoto, Gwandu, and Zaria. This phase corresponded to the growth of plantations near the established commercial centres of the western Sudan, which were located along the middle Niger valley, Futa Jallon, and in the Senegambia region. In the second half of the century, the areas of plantation development spread to the Benue River valley (Yola) and neighbouring areas near the confluence of the Niger and Benue (Nupe and Ilorin), although new plantations continued to be established in the core area, which gradually expanded outward, during this second phase too. This consolidation of a plantation sector in the southern parts of the savanna was similar to the expansion of the plantation system into the area of Samori, Odienne, and Kabadugu. Some emirates were exceptions to this general southern extension of plantations. Bauchí (south-east of Kano) developed earlier than Yola and effectively became associated with metropolitan Hausaland, while Liptako (west of the Niger) was in the northern part of the savanna but as a frontier region developed after the core emirates.[41]

Sokoto and Gwandu, together with Wurno, Jega, and other towns, were established in the river valleys of western Hausaland in the heartlands of the old states of Kebbi and Gobir. The intensity of the fighting in this area resulted in the displacement of virtually the whole population. Many people were enslaved; many more slaves were accepted as tribute from other emirates in the caliphate. By the end of the nineteenth century, these valleys were densely inhabited, and slaves comprised the great majority of the population. In neighbouring Zamfara, the slave population was less because the indigenous inhabitants stayed. None the less, around Talata Mafara, Kaura Namoda, and other towns, plantations were also common. With its relatively high proportion of peasants, Zamfara remained the exception in the central caliphate.

Kano, Katsina, and Zaria – the other large emirates in the central caliphate – were also densely populated, and slaves formed upwards of 50 per cent of the population. Kano was surrounded by 40 walled towns within a radius of 50 km; most people in Katsina emirate lived in the city, in an area south-east of the city that bordered Kano emirate, or in extreme southern Katsina (west of Kano). The population of Zaria was largely confined to the city and numerous towns on the northern border with Kano emirate. There were plantations in all these areas.

The earliest developments occurred in the Hausa region that became the centre of the caliphate. The Muslim reformers assumed ownership of the land seized in the *jihad*, so that as the old governments were displaced the peasants found themselves tenants on the vast holdings of the victors. Furthermore, many people were enslaved during the initial *jihad* (1804–8) or in the rebellions that flared in Zamfara and elsewhere in 1817. Those who were slaves at the time of the *jihad* and did not flee to the camps of the Muslim reformers were re-enslaved, while the war with Borno and the revolts of sympathizers beyond Hausaland resulted in more slaves. By 1820, the ideological phase of the war was over; the established governments had been overthrown in the name of Islam, and the way was set for the consolidation of Islamic government. Thereafter, *jihad* was largely confined to slave raiding as a means of expanding the frontiers of the caliphate and amassing slave labour for settlement within the caliphate.[42]

The economic and social development of the caliphate is associated with the policies of Muhammad Bello, son of Usuman dan Fodio and leader of the pragmatic faction in the *jihad* leadership.[43] In contrast to Usuman's brother. Abdullahi, who shared power with Muhammad Bello through the creation of a dual caliphate, with centres at Gwandu and Sokoto, Muhammad Bello believed that only through the encouragement of trade and industry could the success of *jihad* be secured. While Abdullahi wanted to continue fighting at almost any cost, in the expectation that the purification of the world would be rewarded in heaven, Muhammad Bello sought to regularize caliphate government. This required compromises with the Fulani clan leaders, who were not always the most devout Muslims but who had formed the back-bone of the military. These clan leaders, together with truly religious leaders, became the landowners in whom Bello invested the future of the caliphate.

The scale of slave holdings in the central emirates can be assessed from the observations of Imam Imoru, the learned jurist and author whose knowledge of the Sokoto Caliphate, where he was born, and the Muslim centres along the trade routes to Asante, where he lived for many years, was extensive:

There are slave owners in Hausaland who have purchased 100 and 200 slaves, and there are some slave owners with 400 or 500 slaves. But in my lifetime, I have heard of only one person who was not an official, who had 1,000 slaves in Kano: his name was Kaushe ... In Hausaland, commoners buy slaves, but they are unable to buy 1,000 of them. Officials have more than 1,000 because they do not buy them: they seize them during war campaigns.[44]

Local tradition remembers Kaushe as the wealthiest merchant in Kano, but there were many others who had large holdings too – on the scale that Imoru claims.

The plantations of the aristocracy fell into three categories. Firstly, individuals had private holdings. Secondly, estates were attached to particular offices. Thirdly, aristocratic lineages owned estates collectively. M. G. Smith, in his analysis of the Zaria economy, identified 51 plantations (*rinji*) owned by the Zaria aristocracy around 1900.[45] These ranged in size from small estates, such as the forty slaves at Hanwa a few kilometres from Zaria, to the huge one at Taban Sani, with its population of 3,000.[46] The Emir of Kano had a number of plantations scattered throughout the countryside; the largest included estates at Nasarawa, just outside one of the city walls; at Fanisau, which also served as a country estate; and at Wudil, south-east of Kano. In Katsina, Tuareg and other merchants had plantations at Shibdawa, Doro, Ingawa, and other towns south-east of the city, while in the far southern part of the emirate enterprising merchants settled slaves to grow cotton and grain – the cotton being exported to southern Kano to supply the textile industry there; the grain entering desert-side trade.[47]

This plantation economy spread to the south within a few decades after the *jihad* was won in the central emirates. Bauchi was the first to benefit. The local Fulbe population already had dry-season camps, which were based around slave villages that grew foodstuffs for the nomadic population. Some of these became the model for the development of plantations that were not associated with the transhumance of the nomads. There were at least fourteen Fulani plantations in the Bauchi area before the *jihad* was won there; subsequently, slaves were settled around the emirate capital, and other towns that had their own plantations were founded or seized to the south, especially at Wase.[48] These developments marked the extension of the plantation system to the south. Bauchi itself became a Hausa town, so that the concentration of population in its vicinity represented a cultural extension of Hausaland.

The major developments in the southern parts of the caliphate took place in Yola (in the east), Nupe (due south of Hausaland), and Ilorin (in the heart of the old Oyo state). In these three locations, slave raiding and frontier warfare resulted in the massive concentration of slaves. Yola, located on the Benue River near the centre of several pagan Jukun states that had dominated the region since the sixteenth century at least, became the capital of the Emirate of Fombina (Adamawa), which geographically became the

Table 9.2 *Foundation dates of Nupe 'tungazi'*

District	1857–9	1859–73	1873–82	1882–95	1895–1901
Lemu	30	386	137	168	19
Jima	7	149	109	20	0
Kachia	4	35	136	7	2
Badeggi	0	60	71	47	1
Kutigi	8	52	20	66	35
Mokwa	6	12	1	3	0
TOTAL	55	694	474	311	57

Source: Mason 1973, p. 459.

largest emirate in the caliphate. The Fulbe in the Benue valley were able to unite against a diverse population. The allegiance to Sokoto provided the basis of cooperation for widely scattered Fulbe clans coalesced around the first Emir of Yola, Adamu, and successfully established a state. Yola was founded in the 1850s, and the Fulani forces swept the plains of the Benue valley clean of people, and then war captives were settled on plantations in the deserted savanna near Yola. Already by 1853, the Emir of Yola, Muhammad Lawal, had 'all his slaves settled in rumde or slave villages, where they cultivate grain for his use or profit.'[49] Chomyel Abba, Doulabi, Golomba, Langui, Wuro Dole, Kirngabu, Konkol, Pette, and Yolel were new plantation villages near Yola that were settled after 1850, while nearly all the villages in Namtari, Girei, and Gurin districts were also slave plantations. In this way, the Yola region once again was populated, but the terms of occupancy were based on slavery.[50]

In Nupe, a similar development occurred. The first capital of the *jihad* forces was at Raba, an important crossing-point for caravans on the Niger River. But Raba was destroyed in the civil war that was associated with *jihad* in Nupe. When the capital was shifted to Bida in 1857, the centre of political and economic development moved inland from the Niger valley to a more defensible position.[51] While there may well have been plantations in the Raba period, the growth of slave settlements (*tungazi*) was truly astonishing after 1857. Virtually the whole of Nupe was slave, with the major settlement of war captives taking place between 1859 and 1895 (see table 9.2). Many of these slave villages consisted of resettled Nupe prisoners, seized in the civil wars and forced to live under the new regime (see table 9.3). Because they were culturally part of Nupe society, the terms of slavery appear to have been different from those for slaves brought from elsewhere. Their terms of servitude involved tribute payments to particular aristocrats, which set these captives off from those slaves seized south of the Niger or bought from merchants coming from the north. None the less, even this variation in slavery is instructive. The *jihad* leadership interpreted its mandate in

Table 9.3 *Ethnic origins of settlers on 'tungazi'*

Ethnic group	1857–9	1859–73	1873–82	1882–95	1895–1901
Nupe[a]	40	496	310	200	38
Yoruba[b]	1	56	19	11	—
Afenmai	—	11	2	3	—
Igbirra	—	6	1	1	—
Gbari	1	11	9	8	1
Koro	—	—	1	—	—
Bassa	—	—	1	—	—
Kamberri	3	1	5	1	—
Hausa	4	20	11	6	—
Fulani	2	14	15	9	1
Unknown	—	79	—	—	17
TOTAL	51	694	374	239	57

[a] Includes Bini, Ebe, Gbedegi, Cekpa, Benu, Dibo, Agabi, Gwagba, and 'Mokwa'.
[b] Includes 'Yoruba', Yagba, Bunu, Akoko, and Igbomina.
Source: Mason 1973, p. 460.

terms of servitude. Subjugated people were expected to pay for their resistance; those who refused could be sold to travelling merchants.

The growth of the plantation sector in Nupe was a product of the policies of Emir Masaba (1859–73), who followed the example of Muhammad Bello and the northern emirs in using slaves for economic development. Foreign demand for slaves still existed during Masaba's reign, but he believed that slave labour could produce commodities in demand on the Niger River. European merchants had opened the Niger and Benue to direct trade with Europe by the late 1850s; sheabutter – wanted for its oil – and peanuts were the 'legitimate' goods exported from Nupe. Between 1864 and 1879, sheabutter exports rose from less than 7 tons to almost 1,500 tons, and by the first decade of the twentieth century the volume exceeded 8,000 tons. Peanuts became important more slowly; by the first decade of the twentieth century, exports varied between 500 and 2,000 tons per year; in the previous two decades, peanut sales were nowhere near as important as in the Senegambia region.[52]

The importance of slavery in the Ilorin area is more difficult to assess, but the trend there appears to have been similar to the pattern in Nupe and Yola. Ilorin emerged triumphant in the 1830s. The old city of Oyo was destroyed, and the massive flight of Oyo refugees that had begun a decade and more earlier left the area to the west of Ilorin deserted. Ilorin pursued the *jihad* against the Yoruba states in the south, and captives were settled around Ilorin in order to repopulate the northern Yoruba country. Ilorin was the centre of a thriving slave trade until the last decade of the nineteenth century; slaves were brought from further north, and Yoruba merchants from the south who were granted immunity from the continuing hostilities came to Ilorin to buy slaves.[53] Although the development of a plantation economy around Ilorin was not as pronounced as in Nupe and Yola, there was no other means by which the population of Ilorin could have been promoted.

THE REGION EAST OF LAKE CHAD

The agents of Islamic reform came later to the region east of Lake Chad. The dominant influence there was external – the Turkish regime in Egypt – and *jihad* became a significant factor only in the 1880s when local reaction against Egyptian colonialism coalesced in the Nilotic Sudan under the Mahdi. None the less, the trend toward greater concentration of slaves and their use in production was similar to the pattern in the western and central Sudan, and the division between a northern phase – roughly before mid-century – and a southern expansion of slavery – in the second half of the century – was also similar. The initial expansion in productive slavery was centred in Wadai, Dar Fur, and the Nile valley above Sennar, but as slave raiding, ivory hunting, and political consolidation spread southward, slavery became more prevalent there too.

In the first two decades of the nineteenth century, Wadai, Dar Fur, and the Funj Sultanate of Sennar were the centres of slavery. The concentrations of slaves in Dar Fur and Sennar had already been assembled in the eighteenth century. As late as 1825, the sultan's garrison villages around Sennar – inhabited by slaves since the seventeenth century – had an estimated population of 30,000 while other aristocrats owned thousands of other slaves.[54] In Dar Fur, the policy of settling slaves on Jabal Marra and elsewhere, which had been pursued by the sultans of the eighteenth century, continued. The influx of merchants from the Nile and the seizure of Kordofan from Sennar accelerated the accumulation of slaves.[55] Wadai began a period of expansion in the first decade of the nineteenth century that resulted in the acquisition of slaves too. Benefiting from the war between Borno and the Sokoto Caliphate, the Wadai army marched on Bagirmi, which had been a dependency of Borno. This initiated a general push towards the south, which allowed the Wadai state to export slaves and other goods across the Sahara via a new trade-route opened in the nineteenth century. Under the reign of Muhammad Ali (1858–74), 12,000 to 15,000 people from Bagirmi were brought to Abeche, the Wadai capital. Many of these people were slaves already, but even those who technically were free men suffered. The Wadai sultan also had slave settlements scattered throughout ten districts of the country.[56]

The major changes occurred along the Nile valley after the Turko-Egyptian conquest of Sennar in 1820. While slaves were already numerous around Sennar, there were few slaves to the north of the Nile confluence. In the Shaiqiya country, for example, there were hardly any slaves, in sharp contrast to the capital. At the time of the Egyptian conquest, there were only

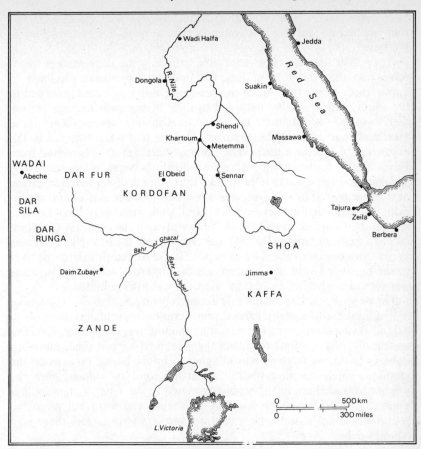

6 The Eastern Sudan in the nineteenth century

4,500 slaves between Wadi Halfa and the Fourth Cataract, amounting to approximately 4 per cent of the population. By the end of the nineteenth century, slaves constituted a third of the population.[57]

The injection of vast numbers of slaves into the riverine districts was a consequence of Egyptian policies. In the quest for slave recruits for the Egyptian army from 1820 to 1840, new captives became so numerous that the domestic market was flooded. Egyptian soldiers were often paid in slaves, who were then sold, while occasionally military expeditions were so successful that it was impossible to export all the captives. The Egyptian government also accepted slaves as payment for taxes, although eventually coin largely replaced slaves in this capacity. Sometimes, government forces simply commandeered slaves when it was necessary to fill export quotas. All of these measures assured the increased circulation of slaves within

Sudanese society, so that an institution that had once been controlled by the Funj aristocracy now became common among merchants and small land-holders.[58]

After 1840, the Sudanese were able to supply the slave market themselves, so that the role of Egyptian military expeditions declined in importance. At the time of the conquest, the indigenous merchants fled to the south, and while they returned to their homes once the new regime demonstrated its intention to promote economic development, these merchants had consolidated commercial links that were essential in the expansion of the slave trade. The existing merchant class benefited from Egyptian rule to the extent that many individuals began to buy land along the river and settle slaves to farm. The introduction of improved irrigation devices, imported from Egypt, was associated with this agricultural expansion. Because irrigation devices were taxed, landowners were encouraged to exploit their land intensively, and the low price of slaves meant that slave labour expanded rapidly. By 1845, the region along the Blue Nile had come under extensive cultivation, for example. Dry-season cultivation of the river banks expanded with the construction of numerous water-wheels, while wet-season cultivation away from the river was also extended.[59]

The new landowners did not rely exclusively on slave labour; a system of agricultural credit already existed that permitted speculators in grain to extend their control over the peasant communities. Known as *sheil*, this system allowed creditors to collect their debts at harvest time, but often debtors could not pay and had to agree to future labour services on the creditor's land. Another traditional labour contract, *teddan*, gave the worker a fixed share of the crop, negotiated at the time of planting, but gradually contract workers lost out to slaves, who were not given the traditional compensation. Now contract workers were largely those who were in debt.

The consolidation of land holdings and the importation of slaves pushed many peasants off the land, particularly Danaqla, Shaiqiya, and Ja'aliyin peasants, who went south as merchants. They travelled throughout the Jellaba commercial network and returned north only if they acquired slaves and could purchase or reclaim land. These migrants usually left their women and children behind, in part because they could not afford to take them, considering the expense and risks involved in long-distance travel, and in part because the presence of women in the riverain communities protected the interests of their husbands and fathers in local land-claims.

Slaves were also enrolled in the private armies of the merchant-adventurers who benefited most from Egyptian occupation, with its concern to acquire slaves for export to Egypt. Perhaps the most successful of these Jellaba was one Jali merchant, the famous Al-Zubayr, who settled in the Bahr el Ghazal in 1856 with an army of one thousand troops. His son, Sulaiman, had even more soldiers, an estimated 6,400 stationed at thirty-one *zeribas* in 1878.

Slaves were involved in agricultural production, both along the Nile River and in the *zeriba* country to the south and west. Al-Zubayr's centre at Daym Zubayr was surrounded by hundreds of farms and plantations. His ability to send thousands of slaves north through Kordofan depended upon this agricultural production, as well as his commercial contacts with the Rizeiqat Arab nomads and the Zande principalities. Sulaiman consolidated this productive and commercial system further. At one centre alone, he stationed a force of 1,500 soldiers, who maintained control over a subject population of 11,000 farmers. This *zeriba* system stretched to Dar al-Kuti in the west and into Zande country to the south-west.[60]

In the 1880s, the foreign occupation of the Nilotic Sudan temporarily ended, but slavery continued to play an important role in the local economy. Indeed, the Mahdist state relied as heavily on slave labour as other reform governments across the savanna. The major change under the Mahdist state was the collapse of the export trade in slaves – effectively eliminated because of the British and Egyptian blockade. The termination of the trade meant, however, that slaves were now directed exclusively into the local economy. Even if the number of new captives decreased, and it seems likely that organized enslavement was on a smaller scale for military reasons, the incidence of slavery in the Nilotic Sudan did not fall off.[61]

Furthermore, the states and armies of the *zeriba* system, many of which pledged their loyalty to the Mahdi, continued to operate, even though they could not export slaves and ivory as efficiently as had been possible under Turkish–Egyptian rule. Trade continued north through Wadai and Dar Fur, which allowed the importation of firearms necessary to maintain military supremacy. The result was a series of wars in the south. These culminated in the career of Rabeh Fadlallah, a disciple of the Mahdi, who swept across the area south of Wadai, seizing Bagirmi in the late 1880s and Borno in 1893. Rabeh too relied on slaves, but he never consolidated his rule sufficiently to establish a viable plantation economy.[62]

The Ethiopian highlands participated in the general expansion in the incidence of slavery. The proximity of the area to the markets of Arabia and Egypt encouraged the continuation of the slave trade; the commercial domination of Muslim merchants meant that developments in the creation of a slave economy were similar to those that took place in the northern savanna, although *jihad* only affected the Somali coast in the last decade of the century and hence was not an important factor in most of the area.

The proportion of slaves in the general population of Christian Ethiopia and the various Galla and Muslim principalities was very high throughout the nineteenth century. In the province of Shoa in the 1840s, for example, 'from the governor to the humblest peasant every house possesses slaves of both sexes, in proportion to the wealth of the proprietor.'[63] The same was true in Jimma and Kaffa, two of the southern principalities, where at least half the population was slave. In 1897, it was reported that the slave population of Kaffa numbered 80,000.[64] The most substantial holdings were those of the aristocracy, whether Christian or Muslim, with some officials reportedly possessing several thousand slaves.

These estimates, as scattered and rough as they are, help to establish that slavery had been transformed in the northern savanna and at least in parts of the Ethiopian region. Slavery had become essential to production. Despite the ties to the outside world through the export of some 'legitimate' commodities, this transformation was essentially an internal development. Productive slavery was already an established feature of Muslim savanna society, but in the nineteenth century it expanded to an unprecedented level. Other forms of slavery, including the use of slaves in the military, government administration, and harems, continued too. None the less, the exploitation of slave labour in production was the characteristic feature of the era.

THE ORGANIZATION OF THE PLANTATION SECTOR

The organization of the plantation sector included a variety of work regimes and management strategies. In some cases, slaves worked in a regimented fashion on the fields of the master under an overseer who was either slave or free. Plantation crops were the same throughout the savanna, there being more variations with latitude than between regions across the savanna. Cotton, indigo, tobacco, sorghum, bulrush millet, pepper, and vegetables were staple crops almost everywhere. Slaves usually had their own fields, too, which they worked during their spare time. In other cases, slaves lived in their own villages and were subject to fixed payments; in these less regimented arrangements, slaves sometimes worked a central field together but often farmed their own fields separately. Slave masters usually could extract more labour from slaves when tight management was maintained, but sometimes it was in the interest of the master to allow greater autonomy, especially over slaves born into captivity. Often labour obligations changed as slaves were assimilated, so that individual estates and villages could combine a number of work regimes.[65]

On most plantations in the Islamic states, slaves lived in their own quarters, working for their masters five or six days each week and occasionally even more.[66] Usually, they were in the master's field from sunrise until 2.00 p.m., these times coinciding with two of the five regular prayers said during the day by Muslims, as Hugh Clapperton, the British envoy to the Sokoto Caliphate in 1824, observed at Magaria, near Sokoto, where some Caliphate nobles had their estates:

> When the time for cultivating the ground and sowing the seed comes on, the owner points out what he requires, and what is to be sown on it. The slave is then allowed to enclose a part for himself and family. The hours of labor, for his master, are from daylight until mid-day [2 p.m.]; the remainder of the day is employed on his own, or in any other way he may think proper. At the time of

206

harvest, when they cut and tie up the grain, each slave gets a bundle of the different sorts of grain, about a bushel of our measure, for himself. The grain on his own ground is entirely left for his own use, and he may dispose of it as he thinks proper.[67]

Usually after the 4.00 p.m. prayer, slaves worked their own gardens, unless there were special assignments on the master's land. Clapperton's observations confirm the essential features of plantation organization. The main field belonged to the master, with separate gardens for the use of slave families. Some of the provisioning was the responsibility of the master, including the bundle of grain from the main field, and almost certainly the mid-day meal that broke the day's labour. Slaves were expected to feed themselves except during the time when they were actually employed on the master's behalf. Masters normally provided one item of clothing per year for each slave and a spouse for young people born into slavery, as well as those first-generation slaves who had proved themselves. In all cases, slave children belonged to their mother's master, and he could assign them tasks that would remove them from their parents. In most communities, the sale of slave children was rare. Public opinion was strongly against sale of those born into slavery. Legally, masters still had the right to sale, but it was usually exercised only in cases related to the settlement of a debt, inheritance decisions in which the master's family could not divide the slaves evenly among children, or bad behaviour on the part of individual slaves.

During the rainy season the principal labour was field work. The slaves often worked in gangs under an overseer who was usually a slave himself. Failure to work hard enough or other insubordination was punished severely, often by whipping, being tied up in the sun, or being placed in irons. Ultimately, difficult slaves were sold. During the dry season, there were many other activities, including house building and repair. Houses were made from mud-bricks, which deteriorated in the rains. Roofs, too, had to be patched or made anew. Slaves also made mats and baskets, corn-stalk beds, transported manure to the fields, and loaded animals for caravan trading. Sometimes slaves were assigned petty trading on their master's account, and many slaves, perhaps most, were involved in textile production. Female slaves spun thread, and male slaves wove. In all these activities, slaves often had time to pursue a craft or trade on their own, and some of the cloth or thread they produced could be sold for their own profit. Occasionally, masters allowed slaves even more time to work for themselves, in exchange for a cash payment in cowries or other currency. Slaves who were able to save money could apply to purchase their freedom. But there were many obstacles to emancipation, including the difficulty of buying the freedom of spouses and children and the hardships of old age, when the master would no longer be responsible. Even when slaves did secure their freedom, they often remained close to the former master's household, becoming a client of the master instead of a slave. As a consequence, some slaves – at least in Malinke society – chose to buy slaves of their own rather than to purchase their own freedom.[68] Technically, the slave of a slave still belonged to the master, but custom allowed the slave to benefit from his own property.

Throughout the savanna where slave plantations were important, agricultural produce was distributed both locally and over considerable distances. The local economy depended upon the movement of goods because harvests could vary from year to year. The general pattern involved the transport of grain northward towards the desert, where local conditions could be extremely good in a particular year but where there was a predictable demand for grain among the desert nomads, trans-Saharan merchants, and farmers whose crops had failed. When local harvests in areas near the desert were very good, grain could be sent south or north, but these supplies could not be counted on every year. Consequently, many plantation owners along the southern edge of the Sahara settled slaves at several locations over a wide area. This provided some insurance against local crop failure, and it also permitted herds of livestock to be moved from one location to another, grazing on the stubble fields after harvest and in the process manuring the land for the next planting season. Often desert nomads had plantations far to the south, located on the routes to savanna markets where livestock, desert salt, dates, and trans-Saharan imports were sold and where textiles, leather goods, and grain could be purchased most cheaply. The nomads grazed their herds near these plantations while they traded. The presence of these herds in the savanna economy was a source of cheap transport. Camels, oxen, and donkeys were available to move farm produce, particularly grain and cotton, within the savanna.

In the central emirates of the Sokoto Caliphate, for example, cotton and grain were transported into the heavily populated textile belt of Kano and Zaria, which also produced cotton and grain, but not enough to supply the local market. The textile industry supplied much of West Africa, although there were many other textile centres elsewhere that were not as big. The Maraka towns of Sinsani, Nyamina, and Banamba also were important, and the pattern was not so different there, despite the reduced scale of production. The spinning and weaving of cloth, largely done by slave women and men respectively, had to be organized over an extensive area in order to supply the dyeing centres. In the Sokoto Caliphate, raw cotton was sometimes moved several hundred kilometres to places where it was spun and woven, and the cloth was then transported another hundred kilometres or more to the dyeing centres. The finished cloth was then exported widely.[69]

The crops grown on the savanna plantations included millet, sorghum, cotton, indigo, cow peas, peanuts, and tobacco. The staples were grown during the rainy season on land that was sown shortly after the first rains, either in May or June, depending upon the year and the latitude. Other crops were planted on low-lying land or along river beds and relied on irrigation. These fields were often quite small, no more than gardens, but their output was significant because these lands were the source of wheat, cassava, tobacco, indigo, onions, peppers, and many vegetables and condiments. The irrigated plots often produced well into the dry season. Because of the different harvest-times for grain, cotton, and irrigated produce, there was work for most of the year. The initial planting of grain was a peak period, since the labour of breaking the barren ground, even when some moisture had returned with the rains, was very heavy. Ridges and occasionally mounds were constructed on which the millet and sorghum were planted. These protected the shoots from being washed away during the torrential storms that characterized the rainy season and also retained water around the roots, despite the heavy run-off after each shower. Subsequently, there were two or more weedings, at which time the ridges and mounds were reconstructed. The work on both irrigated gardens and the grain and cotton fields was done with a small, short-handled hoe. Irrigation was most frequently done with the *shadduf*, which in its most simple design included a container, usually a calabash or gourd, hanging by a rope on a pole that could be lowered to a water source, either a pond or pits hollowed out of a dry river-bed. If necessary, water was also carried to the irrigated plots.

Treatment of slaves could be severe. The account of an escaped slave seized at Keffi, one of the towns near the confluence of the Niger and Benue rivers, demonstrates this. At the orders of the town's official the slave was stripped of the clothes he had stolen and 'sent to work in his plantations'. The slave, depressed at his inability to carry off his escape, proved to be a poor field hand: 'And thus, when I failed to do good work, I got many a flogging from the overseer of the governor's plantation; and one day it was said to me that as I was a worthless slave I should be sold in the market.'[70] In cases of continued disobedience, such as the one reported here, slaves were sold and taken elsewhere. Since slaves knew well the risks involved in travel, they often feared this form of punishment above all others.

When the French administrator for Bamako investigated plantation slavery in the early years of the French occupation, he found that:

> slaves are poorly fed, mistreated, and poorly clothed. Masters rarely give them their two days free (which is theirs) by custom. They prefer to feed them poorly and to be assured all their labour all the time ... Moko Tala, a slave of Touba, belongs to a master who 'generously' gives three *moules* of millet [about six kilograms] for the rations of twenty-five slaves. The *services administratifs* estimated that a daily ration is one kilogram per person per day. Another slave called Hinebahlafe Konati, also of Touba, told us that the twenty slaves of his master were given four kilograms per day.[71]

Certainly conditions varied over the century and in different places, but whether or not slaves were treated as badly as those interviewed by Brevié, plantation slaves were involved in productive activities that demonstrate a type of slave regime that was far different from the stereotype of a benign African slavery.

209

SLAVERY IN THE SAHEL

The sahel and southern Sahara was a region of specialized production and trade that relied extensively on slave labour. For ecological reasons, the inhabitants of this region had to be mobile; even farming populations were usually involved in trade for part of their livelihood, and when rains failed or were inadequate people had to move elsewhere, at least temporarily. Population tended to concentrate around oases or valleys that had relatively easy access to water, and in these locations agriculture could be very productive. Millet especially grew well, so that farmers usually found themselves with a surplus to trade, unless the farmers were servile and were expected to provide substantial amounts of grain to their masters. Other farmers hunted ostrichs, collected gum arabic, raised livestock, or produced salt, which tied them into the commercial economy yet again. Indeed, in the nineteenth century, demand increased for commodities, either as exports to Europe (gum arabic, hides and skins, ostrich feathers) or as exports to the savanna (salt, livestock, grain). For those individuals who could control producers, either through slavery or other means, the nineteenth century was a period of relative prosperity.

The Moors, who lived to the north of the Senegal River, employed slaves in virtually every economic activity. Slaves cultivated millet in the flood plains of the retreating rivers and streams; they gathered gum arabic, the main export to Europe; they fetched water for livestock; they dug wells; and they gathered dung and wood for cooking. Caillié observed the collection of gum arabic in 1821, which was organized in gangs under the supervision of several *marabouts*, or free Muslims. A central camp was situated at the site of a well, where:

> the slaves cut straw to make huts; a single marabout superintends the slaves of his whole family, or of several of his friends; and he assembles them all, sometimes to the number of forty or fifty under the same hut. Every marabout sends as many slaves as he can spare ... The slaves fill their leather bags with water every morning, and furnished with a great forked stick, they traverse the fields in search of gum; as the gum-bearing trees are all thorny, this stick is used to knock off from the higher branches the lumps of gum which could not be reached by hand. As they pick it up they put it in their leather bags; and thus they spend the day, without any thing but a little water to refresh them ... The superintending marabout receives a proportion of the gum; the slaves work five days for their master, and the sixth for the superintendent, who thus comes in for the greater part of the produce.[72]

The export of gum was as important as the export of slaves by 1800; the volume of the trade continued to expand, reaching record levels in the 1830s, 1840s, and 1850s.

Elsewhere along the southern edge of the desert, nomadic merchants and stock breeders also owned large numbers of slaves acquired in raids and through trade with the savanna. Slaves performed virtually all of the hard labour, including well construction and the watering of animals, the collection of manure and brush for fires, and the minding of herds of goats, sheep, and other animals. They loaded and unloaded the camels, prepared food, and waited on their masters. The servile farming population provided resting places for the nomads during livestock movements and caravan expeditions. The nomads themselves were engaged in livestock production and trade, which were closely integrated activities because herds had to be moved in order to obtain water and pasture. This necessity was turned to advantage for the purposes of trade. Camels and oxen could be loaded with salt and dates in the desert and driven south, where the animals could be pastured and the salt and dates sold. Grain, textiles, and other goods could then be taken back north into the desert, and while the livestock were in the savanna they could be used to transport local produce. Slave estates were vital staging points for integrating commercial activities that involved importing salt and dates, purchasing grain and textiles, and selling transport services locally. In addition, the desert nomads made their animals available to the trans-Saharan trade and were directly interested in slave exports and 'legitimate' trade.[73]

The Tichit Moors dominated the salt trade from Ijil to Sinsani, Banamba, and other Maraka towns. One particularly important family, Haidara, operated salt caravans from Ijil through Banamba. Mulay al-Mahdi Haidara, for example, was a Sharif from the Oued Noun who traded throughout the Hodh in the 1850s. He then settled in Tichit and concentrated on wholesale trading; his sons became his agents in the towns to the south. Slaves were settled at Banamba to farm and conduct business for the family. These slaves took caravans to Ijil and Tichit to collect salt, which was later sold wholesale to Juula merchants. The Haidara salt caravans travelled to all the major centres: Gumbu, Nara, Nioro, Balle, Tichit, Nema, Walata, and Segala-Sokolo.[74]

The desert-side trade periodically threw off migrants as a result of drought, localized hardship, or business opportunities. In the 1890s, for example, an emigration of 3,000 people, many of whom had been slaves, left the Tichit and other parts of the sahel because of a bad drought in 1889. Many of these ex-slaves, the Maxanbinnu, settled at Nioro, Murja, Sanamba, Tienbugu, Kita, and Banamba and became agents in the trade between the desert and savanna. They had received their freedom in Tichit when drought conditions became severe. Some of these migrants became prosperous merchants and cultivators, such as the Sibi family, which was of Soninke origin. Some members of the family settled at Nema, where they acquired date-palm groves worked by slaves. Other kin moved to Banamba in the early 1890s, where they conducted a trade in salt, peanuts, grain, cloth, and hides and skins. The Banamba residents, too, employed slaves, including some who farmed.[75]

The principal groups of Tuareg along the southern edge of the Sahara were the Kel Air (comprised of the Kel Ewey, Kel Tamat, Kel Fady, and Kel

Ferwan), the Kel Tademekket and Tingeregif (in the region of Timbuktu), and the Iwllammedan (including the Kel Attaram in the west and the Kel Dinnik in the east). There were other Tuareg centred in the Sahara, (Kel Ajjer, Kel Ahaggar, and Kel Adragh or Ifogha) but they were less numerous than those operating in the sahel. Among those southern Tuareg, 70 to 90 per cent of the population was servile, and many of these servile people were slaves (*iklan*), or freed slaves.[76]

There were three principal corridors of trade and production in the central Sudan; one dominated by the Kel Ewey, another by the Kel Gress, and a third by the Kel Dinnik. A class of aristocrats (*imajeren*) had nearly exclusive control of wealth and power that was accumulated through the domination of the different strata in the social formation. The *imajeren*, who constituted about 10 per cent of the Tuareg population, acted as if they were managers of large firms. They alone decided on war and peace; from their ranks came the political leaders; and they were the main patrons of the Muslim clerics. The use of the Tuareg language (Tamashek) effectively served as specialized language that helped these nomads maintain the desert-side sector as a distinct network within the larger region of the central Sudan.[77]

The Kel Ewey Tuareg, for example, operated from the Air Massif, which was conveniently located on the major trans-Saharan route north from the Sokoto Caliphate to Ghat, Ghadames, and North Africa. As well as hides and skins, ostrich feathers, gold, and other goods, several thousand slaves a year were exported along this route in the nineteenth century. The Kel Ewey were a major link in this network because they provided much of the camel transport, but 'legitimate' trade and slave exports were only one aspect of their economy. These nomads had many camels, horses, cattle, goats, and sheep, and the sale of animals provided a large portion of their income. They were also involved in the salt and date trade, travelling several hundred kilometres to the east of the Air Massif to the salt oases of Kawar and Fachi, where they sold grain and manufactures for the salt cones and cakes of Bilma and other salt sites. This salt they transported to the savanna markets, particularly Zinder, Katsina, and Kano.[78]

Tuareg social structure was characterized by gradations of status: below the aristocrats were various categories of dependants, including tenant farmers, herders who worked on contract, vassals, and slaves. The status of each depended on the position held in the larger desert-edge system, and each was attached to a specific noble or group of nobles. Dependent groups of nomads received livestock from the nobles under a variety of contracts, and they were allowed to breed their own herds – but usually not camels.

These Tuareg nobles settled slaves in the Air Massif and Damergu to the immediate south; they also had estates further south in Tessawa, Damagaram, and elsewhere. The Kel Ewey leader (*anastafidet*), for example, had estates in the Air Massif and elsewhere, while the Imezureg, whose wealth in the late nineteenth century derived from the collection of ostrich feathers for the trans-Saharan trade, had a similar network. *Iklan* belonging to the *anastafidet* lived in several villages near Olelewa; not far away were the estates worked by slaves of the Imezureg, whose capital was at Gangara.[79]

The Tuareg allowed their plantation slaves an amazing degree of movement. To some extent this was a natural feature of the environment. Slaves had to be free to move in case of drought, but the Tuareg allowed even greater liberty. Many of their slaves also traded, either for their masters or on their own account. Heinrich Barth, who travelled with a Tuareg caravan in 1850, visited one of these plantations near Tessawa. The estate belonged to Annur, one of the leading Kel Ewey figures in the nineteenth century and the leader of Barth's caravan:

> The estate is very extensive, and consists of a great many clusters of huts scattered over the fields, while isolated dumpalms give the whole a peculiar feature. The people, all followers and mostly domestic slaves of Annur, seemed to live in tolerable ease and comfort, as far as I was able to see, my companion introducing me into several huts. Indeed, every candid person, however opposed to slavery he may be, must acknowledge that the Tawarek in general, and particularly the Kel owi, treat their slaves not only humanely, but with the utmost indulgence and affability, and scarcely let them feel their bondage at all. Of course there are exceptions.[80]

Barth visited other Tuareg plantations on his journey, and he was surprised to find these located far to the south, in Katsina and Kano emirates in the heart of the savanna. These included estates owned by Annur and his brother, Elaiji. These brothers controlled the movement of thousands of camels and owned estates at Kazaure, Gezawa, Zinder, in Damergu and the Air Massif, as well as at Tessawa.

The Tuareg allowed many of their slaves to pursue an occupation. Some slaves, once they had proven their loyalty, were given animals to herd, and as an incentive, the slaves were given a share in new animals and the right to dairy products. Settled slaves, who lacked close supervision for much of the year, were allowed to trade on their own account. The Tuareg even gave them goods to retail, especially salt and dates. Eventually, slaves might purchase their freedom and invest in caravan trade.

Many of the inhabitants of the most southerly estates of the Tuareg were *irewelen*, freed slaves who had been allowed to emigrate from the sahel but who maintained some contact with their former masters, often providing free accommodation and nominal tribute. These *irewelen* were particularly numerous in Katsina, Kano, and Zamfara, where many were called 'Agalawa', or 'people of the south'. These freedmen and their descendants became prosperous merchants in their own right.[81]

Some *irewelen* were nomadic, receiving livestock from their former masters on contract in much the same way that vassal groups of nomads often did. They tended these livestock, taking a portion of new stock and selling the dairy products of the herd as compensation. The nobles told these *irewelen* where to herd, and whenever the nobles wanted livestock to sell or to replenish their own herds they took their animals. This system allowed the class of nobles to safeguard their own interests. In times of plenty, they distributed livestock to their dependants; in hard times, they took their animals back and indirectly forced their clients to emigrate. Slavery was essential to this system, for slavery was a principal means of acquiring new dependants who could be allowed to work their way up through the ranks. In the meantime, slaves performed most of the work for the nobles, including the care of livestock in the nobles' camps, constructing and maintaining wells, and farming.[82]

ASSIMILATION OF SLAVES

Despite the prevalence of plantation slavery, and other economic uses for slaves, many slaves could hope to achieve their freedom through hard work or emancipation from a pious owner, and some slaves actually were freed. This patriarchal aspect of slavery was part of the Islamic tradition of slavery. Even some plantation slaves had opportunities that permitted social mobility. Hence the dichotomy between plantation slavery and other forms of slavery was not always a sharp one. While the trend was towards the greater exploitation of slaves, the administrative and domestic uses attest to a resilience of social and political institutions that was remarkably different from practices in plantation America.

Because so many slaves were women, one feature of slavery in the Muslim savanna was the assimilation of females through concubinage and marriage and the automatic emancipation of children by slave women, if the master accepted paternity. Martin Klein's analysis of the French census data on slavery in the western Sudan has shown that female slaves often outnumbered male slaves by two to one, although this was not always the case.[83] In those *cercles* for which an attempt was made to tabulate the number of men, women and children, female slaves were more numerous than males. In a sample of 345,400 slaves, women formed 39.3 per cent of the population; while the comparable proportions for males and children were 30.9 per cent and 29.8 per cent respectively (see table 9.1). Klein argues that women were probably under-represented in the sample, since those concubines and slave wives who had given birth may well have been excluded from the census. None the less, by 1904 many slaves had escaped, and escapees more often than not were males; hence it is not possible to determine to what extent women were more numerous than men. Women formed 56 per cent of the adult population of 244,300 slaves recorded in the census. Even though marriage and concubinage did serve as avenues leading to emancipation and assimilation, the sexual imbalance appears still to have existed.

Those women who were not concubines or wives of free men worked as hard as male slaves, and sometimes at the same tasks. While a sexual division of labour was common in textile production and farming, women were still expected to work as many hours as men, and because of child rearing and food preparation many women probably worked longer than men. Spinning and carding of cotton, for example, was a woman's occupation, but it took a woman eight hours to spin enough thread to keep a male slave weaving an hour. Among the Maraka, the cultivation of indigo was woman's work, since women did the dyeing, but in many villages, both men and women worked in the fields, although usually not together. Men planted cotton, while women harvested it.

Many savanna-based merchants, for example, were servile in origin but became prosperous men, owning many slaves of their own. These merchants adopted corporate names for themselves that revealed their origins but also provided a means of identification that proved useful in business. The more important of these groups in the central Sudan were the Agalawa, Tokarawa, and Adarawa.[84] These merchants spoke Hausa as their first language, not the Tuareg tongue. Their homes were in or around the Hausa towns of the Sokoto Caliphate or the adjacent Hausa towns in the stretch of independent territory between the Caliphate and the Air Massif to the north. Many traded to Asante and Adamawa, dealing in kola nuts, salt, textiles, slaves, and other goods. Some amassed so many slaves that they established their own plantations. They did not treat their own slaves with the same leniency as the Tuareg. There was no reason to do so. It was possible to manage these slaves more closely, despite the itinerant trade in which they were involved, and as a result they allowed less autonomy. After all, the humble origins of these merchants had necessitated hard work. Frugality in business and the desire for social mobility in caliphate society were not compatible with a particularly generous policy towards slavery. Instead, the Agalawa, Tokarawa, and Adarawa drove their slaves, using plantation output to provision their business operations and selling surplus on the market in order to raise more capital for their trade.

There are many examples of the gradual change in status of domestic slaves. It was possible for slaves in merchant households to acquire enough expertise and trust to operate on their master's account. A leading Hausa merchant in Abeche, the late-nineteenth-century capital of Wadai, is a case in point.[85] This man, Hasan Babalay, settled in Abeche sometime in the 1880s and established a flourishing commerce in slaves, ivory, livestock, ostrich feathers, textiles, kola nuts, and other goods. At the height of his business, he had some twenty slave assistants in his firm, some of whom were responsible for caravans travelling to the slave-raiding lands south of Wadai, and one who accompanied a caravan across the Sahara. Babalay's business extended to Kordofan and Dar Fur in the east, Dar Runga and Dar Sila in the south, Bagirmi, Borno, and the Sokoto Caliphate in the west, and Cairo and Tripoli in the north. His use of slave assistants was part of a long-standing commercial tradition in Islamic Africa, and even when a trusted slave stole his capital in one trans-Saharan venture he continued to rely on domestic slaves.

215

Indeed, Babalay's ancestry conveys the true dimensions of this tradition of commercial apprenticeship, for he was of Agalawa descent. His family apparently came from Kano Emirate, where many other Agalawa merchants also lived. Babalay established his business in distant Abeche in the 1880s, where he joined the prosperous, slave-owning merchant class of the Wadai capital. The successful operation of his firm required more than a staff of trusted assistants. To feed clients, slaves in transit, and the numerous pilgrims who also lodged at his house in Abeche, Babalay needed large quantities of foodstuffs. Again, commercial tradition dictated that much of this produce had to be grown on his own lands, undoubtedly by slave labour. Resident brokers housed visiting merchants free, in the expectation of profit from commission sales. Babalay had wives and concubines, thirty in all, to oversee this aspect of his business. We do not know how many slaves he had in the countryside, but it could easily have been hundreds, to judge by a comparison with the holdings of other successful merchants.

Besides their importance in commerce, slaves continued to be employed in the army, administration, and domestic service in the nineteenth century. The long tradition of such practices reserved a place for slaves in government and society, whether Muslim or Christian. It appeared to H. Salt, as he travelled through Ethiopia in the early nineteenth century, that:

> The situation of slaves is rather honourable than disgraceful ... and the difference between their state and that of Western slaves is strikingly apparent. They have no long voyage to make, no violent change of habits to undergo, no outdoor labour to perform, no 'white man's scorn' to endure, but on the contrary, are frequently adopted, like children, into the family.[86]

Because this aspect of slavery continued to be important, women and children continued to be in greater demand than men, despite the economically more significant function that men could perform. None the less, most slaves still found themselves in an unenviable position, as a nineteenth-century tradition from Dar Fur makes clear:

> The slaves must do the work in the house; if they are unwilling to work they must be beaten with the whip or must be beaten with the stick. Then they begin to cry [and] be willing to work. Their language is difficult; people don't understand them. If we find a girl among them, who pleases us, then she doesn't need to do any housework. I make her my wife, so that we can sleep together in bed and 'eat the skin', so that we will have children. Then she becomes pregnant and has a child. If it is a boy, then everything is fine.[87]

Slaves performed the menial labour of the household, except for the pretty females, who became the wives or concubines of the master. This practice was traditional in Islamic society, being no different than the customs that prevailed in the savanna from the medieval era until European colonialism ended slavery. There was no room for insubordination in either situation; servants had to perform their daily tasks, and women had to accept their sexual subjugation to the master. There was room for emancipation in Islamic society, as there always had been. For the woman, the birth of a child, even if not the desired male, brought eventual freedom. For the servant, hard work, some intelligence, and much loyalty were rewarded with greater responsibilities and *de facto* change in status, whether or not the master chose to grant legal freedom.

Emancipation, recognized as a pious act and therefore very common in societies dedicated to a renewal of faith, was a feature of savanna slavery that distinguished it from other slave systems. Death-bed grants, court decrees, arrangements for self-purchase, ransoming, and the freeing of concubines with children were common practices. Hence masters could arrange to free those slaves who assisted on caravan journeys and who could be trusted to act as agents. Similarly, slaves who traded on their own account could be allowed to purchase their freedom by paying regular instalments. The status of slave officials placed them in a category of persons that for most purposes should be included as 'free'. That slave officials were not technically free related to their constitutional position. They held appointments that were defined as slave and that were not open to free-born citizens. None the less, their status should not be confused with that of most slaves, who never had access to such privileges.

In allowing slaves to earn a private income, masters recognized that the ownership of slaves had advantages other than the direct exploitation of their labour. In Bauchi, for example, slaves could hire themselves out by paying a fixed sum of cowries – 50, 100 or 300 – to their master, and for a sum of 5,000 cowries a slave could be free to work on his own for a whole year.[88] In the western Sudan, the amount paid to the master under similar arrangements varied widely. A Wolof slave paid about 35 kg of millet, while a Soninke slave was responsible for almost ten times that amount (337 kg). Klein calculates that the average was 200 to 300 kg, roughly equivalent to the amount of grain needed to feed an adult in a year.[89]

The range of uses to which slaves were put and the various avenues to freedom within Muslim society illustrate the particular operation of slavery as an institution in the northern savanna. But the context for these practices must be kept in mind. Most slaves not only lacked special privileges but also lived close to the subsistence level. They worked hard in the fields during the rainy season, spun and wove cotton during the dry season, carried firewood, repaired and built houses, and dug wells. They were granted their own plots and allowed to raise small livestock, but they were also expected to feed themselves when they were not working on the main plantation fields. Extra earnings from retail trading were reduced through payments to their masters, and even their free day or two per week could be cancelled when necessary. The possibilities of social mobility, however, still existed, in large part because newly captured slaves were readily available. Islamic norms encouraged emancipation, but the distinguishing feature of slavery in the northern savanna was the close relationship between the practice of slavery

217

and the availability of more slaves. Slaves could be freed, because slaves were cheap and could be easily replaced.

SLAVERY ON THE PERIPHERY

There were areas in the savanna where slavery was not particularly important, even in the nineteenth century. In the regions of the upper Volta basin, for example, slaves do not appear to have constituted a significantly large proportion of the population. The aristocracy of the small Mossi states had some slaves; these were concentrated in household establishments, although a few of the wealthiest members of the elite had villages of slaves that can be compared with the plantations common elsewhere in the Muslim savanna. The Muslim merchants of these Mossi states also bought slaves for their own households, and these slaves were most probably employed in a manner similar to other parts of the Islamic savanna, that is, for agriculture, domestic chores, textile production, and commercial agency. Blacksmiths, too, bought a few slaves to perform menial tasks if male or to become wives if female. Even the great expansion in slave raiding that occurred on the frontiers surrounding these Mossi communities does not seem to have affected the course of slavery here.[90] Most of the slaves captured in the wars of Babatu and other war-lords – especially among the Gurunsi – were sent south to Asante. Few appear to have been incorporated into local society. The peasant communities scattered through this region did not possess many slaves either. These peasants were more a source of slaves than employers of slaves. In times of famine and feud, slaves were exported, while the centres of political power, located in such towns as Sansanne Mango and Gambaga, were focal points for slave raiding into the countryside. Many of these towns recognized the political sovereignty of Asante until 1874, and slaves were forwarded to Kumasi as tribute.

Beyond the borders of the Islamic states, in the hill retreats of independent peasants, in walled towns of ousted aristocracies, and on the plains of the savanna, hidden by the vastness of space, were people who practised forms of slavery that differed from the Islamic norm. These were the people who were subjected to slave raids and the expansive wars of the *jihad* states. Many were forced into tributary relationships. Others found themselves dependent on the very states they fought. Slavery appears to have been found everywhere, but the incidence was much lower than near the Islamic centres. The legal perception of the institution was based sometimes on kinship and sometimes on Islam, and the rate of assimilation varied. It is likely that the types of slavery found in these more segmentary societies were exceedingly old. A crucial dimension of this institution, however, was its marginality, in the sense that slavery among such people as the Margi, who lived on the borders of the Sokoto Caliphate, permitted the sale of individuals in times of crisis in order to maintain their independence from the Islamic states.[91] Often the Margi and other people on the frontiers of the major states were forced to fight each other over scarce resources, including people who were passed on as tribute, so that the interaction between these societies and the Islamic states could be indirect and complex. Slavery was a vital institution in this relationship. It allowed the tight control over land and other resources among people who faced the perpetual danger of raids, famine, and the unexpected inability to trade for necessities. Enslavement and the slave trade connected the dominant pattern of slavery in the Islamic states with these peripheral areas. To consider them in isolation is to miss a fundamental feature that has influenced the relationship between Muslims and non-Muslims of the savanna country for centuries.

10

Slavery in central, southern, and eastern Africa in the nineteenth century

THE EXPANSION OF THE EXTERNAL ENCLAVES

In the eighteenth century, Europeans and their Euro-African descendants owned slaves at scattered points along the coast. The greatest concentrations were near Luanda, Cape Town, and the Zambezi valley. Despite the relative isolation of these holdings from the main developments in the institution of slavery in African societies before 1800, these European enclaves were the basis of a new order in central, southern, and eastern Africa in the nineteenth century. As these European enclaves expanded, a modified version of the slavery of the Americas expanded too. Despite the presence of a few plantations owned by Brazilians in Dahomey and the attempts at plantation development in Sierra Leone in the 1790s, slave masters in West Africa generally developed slavery into a productive system without the American example. Slave masters adapted the practices and traditions of their own societies – Akan, Yoruba, Igbo, or otherwise – so that European conceptions of slavery continued to be marginal, even as the economic importance of slavery increased. The situation in the southern third of the continent, therefore, was different from the experience of West Africa.

A parallel can be found in the adaptation of Islamic views of slavery in the northern savanna, where slavery was reinterpreted over the centuries in terms of Islam. The consolidation of slavery in the Muslim context represented an ongoing adjustment to the spread of Islam, the continued trade across the Sahara and the Red Sea, and the use of slaves in a variety of functions – the military, administration, domestic service, concubinage, and production. This kind of transformation had been largely absent along the Atlantic shores of Africa where Christian Europeans were present. In the nineteenth century, this situation changed.

The expansion of the external enclaves was related to the development of plantation agriculture on the islands in the Indian Ocean and the Gulf of Guinea, which provided an example for Europeans, Euro-Africans, and others on the mainland. Thousands of slaves were shipped to the offshore islands, initially as slaves and then under other names. Because these islands were relatively close to Africa, their importance as plantation colonies continued longer than many places in the Americas. Efforts to patrol the waters of East Africa and the southern Guinea coast came relatively late, and consequently it was feasible to continue plantation slavery until the end of the century.

The Mascarenes were the first islands to benefit from this new attention.[1] After the Napoleonic wars, sugar-cane, cotton, indigo, cloves, and other spices were grown for export. Sugar-cane was by far the most important crop. Great Britain had seized these islands in 1810 and kept Mauritius and the Seychelles archipelago, but Réunion was returned to France. Planters on Mauritius and the Seychelles imported slaves from Africa during the second and third decades of the nineteenth century, even though the trade was officially abolished to British possessions. Perhaps 20,000 slaves were imported between 1810 and 1820, but the trade gradually declined, until in the 1830s, the British islands looked to India for indentured labour and no longer sought African supplies, although a few liberated slaves seized from slave ships in the Indian Ocean were landed on the islands. Réunion, by contrast, continued to import slaves and *engagés à temps* throughout the first two-thirds of the century. The French added Nossi Bé and Mayotte in the Comoros in the 1840s, and while these islands never became as important as Réunion, sugar-cane and other crops were grown there too. Nossi Bé and Sainte-Marie had an estimated 12,000 slaves in the early 1840s; Mayotte had 2,733 slaves in 1846. After the annexation of these islands, the French passed an emancipation decree that prompted many local Muslim slave-owners to emigrate to other islands in the Comoros, especially to Anjouin, where a plantation economy already existed.[2] This displacement enabled the French to grant concessions to planters from Réunion and also substitute the *engagé* system for slavery, so that the importation of labour from East Africa and Madagascar continued in the middle decades of the century. While these *engagés* were technically free on the French islands, they were slaves when they left Africa.

The heritage of European settlement in the southern third of Africa was also a component of the transformation in slavery that occurred in the nineteenth century. The mainland Portuguese communities in Zambezia and Angola expanded, while São Thomé and Princípe once again became a focus of plantation agriculture after two centuries of stagnation. In South Africa, the Dutch settlers at Cape Town spread inland to the high veld. The abolition of the trans-Atlantic slave trade and the emancipation of slaves in the Americas encouraged the intensified use of slaves in these communities. In effect, the locus of plantation agriculture and other ways of exploiting slaves shifted nearer to the source of slaves in Africa because of the greater risks in transporting slaves across the Atlantic and because slavery itself was abolished in one place after another. As was the case with the Mascarenes and Comoros, farmers and planters on the mainland could compete because the cost of labour was cheaper than in the Americas. A peculiar hybrid emerged that was neither American nor African.

Despite the distant roots in the Americas and Europe, there were a number of unique features of the new slavery in its African context. Firstly, the most important sector was on the East African coast and the islands of Zanzibar and Pemba, where Omani and Swahili slave-owners developed a plantation economy to produce cloves, coconuts, and grain. In this sector, while largely external in origin (the Omanis came from Arabia; capital came largely from India; the inspiration for plantation agriculture came from the Mascarenes and Comoros, and thus indirectly from the Americas), the form of slavery was Islamic, not European or Christian. None the less, this plantation system was similar to the other sectors on the Mascarenes, Comoros, São Thomé, Principé, and the mainland Portuguese enclaves in that production was primarily for foreign markets – in this case principally India – and most slave owners had non-African origins.

Secondly, abolitionism influenced the form of slavery in the European sectors; this new slavery was not a simple copy of earlier forms of American slavery because the rhetoric of abolition required that slave masters should disguise the nature of their exploitation under a variety of new terms. Among the Boers, slaves were called apprentices, as a means of satisfying British laws of emancipation that allowed a period of apprenticeship after the ending of slavery in 1833; except that the movement of the Boers inland beyond the effective control of British rule resulted in the continuation of the apprenticeship system until the Anglo-Boer war in 1899–1902. Similarly, the French and Portuguese purchased slaves for use in agriculture and other economic activities but called them *engagés*, *libertos*, or other names. In all these cases, the presence of the British at Luanda, Cape Town, Zanzibar, and other places required the adaptation of slavery to appease British diplomatic pressure. The new ideology – European in origin – was paternalistic and capitalist. Slavery was perceived in terms of protecting 'primitive' Africans as they experienced the transition to civilized life; the new labour systems were intended as a related transition toward the establishment of wage labour, with the abolition of slavery as an inevitable byproduct.

Thirdly, many slave-owners, particularly in Portuguese areas, were Euro-Africans or non-European immigrants. These included Ambakistas, Indians, and others. Hence the presence of Omanis and Indians in Zanzibar and Pemba was not so different, in that these slave owners also identified with an alien origin, although there were differences between those who associated with Europe, the Islamic Middle East, and India. The Ambakistas spoke Portuguese and were nominally Catholic; the Indians came from either Goa, the Portuguese port in India, or numerous other places. These varied ethnic origins among the entrepreneurs of this new slave economy fell on a continuum from those who were Europeans, Omanis, or Indians to persons of mixed Afro-Omani, Afro-Indian, or Afro-European ancestry to

African slave-owners whose origins were connected with the external presence as mercenaries, commercial agents, or slave descendants. Groups like the *achikunda* (who were associated with the Portuguese *prazo*-holders in the Zambezi valley), the Yao (who were agents for the Swahili and Omani plantation sector of the East African coast), and the Merina (who provided many of the slaves for the Mascarenes) developed plantations of their own that were linked to the external-centred systems of the Portuguese, Omani, and French.

Lineage slavery still existed, but in the context of commercial expansion its relative importance decreased. Lineage-based societies continued to serve as a source of slaves for raiders; they were the prey for marauding bands and consequently incorporated slaves when possible as a means of enlarging kin groups. None the less, lineage slavery was not the most dynamic institution in the nineteenth century, although under some circumstances a partial transformation of slavery occurred, especially when slavery was adapted to military ends or for hunting purposes. Thus the Cokwe and the warrior bands of the *dificane* used slaves as a means of incorporating women and soldiers on a scale that prevented the functioning of real kinship structures, even though slavery was interpreted in the context of kinship.

THE OMANI–SWAHILI SECTOR

The first clove plantations on Zanzibar were in production by the early 1820s, primarily as the result of experiments by Saleh b. Haramil al-Abray, born in Muscat in 1770. He travelled to the Seychelles, Ile de France (Mauritius), and Bourbon (Réunion) and observed the French plantation economy. Saleh and other Omani merchants experimented with sugar-cane and other crops first, but cloves proved most successful. Sultan Sayyid Sa'id of Oman saw in the clove industry the possibilities of a personal fortune. He moved to Zanzibar in 1828 to promote his own interests in clove production. This included the confiscation of Saleh's plantations and the purchase of other rival estates. Thus Sayyid Sa'id became the largest clove producer on the island, and despite the entry of other planters and merchants into the industry, the sultan's family never lost its pre-eminence in the trade.[3]

After the modest beginnings in the 1820s, the clove industry grew dramatically in the 1840s. Exports rose from 280,000 lb in 1840 to over a million lb in 1843–4 to almost five million lb per year in the 1850s. By 1845, private estates outproduced the royal estates by almost two to one, and clove production spread to neighbouring Pemba Island. The expansion on both islands continued for the next few decades, until a hurricane destroyed many of the trees on Zanzibar in 1872. Because of this disaster, Pemba exported more cloves than Zanzibar, reaching two-thirds to three-quarters of clove sales by the 1890s.[4]

The slave population of Zanzibar Island rose from about 15,000 in 1819,

223

before the boom in clove production, to well over 100,000 by the 1830s. For the rest of the century, estimates, some of them partial calculations, indicate that the slave population remained at this level or higher. Mortality rates among slaves were extremely high – 15–20 per cent per year – which meant that 9,000 to 12,000 slaves had to be imported each year in order to maintain the slave population. In 1860, estimates indicated that the majority of slaves arriving at Zanzibar, perhaps 15,000 out of 19,000 slave imports, came from the area of Lake Malawi. The other 4,000 came from the Mrima coast, opposite Zanzibar.[5]

By the 1870s, the sultan had some 4,000 slaves on his plantations, and other wealthy planters had 1,000 to 2,000 slaves, all supervised by overseers. A major plantation could contain 10,000 trees, and some planters owned more than one. In 1895, one planter, Abdalla bin Salim owned 6 plantations with 3,000 slaves. His wife owned 7 smaller plantations with 1,600 slaves. Five other planters at this time owned over 250 slaves each. In Pemba, Mohamed bin Juma bin Said had 7 plantations and 2,000 slaves, and he had holdings in Zanzibar too. Other planters on Pemba reputedly owned as many as 500 slaves each. By 1860, Indians owned 8,000 slaves in Zanzibar, two-thirds of whom were on plantations. The rest were domestic servants, porters, and menial labourers in the Indian commercial firms. The largest owner was Jairam Sewji, who owned 460, although most Indian households had only a few slaves. Despite the scale of some holdings, there were many with only 50 or 60 slaves, and the average size was about 30 slaves per plantation.[6]

There were two clove harvests, the heaviest in November and December and a protracted, smaller one from July to September. The clove buds had to be broken off from the tips of the branches, without damaging the delicate limbs. Each tree had to be picked several times, and since the major harvest overlapped with the rainy season, working conditions were unpleasant and the task of drying the cloves was difficult. Supervision of slaves had to be carefully arranged, in order to prevent damage to trees. Female slaves were responsible for separating the buds from the stems and spreading the cloves on mats to dry. Then they were packed in sacks for transport to town. Masters hired out their slaves during harvests when they could afford to do so, and many slaves were paid according to the amount of cloves they picked. Because of the delicate nature of the labour, piece-work provided an incentive for careful and thorough slaves that might seem inconsistent with plantation slavery but is logical in the context of this particular system. Slaves who were careless or lazy were beaten and deprived of holidays. Slaves were provided with food, clothing, and accommodation, and in most cases they also received a small plot of land for a family garden.[7]

The plantation sector spread to the mainland opposite Pemba and Zanzibar, especially along a 110-km stretch of coast from Mtwapa to Mambrui, but including other places as far north as the Banadir coast and as far south as Mozambique.[8] Grain, coconuts, and oil seeds were the principal exports, although some other foodstuffs and gum copra – used to make varnish – were important locally. The earliest developments began in the 1830s, with the major expansion occurring in the 1850s and 1860s. The peak of the plantation economy was reached between 1875 and 1884, when there were 43,000 to 47,000 slaves on the Kenyan coast, which represented 44 per cent of the population; the largest concentrations were in the Malindi–Mambrui region, near Takaungu, and in the area of Lamu and Pate, although there were smaller numbers of slaves at Mombasa, Vanga, and other places.[9]

One of the earliest centres was Takaungu, founded in 1837 by the Mazrui family who had fled Mombasa to escape Zanzibar rule. In the 1840s, gum copra – gathered in the Watamu area – was the main export; thereafter foodstuffs were more important. The period of greatest expansion occurred in the 1860s when such slave villages as those at Konjora were founded. Slave villages usually had 300 to 400 slaves, organized under an overseer. Now maize and millet were grown for export, and by the 1880s the Takaungu area exported 5,400 tons of grain, sesame seed, rice, and beans per year.[10]

Some of the largest plantations were established in the Malindi–Mambrui region after 1861, when Malindi was resettled. Malindi had been an ancient town but was abandoned in the late eighteenth century. Immigrants from Zanzibar moved to the mainland to grow grain, and by 1884 exports were almost 13,500 tons per year, twice the output of Takaungu. By this time, there were several hundred individual farms, with the size of slave holdings averaging from 10 to 20. Some masters, however, had several locations, with one owner having 10 farms. Suleiman bin Abdallah al-Mauli was one of the largest planters; in the 1890s, he owned 261 slaves who worked 2,500 hectares of grain as well as several coconut groves. He was one of 6 planters owning over 2,500 hectares. There were many other planters with holdings that ranged from 24 to 120 slaves. In fact, the 13 largest planters, each of whom had over 1,200 hectares of land, accounted for 56 per cent of the cultivated land at Malindi. The total slave population reached 4,000 to 5,000 by 1873, reaching a peak of 6,000 in the late 1870s.[11]

The other large concentration of slaves was on the coast opposite Lamu and Pate; in 1897, 9,624 slaves were counted, although the slave population was probably larger in the 1870s before the coastal area was hit by raids from the interior. Lamu exported grain to Arabia, the Persian Gulf, India, and other parts of the coast. By 1859, sesame was also a major export. The 3,900 tons exported in that year exceeded the volume of sesame sales from the rest of the coast combined. Rice, millet, maize, sorghum, beans, and coir completed the list of crops grown by slaves.[12]

There were fewer slaves at Mombasa, Gasi, Wasini, and Vanga, although slaves were involved in production at these centres. Of these, Mombasa was the most important. Agricultural holdings there averaged about 3 hectares – in sharp contrast to the large plantations elsewhere. Only 3 land-lords at Mombasa had over 250 hectares. Because Mombasa was older than

Malindi, Takaungu, and other centres of plantation development the pattern of small holdings was already established before the years of economic expansion after mid-century. Farmers at Mombasa responded to the demand for grain as the market grew, but there was not sufficient land to develop extensive plantations. In 1884, almost 1,800 tons of millet were exported, which was only a tenth of the combined output of Takaungu and Malindi. The slave population was still relatively large, however. In 1897, there were 4,667 slaves in Mombasa. Vanga and Gasi were even less important as centres of slavery. Not only were exports smaller, but there were only 2,153 slaves in the area in 1897.[13]

On the larger plantations – if the estate of Suleiman bin Abdallah of Malindi can be taken as representative – slaves worked in gangs of 5 to 20 under a headman who was also a slave.[14] The hours of work ranged from 8.00 a.m. to 5.00 p.m. during slack periods and the dry season and from sunrise to late afternoon during planting and harvesting, although the average work week on the master's fields there and elsewhere usually did not exceed 40 to 50 hours per week even during peak periods of the agricultural season. On the estate, slaves had Fridays off during the rainy season and Thursdays as well during the dry season. Each slave received a daily grain ration while working for the master, but slaves also were given their own plots to grow additional food for themselves. The men were assigned a fixed piece of land to work during clearing and weeding. Women took produce to market, scared birds away from the fields, and prepared food. Unlike the men, they did not have free days.

The Muslim push into the interior of East Africa involved a combination of 'legitimate' trade, slave raiding, and political consolidation. The first Arab merchants reached the commercial centre at Tabora, half-way between the coast and Lake Tanganyika, in the 1830s, and thereafter the Muslim presence in the interior grew at a phenomenal rate. Muslims, including Arabs, Swahili, and converts among the Nyamwezi and Yao, dominated a vast network of trade routes that stretched beyond the lake country to the basin of the Zaire River by the 1870s.[15] Arabs were operating at Ujiji, the main port on the eastern shore of Lake Tanganyika, in 1840. They moved across the lake and, under the leadership of the colourful Tippu Tip, occupied territory along the upper Zaire (Lualaba). Tabora, Ujiji, Kirando, Kasongo, Riba-Riba, Mataka: these were some of the towns that dotted the trade routes over which copper from Katanga, salt from Ivuna, Uvinza, and elsewhere, textiles and other imports from the coast, and other goods moved. The Muslims were after slaves and ivory, particularly the latter, which constituted the most valuable export from East Africa. Few slaves reached the coast through Nyamwezi country; they were incorporated into the local economy and society instead.

In the internal sector, many slaves were needed at the commercial centres, particularly on plantations that supplied the caravan trade with provisions. Since porters were the principal means of transporting cargo, it was necessary to acquire food at staging points along the caravan trails. Plantation output provided much of this market at the major centres. At Ujiji, for example, slaves constituted the great majority of the local population by the 1880s. The model for Ujiji society was fashioned after the Swahili–Arab coast. Tippu Tip followed in his father's steps as a trader in the interior, investing in plantations both on Zanzibar and in the interior.[16] Along the river, north of Kasongo, Tippu Tip established at least twenty plantations in the early 1880s, thus assuring adequate food supplies for the riverine trade. At Kasongo, on the Lualaba river west of Lake Tanganyika, slaves assembled at the sound of a gong and marched together to the fields, where they worked in gangs.[17] Slaves were found not only on plantations, but also in the harems of wealthy merchants and among the domestic staff of commercial establishments. Some dependants of the merchants and other petty traders were themselves descendants of slaves or had purchased their own freedom. These were known as Ngwana, and they often traded along the less frequented routes, handling small quantities of goods that they bulked for the bigger firms.

THE SOUTH-EASTERN COAST AND THE LAKE MALAWI CORRIDOR

The Muslim network extended down the East African coast, where it overlapped with a rival Afro-Portuguese network. Both networks pursued the slave trade, branched into the ivory trade, and invested in slave labour. Like elsewhere, slave owners shifted to the production of 'legitimate' goods when market demand made it profitable to do so, but they continued to export slaves as long as possible. Kilwa, for example, was the main port for the shipment of slaves to the plantation areas of the northern coast, as well as a supply area for more distant places. Even when British intervention made shipping difficult, the merchants at Kilwa still exported slaves, only now the slaves were sent overland.[18] The other Muslim towns to the south – Angoche, Sancul, and Kitangonya – served the important function of smuggling centres once British pressure on the Portuguese closed Mozambique Island and Quelimane to the slavers.[19] Despite competition between the Muslim and Afro-Portuguese networks that sporadically flared into violence, the two networks were part of the same expansion of slavery.

The Swahili communities began to produce goods for export by mid-century. At Kilwa, slaves gathered gum copra, rubber, and sesame seeds, and they grew grain for export too. The production and collection of 'legitimate' goods encouraged the immigration of Indian merchants. There were 87 in 1873, while in 1886 the number had risen to 242. Sugar-cane and rice were the staple crops in the Pangani valley; gum was common at Lindi, and copra also came from Dar es Salaam.[20]

The Afro-Portuguese communities experienced a similar development. At Ibo, slaves were also used to separate the tiny sesame seeds for export. In 1880, the estates near Ibo ranged in size from 120 to 1,200 hectares, each employing 20 to 50 slaves. By the end of the century, there were also 6 to 10 coffee plantations.[21] At Mozambique Island, more than half the population was slave (total population: 5,800) in 1875, while in the mainland district across from the island, there were 12,000 slaves registered with the government at the time Portugal officially 'freed' the slaves in 1875. Another 9,000 slaves were registered at Quelimane, although at both places there were many masters who did not bother to declare their slave holdings or who did not declare all their slaves. Further down the coast, Inhambane had 3,116 slaves in 1861, while Lourenco Marques had 276 in the same year.[22]

The Portuguese community comprised a mixed population of Goans, Portuguese, and mulattos, who were primarily involved in the export of slaves under various guises and other commodities grown along the coast and in the immediate interior. Even in the 1850s, the Portuguese armed forces at Mozambique Island relied on slave levies, and local officials often had large holdings of slaves. Candido da Costa Soares, for example, was one such official; he and others like him owned as many as 200 slaves.[23] Like their Swahili counterparts at Sancul, Kitangonya, and Angoche, they became involved in the production of 'legitimate' goods as the market for oil seed, grain, and other goods became important in the 1860s and 1870s. Frederic Elton, the British consul at Mozambique in 1875, provided an eyewitness account of the importance of slavery at Mozambique Island, the year Portugal nominally freed slaves by decreeing that henceforth slaves would be *libertos*:

> All the owners of property on the mainland hold *libertos* and slaves. Slave discipline is still carried on. Slave punishments are not discontinued, such as working with a heavy log attached to the leg by a chain. Slaves are let out to work for hire – are lent to foreign commercial houses for a consideration and whether termed *libertos* or slaves fall under the English interpretation of the word slave. For in the case of the *liberto* the equivalent of his labour is never received by him – he is not in the position of a man engaged for a term for certain work. He can be put to work for any person whom his master chooses to hire him, on the terms his master chooses to agree to.[24]

Elsewhere in the Portuguese domain, slaves continued to be as important as they were at Mozambique and Quelimane. The *prazos* in the interior still organized large slave armies of *achikunda*, who terrorized peasants into supplying produce, and these armies seized slaves for the export trade that flourished in the first half of the nineteenth century. In 1806, the *prazo*-holders owned some 20,000 slaves on their Zambezi estates, but most of these were soldiers and their families. *Achikunda* were now employed in caravan trading and elephant hunting, which were natural extensions of their warrior functions from the previous century. They journeyed far into the interior in search of ivory, which they purchased or hunted. Because of the journeys they became virtually autonomous. Portuguese estate holders had to secure the permission of the 'slave' leaders before punishing or selling individuals; it is perhaps at this time that destitute men in search of a protector voluntarily enslaved themselves.[25] The conditions of servitude were hardly onerous, and the opportunities for adventure and commercial success were relatively great. Increasing numbers of *achikunda* severed their ties with the *prazos*, establishing their independence as hunters and traders.

This steady dispersion of *achikunda* was part of a larger transformation in the Zambezi basin. *Prazo*-holders were able to replenish their warrior bands without much difficulty, at least until the 1820s; the export trade in ivory and slaves was sufficiently rewarding for the *prazo*-holders to abuse the free commoners on their estates, extracting agricultural surplus and even enslaving people for export. In the early 1820s, famine and drought hit many parts of the Zambezi valley; between 1826 and 1830, contenders for the Barue throne devastated a number of *prazos*, and in the 1830s, the *dificane* struck the Zambezi valley. Nguni invaders effectively established control over most of the lower Zambezi by 1840. The consequence of these disasters was that *achikunda* fled the region in greater numbers, taking with them a commitment to slavery. Some successfully established bases further up the Zambezi; others travelled into the area west of Lake Malawi; still others went further inland.[26]

Along the Zambezi itself, this population displacement eventually made it possible to reorganize production in scattered locations so that slavery became even more important than it had been. Some slaves were still employed in gold prospecting, as they had been in the eighteenth century and earlier. In 1831, for example, the Italian agent Gamitto observed how slaves were organized by the *prazos* in order to exploit the gold deposits of the Zambezi valley:

> The slaves employed at the mine are divided into *Insakas* as usual, but each of these has six negresses, it being ... only women who mine. Each *Insaka* is under the charge of a *Nyakoda* who gives a weekly account of the work of her people. These weeks are of four days, and each woman has to account for six *tangas* a week; this satisfied, the rest is hers. It often happens that a woman gets enough on the first day to pay the quota and in this case she is not required to turn up on the following days. Owners of the *Bares* mines usually have imported cloths, beads, etc., at them to sell to their slaves at exorbitant prices; and so these slaves buy from any passing merchant, secretly, what they need.[27]

Gamitto reports a sexual division of labour that may have operated in some places. More often, however, men were employed in the mines too.

By the end of the century, slave-based agriculture became more common along the Zambezi, just as it was expanding along the coast. Portuguese farmers – often mulattos – relied on slave labour at many places along the river. Sir John Willoughby visited one master, Araujo Lobo, who had an estate at Matakania, 25 km below Zumbo. Willoughby's description of working conditions demonstrates that Araujo Lobo, at least, worked his slaves hard:

> two gangs of slaves, each consisting of a dozen women, mostly with little children on their backs, and all chained together by means of heavy lengths of

chain attached to iron rings around their necks ... were being employed in porterage between the stockades and the river ... They were the result of Araujo Lobo's latest raid up the Zambesi for men and women.[28]

Women were particularly valued in the regional trade of the Zambezi valley, as Willoughby's observations make clear. *Achikunda* and other merchants bought slaves in the lower Zambezi, took them inland to sell for ivory, and then sold the ivory for export. Some Tonga in the Gwembe valley of the Zambezi are remembered as especially large slave-owners, buying women and girls who could be attached to their lineages without the usual reciprocal exchanges involved.[29] There is no question that one dimension of owning large numbers of women involved their economic exploitation. The mulatto *prazero* Araujo Lobo was probably not much different in his actions from the Tonga masters of the Gwembe valley.

Along the Shire valley between the Zambezi and Lake Malawi, a similar concentration of slaves took place. Yao, *achikunda*, and others settled slaves in villages to grow crops. The Kololo porters in David Livingstone's anti-slavery expedition even participated in these developments in the 1880s. Once these Kololo left Livingstone's service, they defeated some local *achikunda* and established themselves as overlords of the Manganja. Captives were set to work in large fields of sesame; the seeds were exported to the coast. Yao, Swahili, and other merchants had similar slave villages further north, as the area that had been the great slaving ground for the export trade from south-eastern Africa in the early nineteenth century was transformed into a centre of slave-based production. Only high transport costs limited the consolidation of a plantation economy.[30]

Until the second half of the nineteenth century, the Yao were centred in the area east of Lake Malawi, where successful merchant-princes began to consolidate territorial rule on the basis of clientage and slavery. To achieve political power, a Yao merchant had to convert wealth into a personal following. In part this was done by purchasing slaves from the proceeds of ivory sales, the manufacture of cloth, and other commerce; in part slaves were obtained in slave raids. Free people attached themselves to successful men to avoid raiding, both from Yao strongmen and from bands of the *dificane* that plagued the whole area. By the last few decades of the century, there were at least nine Yao strongmen; one of the most powerful, Mataka I Nyambi (who died in the late 1870s), reportedly had 600 wives scattered in 8 villages. A third were housed in his capital at Mwembe, where there was also a substantial free population in addition to his slave women and male slaves, whose numbers are unknown. When Mataka Nyambi died, 30 boys and 30 girls were killed at his funeral.[31]

THE PORTUGUESE ENCLAVES IN WEST-CENTRAL AFRICA

The transfer of plantation agriculture to west-central Africa was different from the development of plantations in the Indian Ocean basin. The

Portuguese began to discuss the necessity of adjusting to the inevitable collapse of the trans-Atlantic trade even before that trade actually declined. As Lopes de Lima argued in the early 1840s, slave-based agriculture should be promoted in Angola:

> Slavery today is general there [in Angola] in the amount of 12 to 40 per cent among permanent settlers; but the number of slaves will rise as soon as the inhabitants of our cities and *presidios* decide to establish and cultivate lands which can rival those of Brazil ... and when the allied *sovas* [native chiefs] in the interior are convinced that they cannot sell their vassals and prisoners to a foreign country, and who decide that it is better to employ them in extracting profit from their own lands by sending colonial products to markets.[32]

In 1850, there were 6,020 slaves in Luanda alone, out of a total population of 12,565; by 1854, there were 26,000 slaves registered in the whole of the Portuguese colony of Angola.[33] The size of this population had been relatively stable throughout the first half of the century. Despite Lopes de Lima's prediction, therefore, a boom in agricultural production had not taken placed by the middle of the century, although there was a sizeable slave population.

São Thomé and Principé were revitalized in the 1850s, precisely at the time when the export trade from west-central Africa began its final decline. As was the case in the Mascarenes, sugar-cane was the main crop, and contract labour was substituted for slavery, even though this substitution did not affect the process of enslavement and slave trading in Africa and hardly affected the nature of servile relationships on São Thomé and Principé. Coffee soon replaced sugar-cane as the principal crop; then, in the 1880s, cocoa began to replace coffee.[34]

A small plantation sector also developed on the mainland in the same period. Near Ambaca, for example, a group of slave owners of mixed Portuguese and African origins, known as Ambakistas, developed their commercial and plantation interests; the Ambakistas were more or less Portuguese in dress, religion, and manners, but like the mulattos of south-eastern Africa, they represented a mixture of cultures.[35] The same was true in the Cazengo district along the Kwanza River inland from Luanda. The first plantation was established in the 1830s. A Brazilian immigrant bought 25 slaves at the Dondo market for use on his farm. By 1850, local African farmers and European settlers were collecting coffee in the forest and planting trees. In 1870, several large-scale European plantations were using slave labour. Within a decade, much of the fertile land along the river had fallen into the hands of white owners. None the less, the plantation sector in Cazengo remained relatively modest; there were never more than a few plantations until the 1870s and 1880s, and even at the peak of development in the 1890s, there were only 28 coffee plantations with a total slave population of 3,798.[36]

To the south, another small plantation colony was established at Moçamedes in the 1840s, with sugar-cane as the main crop. Cotton was tried in the 1860s and 1870s, when American production was low, and this was the period of Moçamedes' greatest prosperity. The growth of the colony was limited by the environment, however. The area included only four coastal oases and one inland oasis at the foot of the escarpment, and cultivation depended on irrigation. The slaves, who numbered between 2,000 and 4,000, worked from sunrise to sunset, with a two hour break in the middle of the day and Sundays off. Men and women performed the same tasks, working in teams under overseers and drivers who were usually slaves themselves. At Moçamedes, slaves were also used in the fishing industry. Fishermen arrived in the 1860s, and they quickly bought slaves, who did most of the manual labour. Men crewed the ships; women dried and salted fish. Some planters produced foodstuffs for the industry, which by the 1890s was the most important part of the local economy. Fish were exported to São Thomé and Principé, among other places.[37]

APPRENTICESHIP IN SOUTH AFRICA

The most significant difference in South Africa was that the expansion of slavery in the external enclaves there was associated with the movement of the Afrikaner population into the interior. The Dutch community accepted British rule begrudgingly at the best of times, but in the 1830s the Boer trek onto the high veld marked a new era of resistance. In part this expansion was related to the slavery issue, for Dutch society was based on slavery and the exploitation of the non-white population. British abolitionist sentiments only fuelled discontent that was already strong for other reasons. It is no coincidence that the great trek began just as the emancipation of slaves in British colonies was to take effect.

In 1807, there were 1,134 free blacks and 30,000 slaves in the Cape colony, which demonstrates the importance of slavery to this European community of 25,000 whites.[38] The agricultural economy – particularly wine and wheat – continued to depend on the labour of slaves, just as it had in the eighteenth century. The port at Cape Town still relied on slave workers who performed menial tasks in the commercial firms and small shops of the town. But the institution of slavery underwent a fundamental change in the first three decades of the nineteenth century.[39] The campaign against the slave trade and slavery in Great Britain had repercussions in Cape society. When the trade was abolished, the import of slaves into Cape Town virtually ceased. From then on it was possible to obtain relatively few new slaves; they came primarily from skirmishes on the frontier in which captives were taken, but also through intermittent and relatively small-scale trade with African traders across the frontier. As in other slave societies, the slave population at the Cape was not demographically self-sustaining; consequently, the termination of imports from overseas and the inability of the interior to compensate for the import trade meant that the relative importance of slavery would inevitably decline.[40]

Indications of change were first evident in Cape Town; some slave owners there sold some of their slaves to farmers in the interior, because the collapse of the slave market drove up prices, so that individual owners found it profitable to sell their slaves at inflated prices. This shift was reflected in the proportion of slaves in the population of the colony; whereas there were still 32,046 slaves in 1817, they no longer formed the majority of the population in Cape Town and gradually they declined as a percentage of the population of the colony as a whole.[41]

Becuase slavery could no longer satisfy the labour requirements of the colony, reforms were instituted between 1812 and 1828 that were designed to produce alternative sources of labour. The principal source was the Khoikhoi and San population – identified as coloureds – who comprised 17,000 people by 1817. Khoikhoi and San were already an important component of the rural labour force, particularly in areas of livestock production. Now San and Khoikhoi children were incorporated into the work-force through a system of apprenticeship, which lasted until they were twenty-five. These children could not be sold and were technically free, but they received no wages for their labour, and once they reached 'maturity' they were supposed to be paid and could even seek alternative employment, although in fact it was difficult to do so. Furthermore, adults were required to have passes that allowed them to be employed for specific periods: passes were instituted in reaction to uprisings among the Khoikhoi and their alliance with Xhosa and others outside the colony.[42]

The pass system of contract labour, which underwent many modifications after it was introduced in 1809, laid the foundation for alternative supplies of labour, but it took several decades for migrant, contract labour to fill the needs of the expanding South African colony. Between 1809 and 1834, the pressures of an insufficient labour supply, the disappearance of land that could be developed, and friction with both the British government and African people on the frontier of Boer settlement created a situation that was potentially explosive. As the economy expanded – the major development involved the growth of wool production – Boers felt that their interests were not protected sufficiently to warrant their loyalty to the British regime; indeed, many Boers were ready to move beyond the frontier and seize new territory. Cattle and sheep required extensive land, and while slaves and Khoikhoi were available, the frontier seemed to offer better opportunities. Firstly, some slaves were obtainable through raids and purchase, although the government tried to suppress slave raiding and trade. As late as 1828, the 5 eastern districts reported a slave population of 6,598, in a slave population for the colony as a whole of 32,243.[43] While the number of slaves had remained relatively constant since the early years of the century, these figures suggest that the proportion owned in the eastern areas – from where many of the Voortrekkers came – had increased, reaching about 20 per cent of the slave population.

The beginning of the Great Trek coincided with the emancipation of slaves in the British Empire, and the two are hardly unrelated. Between 1834 and 1838, slaves were considered to be apprentices; in effect, the British government attempted to impose a new labour regime, derived from the experience of Khoikhoi and San apprenticeship, on the white settlers. In the long run, the emancipation of slaves and the further consolidation of the apprentice system were important steps towards the evolution of a migrant labour force, based on the issuance of passes to control settlement and employment. In the short run, however, many Boers took their slaves and Khoikhoi apprentices and moved inland to seize land for livestock and agriculture, for the devastation of the *dificane* wars had left the best land for settlement.[44] Beyond the British colony, the apprenticeship system functioned as a thinly disguised form of slavery. The Boers who had left by 1837 took with them perhaps 4,000 apprentices and ex-slaves who continued to be treated as servile. The Trekkers also continued to seize children or buy them for the rest of the century; the Nguni at Delagoa Bay became one source of 'apprentices', who were slaves in the eyes of the Nguni. As late as the 1890s, this modified form of slavery continued in the Transvaal, the Orange Free State and Natal, although by then free, migrant labour was more important as a source of manpower than slavery.[45]

EXPANSION OF AN INDIGENOUS SLAVE MODE OF PRODUCTION

The developments in the external enclaves had important repercussions in some parts of the interior. Merchants and war-lords associated with the trade to the coast were able to take advantage of the foreign market for 'legitimate' goods and the continued demand for slave labour. Except for ivory and rubber (late in the century), transport costs were usually too high for the successful development of agriculture, except to support the major corridors of trade. Hence along the Zambezi and such tributaries as the Shire, or overland to Lake Tanganyika and Lake Malawi, Swahili, Nyamwezi, Yao, and other slave owners created a locally-important plantation sector. In west-central Africa, by contrast, the Cokwe and Bobangi, among others, amassed large numbers of slaves who invariably were used in production too, but the cultural and economic links with the coast and the external enclaves were not as pronounced as in East Africa, where the Muslim and Afro-Portuguese penetration of the interior left identifiable traces. On Madagascar, the rise of the Merina state was associated with a similar intensification of slavery: the link with foreign enclaves – the French and British investment in the Mascarenes and Comoros – provided an incentive to use slave labour on a massive scale perhaps, but the productive employment of slaves soon became significant in its own right and without much connection with the external enclaves. Finally, there were isolated places – the Zambezi flood plains of the Lozi and the equatorial basin of the Zaire – where slavery increased in scale, although the links with the external world were either marginal or not important at all. These cases indicate that economic and political conditions in central Africa could involve the transition to a slave mode of production based on indigenous developments.

The Cokwe were farmers and hunters in the interior of Angola. In the first decades of the nineteenth century, the Cokwe were only marginally involved in the commercial patterns of the region; but, as the demand for ivory, beeswax, and rubber affected the area, their skills and location put them in a favourable position. By the 1850s, they were exporting these 'legitimate' commodities. They were also enslaving many people, particularly women and children, whom they incorporated into their villages, even founding whole villages with such captives.[46] Cokwe elephant-hunters acquired as many wives and small children as they could in order to swell their households. They bought slaves, participated as mercenaries in raiding expeditions, and extended loans in return for pawns who were often treated as slaves. Here was a means of shifting population from those who were weak militarily to those who were strong, from those who were suffering from famine to those who had sufficient food, and from those who wanted capital and had only their kin and slaves as security for a loan to those who could supply the loan. Early twentieth-century reports indicated that 80 per cent of the women in Cokwe villages were 'slaves', a term used by A. A. Mendes Correa in 1916 to include captives, women purchased as slaves, and pawns.[47]

Slave and pawn women who formed the bulk of the servile population were treated similarly. Once they were acquired they became wives in one of the polygnous households in a small village that had as its core a number of men who were related through the maternal line. When the Cokwe men were hunting for elephants, engaged as mercenaries in the internal conflicts of neighbouring states, or collecting beeswax or rubber for export to the coast, the women stayed in the villages and farmed. Kinship lost its significance, as children, regardless of their mother's status as slave or pawn, were full members of their father's lineage. For women and children who entered Cokwe society as slaves or pawns, therefore, emancipation was virtually guaranteed upon marriage, and it was fully assured for the second generation. The status of slave was effectively confined to those individuals who were born outside Cokwe society. Slavery was an institution that was tied to enslavement in war, raids, kidnapping, judicial punishment, and debt. The Cokwe never sold their own slaves or pawns; hence slavery here did not function as a fully developed institution.

The division of labour in the Cokwe village reveals the essentially integrative features of a method of recruiting women without confining them to an inferior social category that is usually associated with slavery. The men cleared the land for planting, but otherwise agricultural work was done by women. The men, forming small hunting or raiding parties, then left the villages for long periods. In this situation, dissatisfied slaves could flee, but there was no such class of slaves. Slavery and pawnship among the Cokwe related more to a division of labour based on sex than to a class structure based on slave and free.

Modifications in the general pattern of slavery also occurred along the trade routes that reached inland from the Loango coast to the Zaire River basin. This commercial network included Tio and Bobangi. The Tio kingdom, which controlled the area near Malebo Pool, had a number of important market towns. In 1852, Mswata on the Zaire River contained 8 or 9 free men, 85 wives of the chief Ngobila, and over 190 slaves. The largest merchants and chiefs in Ntamo had hundreds of slaves and perhaps 20 or more wives. The slaves acted as retainers and manned the caravans to the coast. The women were often related to other chiefs and helped consolidate political and commercial alliances.[48] Such concentration of slaves indicates that slavery in the context of Tio society was an essential element in the economic and social differentiation of a prosperous group of merchant-princes. This pattern was essentially the same one that had prevailed throughout the history of the area's involvement in the trans-Atlantic slave trade, as the discussion of the coastal Vili reveals. The transformation of slavery into a productive institution was only partially achieved along the trade routes. In general, slavery remained a factor in social and political consolidation but only marginally became a factor in production.

The Bobangi of the Zaire River followed a similar pattern, although slavery became more basic to social organization and the domination of river traffic.[49] Slave women became wives and farmers, while slave men became canoemen and commercial agents, with the opportunity for promotion, *de facto* emancipation, and full access to the upper sections of Bobangi society. Slave men could even establish independent commercial firms. By the late nineteenth century, Bobangi society was essentially a loose federation of competing trading firms. Relations between master and slave had become the common form of interaction, not kinship. Merchants amassed large numbers of slaves, who lived in a separate ward with their master. Slaves formed the bulk of the population. At one settlement, at the end of the nineteenth century, there were 290 slaves and only 8 free men, a pattern common at all the Bobangi towns. Male slaves paddled canoes and otherwise performed manual labour, while female slaves did most of the agricultural work, thereby providing food for the firms.

The first years of enslavement were the most dangerous for a slave. The death of an important person resulted in the sacrifice of up to 8 slaves. Slaves were also killed to seal pacts between chiefs, such as price fixing and market agreements, and sometimes just to remind slaves of their position. Masters substituted slaves in compulsory poison ordeals related to witchcraft accusations. Guilty people died during the ordeal; innocent people vomited the poison. None the less, despite these risks, individual slaves could become important and occasionally were allowed to split off from the main firm to found a separate ward. When the master died, the firm did not necessarily pass to a son but rather to the most successful merchant, unless the firm was divided into several segments. Hence the two main features of Bobangi society were the acquisition of large numbers of slaves and the emergence of a few talented subordinates, often slaves themselves, who founded their own firms. Still slavery was only partially associated with production. Slaves were the main field workers in growing cassava and other crops, but these functions remained subordinate to commerce. The structure of society relied on slavery, especially since Bobangi society was only self-sustaining demographically through the acquisition of new slaves. Here slavery was transformed more fully than in most parts of the interior, but its productive potential was only partially realized.

Elsewhere in the equatorial basin of the Zaire, other slave owners also began to acquire slaves for the purpose of agricultural labour. The people in the region of the upper Ngiri and Moeko employed slaves to cultivate fields that had been constructed in the swamps. Manioc was grown in the Alima region, sugar-cane in the area of Lukenye and Lake Mai Ndombe, and vegetable salts were made elsewhere. Some Bapoto masters on the river around Lisala had as many as 100 slaves each. Slaves lived on islands in the river where they gathered palm kernels and made palm oil. The owners visited these islands to bring food and collect the palm produce. By the last decades of the nineteenth century, slaves were used to cultivate the fields along the river at Wangata, Ilebo, Lokolela, and Bulobo.[50]

Another relatively isolated transformation occurred in the interior flood plains of the Zambezi valley, where the Lozi state was divided into a landlord class, an exploited peasantry, and a large number of slaves.[51] Many tens of thousands of people lived in the flood plains, with estimates for the number of slaves ranging between a quarter and well over half of the population. The peasantry was obliged to render corvée labour and pay taxes and rent. Since the peasantry was usually related to the dominant class through ties of kinship and ethnicity, traditional claims could be invoked that provided some protection from extreme exploitation. The brunt of oppression fell on the slaves, who probably constituted a majority of the population as early as the 1880s, and perhaps earlier still.

These slaves farmed, herded livestock, repaired and constructed houses, fetched wood and water, and performed a host of other menial tasks in the Lozi economy. The best lands in the plains were reserved for the masters, and these had to be tended before the small plots relegated for the use of slaves could be worked. Furthermore, slave gardens were most apt to be on poorer soil or lower lands that tended to be flooded first. Slaves were also expected to pay a portion of the produce from their own plots, which amounted to a rent on the land. There were many other disabilities for slaves. They could not eat millet or sorghum, nor use wood and mud for their huts, nor wear certain clothes or jewellery. In addition, slaves had to perform the most labour-intensive corvée projects for the state, including the construction and repair of irrigation ditches, settlement mounds, and royal buildings. They also had to cultivate various royal fields, supply government officials with provisions whenever they were on state visits, and furnish slave children to the state as a form of tribute.

The type of exploitation that characterized Lozi was also found to a lesser extent elsewhere in central Africa, particularly in Lunda and Kazembe. The capital districts depended upon slave labour not unlike that in Lozi, though there was no dependence on irrigation and royal projects. Slaves, particularly women, were the main workers in the countryside.[52] The population of the capital districts usually numbered several thousand people, and the impression of various nineteenth-century observers was that a significant proportion was slave.

As in Lozi, slavery had been transformed into a means of political domination. Despite the relatively weak market forces, slaves could be used in an economic sense in order to buttress state power. Both slaves and free peasants paid tribute, but neither produced for market exchange on a significant level. In the early nineteenth century, Lunda and Kazembe still supplied the external slave trade, but when that trade declined the state faced serious problems of adjustment. The aristocracy fought over access to increasingly scarce resources. Civil war and Cokwe incursions led to political disintegration and the decline of state slavery.

The expansion of slavery in Imerina was related to the political expansion of the state, which conquered most of Madagascar in the course of the nineteenth century.[53] Imerina had been one of the major sources of slaves for the Mascarenes in the late eighteenth century, but foreign trade was only one dimension of Imerina's success. The monarchy organized huge irrigation projects around the capital of Tananarive. Marshes were drained and dykes constructed, and the land was turned into rice fields. In the late eighteenth century, work levies consisted of free men, but by the early nineteenth century slave labour became the basis for the maintenance and extension of these public projects. Slaves also became increasingly important in farming the rice fields because free men had military duties that prevented their involvement in agriculture.[54]

In 1817, the British and King Radama of Imerina signed a treaty that allowed the interception of slave ships in exchange for an annual subsidy in the form of firearms. This gave Imerina a monopoly of firearms on Madagascar, which facilitated military expansion and the enslavement of people for use in the irrigation schemes of the capital district. While Radama had to sacrifice the income gained from exporting slaves, the political advantages gained from military supremacy proved to be considerable. By the middle of the century, the slave population had increased to the point where society was divided into two classes, slave and free. By the end of the century, considerably more than half the population was slave. Slaves did virtually all productive activities; they were used in mining and smelting; they transported wood from the forests; and they were household servants and concubines. The monarchy had a large group of royal slaves to carry out public works, farm the royal fields, and maintain the palace. The slaves worked in gangs under overseers, and they lived in barracks. Strict endogamy was practiced to maintain the distinction between slave and free: marriage between a free man or woman and a slave reduced the status of the children to that of slave.[55]

THE LIMITED TRANSFORMATION OF LINEAGE SLAVERY

Fundamentally, lineage slavery involved social reproduction. Actual practice varied. In some cases, slavery was a means of military recruitment; in others, slaves were valued more for their productive capacities; in others still, slaves were killed in symbolic demonstrations of social solidarity. The significanct difference between these forms of slavery and the plantation slavery of the East African coast was that slaves were not primarily exploited for their potential as producers. Even when slaves performed economic functions, and slaves usually did, these were secondary to their subordinate position in a social unit. The limited extent of market development prevented the transformation of slavery into a productive system. Slave trading and enslavement continued in the interior. While slaves could be exported to places where labour was needed for production, the affected areas of this vast region remained part of an international system of slavery. Hence until mid-century, west-central Africa and south-eastern Africa exported slaves to the Americas, and for this period slavery in the domestic sphere remained a dimension of a larger system. Once the export trade was cut off, and despite the resurgence of slave plantations on São Thomé, and to a lesser extent Principé and the Angolan coast, the foreign trade began to collapse after the 1850s. Then the system of slavery began to disintegrate. In contrast to the West African coast, the domestic economy did not experience the kind of transformation to 'legitimate' trade that could result in the exploitation of slaves in a productive capacity. Consequently, slavery in many parts of the interior reinforced a social order based on dependency but not on the exploitation of slaves in order to produce commodities.

Among the Ila, for example, early twentieth-century reports show that 40 per cent of the population was of slave descent, which was as high a proportion of slaves as in many places where slaves were important in production. None the less, the Ila had little that could be sold on the market; transport costs were too high for Ila slave-owners to become involved in the export economy. Slavery was relatively benign and involved the assimilation of people to a great extent, even when their ancestry was remembered. Slavery was a means of augmenting lineage membership.[56] Kinship relationships were redefined to incorporate slaves, particularly women. Slavery broke the link of reciprocity that underlay the normal functioning of kinship, but it did not lead to exploitation as an institution. Instead slavery remained embedded in social structures and was not transformed into a mode of production.

Throughout much of the interior, slavery continued to be firmly associated with a kinship framework, just as it was among the Ila.[57] Slaves were valuable because they had no kinship connections and could be incorporated despite customary norms. In many matrilineal communities, for example, slave women and slave children could be married or 'adopted' without acquiring the obligations that were connected with people who could turn to a lineage in times of trouble.[58] There were no labour demands from kin. There were no meddlesome relatives who might intervene in marital disputes or who might offer advice on child-rearing practices. Nor were there costly visits from family who would expect to be fed and entertained. In matrilineal societies in which brothers-in-law were a force to reckon with, it was often desirable for men to marry women who had no brothers. In this way, their children had no uncle from whom they inherited nor to whom they could look for access to land and communal protection. A man's children were his own if a slave women bore them. It is no wonder, then, that women were 'assimilated' and that children were 'adopted'.

On the surface, this system of slavery appears far from onerous. Since women, with the help of children, did most of the farming, there was little differentiation in agriculture between slave and free. In fact, marriage effectively emancipated slave women in matrilineal societies, and children also became free as they grew older. They were initiated into the customs and obligations of their master's society in ways very similar to the biological children of their master. Hence slaves, especially those purchased or enslaved in their youth, often became full members of society with the passage of time.

Certainly there were societies in which slavery remained closely associated with marriage and kinship structures and was relatively mild. The Tawana, on the borders of the Kalahari Desert, had few slaves. The roots of slavery in the dependent relationships associated with kinship still could be found here, as A. Schulz observed in the 1890s: 'When talking of slaves amongst natives, the term slaves does not bear the same import as to the European mind ... [The] position between master and slave is more one of relative domesticity than actual slavery.'[59] Here was a society relatively far from the main currents of change, only marginally affected by the wars of the *dificane*, beyond the activities of Portuguese and Muslim merchants and raiders, and only beginning to feel the presence of Europeans. The Tawana lived off a mixed economy of cattle herding and farming. There was certainly need for menial labour, but there was little domestic pressure to exploit slaves in a manner that had become common in many parts of the continent by this time.

The means of assimilating slave women into the family among the Kongo in the late nineteenth century are characteristic of many situations in which slaves were 'incorporated' into kinship groups. As Weeks makes clear, the terminology of kinship was adapted to allow slaves to be perceived in a manner that was meant to be more legitimate, but full integration could only be achieved through a collective failure in memory of slave origins or a

240

significant blurring of slave ancestry through complicated intermarriage and descent:

> The children born of family slaves are frequently called grandchildren (*ntekolo*); and when one of these 'grandchildren' is given as a wife in exchange for a female member of the family, a present is given with her to 'wash her blood' (*nsukula menga*), and thus remove the slave element, that she may be treated as a proper wife, and not as a slave. Her children will belong to the family of her owners, but will be called *ana akwa Kinkenge* – children born of a freed woman of the Kinkenge clan, and not *esi Kinkenge* – clansmen.[60]

This process of emancipation occurred over three generations for female slaves in this matrilineal society. The family slaves that Weeks refers to were at least the first generation born into slavery, and hence their children were in fact the grandchildren of newly acquired slaves and fully acculturated to Kongo society. Yet only through marriage and public ceremony could a female be granted the status of freedom in the context of the lineage, and even then her children were still recognized as different from full lineage members.

The Kongo society that Weeks observed was far different from the sixteenth-century Kongo Kingdom that the Portuguese had first encountered. Where once powerful war-lords had amassed large slave establishments, there were only memories that whole villages were slave in origin. Portuguese missionaries had also acquired slaves in those early centuries, and villages descended from these slaves could still be identified at the time Weeks was in Kongo. In both cases, the memory of slave ancestry is a striking testimony to the failure of Kongo society to incorporate slaves fully into the lineages, despite the persistence of a myth that slaves could be assimilated. Even when economic realities eliminated any significant distinction between free peasants and those tainted with a distant slave origin, the heritage of slavery still cast its shadow over Kongo society, revealing ample evidence of the long and tragic history of slavery here. The most onerous tasks were reserved for newly purchased individuals, not those born into the household. Slaves were still subject to death at funerals, and slavery was still the penalty for sorcery, crime, and sometimes debt. No system of plantation agriculture or military conscription through slavery operated in Kongo in the nineteenth century, however; slavery remained a key institution in this poor society, although only incidental to production.

Those people of slave ancestry in the second and third generations faced the risk that their 'lineage', on whose sufferance they obtained land and the right to take part in community affairs, might find itself in debt or in a difficult political or legal situation. These were the conditions in which pawns and slaves were needed, and slave ancestry meant that unless a more likely candidate was available, second- or third-generation slaves were sold or otherwise transferred with a corresponding fall in status. Free members of a lineage could also be pawned or sold, but usually this happened only in the case of suspected sorcery, crime, or physical or mental disability.

There were also cases of men pawning or selling free children and other relatives, even when slaves were available, but this was done to protect personal wealth at the expense of the lineage.

Although slavery was a means of bypassing kinship in a social framework that emphasized the rights and obligations of lineage membership, the actual pressures of the economy and political institutions often undermined this theoretical model. People knew how society was supposed to function with respect to land, labour, marriage, religious ceremonies, and the reciprocal exchange of goods between kin. None the less, that is not how customary law provided a means of settling a wide variety of problems and of preventing an equally diverse range of potential disputes. People who had military or financial means often twisted custom, and over the course of time they in effect changed the legal tradition. Thus, people were supposed to operate on the basis of kinship, but those who could acquired slaves and pawns. In terms of the model of society that still prevailed in the nineteenth century, such actions subverted customary law, even when the rules of kinship were adjusted to make allowance for pawns and slaves. None the less, the manipulation of legal traditions could work both ways, and often slaves were able to gain full lineage rights. The struggle in these societies was between those who acquired slaves and pawns in such numbers that customary laws regarding kinship could not function smoothly and those servile people who did not have rights under traditional laws to establish a claim to lineage affiliation. When free children were pawned or sold as well, customary law was undermined even more fully. Kinship relationships may have remained the model for how society should function, but individuals caught in the web of slavery or pawnship were not fooled by a theoretical construct. They had to live in the real world.

For the various *dificane* groups the myth was that society was based on kinship structures, but the reality was that many people were incorporated as slaves. Whether it was through military conscription or polygyny, large numbers of slaves found themselves in dependent relationships that had little to do with real kinship ties. The language of social intercourse was often based on kinship terms. Slaves called their master 'father', and the legal rights of slaves were often compared with those of other dependants, particularly children. One can say that the dominant ideology was based on this model of social organization. Such small groups of warriors as the 300 followers of Zwide captured youths for the military and women for the soldiers. As they swept north from southern Africa, they integrated captives through artificial kinship structures. The social myth disguised the violent exploitation inherent in the marauding army. Captives had no freedom. Their choice was to conform to the regimentation of the band or face punishment, death, or sale. Through this technique of expansion, Zwide could transform a force of 300 men into a new society, many thousands strong, and splinter groups founded new societies of their own.[61]

Slavery in this setting was a means of recruitment that carried with it automatic emancipation through incorporation. The exploitation in this system rested more in the initial act of enslavement and the indoctrination that was required before integration was recognized. As an army on the prowl, the *dificane* bands were similar to the Cokwe, *ruga ruga*, and other warriors, although their military technology differed. The ratios of slave to free were extremely high among these groups, except that the adoption of new cultures and languages was relatively easy, and hence slaves ceased to be slaves in reality. Three hundred men could not maintain a separate culture unless there was a rigorous form of indoctrination of captives. People were forcibly removed from other societies and incorporated into a new social order that had to allow for social mobility and effective emancipation. The survival of these groups depended upon finding women. They depopulated whole regions – selling new captives when necessary but incorporating many others – in the search for new homes. The *dificane* was truly 'the crushing'; cattle were stolen to replenish the herds that had been lost in migration; and food was taken wherever it was found. Enslavement was a logical part of a movement based on looting.

In core areas of the *dificane* – Zululand, Swaziland, and the Gaza Kingdom inland from Delagoa Bay – slavery underwent a partial transformation that was not characteristic of the northern portions of the *dificane*. In the Gaza, Swazi, and Zulu Kingdoms, slaves were as numerous as in the northern bands, but the effort to assimilate slaves was overcome by the development of the Boer economy. Slaves did not constitute a class, because the children of slave women were accepted as free with automatic rights to kinship status, and slave men were seldom allowed to marry, thereby limiting the number of children born of slave parents. As elsewhere, slaves were involved in agricultural labour and the herding of livestock. Field work freed the wives of the elite from the normal responsibilities for women, who generally did most of the farming, and, since virtually all cattle belonged to the political elite, the employment of slaves in this sector was an important dimension of their economic position. Slavery reinforced the kinship system, allowing the Nguni and Swazi elites to maintain their political and economic power. By the 1870s, however, slaves became more important in production because they enabled free-born to seek employment as migrant workers in Kimberley and Natal. As the movement of migrants increased in the 1880s and 1890s, the importance of slavery in the domestic economies of Gaza, Zululand, and Swaziland appears to have increased too, but unlike in other places where a transformation to a slave mode of production occurred, slavery here facilitated the consolidation of capitalism by facilitating the evolution of a migrant-labour system. Slave production was not intended for the market; instead, slaves filled the subsistence needs of the domestic sector.[62]

There were many places in central Africa where slavery was an important institution, but not in production. This is particularly clear where slaves were sacrificed at funerals or eaten by cannibals. Again the significance of these actions highlights social relationships. Among the Kuba of the Zaire River basin, the proportion of slaves in society was only about 10 per cent at the end of the nineteenth century, and yet Kuba had been a major market for slaves for several decades at least. Slaves were most heavily concentrated around the Kuba capital, but most households had one or two slaves at most, and many had none at all. The proportion of slaves in society remained small, despite continuous purchases, because a major function of slavery here was to provide sacrificial victims for funerals.[63] In a metaphorical sense, these slaves were assimilated into Kuba society, but their incorporation was in the next world not this. A similar phenomenon, on the metaphorical level, prevailed in cannibal rituals, in which human beings were consumed as a means of strengthening the social organism. Such practices were common in the northern equatorial forests, particularly in the Ubangi River valley.[64] Once more slavery was not transformed into a productive institution. Rather the destruction of slaves was a type of exploitation that required a constant supply of slaves, but for purposes that helped consolidate social institutions that were not themselves based on the productivity of slavery.

If the developments in central, southern, and eastern Africa are compared with developments elsewhere, it is apparent that slavery sometimes became essential to production, but not everywhere. As has been shown above, slavery existed in a relatively mild form at the edge of the major political units and economic regions, and in these peripheral places slavery often allowed for incorporation on the basis of near equality. The striking feature of slavery in the northern savanna and along the West African coast was the division between the military and commercial sectors. This dichotomy was most fully developed for the Islamic areas, but it seems that a similar pattern prevailed along the coast as well. This split between a sector based on enslavement and a sector based on the use of slaves in production widened very rapidly in Bantu Africa during the nineteenth century. Moreover, enslavers and producers tended to be more separated geographically than was the case in the other regions. Elsewhere, slaves were concentrated at the centres of the states responsible for the acquisition of the greatest number of new captives. In central Africa, most productive activity was on the East African coast, along the trade routes that supplied the external trade, and in the European enclaves. The greater isolation of productive slavery from enslavement highlights the most impressive difference that distinguishes the region from the rest of the continent; it experienced less social and economic integration. Despite the tremendous increase in the numbers of slaves everywhere in the nineteenth century, slave raiding and war in central and eastern Africa caused more destruction, particularly since no new political order, comparable to the Islamic states of the northern savanna, emerged to offer the possibility of a new stability. People were transferred, as slaves, into productive activities in central Africa. It is unlikely that the resulting output approached the productive

244

potential that could have been realized if people had been left alone because of the extreme waste of the enslavement process. This scale of destruction brings into focus the overall negative effects of the long history of enslavement, the slave trade, and slavery on African society and economy.[65]

11

The abolitionist impulse

By the last decades of the nineteenth century, the African social order was more firmly rooted in slavery than ever before. This meant that Africa and Europe were on a collision course in which slavery was a major issue, even if Europeans did not always recognize it as such.[1] The imperialist momentum thrust a new social and political system on Africa, in which there was no room for slavery. While the pressure for change came from without, African societies were far from passive participants. The internal dynamics of the political economy were closely associated with the transformation of slavery into a productive system, sometimes connected with the external market and sometimes part of regional developments. The transformation was far from uniform. In large parts of Bantu Africa, slavery was linked to the regeneration of social and political institutions, as before. But along the East African coast, in the northern savanna, and on parts of the West African coast, slavery had become essential to the organization of production, no matter what social and political roles were also satisfied through slave use.

The greater use of slaves, involving a transformation in the means of production, demonstrates an adjustment to the world economy of the nineteenth century. Unfortunately, alternatives to slavery were not seriously considered until late in the century, and then primarily as a result of European pressures on the African political economy. The long history of slavery had established the flexibility of the institution in controlling people, organizing production, arranging marriages, and bypassing custom. As long as slaves were readily available, they could be used in every conceivable capacity. Only when the source of slaves and the means of distributing them within Africa were undermined did slavery cease to be a viable institution. From the middle of the nineteenth century, the European role in the history of slavery was to whittle away at the means of enslavement and distribution. Despite a mythology of abolition, this role was not readily accepted. If there was a passive agent in the history of slavery during the nineteenth century, it was Europe, not Africa. Africa struggled to reform slavery in a changing

246

context. Europe did its best to avoid its commitment to abolition, reluctantly pursuing the fight whenever compromise proved impossible. Abolition was eventually achieved not so much because of the desire of one party to end slavery but because the modern industrial system and a slave-based social formation were incompatible. In Marxist terms, the clash was based on the contradictions between different modes of production. The demise of slavery was inevitable in the context of absorption into a capitalist world-economy.

Europeans instituted conflicting policies that at best can be said to be confusing. European territory was free, so that fugitives should have been free once they entered a colony, but European administrations often returned fugitives to their masters. Furthermore, the British distinguished protectorates from colonies in terms of their legal status. In British colonies, slaves were technically free. In protectorates, British law did not apply, and slaves were not free, even though the slave trade was outlawed. Slaves seldom recognized these fine distinctions. While massive flights from slavery were clearly discouraged by the oscillation in European actions and policies, slaves still saw European outposts as possible havens of freedom.

Some scholars have argued that African servility depended upon attitudes quite unrelated to the concept of 'freedom'. African thought, they claim, did not consider freedom a desirable or possible status.[2] There can be no mistake about this matter. The massive desertions by slaves throughout the nineteenth century and especially at the end of the century when European conquest was well underway, demonstrates that the views of these scholars are incorrect. Many slaves knew exactly what they wanted, and it was not to 'belong' to their master. They wanted to escape and they did so. In this sense they knew what freedom was. It is perhaps possible to quibble over definitions, but one point is clear: slaves wanted a status other than that of slave. When they had the opportunity, many people took advantage of it to escape, despite the uncertainties of flight when European governments were only nominally committed to emancipation and abolition.

In seizing the initiative, slaves were largely responsible for changing the social and economic structures of Africa in the late nineteenth and early twentieth centuries. Only in a few places was slavery altered significantly before then. European laws and actions, often contradictory but none the less encouraging, provided the chance. Slaves ran away; they opened new lands for farms; they provided migrant labour for agriculture and mining; they served as hired porters before railways and roads could break the transportation bottleneck. The aim of slaves was freedom, not the modification of the conditions of slavery, and this often placed Europeans in the position of reforming the institution so that its demise would occur gradually and not in one, single revolutionary action. The colonial regimes became the defenders of slavery and the greatest single impediment to full emancipation.

Missionaries, reformers, and some business circles prompted the mystique that Africa would be uplifted by civilization, Christianity, and commerce, the three 'Cs'. Commerce, as we have seen in previous chapters, had the opposite effect: it increased the number of slaves within Africa. The remaining 'Cs' – civilization in the form of the European colonial conquest and Christianity through the actions of missionaries – had a more profound impact, although not always intended. European rhetoric pushed in the direction of abolition and emancipation; European experience encouraged complicity and often openly supported slavery under the guise that 'domestic slavery' was different from slavery elsewhere.

THE COLONIAL OCCUPATION OF THE WESTERN COAST

Nowhere was this contradiction more apparent than along the West African coast, where the British, followed by other European countries, concentrated their early efforts in the abolition campaign. That campaign had several aspects. Firstly, thousands of slaves were taken off European ships and set free in Sierra Leone, thereby establishing a policy of emancipating slaves. The total number of liberated slaves landed between 1810 and 1864 was about 160,000. Of these, the British accounted for 149,800, while the United States and France were responsible for the rest.[3] This presence of ex-slaves was a potentially corrosive influence on the institution of slavery in Africa.

Secondly, British policy and later that of the other colonial powers involved the negotiation of anti-slave trading treaties with African governments, usually as part of more general commercial agreements. By the closing decades of the nineteenth century, virtually all merchants and rulers along the West African coast had agreed to such provisions, sometimes under direct threat of military intervention, but often more willingly. These treaties abolished the export slave trade only and specifically exempted the domestic slave trade and slavery. The naval instructions of 1844 and 1866 recognized 'the distinction between the export of slaves to which Great Britain is determined to put an end and the system of Domestic Slavery with which she claims no right to interfere'.[4] Here was a major retreat in the struggle against slavery, for this distinction between the domestic trade and the external trade was premised on the ignorance of the European public, which knew nothing about African affairs, other than the European dimension, if that. When Europeans began to report more fully on events in the interior, this permissive attitude towards the internal market was no longer politically acceptable, and a new policy, based on total abolition of slave trading, had to be adopted.

Thirdly, the establishment of freed-slave settlements, first in Sierra Leone and later in other places, was conceived within the same framework that distinguished between internal and external trade. The history of Freetown, the first and most important settlement, provides a striking example of this contradiction. Despite its name, the settlement was a free town only for those slaves taken off European slave-ships and others repatriated from the Americas. The laws abolishing slavery in British colonies were not applicable to the Protectorate of Sierra Leone, where slavery continued to flourish. Slavery flourished, therefore, until very late. Slave dealing was not abolished until 1896, and slavery itself was outlawed only in 1926.[5] Freetown, despite its name, was the capital of one of the last bastions of slavery. This scandalous situation could only prevail because of the myth that domestic slavery was different and therefore acceptable.

Sierra Leoneans had a far greater impact on other parts of West Africa, particularly the Bights of Benin and Biafra, than on the immediate interior of Freetown. Many ex-slaves returned to their home countries, often as Christian converts. The Church Missionary Society (CMS) established itself in Freetown in 1804; the Wesleyan Missionary Society opened a mission in 1811. These missions were successful in converting a majority of freed slaves landed in Sierra Leone, so that when the ex-slaves began returning to their home countries, they spread ideas associated with Christianity. Between 1839 and 1842, 500 ex-slaves went back to Yorubaland, and thereafter the number increased. The returnees became merchants and farmers.[6] A few were missionaries themselves, and Yoruba ex-slaves (*Saro*) even came to dominate the government of Abeokuta through an association known as Egba United Improvement Association. Although the Sierra Leoneans disagreed among themselves on the issue of slavery – some were convinced abolitionists; others were moderates; and still others were in favour of a mild form of domestic slavery – the combined activities of the Sierra Leoneans spread the anti-slavery debate, but not until the 1850s, long after the founding of Sierra Leone. The repatriation of the Sierra Leoneans occurred largely as a result of the initiatives of the ex-slaves themselves. The British government was reluctant to commit itself to any substantial support, and the EUIA was even seen as an embarrassment and openly opposed on many issues. While the CMS and Wesleyans encouraged the extension of Christianity through the medium of the repatriates, neither missionaries nor government wanted the Sierra Leoneans to lead the fight against slavery.

The establishment of Liberia was an even more cautious step towards abolition, which had important implications in the United States but virtually no impact on ending slavery in West Africa. Founded in 1821 as a colony for freed slaves from the United States, only 1,430 Afro-Americans arrived in the first decade. Several times that number arrived in the 1830s, and some slaves seized by American ships off the Guinea coast were landed at Monrovia too – the total number of recaptives only reached 5,722. In part the impact of the Liberians was minimal because they were located on a stretch of coast where there were few slaves; as a community of immigrant farmers and merchants they were also relatively isolated from local African society. Unlike the Sierra Leoneans, moreover, the Liberians did not attempt to return to their ancestral homes, so that their influence remained confined to Monrovia and a few smaller settlements along the Liberian coast. While the United States government provided small subsidies to Liberia (which became an independent republic in 1847), the American influence was otherwise marginal in the fight against slavery.[7]

As in Sierra Leone, the British tried to pursue a policy of non-intervention in the domestic affairs of African states elsewhere along the Guinea coast, although the naval blockade of the coast meant that the British were involved, whether they liked it or not. The blockade strained relations between Great Britain and Asante, for example, and since the British controlled a number of trade-castles on the Gold Coast and acquired others from the Danes and the Dutch, the strained relations with Asante even broke out into open warfare several times in the nineteenth century.[8] Because Asante had to adjust to the collapse of its export trade in slaves, the government had to manage its economy carefully in order to compensate for the decline in revenue. Gold and kola production were increased, but commercial policies associated with this effort antagonized coastal merchants and invariably drew the British into conflict with Asante. Asante was relatively successful in managing its foreign trade as a means of limiting the economic dislocation caused by the ending of slave exports, judged by the European accounts of Asante prosperity in this period, but commercial policies required the tight control of the slave population.

Slave discipline was a serious problem. Not only were slave revolts greatly feared, but slaves appear to have escaped to religious shrines and to European posts on the coast in sufficient numbers to warrant official Asante measures to check these incidents. A royal proclamation issued at the time required 'that all slaves who place themselves in fetish shall be immediately handed over, or the fetish priest will be punished as a thief'.[9] To prevent flights to the coast, the Asante government signed at least one agreement with a European factor – the Dutch – in 1816, which stated 'that fugitive slaves shall be given back'.[10] Even more drastic measures were taken to control the slave population. Many slaves were killed in the early decades of the century, while large numbers of slaves living near Kumasi were relocated elsewhere to reduce the concentration of the slave population.[11]

On the coast itself, the British became the sole European power, once Danes, Dutch, and Brandenbergers were bought out. It fell to the British, therefore, to set the pace for further social change, and despite a brief flirtation with the idea of emancipating fugitive slaves in the 1840s, the British shied away from the slavery issue. Abolitionists charged the local British official, George Maclean, with complicity in sanctioning slavery on the Gold Coast. Sometimes he harboured fugitive slaves; or paid their market value; sometimes he returned them to their owners. British nationals were allowed to own slaves, as the estate of one deceased merchant and the practice of hiring slaves from their masters (common from the 1820s) made clear. One consequence of the debate over Maclean's behaviour was to confirm a policy of non-intervention, which did not please the abolitionists.[12] By attacking the moderate practices of Maclean, the abolitionists inadvertently pushed the British government into a position more tolerant of slavery.

The extradition proceedings worked out by Maclean and others began to break down by the 1850s. Under the governorship of Sir Benjamin Pine, a dedicated abolitionist, fugitives were allowed sanctuary, although efforts were made to keep the numbers small and avoid attracting attention to escapees. Pine and others became convinced that slaves and pawns who were returned to their masters would be sacrificed – a not unlikely fate considering the need to maintain control over the servile population. Despite the attempt to minimize the problem of slavery, the contradiction between an embryonic colonial system that could no longer accept the legality of slavery and an indigenous social formation in which slavery was a central institution was bound to cause a clash. Pine recognized this in 1856, when he observed that 'Our courts could not decide a case of disputed succession or scarcely any other case in which property is concerned without taking consequence of slavery. Slavery meets us at every point.'[13] On the Gold Coast, the significant rupture with the policy of minimal confrontation did not come until 1874, when the defeat of Asante was accompanied with a proclamation abolishing slavery on the Gold Coast.

In the period before 1874, the inconsistency in British policy, both on the Gold Coast, in Sierra Leone, and elsewhere, derived from the difficulty of remaining neutral, especially when Christian missionaries or merchants needed naval protection. The desire was non-intervention, but if British subjects were in danger or if it could be shown that African slave-owners were involved in smuggling slaves past the naval blockade, then the British did intervene directly. In the 1850s, for example, when slaves rebelled at Calabar, the Presbyterian missionaries were endangered because they supported the insurrection. The slaves, particularly those who lived on the plantations outside the town, opposed human sacrifices at funerals. The crisis came to a head in 1854, when 50 slaves were killed at one sacrifice. After a series of riots, the navy bombarded part of the town. Thereafter the practice of killing slaves became less common. Despite the favour this gained among the slaves, the missions were largely isolated as a result of their pursuit of this and other reforms. Consequently, only 1,671 people had been converted by 1875.[14] The slow pace of conversion had a sobering influence on mission activities, both at Calabar and elsewhere.

At other places along the coast, the general policy remained non-intervention, unless local events assumed pre-eminence and forced some modification. The British occupied Lagos in 1851 but refused to confer a legal status on this action until 1861, when Lagos became a colony. The port was seized in order to disrupt the slave trade, which was the usual rationale for military action. Until 1859, domestic slavery was accepted. Benjamin Campbell, the British Consul at Lagos from 1853 to 1859, assured a number of large slave-owners: 'the British Government had no disposition to interfere with the state of domestic slavery existing in Africa.'[15] Many slaves thought otherwise. They saw in the British occupation a signal for escape, and soon the arrival of fugitive slaves reached crisis proportions. Maclean had earlier reported that runaway slaves were a problem on the Gold Coast, but the Lagos situation was far more critical.[16] Maclean had been able to check the flight of slaves. It was not possible to do so at Lagos after 1859. The actions of slaves, as at Calabar, altered British policy, unintentionally but decisively.

Despite some attempts to convince Yoruba masters that the British would respect their ownership of slaves, asylum was granted in almost every case. There were so many slaves by the early 1860s that William McCoskry, the acting governor, provided special accommodation:

> In consequence of the numerous slaves seeking protection here I have found it necessary to appoint a man to take charge of and to find work for them ... In order to make the establishment for liberated slaves self-supporting, I devote a small portion of their earnings to defray the expenses and I consider they suffer no injustice in thus providing for their own protection and in supporting an asylum which will be always open for those of their friends who can effect their escape.[17]

The British soon found work for some of these escaped slaves. They were enlisted into the colonial army, the Hausa Armed Police Force, and became agents in the conquest of a British Empire in Africa.

The recruitment of fugitives as soldiers and police proved to be extremely successful, particularly since ex-slaves were highly motivated and had no loyalties to their master's country. The British, later followed by the French and Germans, pursued these recruitment policies for the rest of the century. The British even sent delegations to Salaga after 1874 in order to buy slaves for the army; the official reason was that slaves were being granted their freedom.[18] None the less, the Salaga merchants were more accurate in their perception of the British recruitment officer: he wanted slaves and was willing to pay the market price. Late in the century, the Belgians wanted to form military units for use in the Congo from among the Hausa and other northern fugitives at Lagos and on the Gold Coast, but the British opposed this move because it might inhibit their own recruitment of police and soldiers. In one sense, European attitudes towards military recruitment fit into an African model in which slaves had long been used in armies. There was a significant difference, however. Soldiers of fugitive origins were exposed to a new ideology, based on the abolition of slavery, and when they marched through the countryside during campaigns other slaves were informed of the new idea and encouraged to escape. While the colonial officials and officers themselves did not openly undermine African societies, their soldiers often did, particularly in the various British campaigns in Yoruba country during the last two decades of the nineteenth century.[19]

The official desire for non-intervention did not change, but the political situation certainly did, especially in the 1870s. The 1874 emancipation decree and the defeat of pro-slavery Asante encouraged thousands of slaves to escape, although officials on the coast attempted to conceal the movement through reference to a 'benign' domestic slavery. In late 1873, James Marshall, chief magistrate and judicial assessor for the Gold Coast Colony could state:

> I have not known any instance of domestic slaves leaving their owners for our castles, forts or settlements on this long line of the coast during the last two years; They are part and parcel of their families, to which they are so much attached as their children are, consequently there is no damage to be apprehended at this point.[20]

Despite this effort to down play the crisis, the temporary collapse of Asante gave slaves their chance, and many took it. The actions of British troops, who encouraged desertion among slaves, and the gradual erosion of the extradition arrangements had their effect too, as did the continued preaching of the Basel and other missionaries. In 1874, it was no longer possible to ignore the flight of slaves, although attempts were still made to minimize its significance. Hence another official reported that 'a series of migrations is going on to and from different parts of the country but whatever exodus takes place from a district is, in general, almost equally balanced by the influx of persons who return to it from other districts where they in like manner have been in servitude.'[21] Basel missionaries reported extensive population movement, too, and their missions became sanctuaries for escaped slaves and pawns.

Whole villages of slaves deserted, especially in Abuakwa, which may have lost as many as 10,000 slaves and pawns in the late 1870s. The Basel missions provided sanctuary; their congregations – consisting almost entirely of fugitives – swelled to several thousand in the 1880s. Krobo and Akwapim also experienced losses, although on a smaller scale, while Ada – the salt-producing area near the mouth of the Volta and a major centre of the palm-oil trade – suffered severely. Almost every master lost a slave; some lost ten or more. By 1893, fugitives had founded at least a dozen villages in the interior of Accra. Although information is most complete on the eastern Gold Coast area, slaves also fled from Fanti areas further west, and slaves from the interior who served as porters to the coast also escaped in increasing numbers.[22]

The missions increasingly served as a catalyst for the turbulence among slaves, especially during the 1870s and later. The missionaries, particularly the Church Missionary Society, had always been troubled over the issue of slavery in African society. They were firmly opposed to the slave trade and enslavement; indeed, the missions were intimately associated with the abolition of the trans-Atlantic slave trade. Their activities in Africa were in fact a direct outgrowth of the abolition movement, but their observations and policies contributed to the justification of actions that were lenient towards domestic slavery. On the one hand, they pledged to fight slavery as part of the general reform of African society associated with the spread of

Christianity; on the other, they generally concluded that conversion to Christianity should precede the abolition of slavery. Slave holders, for example, were allowed to become Christians. Slavery was to be tolerated temporarily, so that the Christian church could be established. Only when Christians were a majority of the population would it be safe to abolish slavery.[23]

Besides the CMS, other missionaries in West Africa included the Southern Baptists, strong in the Yoruba region, the Methodists, centred at Badagry and on the Gold Coast, two Catholic missions, the Holy Ghost Fathers and the Société des Missions Africaines, and the Basel Mission on the Gold Coast. They all experienced their own traumas over the slavery issue, with some individuals offering sanctuary to slaves and openly condemning the institution. In general, however, these more radical views were contained after an initial burst of enthusiasm and some local danger to the missions. By the 1850s and 1860s, a more moderate policy was adopted, although by then the missions were seen as opponents of slavery. Sometimes slaves fled to the mission stations, whether or not they were encouraged to do so. The limiting factor on the number of fugitives was the relatively restricted area of Christian activity, confined principally to a few coastal points, towns along the Niger River, and some Yoruba cities where Christians remained a tiny minority until late in the century. Then one of two patterns emerged. In the Biafran area, abolition and Christianity became intricately linked. Beginning in the 1850s at Calabar and spreading to the Niger delta and up the Niger River in the 1870s, reforms and rebellions were associated with fugitive slaves, slave-converts to Christianity, and mission interference in local affairs. Elsewhere, most missions and the growing number of African Christians reached an accommodation over the issue of slavery, and the radical movement became associated with the CMS alone. The growing crisis involving escaped slaves in the Yoruba area was partly associated with these missions and partly with British army recruitment.[24] Almost certainly, however, the preaching of all Christian ministers contributed to the dissemination of ideas that seriously questioned the established order, and in that sense they fed the flames of discontent.

The movement for a changed status that began in the 1850s at Calabar soon spread to other centres in the Niger delta. It first took the form of resistance to abuse, as it had when the Calabar slaves struggled against the right of their masters to sacrifice slaves at funerals. At Bonny, the ascension of King George Pepple I in 1867 led to an internal movement for emancipation. The King was a Christian, educated in England, and sympathized with the discontent of slaves at their status. Ironically, his struggle for emancipation and association with the Christian faction, which was composed almost entirely of slaves, pitted him against a former slave, Jaja, who had become the wealthiest merchant at Bonny and head of the Annie Pepple establishment. Jaja staged an abortive *coup d'état* against the king, and subsequently removed his followers to Opobo, where he successfully challenged the commercial position of his rivals at Bonny. The case is instructive for several reasons. First of all, it demonstrates the extreme social mobility of some slaves in the delta; Jaja rose from the ranks of newly purchased young slaves to the heights of commercial success and political power.[25] It also shows that many slaves supported the Christian missions in their fight against slavery, thereby revealing extreme dissatisfaction among the servile population, again because of immolation at funerals and economic exploitation.

The struggle between converted slaves and traditional authorities took many forms in the Niger delta. At Bonny in the 1870s, Christian converts were chained and tortured, their heads smashed with clubs. Despite this, over 1,000 slaves had become Christian by 1882. At Brass, an African missionary led his slave converts in a *coup d'état* in 1879, which ended in the destruction of the local shrine.[26] The pattern is clear. Whereas slaves had formerly been subject to the will of their masters, who could kill them, sell them, or donate them for sacrifice at shrines, now it was difficult for masters to punish slaves if they were Christian. Social mobility for slaves continued in the Niger delta, but it was because of their own actions, through the threat of force, that they achieved this.

Because of the abolition movement along the West African coast, slavery was under serious strain by the 1890s, even though this was not the intention of British policy. The initiative came internally. The world depressions of the 1880s and 1890s affected the export of palm oil and kernels adversely, so that large producers, using slave labour, were forced to push their slaves harder. Some slaves probably fled as a result. The presence of missionaries who became bolder in their acceptance of runaways, as the Basel Missions on the Gold Coast did, was also a factor.[27] European military action continued to be directed against the largest slave-owners; expeditions such as the march on Aro Chukwu in 1901 accelerated the collapse of slavery.[28] As slave labour became scarce, farmers and merchants had to use the labour of pawns on an ever-increasing scale.[29] Hence the rise of small producers was matched by the expansion of pawnage, as people were forced into debt in these difficult times. The imposition of colonial rule, therefore, involved a complex readjustment that was closely associated with the decline in slavery. As the final emancipation of slaves in Sierra Leone in 1926 demonstrated, slavery did not end with colonial rule, and its legacy influenced economic and social developments for several more decades. None the less, by 1900 the institution was profoundly altered; the initial stages of its collapse caused as much by the actions of slaves themselves as by any other factor.

CHRISTIAN MISSIONS IN CENTRAL AND EAST AFRICA

The abolitionist impulse came much later to central and East Africa than to the West African coast, and when it came, the missionaries had proportionately greater influence until the 1890s. European official intervention here was very restricted, primarily to Zanzibar, South Africa, and a few scattered places elsewhere. Furthermore, European official attitudes were more mixed. The British pursued policies similar to those in West Africa, but the Portuguese and Belgians were far less susceptible to abolitionist sentiments. The Portuguese promoted the use of slaves in their domains until the early twentieth century, although under different names and with some restrictions. The Belgians were so interested in the extraction of profit from the Zaire basin through the use of force and brutality that the slavery issue only served as a convenient scapegoat. Finally, the distinction between productive slavery and lineage slavery also influenced the course of abolition. Where slavery was a major feature of production, abolitionist pressure, despite the fact that it came late, led to a transition from slavery to other forms of servility and oppression; in general, freedom was not an option. Where lineage slavery was predominant, the imposition of colonialism reduced the institution to a marginal role, more by the requirements of the colonial economy than by the conscious efforts to erase slavery from the social order.

The wrath of the abolitionists was directed at the Muslims, particularly Arabs and Swahili, who were held responsible for the slave trade. When missionaries began to write exposés on the horrors of a savage continent where the slave coffles and the destruction of the slavers were unchecked, there was little concern with domestic slavery, however. David Livingstone initiated this attack in the 1850s and was soon followed by others. The German Wissman, the American Stanley, the Scottish Cameron, among others, rivalled each other in advertising the potential of the region by contrasting glorious projections against a picture of depopulated regions, barbarous customs, and incalculable brutality. In 1874, V. L. Cameron could write from Lake Tanganyika that 'the slave trade is spreading in the interior, and will continue to do so until it is either put down by a strong hand, or dies a natural death from the total destruction of the population. At present events are tending towards depopulation.'[30] Cardinal Lavigerie came to the fore in this attack on the slave trade. Domestic slavery, except as it related to the use of slaves as porters by Arabs and Swahili, was scarcely mentioned in this onslaught. In West Africa domestic slavery was tolerated; in central Africa it was largely ignored.

As was the case in many parts of Africa, the Christian missions were the most active agents in the fight against indigenous slavery, although they too often concentrated on slave raiding and trade rather than the plight of domestic slaves. The CMS established a mission at Rabai, near Mombasa, in 1846, but the missionaries shied away from the slavery issue, and the Rabai community remained very small until the 1870s, when slavery could no longer be ignored. The United Methodist Free Churches founded a mission at Ribe, 10 km from Rabai, in 1862, and by then the problem of fugitive slaves was already serious. The Ribe missionaries still tried to minimize their appeal to the slave community of the Mombasa area, however. The Holy Ghost Fathers, on Zanzibar, began buying slave children for conversion as early as 1860, and they pursued a similar policy at Bagamoyo, on the mainland opposite Zanzibar. Despite the conservative approach of the missionaries – Catholic and Protestant alike – the mission stations gained a reputation as refugee centres for slaves, and by the 1870s the number of fugitive slaves seeking asylum increased. After 1875, when the CMS established Frere Town opposite Mombasa as an industrial mission for liberated slaves, including repatriates from India, the mission communities grew rapidly.[31]

Slave escapes already plagued the Swahili plantation society of the coast before the Christian community became a factor. In the late 1860s, escaped slaves (*watoro*) formed a recognizable portion of the population of Witu, near Lamu, where the exiled Nabahani family of Pate had established itself. In its struggle against Zanzibar, the Nabahani welcomed fugitive slaves, who left the plantations on the mainland opposite Lamu by the hundreds – the total number of escapes may have reached several thousand by the end of the century. These *watoro* plundered the plantation region of the coast, seizing slaves for sale to Somali merchants in the north (in exchange for guns and ammunition), although sometimes the Nabahani sultans tried to restrain the *watoro* in order to stabilize relations with Zanzibar. By the 1880s and 1890s, Witu had developed a plantation economy itself, and some escaped slaves had become slave owners too. Witu offered sanctuary to fugitives not as a matter of principle but as a matter of politics. None the less, both in the Lamu area and elsewhere, slaves could find sanctuary in places, like Witu and to a lesser extent Gasi, which were opposed to the hegemony of Zanzibar.[32]

In the Malindi area, fugitive slaves established an independent community in the early 1870s that became allied with the Christian missions by the end of the 1870s. Fugitives fled into the marshes 20 to 30 km inland from Malindi, and despite repeated expeditions against them maintained communities at Jilore and later at Merikano and Makogeni. In 1875 and again in 1877, the Jilore and Makogeni fugitives sought CMS missionaries, and when Malindi expeditions in March 1878 and 1879 were particularly devastating, many fugitives fled south to the mission stations at Rabai and Ribe. By 1881, fugitive slaves formed a sizeable quarter in the settlement at Rabai.[33]

Another fugitive community associated with missionary activity was established at Fuladoyo, 50 km from Takaungu. Fuladoyo was initially a community of Christians, who had been loosely attached to the CMS at Rabai, and, under the leadership of David Koi, fugitive slaves were welcomed as long as they converted to Christianity. The CMS kept its distance from this community, but over the next fifteen years Fuladoyo became the largest settlement of escaped slaves south of the Tana River. The number of Christians living there surpassed the total Christian population of the mission stations at Frere Town, Rabai, and Ribe, despite the fact that the slave owners at Takaungu organized a devastating raid that destroyed the town in 1883. Koi was taken prisoner and executed, but the fugitives regrouped. Fuladoyo was rebuilt, and retaliatory raids launched against the Takaungu plantations. By 1890, Fuladoyo and its satellite communities had an estimated population of 2,000.[34]

The fugitive issue was a difficult problem for the CMS, whose communities at Frere Town and Rabai were allowed to exist at the tolerance of the Mombasa government. Official CMS policy could not condone the acceptance of fugitives into the mission stations, which was one reason why Fuladoyo, as an independent community, was so successful. The difficulty of controlling over-zealous members of the mission stations plagued the CMS throughout the late 1870s and 1880s. William Henry Jones, for example, who was the deacon at Rabai from 1878 through the 1880s, secretly welcomed fugitives, whose identity he hid from his superiors. Jones, an ex-slave of Yao origin, had been at Rabai since 1864. He had sheltered at least 524 escaped slaves by 1888, when his involvement was uncovered in a special enquiry.[35] An abortive slave rising was even organized at Frere Town in 1880; at last, a mob of Mombasa slave-owners attacked the mission, and it was later admitted that there was a white flag at the mission that had 'freedom' written on it in Swahili. Whether or not there was a real plot is uncertain, but certainly the slave owners of Mombasa thought so, and the CMS tried to restrain its members from any actions that would place the safety of the missions in jeopardy. None the less, the same enquiry that demonstrated that Jones was accepting fugitives at Rabai revealed that over 1,400 escaped slaves had been harboured at the mission stations by 1888. The CMS extricated itself from this situation by convincing the Imperial British East Africa Company to compensate the Mombasa government for these slaves, thereby effectively purchasing their freedom. In all, 1,421 certificates of freedom were issued to runaway slaves.[36]

The introduction of Christian missions into central Africa was also closely associated with the fight against slavery, although the early mission of the Protestant Universities Mission established by its example that slavery was a difficult issue. Founded in the 1860s on the western shores of Lake Malawi, the mission offered sanctuary to fugitive slaves and was annihilated as a result.[37] Not until 1876, and the arrival of the Church of Scotland mission, was there another attempt at founding a Christian community, and even then the European missionaries learned their lesson slowly. At first the policies towards slavery were similar to those adopted by the earlier, abortive UMCA mission. Within a few years, Blantyre was surrounded by seven villages that were inhabited primarily by fugitive slaves, despite local opposition and occasional violence. By March 1978, 'Blantyre has become an asylum for the slave.'[38] The policy was to sabotage local slavery, as can be seen in the comments of the Reverend Macklin on the acceptance of six more fugitives:

258

The Mission in its civil and social aspects is making reasonable and satisfactory progress. As an asylum for the poor, persecuted slave, Blantyre is becoming known and prized. We have now six fellow-creatures rescued from the lash of the driver, and miseries worse than death. And this in turn, prepares them for giving a ready reception to the free offers of the greater emancipation, salvation by grace through Jesus Christ our Lord.[39]

Within two years, however, the mission retreated fully from the issue of slavery. No longer was Blantyre to be a place of refuge. Fugitive slaves were subsequently returned to their masters, even when this resulted in the death of the fugitives. Expediency was again the rule, for the head of the mission, the Reverend Duff MacDonald, was after a different breed of convert and feared the consequences of an anti-slavery crusade:

As I mingled more with our neighbours, I saw that our reception of runaway slaves had alienated many excellent men who might have been our best friends, and who were better able to rule slaves than we. If the colonial work disappeared the purely Missionary work would be more successful, and the colonial work might gradually be suffered to disappear if slave refugees were denied an asylum ... The reception of slaves no doubt had certain advantages. Already nearly 400 had sought an asylum in order to escape death. The Mission had thus saved a great many lives, but at a terrible risk. Its course of action had made enemies of all the slave-owners in the district, and even tended to increase the slave-trade, for when a master saw that his slaves might run to the English, he resolved to sell them off as soon as possible. Again, the reception of persons who had fled to escape death or any of the other hard consequences of slavery, soon led anyone that fancied he had a grievance, to desert his master and seek refuge at the Mission, while the kindly treatment he experienced made him desirous of having his friends or relatives with him to share his advantages. Thus the settlement was in danger of becoming a larger state, composed of all the discontented people of the country.[40]

MacDonald's distinction between 'colonial work' and 'Missionary work', the secular and the spiritual, enabled him to ignore the plight of slaves, something that many other missionaries had difficulty in doing. Despite the restraint of men like MacDonald, the missions became associated with freedom. As MacDonald realized, the possibilities for revolutionary change were present, if slaves were allowed to flee *en masse* and could be brought together as a political force. The risks were too high for the Scottish Church at Blantyre. Direct action would have required military support, either from a colonial government or from an independent force armed and trained by the missionaries themselves. The naive ministers, like Macklin, did not perceive this. The astute men, like MacDonald, did but refused to adopt such a course of action.

The White Fathers, under the inspiration of Cardinal Lavigerie, did attempt a more vigorous approach, partly through the purchase of slaves and partly by providing sanctuary for fugitives. In 1879, a mission was established on Lake Tanganyika at Rumonge, 100 km north of the lake port at Ujiji, and another was founded at Masanze, across the lake, in 1880. Because Ujiji was the centre of Nyamwezi, Swahili, and Arab trade into the interior, and there were many slave plantations around the town, the slavery policy inevitably embroiled the White Fathers in local politics, and in 1881 the station was destroyed. Unlike the Scottish Church, however, the White Fathers moved ahead, establishing a new post at Kibanga on the west side of the lake in 1883, and within five years the mission had grown to 2000, including 300 slave children in its orphanage and 200 adults who had been bought as slaves. Many of the other converts were fugitives. Kibanga was on its way to becoming a small Christian kingdom in the heart of central Africa.[41]

The Christian missions provided the catalyst through their purchase of slaves and offers of sanctuary, but the record shows clearly that the slaves themselves were primarily responsible for taking the initiative that began to undermine slavery. Despite mission efforts to prevent these, slave escapes became increasingly common in the 1890s and the first decade of the twentieth century. Many slaves escaped to the missions or into the interior during the revolts on the Kenyan coast in the 1890s. *Maji-maji* uprisings against the Germans in the first decade of the twentieth century offered similar opportunities for slaves there.[42]

Because slavery had not been transformed into a productive system in most of the interior, the colonial regimes were not especially concerned with the plight of slaves. All five European governments – French, Belgian, Portuguese, British, and German – instituted taxation and labour policies designed to force Africans to work for European firms or to provide raw materials for export. These policies had little to do with lineage slavery, which was seen neither as an impediment nor as an asset in the mobilization of the African population. The Belgians instituted an especially harsh system of exploitation. In the 1890s, the Congo Free State granted concessions to giant companies whose profits were based on the extraction of raw materials with the use of forced labour. No distinctions were made between slave and free; the existing social order was largely ignored, and even when the Belgian colonial regime assumed control of the Zaire basin in 1908, the emphasis was on the extraction of agricultural products and other goods through the power of the state and large, foreign companies.[43] Slavery continued as a marginal institution. Cannibalism and funeral sacrifices were outlawed, so that slavery soon lost some functions it had provided in the old social order. When the African population as a whole was being reduced to a migrant labour-force for the mines and an exploited peasantry forced to cultivate select crops for the state and private companies, these older social distinctions had little relevance.

The British, too, largely ignored slavery, once the slave supply-mechanism that fed the plantations of the east coast was disassembled. Instead, racial segregation became the basis of an altered means of separating the working population from its employers. Again, as in the

Congo, a migrant labour-force was needed, and racism provided a strong justification for mobilizing Africans into a malleable working class. Again, the slavery of old had little place in this new industrial system, and even the Boer system of apprenticeship gave way to migrant labour. Only where slavery had been essential to production, as on Zanzibar and Pemba, was there a particularly difficult transition, but the island setting prevented escape. Various measures were enacted so that the ex-slaves would continue to work on the plantations. These included vagrancy laws, manipulation of credit, control over land, and other resources that bear comparison with the West Indies after emancipation there.[44] The Portuguese enacted laws that perpetuated forms of labour that were similar to slavery under different names.[45] In all these cases, slavery became lost in the colonial dictatorship. On a much reduced scale, lineage slavery continued to function on the margins of society, but its social and political importance ended with the establishment of colonial rule.

THE IMPERIALIST JUSTIFICATION OF ISLAMIC SLAVERY

In contrast to the other parts of Africa, in the northern savanna missionaries had scarcely any impact at all on the abolition of slavery, at least, not until the twentieth century. The campaign in these Islamic lands was confined almost exclusively to official government actions, the French in the western Sudan and the British in northern Nigeria and the Nile valley. Ethiopia was different still, for in maintaining its independence from European control until the 1930s it also retained slavery as a major feature of society even when international pressures for abolition began to mount in the 1920s. Consequently, the concern here is with the Islamic lands only and the evolution of French and British policies. In general the French and British attempted to reach an accommodation with Islamic leaders, and for this reason Christian missionaries were excluded from many areas and confined to border regions away from the centres of power whenever possible. Otherwise missions proved to be a vexing problem, as the French found out in Mali, Guinea, and Senegal. In reaching a settlement with African rulers, both colonial states found it necessary to dispose of militant Muslim leaders; for the French, this list included Ahmadu of Segu Tukulor, defeated in 1893, Samori, whose forces in southern Mali and adjacent areas were eliminated in 1898, and Rabeh, who controlled parts of southern Chad and Borno, also crushed in 1898. For the British, only the Mahdiyya, under the leadership of Caliph 'Abdallah, were a comparable enemy, and he was crushed in 1898. The British replaced the leadership of the Sokoto Caliphate, but it was not necessary to dismantle the state, as was the case elsewhere. All these actions came late, and by this time the general policy towards slavery had already been established.

The early attack on slavery in the western Sudan was directed mainly at the trade in slaves, not their indigenous use, even though the French introduced the *engagés à temps* system in 1817 and emancipated some slaves in 1848. The *engagé* system, requiring the indenture of slaves for periods ranging from 10 to 14 years, was a subterfuge that allowed the Senegalese government to acquire slaves for its own use, including military conscription.[46] The 1848 decree covered emancipated slaves throughout the French empire, but the French sphere in Senegambia was narrowly defined to include only the four communes. The colonial regime took strong measures to prevent Saint Louis and Gorée from becoming sanctuaries for fugitives. Escaped slaves were expelled as vagrants and returned to their masters. A modified form of slavery even continued in the towns themselves under the myth that slave children were 'adopted' into local families. Not until the 1870s did the abolitionist forces have a serious influence on French policy towards slavery.[47]

In 1876, the French temporarily annexed Walo and Dimar, after defeating the anti-colonial forces of Bubakar. Annexation automatically extended emancipation laws into the new provinces, and as a result an estimated 3,000 people – large slave-owners and their slaves – moved east. Although the French regime quickly reversed its annexation decree in order to placate slave owners and encourage the return of the exiles, the gradual move towards the end of slavery once more was apparent. By 1883, fugitive slaves were free upon reaching the communes, although escaped slaves were still discouraged from living in the towns. In 1892, a conference was held with political leaders from the region in which the French recognized that domestic slaves were servants and not slaves. The newly classified 'servants' had the right to buy their freedom and to receive a certificate of liberty from the French. The leaders of Kayor, Sine, Saalum, and Dimar accepted these terms; in 1894, the Futa Toro government nominally agreed too. The effects, however, were minimal, as was expected. In Futa Toro, for example, only a few hundred certificates were issued each year between 1895 and 1903, and most of these were to women who had probably borne children by their masters and could expect to be freed anyway.[48] In the far interior, there was no active intervention against slavery – not even in these superficial ways – until it became expedient to encourage the slaves of belligerent states to flee to the French as a means of undermining the power of opponents.

The other nominal commitment to abolition was the establishment of *villages de liberté* along the lines of military advance. These villages became the homes of those slaves who escaped from enemy territory, but their name was even more deceptive than Freetown, Sierra Leone. Villages were located along supply lines to produce crops, and locally their inhabitants were often seen as slaves of the French government, not freed slaves. The *villages de liberté* resembled the plantations from which many of the fugitives had fled, and fugitives frequently used them as a temporary place of refuge before deserting to some place else. Slave owners could even claim their slaves from these settlements within a month of their escape. Since masters from belligerent states were unlikely to do so, this policy effectively guaranteed that the slaves of masters in friendly territory would not escape. Furthermore, the heavy labour obligations in the villages acted as a deterrent against more massive desertions.[49]

As was the case in the use of slaves in the British colonial armies, the French also relied on slaves for its Senegalese *tirailleurs* as well as for its auxiliaries. Since the French never had more than 4,000 troops in West Africa, the conquest of the western Sudan depended upon African recruits, so that – as elsewhere – a force including many ex-slaves conquered Africa for the colonialists.[50] In a very real sense, the French created a slave force reminiscent of the old *tyeddo* slave warriors who were overthrown by the Muslim reformers of the nineteenth century. Even as the French commitment to abolition became firmer – despite the individual actions of administrators – the French slave-army continued to recruit slaves, almost as if the military was tied to some archaic tradition that French officials conveniently did not understand. This atavism was carried to extremes. As late as 1891, the *commandant* at Kita could report to his superior that some of the slaves – especially women – seized during military campaigns were being parcelled out to the soldiers, in partial compensation for salary: 'I am going to distribute the slaves in order to have fewer mouths to feed. Of course, I will keep a certain number for your men, who will be available to them after your campaign: you can tell them that for me in order to stimulate them a little.'[51] Like the *engagés à temps* and the *villages de liberté*, slavery was adapted to colonial ambitions when possible; only the propaganda changed in order to disguise colonial exploitation in the language of abolition. As late as 1895, the French administrator Penel tried to convince pro-abolitionist governor Grodet:

> no man of good sense having experience of the land will counsel immediate abolition of slavery. That would provoke a general uprising, to which also slaves would participate and which would ruin the colony ... Commerce, which is progressing, would be paralyzed. Thus we are under an obligation to accommodate ourselves for the time being to the institution of slavery. Previously, and at every occasion, we have formally promised the natives that we will not directly suppress slavery ... In all our dealings with the Blacks, it is necessary to be loyal, consistent, or lose moral credibility in their eyes.[52]

The issue was a convenient ruse to gain public support in Europe for imperialist ambitions. It was usually difficult for government officials to resist some kind of public statement that supported the humanitarian cry to end the slave trade and slavery. At times it proved useful for one European country to condemn another because too little was being done to end the evil institution. Penel's remarks, none the less, reveal another twist. For him, supporting slavery became an indication of loyalty and consistency, despite over half a century of verbal commitment to abolition. The real battle over abolition may have waxed and waned during the period, but the trend was clear, as Penel himself realized. Slavery had to end; the colonial occupation would inevitably eliminate enslavement as a means of adding to the slave population. The slave trade, too, would subside and eventually stop. Surely, Penel could not really believe that the French position raised questions of morality, as he stated. Supporting slavery was expedient, but it had nothing to do with maintaining moral credibility.

The British concentrated their efforts on ending the trans-Saharan and Red Sea slave trade, and their intervention in the Nile valley, under the auspices of Ottoman and Egyptian authority, was an extension of this campaign. British policy was no more directed against indigenous slavery than elsewhere in the savanna. European administrators pursued the attack on the slave trade most zealously in the late 1870s and early 1880s. England wanted to clean up the image of the Egyptian government, which had become increasingly visual to the European public with the opening of the strategically-vital Suez Canal. These efforts collapsed in 1884 with the emergence of the Mahdist state. The British were able to contain the export trade in slaves, except along the Wadai–Kufra route across the Sahara, but they had no effect on indigenous slavery, raiding, or trade until the reoccupation of the Sudan in 1896. Because the Mahdist state was strongly committed to slavery, the colonial regime refused to emancipate slaves and thereby rekindle the flames of discontent over the issue that had been a major factor in the Mahdist success. Instead, the continuation of slavery was accepted on the basis of British-interpreted Islamic law.[53]

Kitchener, the British governor of Sudan after the reconquest, issued the following instructions to his provincial officers in 1899:

> Slavery is not recognized in the Soudan, but as long as service is willingly rendered by servants to masters it is unnecessary to interfere in the conditions existing between them. . . . I leave it to your discretion to adopt the best methods of gradually eradicating the habit of depending upon the slave labour which has so long been part of the religious creed and customs of this country, and which it is impossible to remove at once without doing great violence to the feelings and injuring the prosperity of the inhabitants. Without proclaiming any intention of abruptly doing away with all slave-holding, much can be done in the way of discouraging it and teaching the people to get on without it.[54]

The British regime went further. Its officials became experts in Islamic law, and they interpreted the provisions on slavery in a manner that would justify its continuation, with modifications. Slave officials were eased out of office, but concubinage was left intact. Slave labour remained an essential component of the economy until the pilgrimage traffic from West Africa brought a migrant labour-force to replace slavery. There was nothing radical in the policy towards slavery, only in the abolition of the slave trade and the termination of large-scale enslavement. These changes invariably affected the ability to replenish the supply of slaves. Islamic ideals, the conversion of slaves, their emancipation, and eventual incorporation into society as clients were officially promoted. The British eliminated some elements of the slave system and encouraged its patrimonial dimensions. Ironically, slavery became more 'Islamic' under the British regime than previously.

This policy of using Islamic law and customary treatment of slaves in order to contain a potentially explosive issue was well established when the British marched on the central provinces of the Sokoto Caliphate in the first three years of the twentieth century. Slavery was being manipulated for imperial purposes. Joseph Chamberlain, British Colonial Secretary from 1895 to 1903, thought that 'sooner or later we shall have to fight some of the slave dealing tribes and we cannot have a better *casus belli* . . . Public opinion here requires that we shall justify imperial control of these savage countries by some serious effort to put down slave dealing.'[55]

By the time the British conquered the central provinces of the Sokoto Caliphate in 1903, a slavery policy already existed. Its architect, Sir Frederick (later Lord) Lugard, combined elements of British experience in the Lake Malawi region, the Anglo-Egyptian Sudan, and coastal West Africa. Lugard brought to the Sokoto Caliphate a sense of political realism that excluded the abolition of slavery. In his instructions to his subordinates in 1906, Lugard explained his position in the following terms:

> to prematurely abolish the almost universal form of labour contract, before a better system had been developed to take its place, would not only be an act of administrative folly, but would be an injustice to the masters, since Domestic Slavery is an institution sanctioned by the law of Islam, and property in slaves was as real as any other form of property among the Mohammedan population at the time that the British assumed the Government, a nullification of which would amount to nothing less than wholesale confiscation.[56]

Faced with a population that contained as many as a million slaves, Lugard successfully established British colonialism without disrupting the social order. As in the Anglo-Egyptian Sudan, he interpreted Islamic law in new ways in order to modify the institution of slavery and to permit a transition to wage labour and tenant farming peacefully. These modifications included a reliance on acts of emancipation that would offer an incentive for slaves to accept the new order willingly.

The institution of *murgu* was the cornerstone of this reform. In the nineteenth century, masters could let slaves work on their own account, in return for a fixed payment. Sometimes slaves earned enough capital to purchase their freedom, if the owner agreed to set a price and the price was reasonable. The act was considered pious because an owner who set a relatively low price was effectively assuming a financial loss in allowing the slave his freedom. The British changed this. Now a master had to agree to set a fair price on any slave who requested the arrangement of *murgu*. Failure to do so was a matter for the courts. This was not the only reform. As in the Anglo-Egyptian Sudan, slave officials were gradually displaced, and the prison for recalcitrant slaves was closed. Finally, the British decreed that all persons born after 1 April 1901 were technically free, so that by the 1930s the slave population was well on its way to extinction.[57]

A crucial dimension of both British and French policies involved the treatment of escaped slaves. At the same time that slaves who stayed with their master were given greater rights and the lure of eventual emancipation, if not for themselves then for their children, the lot of escaped slaves was made as difficult as possible. The freed-slave villages of the French along railway lines and supply routes hardly encouraged escapes in the western Sudan, although slaves sometimes used the villages as temporary refuges before fleeing further. The British enacted vagrancy laws in which the government prevented new settlers from obtaining land in a village unless they had sufficient capital to provision themselves for a year. This was designed to impede the movement of fugitive slaves. The British also destroyed some fugitive-slave villages in areas where slaves had retreated into defensible hill locations. The military solution took several decades, and not until the 1930s were all the hill retreats in Nigeria 'pacified'.

None the less, all these measures, including the efforts of the colonial regimes to disguise the slavery issue, failed to prevent the massive flight of slaves in the 1890s and the first decade of the twentieth century. Throughout the savanna, slaves ran away, particularly slaves who had been on plantations. The most dramatic struggle occurred in French areas, from Banamba, Kankan, Tuba, Gumbu, and other centres of plantation agriculture.[58] Escape had long been a factor in resistance to slavery, as we have seen with respect to the problems encountered by the French and English in curtailing the influx of fugitives into occupied territory. The French had encouraged slave desertions among their enemies because it was expedient. The British had promoted similar actions in the Nile valley before their expulsion in 1884. The events of the 1890s and after were of a different order. The scale was so great that it shook the foundations of the Muslim states as much or more than the colonial conquest itself. While the French had wanted to weaken the economies of Segu Tukulor, Samori, Rabeh, and other enemies, they did not want a social revolution. Nor did the British, as Lugard's expressed fears reveal: 'If ... slaves were to be encouraged to assert their freedom unnecessarily in large numbers, or if those so asserting it, by leaving their masters without some good cause, were indiscriminately upheld in their action by Political Officers, a state of anarchy and chaos would result, and the whole social system of the Mohammedan States would be dislocated.'[59]

Beginning around 1895, slaves took the initiative in French West Africa at an accelerating rate. The advancing colonial armies provided the opportunity, since the Muslim governments were preoccupied or in disarray. A revolt shook Banamba in 1895, along with many escapes, but a few individual slaves were recaptured and severely punished, with the full support of the French, in order to check other insubordination. In 1896, over 1,000 fugitive slaves were settled in a single *village de liberté* near Bakel, until the majority could be sent back to their masters.[60] Complaints from slaves concerning overwork, underfeeding, and other abuses began to reach French officials, who now realized how explosive the situation really was. Work-stoppages, a steady trickle of escapes, and occasional violence against masters continued into the first three years of the twentieth century. French political and judicial reforms did not help the situation. New laws in 1903 and 1905 reduced the status of slavery to a matter that was no longer recognized in French courts. Despite French reluctance to deal with slave complaints, the slaves found that they could receive an audience, even if it was only indirectly through colonial reaction to potential insurrection. In 1905 and continuing into 1906, slavery collapsed in the French western Sudan. Some semblance of order was subsequently re-established, but not before several hundred thousand slaves had fled.[61] They ran away from virtually everywhere, many heading south towards their home country in the lands that Samori and Babemba had devastated. The population of the Bougouni *cercle*, for example, increased from several thousand in the late nineteenth century to 95,592 in 1905, to 162,343 in 1913.

The *cercles* of Sikasso, Koutiala, and Koury experienced a dramatic increase in population too (table 11.1). Better census techniques and natural increase may have accounted for some of the difference, but it is likely that 250,000 people moved into these *cercles* as a result of the slave exodus. Even if allowance is made for natural increase in the order of 1–2 per cent per year, the rise in population was still 35 per cent. Many slaves fled elsewhere too, particularly to the peanut-producing regions, railway construction-sites, and government recruiting-centres for porters.[62]

The scale of the exodus was so large that it represents one of the most significant slave revolts in history. There were many efforts to stop the flight before 1905, but once the exodus began nothing could be done. The French simply let the slaves go, and for the first time the French restrained the masters. Once the dust had settled, the remnants of the slave system were reassembled, only now the more patriarchal dimensions of slavery were predominant. The French, like the British in the Nile valley and the Sokoto Caliphate, upheld Islamic law and custom in supporting slavery, with the expectation that slavery would gradually disappear now that the most disgruntled elements of the slave population were on their own.

Table 11.1 *Population increases, selected 'cercles', western Sudan*

Cercle	1905	1913	Increase	%
Bougouni	95,592	162,343	66,751	69.8
Sikasso	164,410	223,719	59,309	36.1
Koutiala	223,403	353,815	130,412	58.4
Koury	224,266	322,083	97,817	43.6
TOTAL	707,671	1,061,960	354,289	50.1

Source: M. Klein forthcoming.

The flight of slaves was less dramatic in northern Nigeria. The British had watched slaves escape from Nupe, Lafia, and Wase across the Niger and Benue Rivers since the middle of the 1890s. When slaves started deserting the farms around Yola, local slave-owners became so agitated that a mob attacked the British fort in 1902.[63] Slave escapes also spread to Kano and Sokoto, once they fell to the British in 1903; in the next couple of years, slaves left in large numbers. Some masters awoke in the morning to find their slaves gathered together, armed with bows and arrows, hoes, and knives, defiantly taunting their masters to stop them from leaving. Many returned to the areas between the emirates, where slave raiding had cleared the land. Other slaves waited to see what the British regime would do, however, and consequently the exodus was on a smaller scale than in the French areas further west. None the less, the movement continued for many years. The rapid expansion of peanut exports from Kano in 1911 introduced a level of prosperity in the rural areas that helped limit the flight. Because the British were more supportive of the caliphate aristocracy and were particularly favourable to the merchant class, the slave owners were more unified than was the case in the areas conquered by the French. This, too, helped check the exodus. None the less, many masters lost their slaves.[64]

Once again slaves had taken the initiative, just as they had done along the West African coast and in parts of central and eastern Africa. The inability to replenish the slave supply through the acquisition of new captives and through trade was a serious blow to the slave system, but the action of the slaves themselves was equally decisive. Ex-slaves became migrant workers; they opened new lands that were now safe from slave raiding; and they moved to the towns of the colonial states.[65] Many slaves did not escape, but the institution had been changed dramatically. Without the possibilities of more slaves, slavery became more firmly embedded in patriarchal structures, and hence slave conditions were better. By the 1930s, slavery ceased to exist or was well on the way to extinction almost everywhere. It had largely died the 'natural death' that Lugard and other colonialists anticipated.

12

Slavery in the political economy of Africa

In analysing the role of slavery in the political economy of Africa before 1900, I have applied a number of concepts (including 'mode of production', 'social formation', and 'transformation') in order to examine the expansion of productive slavery. This emphasis draws on the contributions of Marxian theorists,[1] particularly those who have explored different modes of production.[2] While a number of scholars have recognized the importance of slavery to the political economy, only a few have argued that slavery assumed a crucial role. Foremost among these is E. Terray.[3]

According to Terray, 'a social formation cannot be understood except by beginning with an analysis of the relations of production which are its base',[4] and for Gyaman, and indeed for Asante as a whole, Terray establishes 'the decisive importance of the exploitation of captives in the functioning of the social formation'.[5]

> We have tried to bring to light the existence of an Abron social formation with a mode of production based on slavery, which organizes a considerable part of the work in three essential sectors of the economy: agriculture, gold mining and transport [portage]. But one must immediately point out that this mode of production contains specific characteristics concerning the reproduction of the social relations which constitute it. We have already alluded to these peculiarities, which can be summarized as follows: there is no natural or biological reproduction of the captive population.[6]

This last point is crucial to Terray's model. The inability of the social formation to maintain itself without the acquisition of new slaves illustrates one of the essential characteristics of the slave mode of production, the need for continued enslavement and slave trading in order to sustain the social order and the economic base of the state.

The concept 'mode of production', therefore, involves a complex interaction between economy, society, and the state in a form that reproduces these relationships.[7] The essential ingredients include the prevalence of slave labour in vital sectors of the economy, the development of class relationships based on the relegation of slaves to the bottom of the social order, and the consolidation of a political and commercial infrastructure that can maintain these forms of exploitation. Slaves need not predominate in every sector of the economy, but they must be involved in production, whatever other functions they may also fulfil. Slave owners may have many sources of income, but a substantial portion must derive from activities related to enslavement, trade in slaves, and the appropriation of the product of slave labour. When these activities are important to the political economy, then other relationships, such as those based on kinship, tribute, taxation, and plunder, are usually affected and may become dependent on relationships associated with slavery. For example, kinship structures among free peasants may become stronger as a result of the danger of slave raids. Tribute payments and taxation were often alternatives to enslavement, and the power of the state could be used to punish those who failed to maintain such subordinate relationships.

This study has pursued Terray's formulation in the following ways: it has considered where and when slavery was a fundamental aspect of the social formation of different African societies. As a theoretical construct, a slave mode of production prevailed whenever slavery was crucial to the productive process in general or to some sector of the economy, particularly if that sector was tied to the export trade. Often this condition involved the exploitation of slave labour on a large scale, on plantations, in mines, and in the harvesting or gathering of wild products. Each of these situations involved considerable differences in the organization of production. To characterize them under a common conceptual label is to emphasize the basis of the social division of labour, not the degree of market development in the economy. The cultivation of agricultural goods under plantation conditions sometimes reflected extensive market development and sometimes not. Plantation output could be used to feed armies and palaces or it could be exported. The low level of technology meant that there was relatively little investment in capital or the improvement of land, although both forms of investment could occur, as in Madagascar (hydraulic works) or Zanzibar (clove trees). Gold mining, as in Asante or Buré, could involve an even stronger market orientation than plantations. There was an investment in pits, and hence production required some input besides the labour of slaves. None the less, since the technology was relatively simple, this investment was virtually destroyed by the rains every year, so that labour was the key variable too. The gathering of wild produce, such as gum arabic, beeswax, and rubber was even more labour intensive. Other than in very rudimentary tools, there was no investment in maintaining or increasing production. In all three situations, therefore, the crucial aspect of production was the coordination of labour in order to exploit economic resources. Labour was almost the only resource that could be mobilized in a manner to affect production.

Slavery was an effective alternative to other forms of organizing labour, and hence when slavery was crucial to the productive process we can distinguish a slave mode of production from other modes. The extraction of tribute from free peasants, the coordination of labour on the basis of kinship, the output of independent peasants in response to limited market development, the development of a labour pool through debt-bondage, and other means of production existed alongside slavery. The identification of a slave mode of production does not diminish the importance of these methods of labour organization, but it correctly establishes the dynamic portion of the political economy in the period from 1000 to 1900.

A wide historical and geographical perspective allows an identification of the two prerequisites for a slave mode of production. Firstly, a slave mode of production required instruments of enslavement, and these had to be institutionalized on the political level. While specific wars may not have been fought for the sole purpose of acquiring slaves, the enslavement of prisoners had to become an acceptable, indeed a likely, fate for captives. The ransoming of prisoners and elaborate justifications for determining who could and could not be enslaved only serve to demonstrate that such adjustments took place relatively early wherever the export of slaves was possible, and indeed in other places, too. Legal, religious, and economic methods of enslavement, as varied as these were, only highlight the institutionalization of enslavement even further. Secondly, the distribution of slaves, especially through trade, also had to achieve a comparable level of organization. Slaves could be dispersed as tribute or war booty, but the market mechanism was most important in this aspect of slavery. Those who controlled these mechanisms of supply and distribution invariably were the ones who benefited from slavery as an institution. Their economic and political position was based on control over the 'means of destruction', to employ the terminology of Jack Goody, and the mechanisms of commercial exchange.[8]

Enslavement and slave trading were essential because slave populations did not reproduce themselves. Data on this demographic failure are clearest from the nineteenth century, but it is likely that wherever slavery was the basis of a mode of production a continuous influx of new slaves had to be maintained. Morton's work on the East African coast, for example, demonstrates that slave mortality was as high as 20 per cent on Pemba (1883), 10–12 per cent on Zanzibar (1883) and 10 per cent at Malindi (1873). He estimates that mortality was probably higher in the 1850s.[9] Despite other important factors, slave families appear to have been reluctant to have children. Harms reports similar conclusions for the Bobangi on the Zaire River; people did not want children, in part because it limited mobility and in part because it was cheaper and easier to buy children. The Bobangi population, therefore, was an unstable population demo- graphically.[10] Comparable patterns are evident in Madagascar, the western Sudan, and elsewhere. The incorporation of women through marriage and concubinage (whose children were considered free) accounts for the

271

necessity of acquiring new slaves to some extent, but as Meillassoux has argued even when the freed offspring of slave women are taken into consideration the birth-rate was very low.[11] Slavery was simply not a self-sustaining institution through biological reproduction.

The external trade was an essential sector of this infrastructure. Not all slaves were captured with export in mind. None the less, it was necessary that most slaves be moved a considerable distance from their point of enslavement. Here was a 'push' factor in the economy that fed the export sector. Whether or not the external market provided a 'pull' for slaves, there was an indigenous force that moved captives. When external demand influenced price, then it was only logical that the two factors should reinforce the flow of slaves from Africa. Once the link to the export market became established, and indeed while it continued to expand, the political economy invariably became more intimately connected with the export trade. The same logic suggests that the collapse of the external market would have equally profound effects on the internal slave system, as indeed has been shown in the preceding chapters.

In broad outline, this external trade included both the export of slaves to the Muslim countries outside black Africa and the shipment of slaves across the Atlantic to the Americas. Indeed, the development of the trans-Atlantic trade resulted in changes in the political economy of the Guinea coast, and the history of slavery in the different portions of that coast can only be understood in the context of the export trade. Indigenous institutions were either developed or modified in order to accommodate that trade, and the result was the evolution of distinctive slave systems that varied as much one from another as they differed from the type of slavery that predominated in the Muslim regions.

The recognition of the importance of the external market for slaves permits a fuller analysis of slavery during the period when the forces of abolition began to affect the nature of the institution. The abolition movement highlights the crucial impact of the external market in reverse. The collapse of that market and the extension of abolitionist doctrines presented a serious challenge to those social formations in which slavery was a major institution. The impact varied, and the form of change differed considerably, as outlined in the preceding chapters. None the less, the transition from a slave mode of production to capitalism has involved fundamental structural changes in the social formation. The recognition that the nature of this transition involved a shift from a political economy based on slavery to one in which slavery withered away has considerable theoretical significance, as well as empirical accuracy. The mass escape of slaves, the colonial accommodation with slave owners, and the reluctance of the colonial regime to enforce abolition until the capitalist economy could absorb the labour released by emancipation all demonstrate this significance.

272

The association of slavery with the external trade clearly distinguishes my interpretation from that of many scholars who argue that the export sector had a marginal impact on African society and economy.[12] The threat of sale to merchants associated with the export trade was as important in the control of slaves as the fear of whipping was on the plantations of the Americas. The interaction between the external trade and the indigenous institution was a dialectical relationship. Both changed over time, and the influences of these changes flowed both ways, constantly producing a new situation in the two spheres. The long-term effects could be significant indeed, as a comparison between west-central Africa and the Islamic savanna reveals. Where women and children could be absorbed easily, as in the societies of west-central Africa, slavery remained associated with a mode of production based on kinship. Males were exported in disproportionate numbers, and women and children were placed in subordinate positions within a lineage. The means of production were not specifically associated with slavery, for most agricultural labour was the responsibility of women and children anyway. In the northern savanna, by contrast, the external market was for women and children, despite a domestic preference for these very same slaves. Unlike west-central Africa, the domestic market and the external market competed for the same slaves, and the value of male slaves was depressed accordingly. It was possible in this context to employ males in productive activities, thereby changing the organization of production. Another important difference directly related to the external trade was the scale of exports, usually a steady but relatively modest level for the northern savanna, but a more substantial volume for west-central Africa, particularly in the eighteenth and early nineteenth centuries. This variation suggests that the pattern of slavery found in west-central Africa was reinforced and indeed extended further into the interior, so that the use of slaves in productive capacities that required a fundamental shift in the social formation did not occur. During this same period, the northern savanna was relatively stable; the existing social formation continued to function as it had for centuries.

These generalizations help confirm the important role of the external trade, including the significance of export volume, the link to the institutions of enslavement and trade, and the negative and positive associations of the trade to the political fragmentation of Africa. The volume helps to establish the scale of slavery in the domestic sector as well as the number of people actually taken from Africa – both the domestic population and the export population resulted from the same mechanisms of slave supply. This interrelationship was characteristic of the slave mode of production along the Guinea coast and other areas feeding the trans-Atlantic trade in the eighteenth and first half of the nineteenth centuries, but the existence of the export trade was not necessary for the continued functioning of a slave mode of production, even though the rise of slave exports had contributed to the transformation of slavery.

Slavery was transformed in Africa, to recount Finley's crucial distinction examined in chapter 1,[13] once slavery became an important component in production, particularly agriculture. Finley's insight accords well with Terray's discussion of a slave mode of production, for Terray, too, emphasizes the role of slaves in the productive process. I have expanded upon Finley's notion, moreover, just as I elaborated Terray's model. The transformations were many, and they often involved changes that affected production in the narrow sense that Finley intended. The origins and development of various plantation systems, the use of slaves in mining and handicrafts, and the employment of slaves in livestock breeding are all manifestations of this transformation of slavery into an instrument of production. Finley has indeed identified a crucial element in the reconstruction of slavery in African history. Slavery was transformed, and slave societies emerged. I have referred to this transformation in terms of the development of a social formation that incorporated a slave mode of production.

The transformations in slavery were more complex than the essential one identified by Finley, and the theoretical significance of this concept is particularly useful in distinguishing between the various kinds of changes that occurred in the history of slavery in Africa. The emphasis on transformations helps identify important factors in the evolution of slavery, including changes in the external market, different responses to the export trade, and particular adjustments in the availability of slaves for domestic assignment. Slavery could be transformed into a productive institution, but the social formation itself could be transformed in different ways in conjunction with the development of slavery.

In order to consider these transformations, it is necessary to distinguish once again between the three sectors of the African slave system: the process of enslavement, the mechanism of slave distribution, and the role of slaves in the social formation. The history of slavery in Africa reveals transformations in each of these sectors, sometimes individually and sometimes in combination. These differences become clearer when various regions of Africa are contrasted. In west-central Africa, institutions of enslavement and trade developed that resulted in fundamental changes to the structure of the political economy. The region became a source of supply for the trans-Atlantic trade, despite the fact that slavery was not transformed into a productive institution. Slaves were used in production, but their tasks related more to the sexual division of labour that characterized the organization of labour among lineage members – that is, women did most of the agricultural labour anyway; hence the acquisition of women enabled men to combine their desires for labour, sexual access, and children. Slavery was not essential to production, so that the kind of transformation that Finley identifies as crucial in the development of a slave society did not take

274

place. None the less, slavery was central to the social formation. Slaves were an item of export, and enslavement was a means of social control in a political system based on tributary relationships between a military elite and dependent lineages. Within this system, slavery filled a variety of functions, including military conscription, porterage in long-distance trade, marriage, and funeral sacrifices. The lack of transformation in the productive process should not disguise the transformation in enslavement and trade. Here the dominant mode of production was based on the extraction of tribute, often in the form of slaves. Tribute collection involving slaves was also prevalent along the West African coast and in the northern savanna, but there slavery assumed a productive dimension as well.

Along the Zaire River and in the Niger delta, the most significant transformation was in the relationship between slavery and the commercial infrastructure. Slaves were incorporated into the firms of merchants, and activities directly related to enslavement and production were usually of secondary importance. This incomplete transformation of slavery was also connected with the export trade in slaves. Again there was a structural change in slavery, despite the relative absence of slaves in production. In these commercial situations, slaves were again crucial to the social formation, since the incorporation of slaves was essential to the operation of business. Slave labour was directly related to the consolidation of the commercial infrastructure that was necessary for the export of slaves. Parallels can be found in the use of slaves as porters and stock boys along the caravan routes of the interior. The use of slaves in commerce was connected to the distribution of other goods too.

For purposes of analysis it is important to isolate the use of slaves in military service, and hence as an agency in the enslavement process, from the employment of slaves in production. In the military slaves were not used for productive purposes, except in the sense that soldiers 'produced' slaves through wars and raids.[14] The incorporation of slaves into the army was, therefore, essential to the perpetuation of slavery as an institution, but the transformation was no more related to productive activities than changes in commercial organization or kinship relationships were.

The maintenance of the trans-Saharan, Red Sea, and Indian Ocean trade in slaves, the development of the trans-Atlantic trade, and the abolition of each of these trades involved transformations in the mechanisms of slave supply as Africa became linked to an international system of slavery and then severed from its external market. The establishment of this structure facilitated the emergence of a slave mode of production within Africa. Clearly this transformation occurred less often than the transformations in the supply mechanism alone. Both could take place together, but the connection was not inevitable, at least not in the same place.

The international system of slavery that developed after the sixteenth century had its African and non-African parts; it was not confined to the African continent. If west-central Africa is examined in isolation from the

Americas, then only a partial transformation took place, but if the mechanisms of slave supply are attached to the receiving area for the slaves, then a full transformation can be perceived. Thus west-central Africa must be seen in conjunction with the development of plantation slavery in the Americas, where slavery was the basis of production but where the institutions of enslavement were absent. Taken together, this sophisticated slave mode of production was separated into distinct parts – enslavement in Africa, productive slavery in the Americas – and a mechanism of slave distribution connected the two sectors. Once the forces of abolition began to sever the link in this intercontinental system, slavery was confined to an African context. The separation continued, with slaves taken to São Thomé and Principé, scattered places along the Angolan coast, and the Arab–Swahili plantations of Zanzibar, Pemba, and the east coast. This transformation presaged the collapse of the system, for the emancipation of slaves in these locations eliminated the need for continued enslavement. Those areas where slavery had not been transformed into a productive institution lost the crucial function of supplying slaves. Elsewhere, the separation between slave supply and the use of slaves in production was far less, and it is possible, therefore, to examine the interaction between the separate sectors in the same social formation.

ARTICULATION WITH CAPITALISM

In the nineteenth century, slavery was harnessed to capitalism. The pressure on the external trade forced the redirection of slaves within Africa on an unprecedented scale. Commercial expansion resulted in the employment of slaves in trade and production; now Africa internalized slavery as a mode of production, whereas previously African slavery had been part of a larger, intercontinental network. This intensification of slavery, reflected in the vehemence of European anti-slavery rhetoric, presaged the collapse of slavery as a mode of production. Conflict was inevitable because the economic interests of Europe, the pressure of abolitionists in the missions and the popular press, and the rivalries of European governments that spilled over into the tropical world eventually undermined slavery. European merchants cooperated with their African counterparts – who were the largest slave-owners – when times were prosperous, but during the series of economic crises at the end of the nineteenth century, European firms moved to bypass their African intermediaries in order to cut costs and increase profits. As African merchants and producers found themselves hard pressed, they demanded more from their slaves. Abolitionists, even when in favour of reform and not immediate emancipation, spread dangerous propaganda among slaves. While their missions were little more than symbols of freedom – the actual numbers of fugitives and ex-slaves at the missions was relatively small when compared with the total slave population – African catechists spread the subversive doctrines of freedom. It took

European colonial expansion to provide slaves with the opportunity to escape. During the chaos of conquest, law and order temporarily broke down; slave masters who had opposed European expansion were in no position to assert their authority over their slaves, and the new colonial regimes could not prevent individuals and small groups from leaving.

This process of intensified slave use and then the collapse of slavery reveals a wider phenomenon – the articulation of a slave mode of production with capitalism. This articulation began with the incorporation of the Guinea coast into the southern Atlantic system of slave supply for the Americas. Africa was invariably tied to the Americas until this supply function was terminated in the nineteenth century; hence developments in slavery along the Guinea coast were subordinate to the emergence of productive slavery in the Americas. Commercial links with Europe and India demonstrate the extent of this involvement, but the nature of the exchange in itself served as a barrier to the transfer of capitalism to Africa. At the height of the slave trade in the eighteenth century, Europe, the Americas, and Africa formed three distinct sectors of the world economy; capitalism emerged triumphant only in Europe, while the Americas and Africa remained subordinate partners.

This subordination shaped slavery in the Americas – which many scholars have recognized – but it also shaped slavery in Africa, at least in those parts of Africa catering to the export trade.[15] In this case, slavery developed within the context of slave supply: the retention of greater numbers of women and children, the use of slaves in the military, and the employment of slaves in production related to the maintenance of a class of merchants and war-lords who were essential to the functioning of an international system of slavery in the seventeenth and eighteenth centuries. This interaction continued into the nineteenth century, only the abolition crusade increasingly hampered the ability to supply slaves.

The strongest economic forces in the nineteenth century were capitalist – the expansion of world markets for 'legitimate' commodities. The growth of the market for oils, ivory, ostrich feathers, and other goods – some for luxury consumption associated with European prosperity and others for the industry that characterized the capitalist order – provided a ready outlet for slave labour. Masters assigned their slaves to the production of export commodities, although production for household consumption and regional markets continued as before, as did the continued use of slaves in non-economic functions. Hence the transformation was more relative than absolute. Slaves were already used in economic capacities; now more slaves were so employed. Older forms of slavery associated with slave supply – military position, administrative appointment, commercial agency – were still important because it was still necessary to supply slaves for the African market, but the relative importance of these functions declined in comparison with the productive employment of slaves.

The emergence of a slave mode of production in Africa was very different from the development of the slave systems of the Americas, despite the fact that both were subordinate to capitalism and ultimately associated with the consolidation of capitalism. In the American context, slavery was introduced from outside and always relied on the importation of slaves and the continued identification of masters with Europe. In Africa, slavery evolved from indigenous institutions, and, except for the relatively small plantation sector in central, eastern, and southern Africa, slave owners were also Africans. Furthermore, the African social formation always included an important – often dominant – regional orientation, while the Americas were more closely integrated with the world market than Africa, and the regional economy was comparatively unimportant. The reliance on race as a method of social control was also peculiarly American, although African slave-owners established their own methods of domination. These and other differences are crucial in distinguishing the form of slavery.

There were significant variations in slavery as a mode of production in different parts of Africa too. Plantation slavery was most widespread in the northern savanna, where religious motivation had been successfully channelled to justify the economic exploitation of captives. Regional economies were by far more important than the export sector, except for the Senegambia area. Hence the articulation between slavery and capitalism was weakest here, even though the number of slaves was greatest. Along the West African coast, slavery was a significant factor in production, although in the Igbo–Ibibio palm-oil belt – the largest source of palm products – slavery was not as important as elsewhere along the West African coast. It is clear from these variations that the dominance of slavery was not a requirement for the integration into the world economy. Local factors had a strong influence on the role slavery played. Where state structures were particularly centralized, as on the Gold Coast and in the Bight of Benin interior, slaves were more numerous than in the Biafran hinterland, which lacked centralized states. Finally, in southern, central, and eastern Africa, the external enclaves relied on slavery to produce commodities for the market, while there were virtually no foreign enclaves that relied on slavery elsewhere (in the Turco-Egyptian Sudan, the indigenous slave owners dominated production; the colonial state was not a major factor in production). The articulation of slavery with capitalism was more pronounced in these enclaves than anywhere else, but the expansion of these enclaves was relatively limited. Except for a few places along trade routes, slavery remained incompletely transformed in most of the interior.

Other forms of labour – share cropping, migrant labour, pawnage – existed alongside slavery in the nineteenth century, and these forms of labour were often associated with slavery. This association can be demonstrated with reference to four examples. Senegambian migrant farmers were sometimes slaves, and whether slave or free they – or their masters – had access to land through the payment of 10 per cent of their peanut harvests to their landlords, who were usually the largest slave owners employing slaves on their own.[16] The leasing of slaves on the Gold Coast and elsewhere solved a bottleneck in the movement of labour from those who had excess manpower to those who needed temporary workers, such as European commercial firms, but the slaves did not have control over their earnings.[17] Migrant labour became important in South Africa in the 1870s; some migrants were slaves by origin, but many were free men who were able to seek employment on European farms and in the new mines of Kimberley because slaves were employed in domestic tasks back home.[18] Pawnage – which already shared centre stage with slavery – had become a source of slaves when customary laws were ignored, but in the late nineteenth century and continuing into the twentieth century pawnage assumed a new importance as a method of labour mobilization. The incidence of pawnage actually increased as slavery began to die, at least in Yorubaland, the middle Niger valley, and perhaps Asante.[19] The erosion of slavery as a mode of production freed these alternative forms of labour, which in one way or another marked the transition to a more complete articulation with capitalism. The transformation of these forms occurred under colonialism.[20]

The conquest of Africa and the extension of European economic domination proceeded together under the banner of anti-slavery. As has been demonstrated, however, the anti-slavery cause was a reluctant one, seldom providing the motivation for European economic or political action. None the less, as an ideology, the anti-slavery rhetoric of missionaries and reformers provided a rationale for expanson that was logically connected with the progression of captialism and imperialism.[21] The literature of nineteenth-century missionaries, explorers, diplomats, and reconnaissance officers maintained the anti-slavery cause. Such authors as Buxton, Schoelcher, André, Berlioux, and Lacour wrote books specifically on the slavery issue, while the anti-slavery movement of Lavigerie and the various societies for suppression of slavery played an active role in promoting expansion by justifying intervention in the name of abolition.[22] Although missionaries and colonial officials in Africa were usually more cautious, political expediency and safety dictated a gradualist policy anyway. Slavery was an explosive issue best left alone, despite its value for propaganda.

None the less, the ideology of anti-slavery was an accurate indicator of larger changes that were inevitable, and as such the observations and aims of reformers and reactionaries alike reveal changes that were taking place, often against the wishes of the observers themselves. The flight of slaves, the hiring of slaves to secure a wage-labour force, reforms imposed on local practice to appease the abolitionist movement, and other developments were important steps in the ending of slavery. The rhetoric influenced the nature of social change and thereby contributed to the transition from a social formation in which slavery was important to the peripheral capitalism of the colonial era.

The imposition of colonialism terminated slavery as a mode of production and marked the fuller integration of Africa into the orbit of capitalism.

Imperialism used the rhetoric of anti-slavery, but the crucial developments involved military expansion and the commercial supremacy of European firms in Africa. While Africa remained on the periphery of capitalism, the colonial dictatorship none the less facilitated the final transformation of slavery – the slave mode of production was dismantled by ending the major forms of enslavement and curtailing most slave trading. Kidnapping and smuggling continued for several decades – and still continue on a small scale in a few places – but slave raiding, warfare, and public slave-marketing ceased virtually everywhere by the first decade of colonial rule. Because of the essential functions of enslavement and trade in the maintenance of the slave population, the curtailment of these activities resulted in the rapid decline in the number of slaves. The flight of slaves and reformed emancipation procedures also reduced the slave population, so that kidnapping, slave smuggling, and the birth of children to slave parents whose servile status was retained could not sustain slavery as a mode of production. European administrators could afford to accommodate slave masters in the interests of social stability because the abolition of slavery was on an irreversible course.

Africa remained peripheral to capitalism, even as slavery was disassembled. The new forms of labour organization – migration, peasant production, colonial coercion through taxation and corvée projects, and military conscription – were associated with the colonial dictatorship.[23] By the time anthropologists and historians concentrated on studying slavery, only the legacy of a slave mode still existed.

THE LEGACY OF SLAVERY

When slavery has been a central institution in society, its legacy lives on, and with it problems confronting Africa. Reports of kidnapped children, young girls taken to Mecca as 'pilgrims' but who end up in harems, and the insistence of some old men that they are still slaves because of the status and benefits that such an assertion still holds, attest to this legacy.[24] Now, however, there is no institution of slavery, despite the evidence for individual cases of slavery. By the 1930s, abolition was well on its way to becoming an accomplished fact virtually everywhere. Even when slaves were not formally emancipated or locally were not recognized as free, the social and political setting had changed irrevocably.

Within Africa, the legacy is often apparent, although issues of the past are now disguised under new labels. Differences between Muslims and Christians can well relate to who was raiding whom for slaves, a division revealed to me in the mid-1970s when university students began to argue among themselves over the historical significance of this religious difference.[25] Many questions about this legacy remain to be examined in the course of future research, particularly the relationship of slave ancestry to migrant labour, the movement of people to the towns and cities, ethnic identification, as well as religious conversion. These and related topics are beyond the scope of this book.

One aspect of the history of slavery and abolition should be readily apparent. Those who focus on slavery in the Americas without reference to slavery in Africa have neglected a major problem in the history of Africans. Africans experienced slavery not only in the Americas but also in Africa. Furthermore, emancipation came much later in Africa. To concentrate on the struggle for freedom in the United States, the West Indies, or other parts of the Americas without recognizing the plight of slaves in Africa introduces a major distortion into our understanding of slave history. The emergence of an international system of slavery tied the Americas and Africa together, just as the earlier history of slavery in Muslim countries had drawn some parts of Africa into the Islamic orbit. The disassembly of that international system required more than the freeing of slaves in the Americas, and the legacy of oppression and racism in the Americas is only one aspect of the tragic heritage of slavery.

In the African context, the legacy of slavery has been so enormous that it has not always been obvious. In order to focus on specific problems, scholars have failed to recognize or have blurred the larger issue, whether they have been conscious of this distortion or not. The colonial dictatorship, the role of the international economy, the racial dimension involved in the relationships between Europeans and Africans, the struggle for political independence, the consolidation of military rule, the revolutionary struggle in southern Africa, and other topics are often perceived in a relatively shallow historical framework, despite – some would say because of – the popularity of dependency theory, Marxist analysis, and the interdisciplinary interaction between anthropology, economics, political science, sociology, and history. Although Cooper's work is a remarkable exception, most scholars concerned with the development of a labour force in the colonial and post-colonial periods have not examined the organization of labour in the immediate pre-colonial era. Yet it should be clear that the transition to colonial rule and political independence occurred in the context of the collapse of slavery.[26] The degree to which this transition marked a major departure in history has not been analysed adequately. Where old elites survived, despite the turmoil of the colonial years, then the transition was less abrupt. Where the old elite was eliminated, slaves could sometimes assert themselves sooner and more fully. None the less, the question is not whether or not there was a dramatic break with the past, but the ways in which people were able to shape the new order, preserving the old or rising above it. Much colonial and post-colonial scholarship has to be re-examined with the problem of abolition in mind.

On the political level, more biographical studies are needed to establish the ancestry of the African leaders of the past eighty years. How many are of slave descent? How were they able to rise above the handicap? Are there any patterns in the policies that individuals of various backgrounds have pursued? With a military heritage involving the recruitment of fugitive slaves into the colonial armies, it might well prove important to examine the backgrounds of subsequent military personnel, again checking for a link with the slave past. Until such research is completed, it is impossible to conclude that ex-slaves continued to dominate the military, although this is possible unless there was a concerted effort on the part of the old elite or the colonial regimes to change the composition of the military. The results of such research would shed new light on the governments of the past two decades, both military and civilian.

The economic sphere is open to reinterpretation to an extent that probably exceeds a new study of political history. Again Cooper has led the way in exploring some aspects of economic adjustment. His analysis of the Swahili coast demonstrates the ways in which a slave plantation-economy was transformed under colonialism; his study offers the possibility for comparison of economic change in areas where slaves were important in production with other areas where slavery was marginal. Except for Cooper's work, the concentration on economic change and dependency has tended to focus on two aspects of history, the role of African entrepreneurship and the impact of the world economy on a technologically backward continent. This orientation has resulted in the accumulation of considerable knowledge of foreign firms and their means of domination. The extent to which African merchants, farmers, and workers have been able to resist or adjust to this adverse situation has led to considerable understanding of class formation and ethnic stratification. The correspondence between these developments and the legacy of slavery is almost totally unknown. Yet when slavery was such a crucial dimension of the past, it is virtually certain that a closer examination of the links between the precolonial economic order and the colonial economy will unveil new questions of considerable significance.

Appendix: Chronology of measures against slavery

1772 Lord Mansfield's decision: slaves become free upon entering the British Isles, thus making it illegal to repossess fugitive slaves.

1783 The Society of Friends (England) forms an anti-slavery association for the relief of slaves and the discouragement of the slave trade.

1787 The Abolition Society of Samuel Wilberforce founds Freetown, Sierra Leone, as a home for liberated slaves.

1789 The revolutionary constitution of France abolishes slavery in principle (subsequently revoked by Napoleon).

1791 Slaves rebel on the French island of Saint Domingue. The last European forces are evacuated in 1798, and the independent, black government of Haiti is established.

1791, 1794 First United States measures abolishing the slave trade.

1792 Denmark declares its intention to abolish the slave trade.

1799 The Church Missionary Society (England) is founded to pursue humanitarian aims in Africa, including the fight against the slave trade.

1803 Denmark abolishes the slave trade.

1805 British Order-in-Council restricts the import of slaves into colonies captured from France and Holland (i.e., since 1802).

1806 Act of Parliament prohibits British participation in the slave trade to foreign territories, effectively outlawing two-thirds of the British trade.

1807 The Abolition Act prohibits all British subjects from participation in the slave trade as of 1 January 1808. A naval squadron that eventually reaches one-sixth of the total strength of the Royal Navy is dispatched to blockade the West African coast.

1808 Sierra Leone becomes a British colony and a centre of anti-slave trade activities.

1808 USA abolishes slave trade.

1810 Anglo-Portuguese treaty whereby Portugal agrees to restrict its slave trade to its own colonies.

1811 Parliament strengthens the Abolition Act by declaring that British subjects engaged in the slave trade are to be considered pirates.

1813 Anglo-Swedish treaty whereby Sweden outlaws the slave trade.

1814 The Treaty of Paris: France and Britain agree that the slave trade is 'repugnant to the principles of natural justice'. France agrees to limit its trade to its own colonies and to abolish the trade in five years.

1814 Anglo-Netherlands treaty whereby the latter outlaws the slave trade.

1814 Anglo-Spanish treaty whereby Spain limits its slave trade to its own colonies and prohibits the trade north of the equator after 1817 and south of the equator after 1820 in return for £400,000 in compensation.

1815 Anglo-Portuguese treaty whereby Portugal agrees to limit its slave trade to its possessions south of the equator. In return, Britain waives Portugal's war debt of £450,000.

1815 Congress of Vienna: Britain, France, Prussia, Russia, Portugal, Spain, Austria, and Sweden condemn the slave trade as 'repugnant to the principles of humanity and universal morality'.

1817 British convention with Portugal limits the Portuguese slave trade of East Africa to an area from Cape Delgado to the Bay of Lourenco Marques. Portugal also concedes visit and search rights on Portuguese ships suspected of violating this and other agreements.

1817 British treaty with Imerina prohibits the export of slaves from Madagascar in return for compensation of £2,000 per year. Imerina outlaws slave raiding in the Comoro Islands on penalty of being reduced to slavery.

1817 Anglo-Spanish treaty grants Britain the right to detain Spanish ships.

1818 France outlaws the slave trade.

1820 British treaty with Imerina is extended.

1820s Slavery is outlawed throughout the newly independent Spanish countries of Latin America.

1821 Slave imports into Cuba become illegal, although effect is minimal.

1822 The American Colonization Society establishes Liberia as a home for liberated American slaves.

1822 Moresby Treaty between Britain and Muscat prohibits the export of slaves by Europeans in East Africa and establishes a British observer at Zanzibar. Britain recognizes Omani claims in East Africa, including the existence of slavery.

1823 A third treaty with Imerina whereby Britain is authorized to seize slavers; it also provides for the resettlement of liberated slaves.

1823 Society for the Mitigation and Gradual Abolition of Slavery throughout the British Dominions is founded.

1824 Establishment of British protectorate over Mombasa with intention to restrict slave trade; protectorate terminates in 1826 under Zanzibar pressure.

1825 Hugh Clapperton and Dixon Denham report that the Sokoto Caliphate and Borno are willing to end slave exports in return for trade in European goods; this report spurs the first expedition to gain anti-slave trade treaties, although expedition fails with the death of Clapperton in 1827.

1826 Newly independent Brazil accepts Portugal's treaty obligations with Britain and promises to abolish the slave trade in three years.

1831 Anglo-French treaty provides for mutual, limited right to search vessels suspected of carrying slaves.

1833 Britain emancipates slaves in its West Indian colonies, South Africa, and Mauritius, with compensation to slave-owners; emancipation takes effect on 1 August 1834, although a system of apprenticeship lasts for four years in some colonies.

1835 Anglo-Spanish treaty for condemnation of slave ships.

1838 Thomas F. Buxton launches a campaign against slavery, advocating free trade and the colonization of the African interior with freed, Christian slaves. Buxton's efforts result in the strengthening of the British naval squadron off the West African coast and the signing of anti-slave trade treaties with African states.

1839 Convention between Oman (Zanzibar) and Britain, which extends rights of search and seizure.

1839 Joseph Sturge founds the British Anti-Slavery Society.

1839 Buxton establishes the African Civilization Society as part of his abolition campaign.

1830s British agreement with Asante for the extradition of fugitive slaves begins to break down.

1841 The British Aborigines' Protection Society is founded in England.

1841 Britain, France, Austria, Prussia, and Russia agree to extend rights of search and seizure to halt the slave trade, although France refuses to ratify the treaty.

1842 Webster–Ashburton Treaty: Britain and the USA agree to maintain a naval force of at least eighty guns off the African coast as part of a joint commitment to suppress the slave trade.

1843 The legal status of slavery is abolished in India, although slaves are not emancipated.

1843 France initiates *engagé* or 'free labour' emigration in its colonial possessions to circumvent anti-slavery treaties.

1844 Britain signs treaty with Sultanate of Anjouin (Comoro Islands) to prevent French recruitment of *engagé* labour.

1845 Anglo-French treaty: both powers agree to maintain at least 26 cruisers off the African coast as an anti-slave trade force; rights of search and seizure are abrogated. France does not adhere to the treaty, which is allowed to expire after 10 years.

1845 British treaty with Oman (Zanzibar): slave trade is restricted to Oman's possessions in Arabia and East Africa; Britain secures the right of search and seizure.

1846 Tunisia abolishes the slave trade in order to gain British support against the Ottoman Empire.

1847 The Ottoman Empire prohibits the slave trade in the Persian Gulf and closes public slave-markets in Constantinople.

1847 Liberia becomes an independent republic.

1848 Persia bans the maritime slave trade.

1848 France emancipates slaves in its colonies.

1849 French preventative squadron off the West African coast is reduced.

1849 France establishes Libreville, Gabon, as a settlement for freed slaves.

1849 Establishment of British consuls and agents in West Africa to supervise treaty obligations, including anti-slave trade provisions. Royal Navy squadron is strengthened.

1851 Britain deposes the ruler of Lagos for his refusal to take action against the slave trade. Anti-slave trade treaties are signed with Lagos, Dahomey, Porto Novo, Badagry, and Abeokuta.

1851 Anglo-Persian treaty grants Britain right of search and seizure.

1854 Portugal decrees that slaves in its territories are *libertos*.

1854 Egypt bans public slave markets, although trade continues in private.

1854 The Ottoman Empire prohibits the white slave trade.

1855 First of several treaties with principalities on the Red Sea coast that grant right of search and seizure to Britain; official appointed to Berbera.

1857 The Ottoman Empire prohibits the slave trade in its domains, although decree is not enforced.

1859 France abolishes the *engagé* system, although enforcement is not strict.

1861 The Canning Award: Zanzibar and Oman are separated, thereby setting the stage for the further suppression of the slave trade in the Indian Ocean.

1862 Treaty of Washington: USA grants Britain the right of search and seizure.

1865 13th Amendment to the USA Constitution abolishes slavery.

1865 British treaty with Imerina whereby Imerina prohibits the importation of slaves.

1869 Royal Navy begins intensive patrolling against Arab slave trade.

1869 Portugal abolishes slavery.

1870 Ownership of slaves becomes illegal in India.

1873 Kirk–Barghash treaty: Zanzibar bans public slave-markets and promises to protect liberated slaves.

1874 Proclamation for the emancipation of slaves on the Gold Coast, following the British defeat of Asante.

1875 British treaty with Tunisia confirming abolition of slavery and the slave trade.

1876 France incorporates Walo and Dimar into Senegal, thereby abolishing slavery. Annexation subsequently revoked.

1876 British Royal Commission investigates the treatment of fugitive slaves in East Africa but opposes asylum for fugitives except in cases of physical danger.

1877 Anglo-Egyptian treaty prohibits the import, export, and transit of slaves in Egypt; domestic slavery to be outlawed by 1884 in Egypt and 1889 in the Nilotic Sudan.

1877 Britain undertakes to reorganize the Zanzibar army to combat the slave trade in the interior.

1877 Imerina declares all slaves from Mozambique free.

1878 Portugal abolishes legal status of slavery.

1880 Anglo-Ottoman Convention reaffirms the prohibition of the slave trade and grants Britain rights of search.

1882 Colonel Charles Gordon, seeking to check the Mahdist rebellion, rescinds the law banning the slave trade in the Nilotic Sudan.

1883 Morocco rejects the 'friendly appeal' of the British Foreign Office for the abolition of slavery.

1883 The African Department of the British Foreign Office replaces the Slave Trade Department, as the era of 'moral temporizing' ends.

1883 Britain assigns four travelling consuls to East Africa to replace naval action against the slave trade.

1884 France and Britain forbid employees and *protégés* in Morocco to own slaves.

1884 British treaty with Ethiopia grants Ethiopia access to Red Sea through Massawa on condition that slave trade ends in the interior.

1885 Berlin Conference: Britain, France, Austria, Germany, Russia, Spain, Portugal, Holland, Belgium, Italy, the Ottoman Empire, Sweden, Denmark, and the USA agree to 'help in suppressing slavery', although no direct measures are taken against the slave trade in Africa.

1888 Brazil becomes the last American country to abolish slavery.

1888 Cardinal Lavigerie inaugurates a campaign against the slave trade in central Africa, thereby revitalizing the humanitarian cause in Britain and Europe.

1888 Imperial British East Africa Company pays more than £3,000 compensation for 1,400 fugitive slaves at the CMS mission stations near Mombasa.

1888 Germany, Britain, and Italy blockade the coast of Zanzibar, ostensibly to suppress the slave trade.

1889 Zanzibar grants the British and Germans perpetual right of search, decrees that new slaves entering its domains after 1 November 1889 shall be free, and provides for the emancipation of all slave children born after 1 January 1890.

1889 Brussels Conference: the participants of the Berlin Conference, plus Persia, Zanzibar, and the Congo Free State, condemn slavery and the slave trade. Bureaux are established in Brussels and Zanzibar to collate and disseminate information on the slave trade.

1892 Convention between France and the independent states of Senegal in which slaves are recognized as servants; French courts grant certificates of liberty to those slaves buying their freedom.

1893 Renwell Rodd's report to the British parliament recommending the gradual abolition of the slave trade in East Africa.

1894 British emancipation ordinance in the Gambia for gradual termination of slavery; slaves to be free at death of master or payment of £10 (adults) or £5 (children).

1896 Legal status of slavery abolished in Sierra Leone.

1897 Legal status of slavery abolished in Zanzibar.

1897 Slavery is abolished in Madagascar, following the French invasion of Imerina in 1895.

1899 Joint deputation of Quakers and the Anti-Slavery Society meets with the British Under-Secretary for Foreign Affairs to demand emancipation of slaves in Africa.

1900 Britain abolishes the legal status of slavery in the occupied parts of Nigeria with the intention of extending the decree throughout Nigeria.

1909 Institution of slavery abolished in Zanzibar.

1919 Treaty of Saint Germain-en-Laye: the Allies limit (but do not prohibit) the slave trade in Africa. The signatories pledge to 'secure the complete suppression of slavery in all its forms and of the slave trade by land and sea'.

1926 44 countries ratify the slavery convention of the League of Nations.

1928 Institution of slavery is abolished in Sierra Leone.

1930 League of Nations prohibition of slavery is extended to include all forms of forced labour.

1936 League of Nations establishes a Permanent Advisory Committee on the suppression of the slave trade.

1942 Legal status of slavery is abolished in Ethiopia.

1962 Saudi Arabia becomes the last country to abolish the legal status of slavery.

Notes

1 Africa and slavery

1 I have been particularly influenced by Finley 1968 in the following analysis, although other works by Finley have also been consulted, including 1964, 1973, 1979, and 1980.

2 Kopytoff and Miers discuss this in terms of the marginality of slaves; see their 'African "slavery" as an institution of marginality', in Miers and Kopytoff 1977.

3 A particularly perceptive discussion that emphasizes this point is that of Goody 1980.

4 The relationship between control over production and control over reproduction has been argued most fully by Meillassoux; see 1972, 1978a, forthcoming a, and 1976. For a critique of Meillassoux's approach, see O'Laughlin 1977.

5 See the excellent discussion in Meillassoux forthcoming b.

6 Finley 1968, p. 310.

7 I have been influenced by the following works: Terray 1974 and 1979; Foster-Carter 1978; Rey 1971 and 1973; Marx 1965; Jewsiewicki 1977; and Padgug 1976. For a critical survey of the Marxist literature, see Law 1978b and 1981.

8 This is discussed more fully in Lovejoy 1981c.

9 Terray 1974 and 1975b; and Law 1978b, p. 446.

10 Hindess and Hirst 1975; Amin 1976; Bernstein and Depelchin 1978–9; Althusser 1977; and Althusser and Balibar 1970. For an excellent critique of the ahistorical approach of these Marxists, see Law 1981.

11 Terray 1979.

12 Hair 1967; and Miller 1981a.

13 Rey 1975b; Sahlins 1972; and Terray 1969.

14 Meillassoux 1972.

15 This discussion accepts the valuable contribution of Kopytoff and Miers 1977 in understanding slavery as one form of dependency in societies organized on the basis of kinship, but it diverges from their interpretation over the development of institutionalized slavery under the impetus of foreign trade and systematic enslavement. For a discussion of this issue, see Lovejoy 1979b; and Kopytoff 1979. Also see Miller 1981a, pp. 43–63.

16 Douglas explored the institution of pawnship, but not in an historical context, in her pioneering article of 1964. Also see Douglas 1960.

17 There are many important studies of the relationship between marriage and slavery; see, for example, Meillassoux 1972; Kopytoff and Miers 1977; Miller 1981a, pp. 45–6; Rey 1969; and the contributions in Klein and Robertson forthcoming, especially Klein forthcoming; and Meillassoux forthcoming b.

18 Isichei 1976.

288

19 The most perceptive discussion of slavery in the context of Islamic society is Brunschvig 1960. See also Fisher and Fisher 1970; Sanneh forthcoming; Cooper 1981; Hunwick 1978; and Lewis 1976.

20 The debate over the impact of the trans-Atlantic slave trade on Africa is divided into two schools, one arguing that the influence was profound and the other considering the impact marginal. An important article in the debate is Rodney 1966; and see his 1967 occasional paper. Also see Fage 1969; and Klein and Lovejoy 1979. In its simplest formulation, the trans-Atlantic slave trade is seen as the direct cause of social stratification in African societies; for a far more sophisticated interpretation, see Fage 1980. The most important recent study that rejects an interpretation that emphasizes the Atlantic slave trade is Peukert 1978. For a review of this literature, see Lovejoy 1981*d*.

2 On the frontiers of Islam, 1400–1600

1 Austen 1979*a*. Also see Mauny 1961, pp. 377–9; Malowist 1966, pp. 59–72; Pankhurst 1961, pp. 372–88, 409–19; and J. E. Harris 1971, pp. 77–90.

2 Ibn Battuta 1922, vol. IV, p. 445. For a fuller discussion, see Mauny 1961, pp. 377–9.

3 Hunwick forthcoming.

4 Fisher and Fisher 1970, pp. 59–60.

5 Abir forthcoming *b*; and O'Fahey and Spaulding 1974, p. 56.

6 Cadamosto 1937, p. 30. For a fuller discussion, see M. Klein 1977*a*, pp. 339–41.

7 Nicholson 1978.

8 For a discussion of the transformation of slavery in the savanna during these centuries, see Meillassoux 1978*b*; Sanneh forthcoming; and Fisher and Fisher 1970.

9 Levtzion 1973, pp. 65, 112–13; Sanneh forthcoming; and Fisher and Fisher 1970, pp. 129–44.

10 Palmer 1936, p. 218.

11 Palmer 1936, p. 242.

12 Barbour and Jacobs forthcoming.

13 As translated in Barbour and Jacobs forthcoming.

14 Cadamosto 1937, p. 30.

15 Curtin 1971*c*; Verlinden 1955 and 1950; Malowist 1969; and Rau 1970.

16 The nature of agricultural slavery in Songhay is a subject of considerable debate between scholars who attempt to compare the Songhay political economy with feudal Europe and those who do not. None the less, all agree that slaves were used extensively in agriculture. See Tymowski 1970; Kodjo 1976, pp. 805–10; Olivier de Sardan 1975; Ol'derogge 1957; and Hunwick forthcoming.

17 Kodjo 1976, pp. 808–9; also see Lovejoy forthcoming *c*.

18 Kodjo 1976, pp. 790–812; and Lovejoy forthcoming *c*.

19 Fernandes 1938, p. 87. For a fuller discussion, see Terray forthcoming *b*; and Garrard 1980.

20 Mauny 1961, pp. 330, 341; and Lovejoy 1978*a*.

21 Pankhurst 1961, pp. 372–88, 409–19. Also see Abir forthcoming *b* and forthcoming *a*.

22 Freeman-Grenville 1963, pp. 150–2; Kent 1970, pp. 69–71; Mathew 1963, pp. 106, 107, 121.

23 Vogt 1979; and Curtin 1971*c*.

24 The most thorough study of slavery in Europe is the massive study of Verlinden 1955.

25 Rau 1970, pp. 76–7; Malowist 1969; and Curtin 1971*c*, pp. 75–81.

26 Vogt 1979, pp. 57–9, 72.

27 Vogt 1979, pp. 67–8, 73, 76.

28 Cadamosto 1937, p. 30.

29 Curtin 1975*a*, vol. I, pp. 3–13; and Rodney 1966, pp. 431–42.

30 Harrop 1964, 8, 4: 23–4; Fage 1969, pp. 396–7; Blake 1937, p. 93; Graham 1965, pp. 318–19; Wilks 1977, pp. 517–19; and Vogt 1973.

31 Graham 1965, pp. 318–21; and Ryder 1969, pp. 24–84.
32 Vogt 1979, p. 57.
33 Vogt 1979, pp. 57–8, 72, and 1973, pp. 453–67.
34 Vansina 1966, pp. 37–69, and 1962, p. 377; Birmingham 1966; Miller 1976a, pp. 79–84; Thornton 1979, 1981, and forthcoming.
35 Thornton 1981, p. 192.
36 Miller 1976a, pp. 79–84; and Birmingham 1966, pp. 25–6, 32, 40–1.
37 Thornton 1981, p. 192.
38 Thornton 1981, pp. 188, 191–2; Vogt 1979, p. 147; and Miller 1976a, pp. 79–88.
39 Vansina 1966, pp. 37–69, and 1962, p. 377; Birmingham 1966, pp. 48–63; and Miller 1976a, pp. 84–92.
40 This analysis of slavery in Kongo is based on Thornton 1981, p. 187, 1979, pp. 60–2, and forthcoming; Miller 1976a, p. 83; and Orlova 1964, pp. 196–202.
41 Hilton 1981.
42 Probably based on a published account of Philippe Pigafetta, who compiled his information from Duarte Lopez, the Portuguese ambassador to the Kingdom of Kongo, who was in Kongo in the late 1570s. The account here is taken from the further compilations of Confalonieri, and published in Cuvelier and Jadin 1954, p. 135. See also Fage 1980, p. 305.
43 Thornton 1981, p. 191.
44 Garfield 1971, pp. 40, 53, 61, 64.
45 The first plantations were established in São Thomé by 1499; by the middle of the sixteenth century, 2,150 tons of sugar were being produced for export; see Garfield 1971, pp. 20, 52.
46 As cited in Fage 1980, p. 305.
47 As cited in Fage 1980, p. 308.
48 John Hawkins, as quoted in Donnan 1930–5, vol. I, pp. 48–9.
49 Rodney 1966, pp. 431–42.
50 Hair 1975.
51 Hair 1975, p. 67.
52 Rodney's pioneering work on the impact of the slave trade on Africa has long provided inspiration for scholars, but his overly simplistic model has been greatly modified. The most sophisticated treatment of early sources for purposes of analysing social relations in African societies at the time of early European contact on the West African coast is Fage 1980. Fage shows a far more complicated interaction between indigenous developments, foreign trade, and the expansion of servile relationships than Rodney did in his seminal article.

3 The export trade in slaves, 1600–1800

1 This breakthrough has been examined from a number of perspectives. Curtin has examined it in terms of 'intercommunicating zones', from which much of Africa had been isolated previously (forthcoming); Gemery and Hogendorn have employed an economic model, 'vent for surplus', in discussing the opening of trade (1974); Rodney (1966) has considered the social impact; and Fage (1969) has discussed the political repercussions. While the change began in the sixteenth century, the expansion of trade in the seventeenth century was so great that the real breakthrough occurred then.
2 Curtin's pioneering study of the volume of the export trade in slaves (1969) has been revised considerably, including a thorough review by Curtin himself (1975b). The addition of extensive archival materials not available to Curtin has further modified the conclusions of his work. The combined result of this research has contributed significantly to our understanding of the trans-Atlantic trade, and of other sectors of the export traffic that Curtin did not examine. This chapter takes account of this literature in an attempt to synthesize the findings of numerous scholars whose work is cited in the appropriate tables. It should be noted, however, that the extreme revisions of two critics of Curtin's estimates are not accepted; see Inikori 1976a and 1978, pp. 7–8; and Rout 1976, pp. 61–6, who reject the

Curtin projection without providing proof for an alternative total. For a discussion of the Inikori calculations and the reasons for their modification, see Drescher 1977, pp. 205–13. Other revisions are referred to in the appropriate tables. Some changes are also likely as a result of research into local patterns, such as that of Jones and Johnson 1980. In this particular case, however, there is no attempt at a new calculation of the quantity of slave exports, only a shift in the total volume to other sections of the West African coast from the Windward Coast. The implications of this analysis are followed here, but it is likely that additional research will clarify the actual distribution of slaves that have hitherto been assigned to the Windward Coast.

3 LeVeen 1975a; Bean 1975, pp. 68–73, 123–57; and Manning 1982. Also see Curtin 1975a, vol. I, pp. 158–68, vol. II, appendix 8; and Gemery and Hogendorn 1974.

4 See, for example, Curtin 1971c, pp. 86–7.

5 LeVeen 1975a, pp. 9–13. LeVeen further shows that the rise in the price for prime male slaves rose at the same rate in the West Indies and Africa, which again indicates a strong correlation between the demand for slaves and their supply, at least in the aggregate; see LeVeen 1977, p. 8.

6 The overall estimates are supplemented by scattered data in a number of works; see Birmingham 1966, pp. 25–6, 28, 40–1; Martin 1972, pp. 117–35; and Miller 1976a, p. 86.

7 Law 1977a, pp. 217–36; Manning 1979, pp. 107–41; and Morton-Williams 1964.

8 There is considerable disagreement among specialists over the importance of Dahomey and Oyo in the slave trade. Peukert (1978) argues that the slave trade played a far less significant role in Dahomey history than other scholars have thought; Manning (1982) argues the reverse, to the extent that he considers Dahomey to have been more important than Oyo. Finally, Law (1977a, pp. 217–28, 240–1) demonstrates the key role of the slave trade in the development of the Oyo economy, although he presents a balanced view that examines other factors too. The synthesis presented here attempts to assess the relative merits of these conflicting interpretations.

An additional problem in the debate relates to estimates of the volume of the slave trade from the Bight of Benin.

Bight of Benin: estimates of slave exports, 1741–1800

Decade	Manning	Peukert	Lovejoy
1741–50	70,100	140,400	109,900
1751–60	70,500	129,000	98,700
1761–70	102,700	149,500	102,700
1771–80	90,700	175,500	90,700
1781–90	153,100	164,000	117,000
1791–1800	74,000	130,000*	74,000
TOTAL	561,100	888,400	593,000

*1791–97

Sources: Manning 1982; Peukert 1978, pp. 305–6; and table 3.4.

Ironically, Peukert's estimate is the highest, even though he argues that the slave trade was marginal to the local economy. For a discussion of Peukert's figures, see Manning 1982.

9 Davies 1957, p. 226; and Daaku 1970, pp. 28–33, 44–7.

10 Fynn 1971; Kea 1976; and La Torre 1978. La Torre provides an alternative set of data on slave exports from the Gold Coast, although his estimates for the Dutch portion of the trade

conflict in different tables (pp. 431 and 434). La Torre accepts a calculation that includes the region Accra to Cape Lahu, as I have also done in my calculation:

Estimates for Gold Coast slave exports, 1751–1800

Decade	La Torre	Lovejoy
1751–60	86,000	66,300
1761–70	109,000	63,400
1771–80	91,000	56,000
1781–90	87,000	84,200
1791–1800	53,000	74,000
Total	426,000	343,900

Sources: La Torre 1978; and table 3.4.

11 Weiskel 1978, pp. 503–27.
12 For the slave trade in the Bight of Biafra and its impact on the local economy, see Northrup 1978; Latham 1973; and Alagoa 1970 and 1972.
13 Isichei 1978, p. 10, citing John Barbot.
14 Curtin 1975a, vol. i, pp. 162–7.
15 Jones and Johnson 1980; and Rodney 1970, pp. 240–70.
16 Curtin 1969, pp. 202, 254–5.
17 For the trans-Saharan and Red Sea trade in the seventeenth and eighteenth centuries, see Austen 1979a, pp. 30–9; Lavers 1982; Abir forthcoming; Austen 1977b and 1979b; and Walz 1978, pp. 33–4.
18 Walz (1978, pp. 33–4) surveys the various estimates for slave imports into Egypt; he also provides an excellent analysis of the slave trade in Cairo (see pp. 124–30, 173–221). For imports into Morocco, see Meyers 1977.
19 Austen 1979a, p. 68, and 1977b; Martin and Ryan 1977, pp. 72–3; Alpers 1967 and 1970; and Filliot 1974, pp. 113–26.
20 Davies 1957, p. 226.
21 Miller 1981b, p. 413; also see Curtin 1968.
22 Miller 1981b.
23 Miller 1981b, p. 413.
24 For a discussion of sex ratios, see Curtin 1969, pp. 19, 28; H. S. Klein 1978, pp. 149–50, 223; and Bean 1975, pp. 132–4.
25 There is some indication that the age and sex distribution changed over time, resulting in a larger percentage of adult males. See, for example, the calculations on the sex ratios and age distribution of exported slaves, 1637–45:

Category	Guinea	%	Angola	%	Total	%
Male as % of adults	1587	58.9	706	51.2	2293	56.3
Male as % of total		51.4		34.2		44.5
Female as % of adults	1107	41.1	672	48.8	1779	43.7
Female as % of total		35.9		32.6		34.5
Children	392	12.7	686	33.2	1078	20.9
Total	3086		2064		5150	

Source: Van den Boogaart and Emmer 1979, p. 366.

For my purposes, considering the speculative nature of the figures derived from the sex and age data, I have considered the sex and age distribution as constant. When more research has been done on the demography of the trade, it may be possible to refine this analysis.

26 Manning 1981.
27 Thornton 1980.
28 Thornton 1980, p. 427; and Manning 1981. The approach of Manning and Thornton is preferable to that of Anstey and Fage, who both attempt to assess the demographic impact of the slave trade on the total population of Africa; see Anstey 1975*a*, pp. 79–88; and Fage 1978, pp. 263–70. Fage's discussion can be used as an example of this approach. Fage allows a population of 25 million for West Africa in 1700 and argues that slave exports could have done no more than halt population growth. He suggests that the impact may have been more severe in central Africa, with its lower population base, than for West Africa. The problem with this approach is that the total population of Africa – even if it could be measured – was not the reservoir from which slave exports came. Manning's model is preferable because it recognizes that some societies were net exporters and others were not.

4 The enslavement of Africans, 1600–1800

1 Various scholars have approached this problem from different perspectives; see for example, Goody 1971; Law 1976; Bazin 1975; Gemery and Hogendorn 1978; and R. L. Roberts 1980*a*.
2 Nicholson 1978.
3 For a discussion of drought in the seventeenth and eighteenth centuries, see: Cissoko 1968; Lovejoy and Baier 1975, pp. 570–4; and Curtin 1975*a*, vol. II, p. 5.
4 Cissoko 1968; Curtin 1975*a*, vol. II, p. 5; and Lovejoy and Baier 1975, pp. 570–4. For a discussion of the general implications of these climatic conditions, see Lovejoy forthcoming *b*.
5 For slave raiding in Sennar and Dar Fur, see O'Fahey and Spaulding 1974, pp. 56, 80, 161. For Borno, see Adeleye 1971, p. 504; Brenner 1973; p. 25; and Fisher and Fisher 1970, pp. 17–20.
6 The discussion of Ethiopia is based on Abir 1968, pp. 27–43, 53–70, 73–93, and 1980; and Pankhurst 1976.
7 As cited in Hodgkin 1975, pp. 178–9.
8 As translated by Barbour and Jacobs forthcoming.
9 Adeleye 1971, pp. 508–29.
10 This analysis is based on the research of R. L. Roberts 1978, pp. 1–64. Also see Bazin 1975.
11 M. Klein 1977*a*, pp. 344–5, and 1972, pp. 427–9.
12 Curtin 1971*a*; and Rodney 1968.
13 Miller 1976*a*, p. 85.
14 Thornton 1979, pp. 57–8, 110, 217–18.
15 Vansina 1966, pp. 124–54; Miller forthcoming; Birmingham 1966, pp. 48–63.
16 This analysis is based on the research of Miller 1976*b*, 1977, and forthcoming.
17 Miller 1977, pp. 211–22.
18 Miller forthcoming and 1976*b*, pp. 260–1.
19 For a survey of these states, see Vansina 1966, pp. 70–97, 155–79; Vellut 1972; and Cunnison 1961.
20 Alpers 1967 and 1970; and Isaacman 1972*a*.
21 This discussion of the *prazos* is from Isaacman 1972*a*; A. Isaacman and B. Isaacman 1975; and Newitt 1973.

22 Alpers 1975.
23 Shepherd 1980, pp. 74–5.
24 Bloch 1980; Shepherd 1980, p. 76; and Filliot 1974.
25 For a discussion of Oyo, see Law 1977*a*, pp. 217–20.
26 Law 1977*a*, pp. 92, 148–9, 154.
27 Law 1977*a*, pp. 226–7; Manning 1982; for the extent of Oyo hegemony in the eighteenth century, see Law 1977*a*, pp. 89, 119–44.
28 Law 1977*a*, pp. 219–23.
29 For various interpretations of the history of Dahomey, see Law 1977*a*, pp. 221–2; Manning 1982; Peukert 1978; and Akinjogbin 1967.
30 Law 1977*a*, pp. 219–23.
31 Manning 1982. It should be noted that my interpretation of Manning's data differs substantially from Manning's analysis. Manning attributes Aja origins to a very high percentage of total exports, while I do not.
32 Manning 1982, and confirmed by Law 1977*a*, pp. 226–7, who reports that slaves of northern origin were not a major item in the transit trade to the coast until the last decades of the eighteenth century. Slaves of similar origin may have been important earlier but disguised through acculturation or a different system of identifying slaves.
33 This account of Akwamu is based on Kea 1976; and Wilks 1957. Also see Kea 1980.
34 Daaku 1970, pp. 26–7; Fynn 1971, pp. 8–26; and Bean 1974.
35 Fynn 1971, pp. 19–22.
36 Fynn 1971, p. 84; and Wilks 1971*b*.
37 Isichei 1976, pp. 58–64, 77–89; Northrup 1978, pp. 30–176, and 1972.
38 Ekejiuba 1972; Isichei 1976, pp. 58–64, 77–89; and Northrup 1978, pp. 120–245; Afigbo 1971*b*; Alagoa 1970 and 1972; and Latham 1973, pp. 17–51.
39 Northrup 1978, pp. 114–16, 127–8, 130, 133. For a later description, see Isichei 1978, p. 233, quoting an early British military source. See also Ilogu 1957, and Ottenberg 1958.
40 For a discussion of the enslavement process in terms of the relative importance of political and economic factors, see the excellent discussions in Curtin 1975*a*, vol. 1, pp. 156–7; Northrup 1978, pp. 65–84; and LeVeen 1975*a*.
41 As edited in G. I. Jones 1967, p. 75.
42 Vansina 1966, p. 53.
43 See, for example, Curtin 1971*a*, p. 23.
44 As translated in Barbour and Jacobs forthcoming.
45 De La Roncière 1919. For a discussion, see Fisher and Fisher 1970, p. 53 fn.
46 Moore 1738, p. 42.

5 The organization of slave marketing, 1600–1800

1 For a general overview of slave marketing, see Lovejoy and Hogendorn 1979; and Miller 1976*a*.
2 Curtin 1975*a*, vol. 1, p. 155.
3 O'Fahey and Spaulding 1974, p. 56.
4 Adeleye 1971, pp. 502–3.
5 Lavers 1982; and Abir forthcoming.
6 Lovejoy 1980*a*, pp. 58–9, 68–9, 70–1.
7 For various Juula networks, see Curtin 1971*b* and 1975*a*, vol. 1, pp. 59–91; R. L. Roberts 1978, pp. 180–277; Person 1968–75, vol. 1, pp. 95–122; and Izard 1971.
8 Park 1971, pp. 318–19.
9 Lovejoy 1980*a*, pp. 29–74; and Adamu 1978, pp. 37–51, and 1979.
10 Lovejoy 1980*a*, p. 146; and O'Fahey 1971, p. 94.
11 Abir 1970; and Pankhurst 1961, pp. 307–21, 372–88.

12 Mathew 1963, pp. 140–68; Alpers 1969, pp. 406–7; A. Roberts 1970*b*, pp. 47–50; and Alpers 1975, pp. 42–64.
13 Birmingham 1970; Vansina 1962; Birmingham 1966, pp. 78–103; Miller 1979 and 1976*a*.
14 Thornton 1979, pp. 67–8.
15 Miller 1976*a*, p. 98.
16 P. Martin 1970 and 1972, pp. 53–135.
17 Vellut 1972, pp. 84–110.
18 Daaku 1971, 1970; pp. 111–13; Fynn 1971, pp. 13–16; and Kea 1976.
19 Law 1977*a*, pp. 217–36; Morton-Williams 1964; and Manning 1979, pp. 116–36.
20 Law 1977*a*, pp. 219–22.
21 La Torre 1978, p. 422; also see Daaku 1971 and 1970, pp. 167–70.
22 La Torre 1978, p. 433.
23 Law 1977*a*, pp. 235–6; also see Morton-Williams 1964.
24 Manning 1982. It should be noted that Polanyi's analysis of Dahomey's involvement in the slave trade (1966) has been thoroughly revised.
25 Law 1977*a*, p. 223.
26 Kea 1976, citing a 1727 report in the Danish archives.
27 Peukert 1978, pp. 333–7; and Manning 1982.
28 This discussion is based on Manning 1982, although my conclusions are different. Manning has calculated the ethnic origins of slaves exported from the Bight of Benin as follows:

Years	Aja	Yoruba	Voltaic	Nupe	Hausa	Total
1641–1700	217,900	11,800	—	—	—	229,700
1701–1800	873,000	127,400	95,800	7,900	10,500	1,114,600

According to his calculations, 95 per cent of slaves exported in the seventeenth century were Aja; only 5 per cent were Yoruba; in the eighteenth century, 78 per cent were Aja; 11 per cent were Yoruba; 8 per cent were Voltaic; and less than 2 per cent were Hausa and Nupe. Manning argues that the Aja population suffered a decline as a result; in the period 1690 to 1740, he estimates that over 8,500 Aja slaves were exported per year. Furthermore, he concludes that Oyo played a far less significant role in the export trade than previously thought.

    While accepting Manning's analysis of the size of the slave population identified as Aja, I cannot accept the full analysis. Aja slaves could have included acculturated slaves of non-Aja origin, slaves labelled Aja by mistake, slaves called Aja because they came from ports controlled by Aja, as well as Aja war captives and slave descendants. In short, the ethnic identification disguised other developments in the region. Furthermore, Manning's conclusions do not accord with those of Law (1977*a*, pp. 217–28, 240–1) and other scholars who have shown that Yoruba slaves formed a significant proportion of the total export trade.

29 Alagoa 1970; Latham 1973, pp. 17–51; Northrup 1972 and 1978, pp. 85–145; Isichei 1976, pp. 58–67; Ekejiuba 1972, vol. I: 2, pp. 10–21; and R. Smith 1970, pp. 518, 524–7.
30 Isichei 1978, p. 12, citing John Adams' account of 1786–1800.
31 'Report of the Lords of the Committee of Council concerning the present State of the Trade to Africa, and particularly the Trade in Slaves (1789), Part I, Evidence of William James', as cited in Isichei 1973, p. 48.
32 Ekejiuba 1972, vol. I: 1, pp. 13–14; Isichei 1976, pp. 58–67; and Northrup 1978, pp. 114–45.
33 Cookey 1980; Isichei 1976, p. 65; and Oriji forthcoming.
34 Isichei 1976, pp. 51–8; Northrup 1972, pp. 231–6; and Ogedengbe 1971.

35 For a discussion of restrictive practices in West Africa, see Lovejoy and Hogendorn 1979. A crucial dimension to my argument is that profits from trade – including trade in slaves – accrued to merchants in Africa, thereby facilitating the accumulation of slaves. This interpretation conflicts with the approach of Thomas and Bean 1974, pp. 885–94.

36 Curtin 1975*a*, vol. I, pp. 330–1; Bean 1974; Abir forthcoming; and Rodney 1970, pp. 152–70.

37 Mauny 1961, pp. 321–36; Lovejoy 1978*a*; Abir 1966; Pankhurst 1961, pp. 260–2, and 1964.

38 Birmingham 1970, pp. 164–5, 166, 169–70; and Vansina 1962, p. 386.

39 Lovejoy 1980*b*.

40 Curtin 1982; Bean 1974; and M. Johnson 1968.

41 M. Johnson 1970; Lovejoy 1974; Hogendorn 1981; and Kea 1976. Also see Law 1977*a*, p. 98, where the movement of cowries as tribute is discussed.

42 Manning 1982.

43 Curtin 1982 and 1975*a*, vol. I, pp. 261–3, 268–70.

44 Lovejoy 1980*b*, pp. 112–13.

45 Latham 1971.

46 Gemery and Hogendorn 1977.

47 Law 1976.

48 Inikori 1977; Richards 1980; and Gemery and Hogendorn 1978.

49 David Richardson 1979; Curtin 1975*a*, vol. I, pp. 311–34; Northrup 1978, pp. 164–7; P. Martin 1972, pp. 109–13; Rodney 1970, pp. 171–99; Manning 1982; and Verger 1976.

50 For a perceptive discussion of the relationship between gun imports and slaves exports, see Gemery and Hogendorn 1978. Also see Inikori 1977; and Richards 1980. For a criticism of this thesis, see Peukert 1978.

51 Curtin 1975*a*, vol. I, pp. 334–41.

6 Relationships of dependency, 1600–1800

1 Thornton 1980, p. 427.

2 Manning 1981.

3 This discussion is based on various studies of slavery in the northern savanna and Ethiopia. See especially Meillassoux 1978*b*; Cissoko 1969; M. Klein 1977*a*, pp. 337–49; Sanneh 1976 and forthcoming; O'Fahey 1973 and 1977; and Abir forthcoming.

4 Moore 1738, p. 33.

5 Park 1971, pp. 318–19.

6 Barbour and Jacobs forthcoming.

7 Jobson 1623, p. 101.

8 Palmer 1936, p. 247. See also Spaulding 1982.

9 *Kano Chronicle*, as translated in Palmer 1928, vol. III, p. 118.

10 O'Fahey and Spaulding 1974, pp. 64–5.

11 O'Fahey 1973 and 1977.

12 Madden 1837, vol. II, pp. 196–8. For a discussion, see Wilks 1967, p. 164.

13 Rodney 1968; and Baldé 1975.

14 Curtin 1971*a*.

15 Usman 1974.

16 Lovejoy 1978*c*, p. 351. Similar estates probably were found in the Masina area; see M. Johnson 1976*b*, p. 489, although Johnson does not refer to them as plantations. She prefers an analogy to feudalism instead. For a criticism of this approach, see Lovejoy 1979*a*, pp. 1273–4.

17 Perrot 1975; and Augé 1975.

18 Holsoe 1977.

19 MacCormack 1977, pp. 192–3.

20 Terray forthcoming *b*.
21 Brun 1624.
22 Muller 1976, p. 272.
23 Tilleman 1904.
24 Kea 1976. Also see Daaku 1970, pp. 120–2.
25 Terray forthcoming *b*; A. N. Klein 1980; and Wilks 1977, pp. 519–26.
26 Lovejoy 1982*a*.
27 Romer 1760, p. 3.
28 A. N. Klein 1980.
29 Law 1977*a*, pp. 67–70, 82.
30 Law 1977*a*, pp. 10–16, 186, 189.
31 Snelgrave 1734, p. 158. Also see Law 1977*b*, p. 573.
32 Law 1977*a*, pp. 229, 233.
33 G. I. Jones 1967, p. 78. Also see Uchendu 1977; and Northrup 1981, pp. 103–4, 107–8.
34 Isichei 1976, p. 61.
35 R. Smith 1970, pp. 518, 524–7; G. I. Jones 1963, p. 55; and Alagoa 1970, p. 322.
36 Isichei 1978, pp. 118, 234, 275, and 1976, pp. 47–8, 96–7.
37 Thornton 1979, pp. 56, 60, 62.
38 Cited in Thornton 1979, p. 53.
39 Thornton 1979, p. 79.
40 Cited in Thornton 1979, pp. 57–8.
41 Thornton 1980, p. 424, and 1979, pp. 206–7, 217–18.
42 Thornton 1979, p. 60.
43 Orlova 1964, pp. 197–8.
44 Cited in Thornton 1979, p. 58.
45 Thornton 1979, p. 235.
46 Miller 1977, pp. 205–33, and 1976*b*, pp. 151–251.
47 Miller 1977, pp. 211–15, and 1976*b*, pp. 225–51.
48 Miller 1977, pp. 211–19, and 1976*b*, pp. 158–9, 182, 225–51.
49 Thornton 1980, pp. 423–5.
50 P. Martin 1972, pp. 166, 168.
51 P. Martin 1972, pp. 166, 168.
52 Vellut 1972, pp. 74, 77–8, and forthcoming.
53 For Luba, see Reefe 1981, pp. 93, 107, 153–4, although it should be noted that my interpretation differs from Reefe's.
54 Curtin 1975*a*, vol. II, pp. 38–41.
55 Daaku 1970, pp. 44–6; Davies 1957, pp. 244, 251; Rodney 1970, pp. 200–22, 264–8; and Fyfe 1962, p. 54.
56 Cited in Cuvelier and Jadin 1954, p. 452 fn. 2. Also see p. 89.
57 Miller 1976*a*, p. 94, and 1979, pp. 80, 84; and Thornton 1980, pp. 418–19.
58 Thornton 1980, pp. 419–20, 423–4.
59 Katzen 1969, vol. I, pp. 204–8, 224, 232; Guelke 1979, pp. 41–4; Armstrong 1979, pp. 76–84, 100; and Giliomee and Elphick 1979.
60 Armstrong 1979, pp. 85–90; and R. Ross 1978*b*. Also see Greenstein 1973; Edwards 1942; and Kock 1950.
61 Katzen 1969, p. 204; Greenstein 1973, pp. 27, 34; Guelke 1979; Armstrong 1979, p. 92; and Giliomee and Elphick 1979, p. 360.
62 Greenstein 1973, pp. 34–5; Kock 1950, pp. 53–4; and Edwards 1942, p. 15.
63 Armstrong 1979, pp. 94–8.
64 This comparison is made by Armstrong 1979, p. 95, but especially by Greenstein 1973, pp. 25–46.
65 Elphick and Shell 1979; and R. Ross 1978*a*.

66 Greenstein 1973, pp. 34–5; Kock 1950, pp. 53–4; Edwards 1942, p. 15; and Elphick 1979, pp. 21–33.
67 Mist 1920, p. 252. Also see Greenstein 1973, p. 26; and Freund 1979, p. 213.
68 Isaacman 1972*a* and *b*.
69 Fernando de Jesus Maria, p. 73, as cited in Newitt 1973, pp. 196–7.
70 Newitt 1973, pp. 177, 200–1. Also see Isaacman 1972*b*, pp. 452–3.
71 B. Isaacman and A. Isaacman 1977.

7 The nineteenth-century slave trade

1 For the abolition movement, see Drescher 1977; Anstey 1975*a*, pp. 321–402; Miers 1975; Renault 1971*a*; Fyfe 1974; Lloyd 1949; LeVeen 1977; Nwulia 1975; and Eltis and Walvin 1981.
2 The most perceptive analysis of the shift to 'legitimate trade' is Hopkins 1973, pp. 112–66. See also M. Klein 1971. For an opposing view on the importance of the shift, see Austen 1970.
3 The figures accepted here for the Red Sea trade are considerably more conservative than those advanced by Austen (1979*b* and *a*, p. 66) and Pankhurst (1964).
4 La Torre 1978, pp. 426–7.
5 LeVeen 1977, p. 8. Also see Eltis 1978, p. 324. Eltis calculates that the average price of slaves on the West African coast declined from $66 between 1821 and 1837 to $61 between 1838 and 1843.
6 Manning 1982.
7 Tambo 1976.
8 Renault 1971*a*, vol. I, pp. 82–6.
9 LeVeen 1975*b*; and Eltis 1979*b*, pp. 296–7.
10 Manning 1982; Oroge 1971; and Hopkins 1968.
11 Agiri 1981, pp. 124–6, 131–6; and Oroge 1971, chs. 1 and 2.
12 Ajayi 1967, p. 301.
13 Curtin 1967*b*, pp. 326–7.
14 Manning 1982; Oroge 1971, chs. 1 and 2; and Agiri 1981, pp. 124–5.
15 Northrup 1978, pp. 177–223, 1976, and forthcoming *a*, Isichei 1978, pp. 132–5, and 1976, pp. 75–93.
16 Isichei 1978, pp. 132–5, 1976, pp. 75–93, and 1973, p. 49.
17 Horton 1954, pp. 311–16; and Northrup 1979.
18 Isichei 1978, pp. 45, 51, 152, and 1973, p. 49.
19 Northrup 1978, pp. 133–4; Ottenberg 1958; and Cookey 1980.
20 Northrup 1976, pp. 358–9.
21 Chilver 1961; and Afigbo 1973.
22 Isichei 1978, pp. 31, 32, 45, 51, 76, 114, 132–5, 152.
23 See Vansina 1966, pp. 155–248; Vellut 1972; Harms 1981; and Miller 1976*a*, pp. 108–11.
24 Miller 1970.
25 Duffy 1967; and Clarence-Smith 1979*b*.
26 Vail and White 1980, pp. 6–50.
27 Zuccarelli 1962; and Curtin 1969, p. 250.
28 Renault 1976, p. 158; and Vail and White 1980, pp. 31–7, 85–7. It should be noted that I am using a mortality rate of 10 per cent which is lower than the rate used by Renault.
29 Duffy 1967, pp. 11–13, 27, 35, 98.
30 La Torre 1978, p. 415; and personal communication from P. C. Emmer. It should be noted that the immigration from Sierra Leone to the British West Indies is not included, since freed slaves were involved. The scheme was instituted after 1843 and reached a peak in 1847–9; see Asiegbu 1969, pp. 67–71, 91–2, 118.

31 Baer 1969; R. Gray 1961, p. 5; and Walz 1978, pp. 173–221.
32 R. Hill 1959, pp. 5–21.
33 R. Hill 1959, pp. 11, 25, 62–5.
34 Muhammad Ali to the commander-in-chief of the Sudan and Kordofan, 23 September 1823; cited in Hill 1959, p. 13.
35 Abir 1968, p. 106; and R. Gray 1961, pp. 5–6.
36 Hill 1959, pp. 62–5, 103–4; and R. Gray 1961, pp. 44–5, 52, 67–8.
37 For the issue of slavery in the Mahdist victory, see Warburg 1978 and 1981.
38 Abir 1968, pp. 18, 107; and Pankhurst 1968, pp. 73–134.
39 Abir forthcoming; and Pankhurst 1975.
40 Miers 1975, pp. 70–3, 82–6; and Abir 1968, p. 142.
41 Austen 1979a; and Lovejoy 1982b For a survey of the *jihads*, see Last 1974.
42 Cooper 1977. For the demand on the islands in the Indian Ocean, see Shepherd 1980; Benedict 1980; J. Martin 1976, pp. 207–99, and 1973, pp. 45–51; and Campbell 1981.
43 Alpers 1975, pp. 185–203; and Isaacman 1972a, pp. 79–93, 95–110.
44 Cooper 1977, pp. 115–22.
45 For the Nyamwezi, see A. Roberts 1970b; for Yao, see Alpers 1969; for the *achikunda*, see Isaacman 1972b.
46 Isaacman forthcoming b; and Omer-Cooper 1969.
47 See appendix. Also see Miers 1975; Nwulia 1975; and Renault 1971.
48 Burnham 1980; Buttner 1967; and Agiri 1981, pp. 124–5, 137–9.
49 R. Roberts 1978, pp. 70–90.
50 For Samori, see Person 1968–75, vol. III, pp. 1637–1712; and Holden 1970. For Rabeh, see Hallam 1977.
51 The best source on the origins of the movement is Al-Hajj 1975. Also see Adeleye and Stewart forthcoming; Mason 1969; Gleave and Prothero 1971; and Mason's reply in the same place, pp. 324–7. Also see Mason 1970; and Hogendorn 1980.
52 La Torre 1978, p. 238; also see Wilks 1975, pp. 674–5.
53 La Torre 1978, pp. 417–18, 420.
54 Holden 1970 and 1965.
55 Abubakar 1977, p. 103. Also see Adamu 1979, pp. 172–9.
56 M. Klein forthcoming.
57 M. Klein 1981.
58 Agiri 1981, p. 137.
59 See, for example, Isichei 1978, pp. 31, 45, 51, 76, 83, 114, 152.
60 See, for example, Jewsiewicki and Bawele 1981, pp. 73–98, who describe the incorporation of the central Zaire basin into the slaving frontier.

8 Slavery and 'legitimate trade' on the West African coast

1 Hopkins 1973, pp. 112–66.
2 Fyfe 1962; Grace 1975, pp. 1–66; C. I. Foster 1953; and Fyfe 1974. Also see Abraham 1975.
3 Grace 1975, pp. 220–62.
4 MacCormack 1977. For a study of Sierra Leone and its hinterland as a region, see Howard 1979.
5 Grace 1977.
6 Wylie 1973; and Rodney 1966, p. 439.
7 Holsoe 1977.
8 Massing 1977; and Augé 1975.
9 For slavery in Asante and the adjustments to abolition, see the following: A. N. Klein 1980; Wilks 1975, pp. 93–4, 177, 264, 675, 1977, pp. 495–531; Reynolds 1974, pp. 37–71; and

Terray forthcoming *b*. Also see Poku 1969; A. N. Klein 1969; Rattray 1929; Reynolds 1973; La Torre 1978, pp. 92–7, 105–9, 116–21.

10 Binger 1892, vol. II, p. 85.

11 Archives AOF, dossier K21, as quoted in Terray 1975*b*, p. 113.

12 Archives AOF, dossier K21, as quoted in Terray 1975*b*, p. 124.

13 Dupuis 1824, p. lvii. For a discussion, see Terray 1974, p. 328.

14 'Full report on his mission to Ashanti and Gaman, April 14, 1883', P.P. C3687, in vol. XLVIII, 1883, cited in Terray 1974, pp. 528–9.

15 Bowdich 1819, pp. 323–4. Also see Wilks 1975, p. 177.

16 Beecham 1841, pp. 130–1.

17 Bowdich 1821, p. 18. Also see Terray forthcoming *b*; and Wilks 1975, pp. 52, 70, 84.

18 Wilks 1975, pp. 84, 176–8, and 1971*a*; Lovejoy 1980*a*, pp. 11–27; and Terray forthcoming *b*.

19 A.N. Klein 1980; Wilks 1977, p. 526; Terray forthcoming *b*; Wilks 1975, p. 675; La Torre 1978, pp. 108, 117–18; McSheffrey 1983; and Reynolds 1974, pp. 18–19, 82–3, 152–3, and 1981, pp. 141–51.

20 Lovejoy 1980*a*, pp. 18–23, 29–49. Kwame Arhin notes that the scale of slave labour in the rubber boom of Asante (1890s) was considerable and that 'the rubber villages appear to have had "plantation" dimensions' (Arhin 1980, p. 60).

21 A. N. Klein 1980 and 1981; Wilks 1975, p. 86.

22 Weiskel 1979; and Etienne 1976.

23 Perrot 1975, pp. 351–87, and 1969; and Augé 1975.

24 For slavery in this region, see Oroge 1971; Law 1977*b*; Manning 1969; Agiri 1974 and 1981; Hopkins 1966, pp. 138–43, and 1968, pp. 585–91.

25 Law 1977*b*; Manning 1969; Coquery 1971; and D.A. Ross 1965. Also see Aguessy 1970; Kilkenny 1981; Obichere 1978; and Newbury 1960.

26 Forbes 1851, p. 31.

27 Forbes 1851, p.115.

28 Oroge 1971, pp. 159–99.

29 Oroge 1971, pp. 91–5.

30 Johnson 1921, pp. 324–5.

31 Oroge 1971, pp. 175–8.

32 Oroge 1971, pp. 86, 91–5, 138–211; and Agiri 1981, pp. 131–6.

33 Oroge 1971, pp. 160.

34 Oroge 1971, pp. 91–5; and Agiri 1981, p. 135.

35 Church Missionary Society Papers, London, CA2/031, Crowther to Venn, 4 March 1857, cited in Ajayi 1965, p. 105.

36 Cited in Hopkins 1966, p. 140.

37 The following analysis is based on Northrup 1979 and 1981; Latham 1973, pp. 51–62; J. S. Harris 1942; Ogedengbe 1977; R. Harris 1972; Horton 1956 and 1954; G. I. Jones 1961 and 1962; and Uchendu 1967 and 1977.

38 Northrup 1976 and 1978, pp. 177–233.

39 Northrup forthcoming *b*.

40 Oriji 1982.

41 Oriji 1982.

42 Isichei 1976, pp. 102–7.

43 Isichei 1978, p. 256; and Oriji 1982.

44 Isichei 1973, p. 62.

45 Isichei 1973, p. 76.

46 These examples are cited in Ekejiuba 1972, p. 14. Also see Northrup 1978, pp. 220–3; and Latham 1973, pp. 96–102.

47 Isichei 1973, p. 64.

48 Horton 1954, pp. 311–12.

49 G. I. Jones 1963, pp. 43–8; 58–62, 167–73, 183–4.
50 Crowther and Taylor 1859, p. 438.
51 Crowther and Taylor 1859, p. 438. Also see Ogedengbe 1977.
52 Isichei 1976, p. 47.
53 Isichei 1978, p. 256.
54 Isichei 1973, pp. 53, 57–8.
55 Ayandele 1966, pp. 71–100; and Alagoa 1971*b*.
56 Nair 1972, pp. 37–43; Latham 1973, pp. 96–102.
57 Waddell 1863, pp. 319–20.
58 Nair 1972, pp. 43–51; Latham 1973, pp. 91–6; Alagoa 1971*b*, pp. 566–8; and Isichei 1976, pp. 96–7.
59 Uchendu 1977, pp. 127–30.
60 Leith-Ross 1937; and Ogedengbe 1980.

9 Slavery in the savanna during the era of the *jihads*

1 Lovejoy and Baier 1975.
2 Meillassoux (introduction to 1975*a*, p. 17) makes the estimate that 30–50 per cent of the population was slave. Meillassoux provides a fuller discussion in 1978*b*, p. 135. Also see M. Klein forthcoming. An earlier survey of the same archival material is in Deherme 1908, pp. 383–4; and Boutillier 1968. Also see M. Klein 1977*b*; and Roberts and Klein 1981. Other studies confirm these figures; see Bouchez 1901, p. 293; R. L. Roberts 1978, pp. 291–3; and O'Sullivan 1981, pp. 642–7.
3 Lovejoy 1981*b*.
4 Spaulding 1982.
5 Lovejoy 1979*a*. Also see O'Sullivan 1981, pp. 642–7; R. L. Roberts 1981; Warburg 1981; Meillassoux 1973; Spaulding 1982; and McDougall 1980.
6 M. Klein 1972, pp. 429–37.
7 Hanson 1971, pp. 7–8; and M. Klein 1972, p. 429.
8 M. Klein 1977*b* and forthcoming.
9 M. Klein 1972, pp. 424, 438; Brooks 1975, pp.29, 34, 43, 46, 49–50.
10 Swindell 1980, pp. 94, 95, 99–100.
11 Caillié 1830, vol. ɪ, pp. 190, 192.
12 Caillié 1830, vol. ɪ, p. 211.
13 Richard-Molard 1952*a*, *b*, and *c*. Also see Baldé 1975; Patenostre 1930; and Derman 1973, pp. 12–56.
14 R. L. Roberts 1978, pp. 180–277, and 1980*b*; and M. Klein 1977*b*. For other cases, see Pollet and Winter 1968 and 1971; Riesman 1974; and Sanneh 1976.
15 R. L. Roberts, 1978, pp. 307–20, 1980*b*, and 1981, pp. 172–91; and McDougall 1980.
16 Roberts 1980*b*, p. 173.
17 Roberts and Klein 1981, p. 392.
18 Roberts 1978, pp. 292–3.
19 Roberts 1978, p. 291.
20 Meillassoux 1975*b*, p. 432; and McDougall 1980.
21 M. Johnson 1976*b*, pp. 482–94. It should be noted, however, that Johnson refers to slaves as 'serfs'. Elsewhere I have criticized such an approach; see Lovejoy 1979*a*, pp. 1273–4. It should also be noted that Johnson has combined the labour obligations of slaves during the pre-colonial and early colonial periods. The 'rent' on land, which she includes in her discussion of 'feudal' obligations, replaced earlier payments once the French had abolished slavery and encouraged other forms of servility. I wish to thank Martin Klein for discussing this matter with me. For the slave population at Jenne, see M. Klein forthcoming.
22 Caillié 1830, vol. ɪ, p. 181.

23 Caillié 1830, vol. I, pp.283–4.
24 Caillié 1830, vol. I, p. 182.
25 Boutillier 1975, p. 266, although it should be noted that Boutillier calculates the figure as 55 per cent.
26 O'Sullivan 1981, pp. 636, 640–7; and Boutillier 1968, p. 528.
27 Person 1974, vol. II, pp. 290–4, 299–300, and 1968–75, vol. I, pp. 269–576, for a fuller discussion.
28 Peroz 1889, p. 353. Also see Person 1968–75, vol. II, pp. 836–9, 860 fn.
29 M. Klein 1977*b*.
30 Boutillier 1975, p. 266, although Boutillier calculates the figure at 44 per cent. Also see M. Klein 1977*b*.
31 M. Klein 1977*b*.
32 Boutillier 1975, pp. 260, 268–9.
33 Holden 1970.
34 Barth 1857–9, vol. I, p. 523. Also see Lovejoy 1978*c*, pp. 342–4.
35 Barth 1857–9, vol. II, p. 191.
36 Froelich 1954, p. 25. Also see Burnham 1980; and Buttner 1967.
37 Lovejoy 1978*c*.
38 For a discussion of slavery in the Sokoto Caliphate and neighbouring areas, see Lovejoy 1981*b*, 1978*c*, and 1979*a*; Hogendorn 1977; M. G. Smith 1954; P. Hill 1976; Piault 1975; Mason 1973; Burnham 1980; pp. 46–51; Buttner 1967; R. A. Dunbar 1977; Meyers 1971; and Sellnow 1964.
39 Shea 1975; and Lovejoy 1978*c*, pp. 350–60.
40 P. Hill 1976. For a critique of Hill's analysis, see Lovejoy 1979*a*, p. 1279, and 1978*c*, pp. 358–63.
41 Lovejoy 1979*a*, pp. 1275–91, and 1978*c*.
42 Lovejoy 1981*b*, pp. 207–15.
43 For a discussion, see Lovejoy 1978*c*, pp. 351–3.
44 Imam Imoru, in Ferguson 1973, p. 233.
45 M. G. Smith 1955, p. 81.
46 Hogendorn 1977; and M. G. Smith 1954.
47 Lovejoy 1978*c*.
48 Aliyu 1974.
49 Barth 1857–9, vol. II, p. 191.
50 Abubakar 1977, p. 103.
51 Mason 1973.
52 Mason 1981, p. 217; and Hogendorn 1978, pp. 44, 56.
53 Lovejoy 1978*c*, p. 364; and Agiri 1981, pp. 137–8.
54 Spaulding 1982.
55 O'Fahey 1977.
56 Nachtigal 1971, pp. 67–8, 152, 165, 171.
57 Spaulding 1982. For a different interpretation of the role of slavery in the Nilotic Sudan, see 'Ali 1972. 'Ali argues that slavery was not exploitative in the Sudan and that British efforts at the suppression of the slave trade were closely related to political motives, with the result that British views of slavery were distorted.
58 Spaulding 1982.
59 Spaulding 1982.
60 R. Gray 1961, pp. 6–7, 69, 124, 134, 147; Prins 1907; Cordell forthcoming *b*, *a*, and 1977, pp. 236–68; and Mire forthcoming.
61 Warburg 1981, pp. 250–7.
62 For Rabih, see Cordell forthcoming *b*.

63 W. C. Harris 1844, vol. I, p. 198, cited in Pankhurst 1968, p. 74. For a discussion of slavery in nineteenth century Ethiopia, see Pankhurst 1968, pp. 73–134, and 1975.

64 Giaccardi 1939 cited in Pankhurst 1968, p. 75.

65 Hanson 1971, pp. 4–5, 11–13; M. Klein 1981; Abubakar 1977, pp. 103–4; R. Roberts 1978, pp. 296–320; Lovejoy 1979a, pp. 1274, 1283–6, and 1978c, pp. 361–6; and Swindell 1980, pp. 100–1.

66 For a general discussion of plantation agriculture, see Lovejoy 1979a.

67 Clapperton 1829, p. 214.

68 R. L. Roberts 1981, pp. 188–9; and O'Sullivan 1981, p. 644.

69 For a discussion of textiles, see Shea 1975; R. Roberts 1978, pp. 373–422; and Lovejoy 1978c, pp. 355–66.

70 Johnston 1889, p. 111.

71 Brevié's report of 1904, cited in R. Roberts 1978, p. 331.

72 Caillié 1830, vol. I, pp. 90–2. See also Hunkanrin 1964; Curtin 1981, p. 93.

73 For slavery among the Tuareg, see Baier and Lovejoy 1977; Bernus and Bernus 1975; Bonté 1975; and Bourgeot 1975.

74 McDougall 1980.

75 McDougall 1980.

76 Bernus and Bernus 1975, pp. 28–9; Bonté 1975, p. 51.

77 Bonté 1975, p. 51; Bernus and Bernus 1975, p. 28; and Baier and Lovejoy 1977, pp. 397–404.

78 Baier and Lovejoy 1977, pp. 391–411.

79 Baier and Lovejoy 1977, pp. 400–1.

80 Barth 1857–9, vol. I, p. 439. For a fuller discussion, see Baier and Lovejoy 1977, pp. 391–411.

81 Baier and Lovejoy 1977, pp. 402, 406–7; and Lovejoy 1980a, pp. 78–80.

82 Baier and Lovejoy 1977, pp. 400–4; and Lovejoy 1980a, pp. 78–80.

83 M. Klein forthcoming.

84 Lovejoy 1980a, pp. 75–100.

85 Works 1976, pp. 62–78.

86 Salt 1814, p. 382.

87 Quoted in O'Fahey 1977.

88 Lugard 1906, pp. 302–3.

89 M. Klein 1977b; and Klein and Lovejoy 1979, pp. 190–1.

90 For these areas, see Rey-Hulman 1975; Héritier 1975; and Arnaud 1932.

91 Vaughan 1977 and 1970.

10 Slavery in central, southern, and eastern Africa in the nineteenth century

1 Burke 1976; and Benedict 1980, pp. 136–8.

2 Shepherd (1980, pp. 74–99) discusses the origins of the plantation sector on the Comoros and its collapse as a result of raids from Madagascar. By the 1840s, when the French intervened, the Comoros were recovering from these deprivations. Also see J. Martin 1976, pp. 207–33, and 1973, pp. 45–51.

3 Cooper 1977, pp. 50–4; and Sheriff forthcoming.

4 Cooper 1977, pp. 50–4, 131–2.

5 Cooper 1977, pp. 56, 120.

6 Cooper 1977, pp. 44–55, 68–70; and Mackenzie 1895, as cited and discussed in Cooper 1977, p. 69.

7 Cooper 1977, pp. 156–64.

8 The discussion of slavery on the mainland is based on Cooper 1977, pp. 80–113; and Morton 1976.

9 Morton 1976, pp. 44–7, 398–401.
10 Morton 1976, pp. 57–60, 70.
11 Morton 1976, pp. 61–3; Cooper 1977, pp. 81–97.
12 Morton 1976, pp. 64–5.
13 Cooper 1977, pp. 97–110; Morton 1976, pp. 68–9.
14 Morton 1976, pp. 72–4; Cooper 1977, pp. 91, 156–82.
15 For an examination of these developments, see A. Roberts 1970b; Alpers 1969, pp. 411–14; and Renault 1971a, vol. I, pp. 70–7. Related changes, with a corresponding increase in slavery, were occurring at places affected by the expansion of trade; see, for example, Hartwig 1977.
16 Cooper 1977, p. 68.
17 Renault 1971a, vol. I, p. 74; citing 'L'arrivée des Arabes dans la région de Kasongo', *Bulletin militaire (Léopoldville)*, September 1949, pp. 532–4.
18 Cooper 1977, pp. 45, 123.
19 Hafkin 1973, pp. 52–7, 91–4, 151–2, 187.
20 Renault 1971a, vol. I, pp. 285–6; J. Gray 1963, p. 241; and Nicholls 1971, p. 359.
21 Duffy 1967, p. 85 fn.; Renault 1971a, vol. I, p. 286; and Mandala forthcoming.
22 Duffy 1967, pp. 68–9; and Harries 1981, p. 326.
23 Hafkin 1973, pp. 70, 254–5.
24 Frederic Elton to FO, 21 July 1875, FO 84/1411, as quoted in Duffy 1967, p. 68.
25 Isaacman 1972a, p. 41, and b, pp. 447–57.
26 Isaacman 1972b, pp. 448–9, and Vail and White 1980, pp. 26–41.
27 Gamitto 1960, vol. I, p. 58. Also see Newitt 1973, p. 198.
28 As quoted in Duffy 1967, p. 131. Also see the account of H. C. Moore, 1891: 'The farms all the way up the river are worked by slaves', quoted in Duffy, 1967, p. 130.
29 Matthews 1981, pp. 32–5.
30 Mandala forthcoming; and Duffy 1967, p. 85 fn.
31 Alpers 1969, pp. 406–20.
32 Keith 1971, p. 247, quoting Lopes de Lima (1844, vol. I, p. 7).
33 Duffy 1967, p. 11; Bender 1978, p. 139 fn.
34 Duffy 1967, pp. 11–13, 34–5; Clarence-Smith 1979b, p. 64.
35 Miller 1976a, p. 110.
36 Birmingham 1978, pp. 523, 528–9, 535, 538; and Dias 1976, pp. 248–51.
37 Clarence-Smith 1979b, and 1976, pp. 214–23; and Keith 1971.
38 Greenstein 1973, pp. 40, 44.
39 Freund 1979, pp. 215–19; and Newton-King 1980, pp. 173–80, 200.
40 Newton-King 1980, pp. 178–80, 204 fn. It should be noted that Newton-King presents a convincing argument that abolition had a profound effect on the Cape economy, but for a different view, see Edwards 1942, p. 52.
41 Freund 1979, pp. 216–17, 222–3; and Newton-King 1980, p. 179.
42 Newton-King 1980, pp. 173–200; Freund 1979, p. 217; and Giliomee 1979, pp. 318–21. For the continued importance of servile relationships, see Russell 1976; and Silberbauer and Kuper 1966.
43 Newton-King 1980, p. 179.
44 Thompson 1969a, pp. 437, 445; and Trapido 1977.
45 Harries 1981, pp. 316–17, 322; Thompson 1969a; and Bonner 1980, pp. 96–7. Also see Kistner 1952.
46 This discussion is based on Miller 1970 and 1969.
47 As cited in Miller 1969, pp. 15–16.
48 Vansina 1973, pp. 74, 248, 256–7, 276–7, 310.
49 For a discussion of the Bobangi, see Harms 1981.
50 Jewsiewicki and Mumbanza 1981.

51 Clarence-Smith 1979*a*.
52 Vellut 1972, pp. 74–8.
53 Bloch 1980 and 1979; Grandidier 1877; Ratsimamanga 1933.
54 Bloch 1980, pp. 109–10.
55 Bloch 1980, pp. 106–11.
56 Tuden 1970, p. 49.
57 Bonnafé 1975; Cureau 1912; Tisserant 1955; White 1957; Rey 1969 and 1975*a*; Douglas 1964; De Jonghe and Vanhove 1949; De Jonghe 1933*a*; Donny 1911; De Beaucorps 1945; Denolf 1938; Miller 1981*a*, pp. 60–3; and Jewsiewicki and Mumbanza 1981, pp. 79–88.
58 The Isaacmans argue this point persuasively for the patrilineal Sena of the Zambezi valley, see Isaacman and Isaacman 1977.
59 Schulz and Hammar 1897, p. 354, as cited in Tlou 1977, p. 383.
60 Weeks 1969, p. 97. Also see MacGaffey 1977.
61 Isaacman forthcoming *a*.
62 Harries 1981, pp. 318–29.
63 Vansina 1978, pp. 165–8, 205; Wissmann 1891, p. 145.
64 Jewsiewicki and Mumbanza 1981, pp. 75–6.
65 For a similar argument, see Thomas and Bean 1974.

11 The abolitionist impulse

1 This analysis draws heavily upon Miers 1975; Renault 1971*a*; Grace 1975, pp. 22–62; and Van Zwanenberg 1976, pp. 108–27. Also see Tamuno 1964; Fyfe 1974; Nwulia 1975; and Gann 1954.
2 Kopytoff and Miers 1977, pp. 4–5, 17; Miers 1975, pp. 118–20; and Kopytoff 1979, p. 70.
3 Curtin 1969, p. 250. Also see Lloyd 1949, pp. 275–6; and Asiegbu 1969, pp. 191–214.
4 *Instructions*, 1844 and 1866 editions, as cited in Miers 1975, p. 118.
5 Grace 1975, pp. 21–65, 220–60.
6 Fyfe 1974, pp. 47–52; Verger 1976, pp. 442–3.
7 Fyfe 1974, pp. 52–5; and C. I. Foster 1953, p. 60.
8 Wilks 1975, pp. 175–9, 262–3; and Lovejoy 1980*a*, pp. 11–14.
9 As cited in Wilks 1975, p. 137.
10 As cited in Wilks 1975, p. 157. A similar policy was informally pursued in Sierra Leone, although the British government refused to ratify an extradition treaty between Freetown and Loko Temne in 1836, and in 1841 it was officially made clear that fugitive slaves would not be returned to their masters (Grace 1975, p. 62 fn.)
11 Wilks 1975, pp. 679–80.
12 Grace 1975, pp. 23–7; Kaplow 1978, pp. 29–30; Dumett 1981, p. 214 fn.; McSheffrey 1983; and Wilks 1975, p. 219, quoting a letter from Kwaku Dua to Pine, 9 February 1863, which explains the agreement signed by Maclean for the extradition of fugitive slaves to Asante.
13 As quoted in McSheffrey 1983. Also see McSheffrey's discussion of Pine.
14 Ayandele 1966, pp. 23–4, 26; Alagoa 1971*b*; Nair 1972, pp. 37, 46–55; and Latham 1973, pp. 102–9.
15 Campbell to Malmesbury, 4 March 1859, FO 84/1088, as quoted in Oroge 1975*a*, p. 41.
16 Grace 1975, p. 26. There were also some fugitive slaves in Sierra Leone earlier in the century; see Grace 1975, pp. 62 fn., 78.
17 McCoskry to Russell, 3 September 1861, FO 84/1141, as quoted in Oroge 1975*b*, p. 63. Also see Verger 1976, p. 549.
18 Reynolds 1974, pp. 120–1, for recruitment of slaves in the 1850s. Also see McSheffrey 1983, Grace (1975, pp. 75–7) notes that many ex-slaves had joined the Frontier Police in Sierra Leone which was a force of 500 men in 1894.

19 Oroge 1971, pp. 338–9, 363.
20 Marshall to Wolseley, 24 December 1873, C.O. 879/6/39 No. 79, as quoted in A. N. Klein 1980.
21 Chalmers to Strahan, 6 March 1875, C.O. 96/115/2733, as quoted in McSheffrey 1983.
22 McSheffrey 1983.
23 Ajayi 1965, pp. 104–5; and Ayandele 1966, pp. 331–4.
24 Ayandele 1966, p. 47; Isichei 1976, p. 102; and Latham 1973, pp. 102–9.
25 Ayandale 1966, pp. 77–110; and Isichei 1973, pp. 65, 74, 91–2, 103–4.
26 Ayandele 1966, pp. 84–6; and Isichei 1976, p. 102.
27 McSheffrey 1983; Grace (1975, pp. 276–85) provides a list of fugitive slaves at the Customs Post, Kironkeh, Sierra Leone, April 1896 to May 1897: of 187 fugitives, 136 claimed ill treatment as the reason for escape; 31 'desired freedom' and 23 feared the threat of sale. Also see the forthcoming work of Dumett.
28 Afigbo 1971a. Also see Igbafe 1975.
29 Oroge 1975c. I wish to thank Dr Oroge for showing me this valuable paper. In the context of Yorubaland, also see Hopkins 1968 and 1966.
30 Cameron 1888, p. 265. Also see Nwulia 1975.
31 Renault 1971a, vol. I, pp. 140–50; and Morton 1976, pp. 231, 236–7. Also see Akinola 1972.
32 Morton 1976, pp. 137, 154–8. For the northern coast, see Cassanelli forthcoming.
33 Morton 1976, pp. 192–6.
34 Morton 1976, pp. 183, 209–16.
35 Morton 1976, pp. 229–30, 243, 279–80.
36 J. Gray 1963, p. 245; and Morton 1976, pp. 279–80.
37 Renault 1971a, vol. I, pp. 140–50.
38 Miers 1975, p. 155; MacDonald 1882, vol. II, p. 29; and Hanna 1956, pp. 4–10, 34–7, 56–9, 196–7.
39 MacDonald 1882, vol. II, p. 32.
40 MacDonald 1882, vol. II, pp. 198–9.
41 Renault 1971a, vol. I, pp. 184–98. Also see M. Wright 1975.
42 Miers 1975, p. 300.
43 Jewsiewicki and Mumbanza 1981, pp. 88–96.
44 Cooper 1980.
45 Duffy 1967; and Clarence-Smith 1979b.
46 Zuccarelli 1962; and Fauré 1920.
47 For a summary of French policy, see Roberts and Klein 1981, pp. 382–4; Guèye 1966; Pasquier 1967; Renault 1971b; M. Klein 1981; and Oloruntimehin 1971–2, p. 52.
48 Hanson 1971, pp. 22–4.
49 Bouche 1968, pp. 58–64, 79–89, 146–53. The British established similar villages later; see Olusanya 1966.
50 Kersaint-Gilly 1924; Kanya-Forstner 1969, pp. 10, 272–3.
51 Commandant Kita to Commandant Supérieur, 19 January 1891, as quoted in M. Klein forthcoming. Also see Bouche 1968, p. 80.
52 As quoted in R. Roberts 1978, p. 321.
53 Warburg 1981, pp. 257–66. Also see Baer 1969. For a useful analysis of the role of abolition in the history of the Nilotic Sudan, see 'Ali 1972.
54 Memorandum to Mudirs, enclosure in Cromer to Salisbury, 17 March 1899, F.O. 78/5022, as cited in Warburg 1981, p. 258.
55 Minute, 5 April 1900, on Moor to Chamberlain, no. 1 conf., 28 Jan. 1900, C.O. 520/1, as quoted in Miers 1975, p. 294. For the origins of this pro-slavery sentiment as an aspect of British imperialism, see Grace 1975, pp. 22, 40. Grace argues that Mary Kingsley, C. L. Temple, Lugard, and others combined a positive economic policy with a conservationist

social policy in which slavery was one of many 'native' institutions that should be allowed to function in modified form.

56 Lugard 1906, p. 136. Also see Lugard 1896; and Nwulia 1975, pp. 173–5.
57 Lovejoy 1981*b*, pp. 233–6.
58 Roberts and Klein 1981, pp. 385–92.
59 Lugard 1906, p. 136.
60 Roberts and Klein 1981, p. 386.
61 Roberts and Klein 1981, p. 393. Also see O'Sullivan (1981, p. 646), who reports that 8,000–9,000 slaves fled the Odienne area in 1907.
62 M. Klein 1981.
63 Abubakar 1977, p. 151.
64 Lovejoy 1981*b*, pp. 229–32; and Mason 1973, p. 464.
65 For some aspects of the transition from slavery to other forms of labour, see Asiegbu 1970; Renault 1976; M. Klein 1981; and Weiskel 1979.

12 Slavery in the political economy of Africa

1 A useful survey of the early literature can be found in Seddon 1978, which contains excerpts from the work of Maurice Godelier, Claude Meillassoux, Georges Dupré, Pierre Philippe Rey, and others. Also see Suret-Canale 1969; Hindess and Hirst 1975, pp. 109–77; Coquery 1975; Terray 1974 and 1975*b*, pp. 85–134; and Klein and Lovejoy 1979, pp. 207–9.
2 Marx 1965; and Hindess and Hirst 1975.
3 See especially, Terray 1974, and 1975*b*, pp. 85–134. Meillassoux has been the most important scholar among those who have recognized the importance of slavery but who have fallen short of accepting its crucial role; see 1978*a*, introduction to 1975*a* (pp. 18–21), and 1978*b*. For a survey of this debate, see Klein and Lovejoy 1979, pp. 207–12; Cooper 1979; M. Klein 1978; and Harms 1978. Among other scholars who apply the concept 'mode of production' to slavery, see M. Klein 1977*b*, forthcoming, and 1978*b*; Kilkenny 1981; Bloch 1980; and R. L. Roberts 1980*a* and 1981, pp. 171–8.
4 Terray 1974, p.340.
5 Terray 1974, p.341. Also see Terray 1975*b*, pp. 85–134.
6 Terray 1975*a*, p. 437.
7 Terray has explored various aspects of this interaction in a number of his articles, which are in anticipation of a much longer and more detailed study that is currently under way. See, for example, forthcoming *b* and *a*.
8 Goody 1971, pp. 39–56.
9 Morton 1976, p. 398.
10 Harms 1978. Also see his chapter in Klein and Robertson forthcoming.
11 Meillassoux forthcoming *b*.
12 For various interpretations of this impact, see Dantzig 1975; Davidson 1971; M. Johnson 1976*a*; Kilson 1971; Ronon 1971; Uzoigwe 1973; Fage 1969; Wrigley 1971; and Rodney 1966.
13 Finley 1968.
14 Terray 1975*a*, pp. 437–48; Bazin 1975; and R. L. Roberts 1980*a*.
15 Padgug (1976) has examined the subordinate status of the Americas in the rise of capitalism by distinguishing slavery in three contexts: classical antiquity, Asiatic societies, and the Americas. For Padgug, slavery in the Americas was different from other slave systems because of the articulation with capitalism, but he fails to see that slavery in Africa represented a fourth system that was also associated with the rise of capitalism. My approach is indebted to Curtin's conceptual breakthrough in analysing the interrelationship between African slave supply and productive slavery in the Americas as a 'south Atlantic system', although Curtin does not carry his analysis as far as I do. None the less, I consider

the identification of a slave mode of production in Africa as the logical extension of Curtin's framework; see Curtin 1971c, and 1977.

16 Swindell 1980, p. 99.

17 McSheffrey 1983; Dumett 1981, p. 214 fn.; and Kaplow 1978, pp. 29–30.

18 Harries 1981, p. 317. In the Nilotic Sudan, migrant labour was available as a by-product of the pilgrimage traffic to Mecca, and agricultural producers were quick to realize the utility of pilgrim labour as a substitute for slave labour; see Warburg 1981, pp. 265–6 and 1978; McLoughlin 1962, 1966, and 1970.

19 Oroge 1975c; and Ortoli 1939.

20 In an interesting thesis, Hillard Warren Pouncy examines the extent to which the labour code of Great Britain was imposed on West Africa. Vagrancy laws and other measures often reflected out-of-date metropolitan laws but were clearly conceived as the basis of legal means to control labour, even though the laws themselves were seldom enforceable; see Pouncy 1981.

21 Various authors have suggested a close connection between abolitionism and the ideology of imperialism; I have discussed this elsewhere; see 1981c, pp. 26–7. Also see Van Zwanenberg 1976, pp. 108–27; Temperley 1981; and Warburg 1981, pp. 257–66. Olorun-timehin (1971–2) earlier argued that anti-slavery rhetoric was often merely propaganda, while 'Ali (1972, pp. 3–129) has analysed the statements of different observers in the Nilotic Sudan in order to demonstrate the underlying ambiguity of British policy.

22 For examples of the vast literature on abolition, see Buxton 1839; Schoelcher 1880; André 1899; Berlioux 1872 and 1870; and Lacour 1889. Also see the discussion in Miers 1975; and Renault 1971a.

23 See, for example Echenberg 1975 and 1980. I wish to thank Professor Echenberg for information on the importance of slave origins among conscripts.

24 Derrick 1975.

25 Based on my experience at Ahmadu Bello Univeristy, Zaria.

26 Cooper 1980.

Bibliography

Anonymous. 1949. L'arrivée des Arabes dans la région de Kasongo. In *Bulletin militaire, Léopoldville*, 532–4
1979. *The African Slave Trade from the Fifteenth to the Nineteenth Century.* Paris
Abir, M. 1966. Salt trade and politics in Ethiopia in the 'Zamana Masafent'. *Journal of Ethiopian Studies*, 4, 2: 1–10
1968. *Ethiopia: The Era of Princes.* New York
1970. Southern Ethiopia. In Richard Gray and David Birmingham (eds.), *Pre-Colonial African Trade: Essays on Trade in Central and Eastern Africa before 1900*, pp. 119–37. London
1980. *Ethiopia and the Red Sea: The Rise and Decline of the Solomonic Dynasty and Muslim European Rivalry in the Region.* London
forthcoming. The Ethiopian slave trade and its relation to the Islamic world. In J. R. Willis (ed.), *The Servile Estate.* London
Abraham, Arthur. 1975. The institution of 'slavery' in Sierra Leone. *Genève-Afrique*, 14, 2: 46–57
Abubakar, Sa'ad. 1977. *The Lāmībe of Fombina: A Political History of Adamawa, 1809–1901.* Zaria
Adamu, Mahdi. 1978. *The Hausa Factor in West African History.* Zaria
1979. The delivery of slaves from the central Sudan to the Bight of Benin in the eighteenth and nineteenth centuries. In H. A. Gemery and J. S. Hogendorn (eds.), *The Uncommon Market: Essays in the Economic History of the Atlantic Slave Trade*, pp. 163–80. New York
Adeleye, R. A. 1971. Hausaland and Bornu. In J. F. Ade Ajayi and Michael Crowder (eds.), *History of West Africa*, pp. 484–530. London
Adeleye, R. A. and Stewart, C. C. forthcoming. The Sokoto Caliphate in the nineteenth century. In J. F. A. Ajayi and M. Crowder (eds.), *History of West Africa*, rev. ed. London
Afigbo, A. E. 1971*a*. The eclipse of the Aro slaving oligarchy of south-eastern Nigeria, 1901–1927. *Journal of the Historical Society of Nigeria*, 6, 1: 3–24
1971*b*. The Aro of southeastern Nigeria: a socio-historical analysis of legends of their origins. *African Notes*, 6, 2: 31–46
1973. Trade and trade routes of nineteenth century Nsukka. *Journal of the Historical Society of Nigeria*, 8, 1: 77–90
1974. The nineteenth century crisis of the Aro slaving oligarchy in southeastern Nigeria. *Nigeria*, 110–12: 66–73
Agiri, B. A. 1974. Aspects of socio-economic changes among the Awori Egba and Ijebu Remo communities during the nineteenth century. *Journal of the Historical Society of Nigeria*, 7, 3: 465–83

309

1981. Slavery in Yoruba society in the nineteenth century. In Paul E. Lovejoy (ed.), *The Ideology of Slavery in Africa*, pp. 123–48. Beverly Hills

Aguessy, Honorat. 1970. Le Dan-Home du XIX siècle était-il une société esclavagiste? *Revue française d'études politiques africaines*, 50: 71–91

Ajayi, J. F. Ade. 1965. *Christian Missions in Nigeria, 1841–1891.* London

1967. (ed.) The narrative of Samuel Ajayi Crowther. In Philip D. Curtin (ed.), *Africa Remembered: Narratives of West Africans from the Era of the Slave Trade*, pp. 289–316. Madison

Akinjogbin, I. A. 1967. *Dahomey and its Neighbours, 1708–1818.* Cambridge

Akinola, G. A. 1972. Slavery and slave revolts in the Sultanate of Zanzibar in the nineteenth century. *Journal of the Historical Society of Nigeria*, 6, 2: 215–28

Alagoa, E. J. 1970. Long-distance trade and states in the Niger delta. *Journal of African History*, 11, 3: 319–29

1971a. The development of institutions in the states of the eastern Niger delta. *Journal of African History*, 12, 2: 269–79

1971b. Nineteenth century revolutions in the eastern delta states and Calabar. *Journal of the Historical Society of Nigeria*, 5, 4: 565–74

1972. *A History of the Niger Delta.* Ibadan

Al-Hajj, Muhammad. 1975. The meaning of the Sokoto *Jihad.* Unpublished paper presented at the Sokoto Seminar, Sokoto

'Ali, 'Abbas Ibrahim Muhammad. 1972. *The British, the Slave Trade and Slavery in the Sudan, 1820–1881.* Khartoum

Aliyu, Y. A. 1974. The establishment and development of emirate government in Bauchi, 1805–1903. Unpublished PhD thesis, Ahmadu Bello University

Alpers, E. A. 1967. *The East African Slave Trade.* Nairobi.

1969. Trade, state, and society among the Yao in the nineteenth century. *Journal of African History*, 10, 3: 405–20

1970. The French slave trade in East Africa (1721–1810). *Cahiers d'études africaines*, 10, 1: 80–124

1975. *Ivory and Slaves in East Central Africa: Changing Patterns of International Trade to the Later Nineteenth Century.* London

Althusser, Louis. 1977. *For Marx.* London

Althusser, Louis and Balibar, Etienne. 1970. *Reading Capital.* London

Amin, Samir. 1976. *Unequal Development: An Essay on the Social Formations of Peripheral Capitalism*, trans. Brian Pearce. London and New York

André, E. C. 1899. *De l'esclavage à Madagascar.* Paris

Anstey, Roger. 1975a. *The Atlantic Slave Trade and British Abolition, 1760–1810.* London

1975b. The volume of the North American slave-carrying trade from Africa, 1761–1810. *Revue française d'histoire d'outre-mer*, 42, 12: 47–66

1975c. The volume and profitability of the British slave trade, 1761–1807. In S. L. Engerman and E. D. Genovese (eds.), *Race and Slavery in the Western Hemisphere: Quantitative Studies*, pp. 3–31. Princeton

1976. The British slave trade, 1751–1807. *Journal of African History*, 17, 4: 606–7

1977. The slave trade of the continental powers, 1760–1810. *Economic History Review*, 30, 2: 259–68

Anstey, Roger and Hair, P. E. H. (eds.) 1976. *Liverpool, the African Slave Trade, and Abolition: Essays to Illustrate Current Knowledge and Research*, Historic Society of Lancashire and Cheshire, occasional series, vol. II

Arhin, Kwame. 1968. Status differentiation in Ashanti in the nineteenth century: a preliminary study. *Research Review* (Institute of African Studies, University of Ghana), 4, 3: 34–52

1980. The economic and social significance of rubber production and exchange on the Gold and Ivory Coasts, 1880–1900. *Cahiers d'études africaines*, 20, 1–2: 49–62

Armstrong, James C. 1979. The slaves, 1652–1795. In Richard Elphick and Hermann Giliomee (eds.), *The Shaping of South African Society, 1652–1820*, pp. 75–115. Cape Town

Arnaud, Robert. 1932. Les Formes anciennes de l'esclavage dans la Boucle méridionale du Niger. *Études de sociologie et d'ethnologie juridiques*, 12: 23–64

Asiegbu, Johnson U. J. 1969. *Slavery and the Politics of Liberation, 1787–1861: A Study of Liberated African Emigration and British Anti-Slavery Policy*. London

1970. British slave emancipation and 'free' labour recruitment from West Africa. *Sierra Leone Studies*, 26: 37–47

Augé, Marc. 1975. Les Faiseurs d'ombre: servitude et structure lignagère dans la société alladian. In Claude Meillassoux (ed.), *L'Esclavage en Afrique précoloniale*, pp. 455–75. Paris

Austen, Ralph A. 1970. The abolition of the overseas slave trade: a distorted theme in West African history. *Journal of the Historical Society of Nigeria*, 5, 2: 257–74

1977. Slavery among coastal middlemen: the Duala of Cameroon. In S. Miers and I. Kopytoff (eds.), *Slavery in Africa: Historical and Anthropological Perspectives*, pp. 305–33. Madison

1979a. The trans-Saharan slave trade: a tentative census. In H. A. Gemery and J. S. Hogendorn (eds.), *The Uncommon Market: Essays in the Economic History of the Atlantic Slave Trade*, pp. 23–76. New York

1979b. The Islamic Red Sea slave trade: an effort at quantification. In *Proceedings of the Fifth International Conference on Ethiopian Studies*, pp. 443–67. Chicago

1981. From the Atlantic to the Indian Ocean: European abolition, African slave trade, and Asian economic structures. In David Eltis and James Walvin (eds.), *The Abolition of the Atlantic Slave Trade*, pp. 117–39. Madison

forthcoming. The Islamic slave trade out of Africa (Red Sea and Indian Ocean): an effort at quantification. In J. R. Willis (ed.), *The Servile Estate*. London

Ayandele, E. A. 1966. *The Missionary Impact on Modern Nigeria, 1842–1914: A Political and Social Analysis*. London

1967. Observations on some social and economic aspects of slavery in pre-colonial northern Nigeria. *Nigerian Journal of Economic and Social Studies*, 9, 3: 329–38

Baer, Gabriel. 1969. Slavery and its abolition. In *Studies in the Social History of Modern Egypt*, pp. 161–89. Chicago

Baier, Stephen and Lovejoy, Paul E. 1977. The Tuareg of the central Sudan: gradations in servility at the desert-edge (Niger–Nigeria). In S. Miers and I. Kopytoff (eds.), *Slavery in Africa: Historical and Anthropological Perspectives*, pp. 391–411. Madison

Baldé, Mamadou Saliou. 1975. L'Esclavage et la guerre sainte au Fuuta Jalon. In Claude Meillassoux (ed.), *L'Esclavage en Afrique précoloniale*, pp. 183–220. Paris

Baldus, Berd. 1977. Responses to dependence in a servile group; the Machube of northern Benin. In S. Miers and I. Kopytoff (eds.), *Slavery in Africa: Historical and Anthropological Perspectives*, pp. 435–58. Madison

Baravelli, Giulio Cesare. 1935. *The Last Stronghold of Slavery: What Abyssina Is*. Rome

Barbour, Bernard and Jacobs, Michelle. forthcoming. The Mi'rāj: a legal treatise on slavery by Ahmad Baba. In J. R. Willis (ed.), *Islam and the Ideology of Enslavement*. London

Barth, Heinrich. 1857–9. *Travels and Discoveries in North and Central Africa: Being a Journal of an Expedition undertaken under the Auspices of H.B.M.'s Government in the Years 1849–1855* (3 vols.) New York

Batran, Aziz Abdalla. The Ulema of Fas: Mulay Ismail and the issue of the Haratin of Fas. In J. R. Willis (ed.), *The Servile Estate*. London

Bibliography

Bazin, Jean. 1975. Guerre et servitude à Segou. In Claude Meillassous (ed.), *L'Esclavage en Afrique précoloniale*, pp. 135–82. Paris.

Beachy, R. W. 1976. *The Slave Trade of Eastern Africa*. London

1977. Some observations on the volume of the slave trade of eastern Africa in the 19th century. In *African Historical Demography*, pp. 365–72. Centre of African Studies, University of Edinburgh

Bean, Richard. 1974. A note on the relative importance of slaves and gold in West African exports. *Journal of African History*, 15, 3: 351–6

1975. *The British Trans-Atlantic Slave Trade, 1650–1775*. New York

Beecham, John. 1841. *Ashantee and the Gold Coast*, London

Beinart, William. 1980. Production and the material basis of chieftainship: Pondoland, c. 1830–80. In Shula Marks and Anthony Atmore (eds.), *Economy and Society in Pre-Industrial South Africa*, pp. 120–47. London

Bender, Gerald J. 1978. *Angola under the Portuguese: The Myth and the Reality*. London

Benedict, Burton. 1980. Slavery and indenture in Mauritius and Seychelles. In James L. Watson (ed.), *Asian and African Systems of Slavery*, pp. 135–68. Oxford

Berbain, Simone, 1942. *Études sur la traite des noirs au golfe de Guinée: le comptoir français de Juda (Ouidah) au XVIII siècle*. Mémoires de IFAN, 3, Paris. Republished 1968, Amsterdam

Berlioux, E. 1870. *La Traite orientale*. Paris

1872. *The Slave Trade in Africa in 1872*. London

Bernstein, Henry and Depelchin, Jacques. 1978–9. The object of African history: a materialist perspective. *History in Africa*, 5: 1–20; 6: 17–43

Bernus, Edmond and Bernus, Suzanne. 1975. L'Évolution de la condition servile chez les Touregs sahéliens. In Claude Meillassoux (ed.), *L'Esclavage en Afrique précoloniale*, pp. 27–47. Paris

Bethell, Leslie. 1966. The mixed commissions for the suppression of the transatlantic slave trade in the nineteenth century. *Journal of African History*, 7, 1: 79–93

Binger, Louis-Gustave. 1892. *Du Niger au Golfe de Guinée par le pays de Kong et le Mossi (1887–1889)* (2 vols.) Paris

Birmingham, David. 1966. *Trade and Conflict in Angola: The Mbundu and their Neighbors under the Influence of the Portuguese*. Oxford

1970. Early trade in Angola and its hinterland. In Richard Gray and David Birmingham (eds.), *Pre-Colonial African Trade: Essays on Trade in Central and Eastern Africa before 1900*, pp. 163–74. London

1978. The coffee barons of Cazengo. *Journal of African History*, 14, 4: 523–38

Blake, John W. 1937. *European Beginnings in West Africa, 1454–1578*. New York.

Bloch, Maurice. 1975. (ed.), *Marxist Analyses and Social Anthropology*. London

1979. The social implications of freedom for Merina and Zafimaniry Slaves. In Raymond Kent (ed.), *Madagascar in History*, pp. 269–97. Albany, California

1980. Modes of production and slavery in Madagascar: two case studies. In James L. Watson (ed.), *Asian and African Systems of Slavery*, pp. 100–34. Oxford

Boahen, Adu. 1964. *Britain, the Sahara, and the Western Sudan 1788–1861*. London.

Boeseken, A. J. 1977. *Slaves and Free Blacks at the Cape 1658–1700*. Cape Town

Bonnafé, Pierre. 1975. Les Formes d'asservissement chez les Kukuya d'Afrique centrale. In Claude Meillassoux (ed.), *L'Esclavage en Afrique précoloniale*, pp. 529–55. Paris

Bonner, Philip. 1980. Classes, the mode of production and the state in pre-colonial Swaziland. In Shula Marks and Anthony Atmore (eds.), *Economy and Society in Pre-Industrial South Africa*, pp. 80–101. London

Bonté, Pierre. 1975. Esclavage et relations de dépendance chez les Touregs Kel Gress. In Claude Meillassoux, (eds.), *L'Esclavage en Afrique précoloniale*, pp. 49–76. Paris

Bouche, Denise. 1968. *Les villages de liberté en Afrique noire française, 1887–1910*. Paris

312

Bouchez. 1901. Notice sur le Dinguiray. *Revue coloniale*, 1: 282–301, 478–500

Bourgeot, André. 1975. Rapports esclavagistes et conditions d'affranchissement chez les Imuhag. In Claude Meillassoux (ed.), *L'Esclavage en Afrique précoloniale*, pp. 77–98.

Boutillier, J.-L. 1968. Les captifs en A.O.F. (1903–1905). *Bulletin de l'IFAN*, series B, 30, 2: 513–35

1975. Les Trois Esclaves de Bouna. In Claude Meillassoux (ed.), *L'Esclavage en Afrique précoloniale*, pp. 253–80. Paris

Bowdich, Thomas E. 1819. *Mission from Cape Coast Castle to Ashantee*. London

1821. *The British and French Expeditions to Teemb*. Paris

Brenner, Louis. 1973. *The Shehus of Kukawa: A History of the al-Kanemi Dynasty of Bornu*. Oxford

Brooks, George. 1975. Peanuts and colonialism: consequences of the commercialization of peanuts in West Africa, 1830–70. *Journal of African History*, 16, 1: 29–54

Brun, Samuel. 1624. *Schiffarten, welche er in etliche Lander und Insulen ... gethan*. Basle. Reprinted in *Linschoten Vereeniging*, 6 (1913), 77–8

Brunschvig, H. 1960. 'Abd. *The Encyclopaedia of Islam*, vol. I, pp. 24–40. London

Burke, Enid M. 1976. African and Seychellois socio-cultural ties, mid-18th century to present day. *Hadith*, 6: 86–110

Burnham, Philip. 1980. Raiders and traders in Adamawa: slavery as a regional system. In James L. Watson (ed.), *Asian and African Systems of Slavery*, pp. 43–72. Oxford

Buttner, Thea. 1967. On the socio-economic structure of Adamawa in the nineteenth century: slavery or serfdom? In W. Markov (ed.), *Études africaines*, pp. 43–61. Leipzig

Buxton, Thomas Fowell. 1839. *The African Slave Trade*. Philadelphia

Cadamosto, A. da. 1937. *The Voyages of Cadamosto*, trans. G. R. Crone. London

Caillié. René. 1830. *Travels through Central Africa to Timbuctoo* (2 vols.) London

Cameron, V. L. 1888. Slavery in Africa: the disease and the remedy. *National Review*, 10: 260–9

Campbell, Gwyn. 1981. Madagascar and the slave trade, 1810–1895. *Journal of African History*, 22, 2: 203–27

Cassanelli, Lee V. forthcoming. Social constructs on the Somali frontier: Bantu ex-slave communities in nineteenth-century Somaliland. In Igor Kopytoff (ed.), *The Internal African Frontier*, Philadelphia

Chauveau, Jean-Pierre. 1977. Note sur les échanges dans le Baule précolonial. *Cahiers d'études africaines*, 16: 567–601

Chilver, E. M. 1961. Nineteenth century trade in the Bamenda grassfields, southern Cameroons. *Afrika und Ubersee*, 45: 233–58

Chilver, E. M., Kaberry, P. M., and Cornevin, R. 1965. Sources of the nineteenth century slave trade: two comments. *Journal of African History*, 4, 2: 117–20

Cissoko, S. 1968. Famines et épidémies à Tombouctou et dans la Boucle du Niger du XVIe au XVIIIe siècle. *Bulletin de l'IFAN*, 30, 3: 806–21

1969. Traits fondamentaux des sociétés de Soudan occidental de XVIIe au début du XIXe siècle. *Bulletin de l'IFAN*, 31, 1: 1–30

Clapperton, Hugh. 1829. *Journal of a Second Expedition into the Interior of Africa*. London

Clarence-Smith, W. G. 1976. Slavery in coastal southern Angola, 1875–1913. *Journal of Southern African Studies*, 2, 2: 214–23

1979a. Slaves, commoners and landlords in Bulozi, c. 1875 to 1906. *Journal of African History*, 20, 2: 219–34

1979b. *Slaves, Peasants and Capitalists in Southern Angola, 1840–1926*. New York

Cohen, Ronald, et al. 1967. Slavery in Africa. *Trans-Action*, 4: 44–56

Cookey, S. J. S. 1972. An Igbo slave story of the late nineteenth century and its implications. *Ikenga*, 1, 2: 1–9

Bibliography

1980. Review of Northrup, *Trade without Rulers*. *International Journal of African Historical Studies*, 13, 2: 366

Cooper, Frederick. 1973. The treatment of slaves on the Kenya coast in the nineteenth century. *Kenya Historical Review*, 1, 2: 87–108

1977. *Plantation Slavery on the East African Coast*. New Haven

1979. The problem of slavery in African studies. *Journal of African History*, 20, 1: 103–25

1980. *From Slaves to Squatters: Plantation Labor and Agriculture in Zanzibar and Coastal Kenya, 1908–1925*. New Haven

1981. Islam and cultural hegemony: the ideology of slaveowners on the East African coast. In Paul E. Lovejoy (ed.), *The Ideology of Slavery in Africa*, pp. 270–307. Beverly Hills

Coquery, Catherine. 1971. De la traite des esclaves à l'exportation de l'huile de palme et des palmistes au Dahomey: XIXe siècle. In Claude Meillassoux (ed.), *The Development of Indigenous Trade and Markets in West Africa*, pp. 107–23. London

1975. Research on an African mode of production. *Critique of Anthropology*, 4: 38–71

Cordell, Dennis. 1977. Dar Al-Kuti: a history of the slave trade and state formation on the Islamic frontier in northern equatorial Africa (Central African Republic and Chad). Unpublished PhD thesis, University of Wisconsin

forthcoming *a*. Secondary empire and slave-raiding beyond the Islamic frontier in northern equatorial Africa: the case of Bandas Haim and Sa'id Baldas

forthcoming *b*. The Lake Chad–Nile region and the Ubangi-Shari, 1750–1900: the integration of northern equatorial Africa into the international economy.

Craton, Michael (ed.) 1979. *Roots and Branches: Current Directions in Slave Studies*. Toronto

Crone, Patricia. 1980. *Slaves on Horses: The Evolution of the Islamic Polity*. New York

Crowther, Samuel and Taylor, J. 1859. *The Gospel on the Banks of the Niger*. London

Cunnison, Ian. 1961. Kazembe and the Portuguese, 1798–1832. *Journal of African History*, 2, 1: 61–76

Cureau, Adolphe Louis. 1912. *Les Sociétés primitives de l'Afrique equatoriale*. Paris

Curtin, Philip D. 1967*a*. (ed.) *Africa Remembered: Narratives of West Africans from the Era of the Slave Trade*. Madison

1967*b*. Joseph Wright of the Egba. In Philip D. Curtin (ed.) *Africa Remembered*, pp. 317–33. Madison

1968. Epidemiology and the slave trade. *Political Science Quarterly*, 83, 2: 190–216

1969. *The Atlantic Slave Trade: A Census*. Madison

1971*a*. Jihad in West Africa: early phases and interrelations in Mauritania and Senegal. *Journal of African History*, 12, 1: 11–24

1917*b* Pre-colonial trading networks and traders: the Diakhanke. In Claude Meillassoux (ed.), *The Development of Indigenous Trade and Markets in West Africa*, pp. 228–39. London

1971*c*. The slave trade and the Atlantic basin: intercontinental perspectives. In N. I. Huggins, M. Kilson, and D. M. Fox (eds.), *Key Issues in the Afro-American Experience*, vol. I, pp. 74–93. New York

1973. The lure of Bambuk gold. *Journal of African History*, 14, 4: 623–31

1974. The Atlantic slave trade, 1600–1800. In J. F. Ade Ajayi and Michael Crowder (eds.), *History of West Africa*, vol. I, pp. 240–68. London

1975*a*. *Economic Change in Precolonial Africa: Senegambia in the Era of the Slave Trade* (2 vols.) Madison

1975*b*. Measuring the Atlantic slave trade. In S. L. Engerman and E. D. Genovese (eds.), *Race and Slavery in the Western Hemisphere: Quantitative Studies*, pp. 107–28. Princeton

1976. Measuring the Atlantic slave trade once again. *Journal of African History*, 17, 4: 595–605

1977. Slavery and empire. In V. Rubin and A. Tuden (eds.), *Comparative Perspectives on*

Slavery in New World Plantation Societies, pp. 3–11. New York

1981. The abolition of the slave trade from Senegambia. In David Eltis and James Walvin (eds.), *The Abolition of the Atlantic Slave Trade*, pp. 83–97. Madison

1982. Africa and the wider monetary world, 1250–1850. In John Richards (ed.) *Precious Metals in the Medieval and Early Modern Worlds*. Durham, NC.

forthcoming. External trade to 1800. In J. F. Ade Ajayi and Michael Crowder (eds.), *History of West Africa* (3rd ed.) London

Curtin, Philip D. and Vansina, Jan. 1964. Sources of the nineteenth century Atlantic slave trade. *Journal of African History*, 5, 2: 185–208

Cuvelier, J. and Jadin, L. 1954. *L'Ancien Congo d'après les archives romaines (1518–1640)*. Brussels

Daaku, Kwame Yeboa. 1970. *Trade and Politics on the Gold Coast, 1600–1720: A study of the African Reaction to European Trade*. Oxford

1971. Trade and trading patterns of the Akan in the seventeenth and eighteenth centuries. In Claude Meillassoux (ed.), *The Development of Indigenous Trade and Markets in West Africa*, pp. 168–81. London

Dantzig, Albert van. 1975. Effects of the Atlantic slave trade on some West African societies. *Revue française d'histoire d'outre-mer*, 62, 1–2: 252–69

Davenport, T. R. H. 1971. The consolidation of a new society: the Cape colony. In Monica Wilson and Leonard Thompson (eds.), *The Oxford History of South Africa*, vol. I, pp. 272–333. New York.

Davidson, Basil. 1961. *The African Slave Trade*. Boston

1971. Slaves or captives? some notes on fantasy and fact. In Nathan I. Huggins, Martin Kilson, and Daniel M. Fox (eds.), *Key Issues in the Afro-American Experience*, vol. I, pp. 54–73. New York.

Davies, K. G. 1957. *The Royal African Company*. London

De Beaucorps, R. P. 1945. L'Asservissement chez les Basongo de la Luniumga et de la Gobari. *Bulletin des Jurisdictions Indigènes et du Droit Coutumier Congolais*, 6: 161–66

Deerr, Noel. 1949–50. *The History of Sugar* (2 vols.) London

Deherme, G. 1908. *L'Afrique occidentale française: action politique, économique et sociale*. Paris

De Jonghe, E. 1933*a*. A propos de l'esclavage au Congo. *Bulletin de l'Institut royale colonial belge*, 4, 1: 65–88

1933*b*. Enquête ethnographique relative aux diverses formes d'asservissement au Congo. *Bulletin de l'Institut royale colonial belge*, 4, 2: 346–66

De Jonghe, E. and Vanhove, J. 1949. *Les Formes d'asservissement dans les sociétés indigènes du Congo Belge*. Brussels

De La Roncière, C. 1919. Une histoire du Bornou au XVIIe siècle par un chirurgien français captif à Tripoli. *Revue de l'histoire des colonies françaises*, 86–8

Deme, Kalidou 1966. Les Classes sociales dans le Sénégal pré-colonial. *La Pensée*, 130: 11–31

Denolf, F. 1938. De slaven bij de Basho, Bakuba en Baluba. *Revue general de la colonie belge*, 2: 67–79, 197–212, 296–308

Derman, William. 1973. *Serfs, Peasants and Socialists*. Berkeley

Derrick, Jonathan. 1975. *Africa's Slaves Today*. London

Dias, Jill R. 1976. Black chiefs, white traders and colonial policy near the Kwanza: Kabuku Kambilo and the Portuguese, 1873–1896. *Journal of African History*, 17, 2: 245–65

Dieng, A. A. 1974. Classes sociales et mode de production esclavagiste en Afrique de l'Ouest. *Cahiers du Centre d'études et de Recherches Marxistes*. Paris

Diop, Majhemout. 1971. *Histoire des classes sociales dans l'afrique de l'ouest: I. le Mali*. Paris

1973. *Histoire des classes sociales dans l'afrique de l'ouest: II. le Sénégal*. Paris

315

Bibliography

Donnan, E. (ed.) 1930–5. *Documents Illustrative of the Slave Trade to America* (4 vols.) Washington

Donny, L. 1911. Vers la suppression complète de l'esclavage au Congo Belge. *Bulletin de la société belge d'études coloniales*, 18: 177–210

Douglas, Mary, 1960. Blood-debts and clientship among the Lele. *Journal of the Royal Anthropolgical Institute*, 90: 1–28

1964. Matriliny and pawnship in Central Africa. *Africa*, 34, 4: 301–13

Drescher, Seymour. 1977. *Econocide: British Slavery in the Era of Abolition*. Pittsburgh

Duffy, J. 1967. *A Question of Slavery*. Oxford

Dumett, Raymond E. 1981. Pressure groups, bureaucracy and the decision-making process: the case of slavery abolition and colonial expansion in the Gold Coast, 1874. *Journal of Commonwealth History*, 9, 2: 193–215

Dunbar, Edward E. 1861. History of the rise and decline of commercial slavery in America, with reference to the future of Mexico. *The Mexican Papers*, 1: 177–279

Dunbar, Roberta Ann. 1977. Slavery and the evolution of nineteenth-century Damagaram (Zinder, Niger). In S. Miers and I. Kopytoff (eds.), *Slavery in Africa: Historical and Anthropological Perspectives*, pp. 155–80. Madison

Dupuis, J. 1824. *Journal of a Residence in Ashantee*. London

Echenberg, Myron J. 1975. Paying the blood tax: military conscription in French West Africa, 1914–1929. *Canadian Journal of African Studies*, 9, 2: 171–92

1980. Les Migrations militaires en Afrique occidentale française, 1900–1945. *Canadian Journal of African Studies*, 14, 3: 429–50

Edwards, Isobel E. 1942. *Towards Emancipation: A Study in South African Slavery*. Cardiff

Ekejiuba, F. I. 1972. The Aro trade system in the nineteenth century. *Ikenga*, 1, 1: 11–26; 1, 2: 10–21

Elphick, Richard. 1979. The Khoisan to c. 1770. In Richard Elphick and Hermann Giliomee (eds.), *The Shaping of South African Society, 1652–1820*, pp. 3–40. Cape Town

Elphick, Richard and Shell, Robert. 1979. Intergroup relations: Khoikhoi, settlers, slaves and free blacks. In Richard Elphick and Hermann Giliomee (eds.), *The Shaping of South African Society, 1652–1820*, pp. 116–69. Cape Town

Eltis, D. 1977. The export of slaves from Africa, 1821–1843. *Journal of Economic History*, 37, 2: 409–33

1978. The trans-Atlantic slave trade, 1821–1843. Unpublished PhD thesis, University of Rochester

1979a. The British contribution to the nineteenth century transatlantic slave trade. *Economic History Review*, 32, 2: 211–27

1979b. The direction and fluctuation of the transatlantic slave trade, 1821–1843: a revision of the 1845 parliamentary paper. In H. A. Gemery and J. S. Hogendorn (eds.), *The Uncommon Market: Essays in the Economic History of the Atlantic Slave Trade*, pp. 273–301. New York

1981. The direction and fluctuation of the transatlantic trade 1844–67. Unpublished paper presented at the African Studies Association Annual Meeting, Bloomington, Indiana

1982. Nutritional trends in Africa and the Americas: heights of Africans, 1819–1839. *Journal of Interdisciplinary History*, 13

Eltis, David and Walvin, James (eds.) 1981. *The Abolition of The Atlantic Slave Trade*. Madison

Engerman, S. L. and Genovese, E. D. (eds.) 1975. *Race and Slavery in the Western Hemisphere: Quantitative Studies*. Princeton

Etienne, Mona. 1976. Women and slaves: stratification in an African society (the Baule, Ivory

Coast). Unpublished paper presented at the American Anthropological Association, Washington, DC

Fage, J. D. 1969. Slavery and the slave trade in the context of West African History. *Journal of African History*, 10, 3: 393–404

1978. *A History of Africa*. London

1980. Slaves and society in Western Africa, c. 1445 – c. 1700. *Journal of African History* 21, 3: 289–310

Fauré, C. 1920. La Garrison européene du Sénégal (1779–1858). *Revue d'histoire des colonies*, 8: 5–108

Ferguson, Douglas E. 1973. Nineteenth-century Hausaland, being a description by Imam Imoru of the land, economy and society of his people. Unpublished PhD thesis, UCLA

Fernandes, V. 1938. *Description de la Côte occidentale d'Afrique (Sénégal au Cap de Monte, Archipels) par V. Fernandes (1505–1510)*, trans. P. de Cenival and Th. Monod. Paris

Filliot, J. M. 1974. *La Traite des esclaves vers les Mascareignes au XVIIIe siècle*. Paris

Finley, M. I. 1960. (ed.) *Slavery in Classical Antiquity*. Cambridge

1964. Between slavery and freedom. *Comparative Studies in Society and History*, 6: 233–49

1968. Slavery. *International Encyclopedia of the Social Sciences*, 14: 307–13

1973. *The Ancient Economy*. London

1979. Slavery and the historians. *Social History*, 12: 247–61

1980. *Ancient Slavery and Modern Ideology*. London

Fisher, Allan G. B. and Fisher, Humphrey J. 1970. *Slavery and Muslim Society in Africa: The Institution in Saharan and Sudanic Africa and the Trans-Saharan Trade*. London

Fogel, R. and Engerman, S. L. 1974. *Time on the Cross: Evidence and Methods*. Boston

Forbes, F. E. 1851. *Dahomey and the Dahomans*. London

Foster, Charles I. 1953. The colonisation of free Negroes in Liberia. *Journal of Negro History*, 38, 1: 41–66

Foster, Herbert J. 1976. Partners or captives in commerce? The role of Africans in the slave trade. *Journal of Black Studies*, 6, 4; 421–34

Foster-Carter, Aidan. 1978. The modes of production controversy. *New Left Review*, 107–12

Freeman-Grenville, G. S. P. 1963. The coast, 1498–1840. In R. Oliver and G. Mathew (eds.), *History of East Africa*, vol. I, pp. 129–68. Oxford

Freund, William M. 1979. The Cape under the transitional governments, 1795–1814. In Richard Elphick and Hermann Giliomee (eds), *The Shaping of South African Society, 1652–1820*, pp. 211–42. Cape Town

Froelich, J. C. 1954. Le Commandement et l'organisation sociale chez les Foulbe de l'Adamawa. *Études camerounaises*, 45/6: 5–91

Fyfe, Christopher. 1962. *A History of Sierra Leone*. London

1965. A historigraphical survey of the transatlantic slave trade from West Africa. In *The Transatlantic Slave Trade from West Africa*, pp. 1–12. Edinburgh

1974. Reform in West Africa: the abolition of the slave trade. In J. F. Ade Ajayi and Michael Crowder (eds.), *History of West Africa*, vol II, pp. 30–56. London

1977. A brief note on the demographic effects of the transatlantic slave trade on West Africa. In *African Historical Demography*, p. 211. Edinburgh

Fynn, J. K. 1971. *Asante and its Neighbours, 1700–1807*. London

Gamitto, Antonio Candido Pedroso. 1960. *King Kazembe and the Marave, Cheva, Bisa, Bemba, Luanda, and other peoples of Southern Africa being the Diary of the Portuguese expedition to the Potentate in the years 1831 and 1832*, trans. I. Cunnison. Lisbon

Gann, L. H. 1954 The end of the slave trade in British central Africa, 1889–1912. *Rhodes–Livingstone Journal*, 16: 27–51

Bibliography

Garfield, Robert. 1971. A history of São Tomé Island, 1470–1655. Unpublished PhD thesis. Northwestern University

Garrard, Timothy F. 1980. *Akan Gold Weights and the Gold Trade*. London

Gemery, H. A., and Hogendorn, Jan. 1974. The Atlantic slave trade: a tentative economic model. *Journal of African History*, 15, 2: 233–46

1977. A note on the social costs of imported African monies. Unpublished paper presented at the African Studies Association Annual Meeting, Houston

1978. Technological change, slavery and the slave trade. In C. J. Dewey and A. G. Hopkins (eds.), *The Imperial Impact: Studies in the Economic History of Africa and India*, pp. 243–58. London

1979a. (eds.) *The Uncommon Market: Essays in the Economic History of the Atlantic Slave Trade*. New York

1979b. The economic costs of west African participation in the Atlantic slave trade: a preliminary sampling for the eighteenth century. In H. A. Gemery and Jan Hogendorn (eds.), *The Uncommon Market*, pp. 143–61. New York

1979c. Comparative disadvantage: the case of sugar cultivation in West Africa. *Journal of Interdisciplinary History*, 9, 3: 429–49

Giaccardi, A. 1939. La colonizzazione Abissina nel'Ethiopia occidentale. *Annali dell'Africa Italiana*, 2: 192

Gibson, A. E. 1903. Slavery in western Nigeria. *Journal of the Royal African Society*, 3: 17–54

Giliomee, Hermann. 1979. The eastern frontier, 1770–1812. In Richard Elphick and Hermann Giliomee (eds.), *The Shaping of South African Society, 1652–1820*, pp. 291–337. Cape Town

Giliomee, Hermann and Elphick, Richard. 1979. The structure of European domination at the Cape, 1652–1820. In Richard Elphick and Hermann Giliomee (eds.), *The Shaping of South African Society, 1652–1820*, pp. 359–90. Cape Town

Gleave, M. B. and Prothero, R. M. 1971. Population density and 'slave raiding' – a comment. *Journal of African History*, 12, 2: 319–24

Goldstein, Ferdinand. 1908. Die Sklaverei in Nordafrika und im Sudan. *Zeitschrift fur Sozialwissenschaft*, 11: 352–69

Goody, Jack. 1971. *Technology, Tradition and the State in Africa*. London

1980. Slavery in time and space. In James L. Watson (ed.), *Asian and African Systems of Slavery*, pp. 16–42. Oxford

Goulart, Mauricio. 1950. *Escravidão africana no Brasil*. São Paulo

Grace, John. 1975. *Domestic Slavery in West Africa*. New York

1977. Slavery and emancipation among the Mende in Sierra Leone, 1896–1928. In S. Miers and I. Kopytoff (eds.), *Slavery in Africa: Historical and Anthropological Perspectives*, pp. 415–34. Madison

Graham, Richard D. 1965. The slave trade, human sacrifice, and depopulation in Benin history. *Cahiers d'études africaines*, 6: 317–34

Grandidier, Alfred. 1877. L'affranchissement des negres africains à Madagascar. *Bulletin de la société de géographie de Marseille*, 389–94

Gray, John. 1963. Zanzibar and the coastal belt, 1840–84. In R. Oliver and G. Mathew (eds.), *History of East Africa*, vol. I, pp. 212–52. Oxford

Gray, Richard. 1961. *A History of the Southern Sudan, 1839–89*. Oxford

Gray, Richard and Birmingham, David (eds.) 1970. *Pre-Colonial African Trade: Essays on Trade in Central and East Africa before 1900*. London

Greenidge, C. W. W. 1958. *Slavery*. London

Green-Pederson, Svend Erik. 1957. The History of the Danish Negro slave trade, 1733–1807. *Revue française d'histoire d'outre-mer*, 42: 196–220

Greenstein, Lewis J. 1973. Slave and citizen: the South African case. *Race*, 15, 1: 25–46

318

Guelke, Leonard. 1979. The white settlers, 1652–1780. In Richard Elphick and Hermann Giliomee (eds.), *The Shaping of South African Society, 1652–1820*. pp. 41–74. Cape Town.

Guèye, M'Baye. 1965. L'Affaire Chautemps, (Avril 1904) et la supression de l'esclavage: de case au Sénégal. *Bulletin de l'IFAN*, 27, 3–4: 543–59

1966. La Fin de l'esclavage à Saint-Louis et à Gorée en 1848. *Bulletin de l'IFAN*, series B, 28, 3–4; 637–56

Hafkin, Nancy J. 1973. Trade, society and politics in northern Mozambique, *c*. 1753–1913. Unpublished PhD thesis, Boston University

Hair, P.E.H. 1967. Ethnolinguistic continuity on the Upper Guinea coast. *Journal of African History*, 8: 247–68

1975. Sources on early Sierra Leone: (6) Barreira on just enslavement, 1606. *Africana Research Bulletin*, 6: 52–74

1978. *The Atlantic Slave Trade and Black Africa*. London

Hallam, W. K. R. 1977. *The Life and Times of Rabih Fadl Allah*. Devon

Hanna, A. J. 1956. *The Beginning of Nyasaland and North-Eastern Rhodesia, 1859–95*. Oxford.

Hanson, David. 1971. The Maccube of Fouta Toro. Unpublished MA thesis, University of Wisconsin

Harms, Robert. 1978. Slave Systems in Africa. *History in Africa*, 5: 327–35

1981. *River of Wealth, River of Sorrow*. New Haven

Harris, Joseph E. 1971. *The African Presence in Asia: Consequences of the East African Slave Trade*. Evanston

Harris, J. S. 1942. Some aspects of slavery in southeastern Nigeria. *Journal of Negro History*, 27: 37–54

Harries, Patrick. 1981. Slavery, social incorporation and surplus extraction: the nature of free and unfree labour in south-east Africa. *Journal of African History*, 22, 3: 309–30

Harris, Rosemary. 1972. The history of trade at Ikom, eastern Nigeria. *Africa*, 42, 2: 122–39

Harris, W. C. 1844. *The Highlands of Ethiopia* (2 vols.) London

Harrop, Sylvia. 1964. The economy of the West African coast in the sixteenth century. *Economic Bulletin of Ghana*, 8, 3: 15–33; 8, 4: 19–36

Hartwig, Gerald W. 1977. Changing forms of servitude among the Kerebe of Tanzania. In S. Miers and I. Kopytoff (eds.), *Slavery in Africa: Historical and Anthropological Perspectives*, pp. 261–85. Madison

Héritier, Françoise. 1975. Des Cauris et des hommes: production d'esclaves et accumulation de cauris chez les Samo (Haute-Volta). In Claude Meillassoux (ed.), *L'Esclavage en Afrique précoloniale*, pp. 477–508. Paris

Hill, Polly. 1976. From slavery to freedom: the case of farm-slavery in Nigerian Hausaland. *Comparative Studies in Society and History*, 18, 3: 395–426

Hill, Richard. 1959. *Egypt in the Sudan, 1820–1883*. Oxford

Hilliard, Constance. forthcoming. Zurhur al Bastin and Ta-rikh al Turubbe: some legal and ethical aspects of slavery in the Sudan as seen in the works of Shaykh Musa Kamara. In J. R. Willis (ed.), *Islam and the Ideology of Enslavement*. London

Hilton, Anne. 1981. The Jaga reconsidered. *Journal of African History*, 22, 2: 191–202.

Hindess, Barry and Hirst, Paul Q. 1975. *Pre-capitalist Modes of Production*. London

Hiskett, Mervyn. forthcoming. The image of slaves in Hausa literature. In J. R. Willis (ed.), *Islam and the Ideology of Enslavement*. London

Hodgkin, Thomas (ed.) 1975. *Nigerian Perspectives* (2nd ed.) Oxford

Hogendorn, Jan. 1977. The economics of slave use on two 'plantations' in the Zaria Emirate of the Sokoto Caliphate. *International Journal of African Historical Studies*, 10, 3: 369–83

1978. *Nigerian Groundnut Exports: Origins and Early Developments*. Zaria

1980. Slave acquisition and delivery in precolonial Hausaland. In R. Dumett and Ben K. Schwartz (eds.), *West African Culture Dynamics: Archaeological and Historical Perspectives*, pp. 477–93. The Hague

Bibliography

1981. The West African cowrie currency: a new global import series. Unpublished paper presented at the African Studies Association Annual Meeting, Bloomington, Indiana

Hogendorn, Jan and Gemery, Henry A. 1981. Abolition and its impact on monies imported to West Africa. In David Eltis and James Walvin (eds.), *The Abolition of the Atlantic Slave Trade*, pp. 99–115. Madison

Holden, J. J. 1965. The Zabarima of north-west Ghana. *Transactions of the Historical Society of Ghana*, 8: 60–86

1970. The Samorian impact on Buna: an essay in methodology. In C. Allen and R. W. Johnson (eds.), *African Perspectives*, pp. 83–108. Cambridge

Holsoe, Svend E. 1977. Slavery and economic response among the Vai (Liberia and Sierra Leone). In S. Miers and I. Kopytoff (eds.), *Slavery in Africa: Historical and Anthropological Perspectives*, pp. 297–303. Madison

Hopkins, A. G. 1966. The Lagos strike of 1897: an exploration in Nigerian labour history. *Past and Present*, 35: 133–55

1968. Economic imperialism in West Africa: Lagos, 1880–92. *Economic History Review*, 21, 3: 580–606

1973. *An Economic History of West Africa*. London

Horton, W. R. G. 1954. The Ohu system of slavery in a northern Ibo village-group. *Africa*, 24: 311–36

1956. God, man and the land in a northern Ibo village-group. *Africa*, 26: 17–28

Howard, Allen M. 1979. Production, exchange and society in northern coastal Sierra Leone during the 19th century. In V. R. Dorjahn and B. L. Isaac (eds.), *Essays on the Economic Anthropology of Liberia and Sierra Leone*. Philadelphia

Hunkanrin, L. 1964. L'Esclavage en Mauritanie. *Études dahoméenes*, 32–49

Hunwick, J. O. 1978. Black Africans in the Islamic world: an understudied dimension of the black diaspora. *Tarikh*, 5: 20–40

forthcoming. Notes on slavery in the Songhay empire. In J. R. Willis (ed.), *The Servile Estate*. London

Ibn Battuta. 1922. *Voyages*, trans. C. Defremery and B. R. Sanguinetti (4 vols.) Paris

Igbafe, Philip A. 1975. Slavery and emancipation in Benin, 1897–1945. *Journal of African History*, 16, 3: 409–29

Ilogu, E. 1957. Inside Arochukwu. *Nigeria*, 53: 100–18

Inikori, J. E. 1976a. Measuring the Atlantic slave trade: an assessment of Curtin and Anstey. *Journal of African History*, 17, 2: 197–223

1976b. Measuring the Atlantic slave trade. *Journal of African History*, 17, 4: 607–27

1977. The import of firearms into West Africa, 1750–1807: a quantitative analysis. *Journal of African History*, 18, 3: 339–68

1978. The origin of the diaspora: the slave trade from Africa. *Tarikh*, 5, 4: 1–19

Isaacman, A. F. 1972a. *Mozambique: The Africanization of a European Institution: The Zambesi Prazos, 1750–1902*. Madison

1972b. The origin, formation and early history of the Chikunda of south central Africa. *Journal of African History*, 13, 4: 443–62

forthcoming. South-central Africa in the nineteenth century. In J. F. Ade Ajayi (ed.), *UNESCO History of Africa*, vol. VI

Isaacman, Allen and Isaacman, Barbara. 1975. The Prazeros as transfrontiersmen. *International Journal of African Historical Studies*, 8, 1: 1–39

Isaacman, Barbara and Isaacman, Allen. 1977. Slavery and social stratification among the Sena of Mozambique: a study of the Kaporo system. In S. Miers and I. Kopytoff (eds.), *Slavery in Africa: Historical and Anthropological Perspectives*, pp. 105–20. Madison

Isichei, Elizabeth. 1973. *The Ibo People and the Europeans*. London

1976. *A History of the Igbo People*. London and Basingstoke

1978. *Igbo Worlds: An Anthology of Oral Histories and Historical Descriptions*. Philadelphia

Izard, Michel. 1971. Les Yarse et le commerce dans le Yatênga pré-colonial. In Claude Meillassoux (ed.), *The Development of Indigenous Trade and Markets in West Africa*, pp. 214–27. London

1975. Les Captifs royaux dans l'ancien Yatenga. In Claude Meillassoux (ed.), *L'esclavage en Afrique précoloniale*, pp. 281–96. Paris

Jewsiewicki, Bogumil. 1977. L'Anthropologie économique et les 'modes de production'. *Cultures et développement*, 9, 2: 195–246

Jewsiewicki, B. and Mumbanza, mwa Bawele. 1981. The social context of slavery in equatorial Africa during the nineteenth and twentieth centuries. In Paul E. Lovejoy (ed.), *The Ideology of Slavery in Africa*, pp. 72–98. Beverly Hills

Jobson, Richard. 1623. *The Golden Trade, 1620–1621*. London

Johnson, Marion. 1968. The nineteenth-century gold 'Mithqal' in West and North Africa. *Journal of African History*, 9, 4: 547–70

1970. The cowrie currencies of West Africa. *Journal of African History*, 11, 1: 17–49; 11, 3: 331–53

1976*a*. The Atlantic slave trade and the economy of West Africa. In Roger Anstey and P. E. H. Hair (eds.), *Liverpool, the African Slave Trade, and Abolition: Essays to Illustrate Current Knowledge and Research* (Historic Society of Lancashire and Cheshire, Occasional Series, vol. 2), pp. 14–38

1976*b*. The economic foundations of an Islamic theocracy – the case of Masina. *Journal of African History*, 17, 4: 481–95

1980. Polanyi, Peukert and the political economy of Dahomey. *Journal of African History*, 21, 3: 395–8

Johnson, Samuel. 1921. *The History of the Yorubas*. Lagos

Johnston, H. H. 1889. *The History of a Slave*. London

Jones, Adam and Johnson, Marion. 1980. Slaves from the Windward Coast. *Journal of African History*, 21, 1: 17–34

Jones, Gwilym Iwan. 1961. Ecology and social structure among the north-eastern Ibo. *Africa*, 31: 117–34

1962. Ibo age organization with special reference to the Cross River and north-eastern Ibo. *Journal of the Royal Anthropological Institute*, 92, 2: 191–221

1963. *The Trading States of the Oil Rivers*. London

1967. (ed.) Olaudah Equiano of the Niger Ibo. In Philip D. Curtin (ed.), *Africa Remembered: Narratives of West Africans from the Era of the Slave Trade*, pp. 60–98. Madison

Kanya-Forstner, A. S. F. 1969. *The Conquest of the Western Sudan: A Study in French Military Imperialism*. Cambridge

Kaplow, Susan B. 1978. Primitive accumulation and traditional social relations on the nineteenth century Gold Coast. *Canadian Journal of African Studies*, 12, 1: 19–36.

Katzen, M. F. 1969. White settlers and the origin of a new society, 1652–1778. In Monica Wilson and Leonard Thompson (eds.), *The Oxford History of South Africa*, vol. I, pp. 187–232. Oxford

Kea, Raymond A. 1976. Administration and trade in the Akwamu Empire, 1681–1730. Unpublished paper presented at the American Historical Association Annual Meeting, Washington, DC

1980. The 'laboring classes' in 17th and 18th century Gold Coast states: a note on the political economy of pre-capitalist social labor. Unpublished paper presented at the African Studies Association Annual Meeting, Philadelphia

Keith, Henry H. 1971. Masters and slaves in Portuguese Africa in the nineteenth century: first soundings. *Studia*, 33: 235–49

Kent, Raymond. 1970. *Early Kingdoms in Madagascar, 1500–1700*. New York

Kersaint-Gilly, F. de. 1924. Essai sur l'évolution de l'esclavage en Afrique occidentale française: son dernier stade au Soudan française. *Bulletin du Comité études historiques et scientifiques de l'AOF*, 9: 469–78

Kilkenny, Roberta Walker. 1981. The slave mode of production: precolonial Dahomey. In Donald Crummey and C. C. Stewart (eds.), *Modes of Production in Africa: The Pre-colonial Era*, pp. 157–73. Beverly Hills

Kilson, M. D. 1971. West African society and the Atlantic slave trade, 1441–1865. In N. I. Huggins, M. Kilson, and D. M. Fox (eds.), *Key Issues in the Afro-American Experience*, vol. I, pp. 39–53. New York

Kilson, Martin L. and Rotberg, Robert I. (eds.) 1976. *The African Diaspora: Interpretative Essays*. Cambridge, Mass.

Kistner, W. 1952. The anti-slavery agitation against the Transvaal Republic, 1852–1868. In *Archives Yearbook for South African History*, vol. II, pp. 194–278A

Klein, A. Norman. 1969. West African unfree labor before and after the rise of the Atlantic slave trade. In Laura Foner and Eugene D. Genovese (eds.), *Slavery in the new World: A Reader in Comparative History*, pp. 87–95. Englewood Cliffs, New Jersey

1980. Inequality in Asante: a study of the forms and meaning of slavery and social servitude in pre- and early colonial Akan–Asante society and culture. Unpublished PhD thesis, University of Michigan

1981. The two Asantes: competing interpretations of 'slavery' in Akan–Asante culture and society. In Paul E. Lovejoy (ed.), *The Ideology of Slavery in Africa*, pp. 149–67. Beverly Hills

Klein, Herbert S. 1978. *The Middle Passage: Comparative Studies in The Atlantic Slave Trade*. Princeton

Klein, Herbert S. and Engerman, Stanley L. 1979. A note on mortality in the French slave trade in the eighteenth century. In H. A. Gemery and J. S. Hogendorn (eds.), *The Uncommon Market: Essays in the Economic History of the Atlantic Slave Trade*, pp. 261–72. New York

Klein, Martin. 1971. Slavery, the slave trade, and legitimate commerce in late nineteenth century Africa. *Études d'histoire africaine*, 2: 5–28

1972. Social and economic factors in the Muslim revolution in Senegambia. *Journal of African History*, 13, 3: 419–41

1977a. Servitude among the Wolof and Sereer of Senegambia. In S. Miers and I. Kopytoff (eds.), *Slavery in Africa: Historical and Anthropological Perspectives*, pp. 335–66. Madison

1977b. Slave systems of the western Sudan. Unpublished paper, University of Toronto

1978a. The study of slavery in Africa: a review article. *Journal of African History*, 19, 4: 599–609

1978b. Slavery as an institution and slavery as a mode of production: some reflections on African data. Unpublished seminar paper, University of Toronto

1981. The transition from slave labour to free labour: the case of Senegambia. Unpublished paper presented at the Canadian Historical Association Annual Meeting, Halifax

forthcoming. Female slavery in the western Sudan. In Martin Klein and Claire Robertson (eds.) *Women and Slavery in Africa*. Madison

Klein, Martin and Lovejoy, Paul E. 1979. Slavery in West Africa. In H. A. Gemery and J. S. Hogendorn (eds.), *The Uncommon Market: Essays in the Economic History of the Atlantic Slave Trade*, pp. 181–212. New York

Klein, Martin and Robertson, Claire (eds.) forthcoming. *Women and Slavery in Africa*. Madison

Kock, Victor de. 1950. *Those in Bondage: An Account of the Life of the Slaves at the Cape in the Days of the Dutch East India Company*. Cape Town

Kodjo, N. G. 1976. Contribution à l'étude des tribus dites serviles du Songai. *Bulletin de l'IFAN*, 38, 4: 790–812

Kopytoff, Igor. 1979. Commentary one. *Historical Reflections/Reflexions Historiques*, 6, 1: 62–77

Kopytoff, Igor and Miers, Suzanne. 1977. African 'slavery' as an institution of marginality. In S. Miers and I. Kopytoff (eds.), *Slavery in Africa: Historical and Anthropological Perspectives*, pp. 3–81. Madison

Kuczynski, Robert R. 1936. *Population Movements*. Oxford

Lacour, A. 1889. *L'Esclavage africain*. Dunkirk

Lamphear, John. 1970. The Kamba and the northern Mrima coast. In Richard Gray and David Birmingham (eds.), *Pre-Colonial African Trade: Essays on Trade in Central and Eastern Africa before 1900*, pp. 75–101. London

Last, Murray. 1974. Reform in West Africa: the Jihād movements of the nineteenth century. In J. F. Ade Ajayi and Michael Crowder (eds.), *History of West Africa*, vol. II, pp. 1–29. London

Latham, A. J. H. 1971. Currency, credit and capitalism on the Cross River in the pre-colonial era. *Journal of African History*, 12, 4: 599–605

1973. *Old Calabar, 1600–1891: The Impact of the International Economy upon a Traditional Society*. Oxford

La Torre, Joseph R. 1978. Wealth surpasses everything: an economic history of Asante, 1750–1874. Unpublished PhD thesis, University of California at Berkeley

Lavers, John E. 1982. Trans-Saharan trade before 1800: towards quantification. In Habib El-Hesnawi (ed.), *A History of the Trans-Saharan Trade Routes*. Tripoli

Law, R. C. C. 1976. Horses, firearms and political power in pre-colonial West Africa. *Past and Present*, 72: 112–32

1977a. *The Oyo Empire, c. 1600 – c. 1836: A West African Imperialism in the Era of the Atlantic Slave Trade*. Oxford

1977b. Royal monopoly and private enterprise in the Atlantic trade: the case of Dahomey. *Journal of African History*, 18, 4: 555–77

1978a. Slaves, trade and taxes: the material basis of political power in pre-colonial West Africa. *Research in Economic Anthropology*, 1: 37–52

1978b. In search of a Marxist perspective on pre-colonial tropical Africa. *Journal of African History*, 19, 3: 441–52

1981. For Marx but with reservations about Althusser: a comment on Bernstein and Depelchin. *History in Africa*, 8: 247–51

Legassick, Martin. 1980. The frontier tradition in South African historiography. In Shula Marks and Anthony Atmore (eds.), *Economy and Society in Pre-Industrial South Africa*, pp. 44–79, London

Leith-Ross, S. 1937. Notes on the Osu system among the Ibo of Owerri Province, Nigeria. *Africa*, 10, 2: 206–20

LeVeen, E. Phillip. 1975a. The African slave supply response. *African Studies Review*, 18, 1: 9–28

1975b. A quantitative analysis of the impact of British suppression policies on the volume of the nineteenth century slave trade. In S. L. Engerman and E. D. Genovese (eds.), *Race and Slavery in the Western Hemisphere: Quantitative Studies*, pp. 51–81. Princeton

1977. *British Slave Trade Suppression Policies, 1821–1865*. New York

Levine, Nancy E. 1980. Opposition and interdependence: demographic and economic perspectives on Nyinba slavery. In James L. Watson (ed.), *Asian and African Systems of Slavery*, pp. 195–222. Oxford

Levtzion, Nehemia. 1973. *Ancient Ghana and Mali*. London

forthcoming. Slavery and Islamization in Africa. In J. R. Willis (ed.), *Islam and the Ideology of Enslavement*. London

Lewicki, Tadeusz. 1967. Arab trade in Negro slaves up to the end of the XVIth century. *Africana Bulletin*, 6: 109–11

Lewis, Bernard. 1976. The African diaspora and the civilization of Islam. In Martin L. Kilson and Robert Rotberg (eds.), *The African Diaspora*, pp. 37–56. Cambridge, Mass.

323

Bibliography

Lloyd, Christopher. 1949. *The Navy and the Slave Trade: The Suppression of the African Slave Trade in the Nineteenth Century*. London

Lopes de Lima, José Joaquim. 1844. *Ensaios sobre a estatística das possessões portuguesas na Africa Occidental*. Lisbon

Lovejoy, Paul E. 1973. The Kambarin Beriberi: the formation of a specialized group of Hausa kola traders in the nineteenth century. *Journal of African History*, 14, 4: 633–51

1974. Interregional monetary flows in the precolonial trade of Nigeria. *Journal of African History*, 15, 4: 563–85

1978a. The Borno salt industry. *International Journal of African Historical Studies*, 11, 4: 629–68

1978b. The role of the Wangara in the economic transformation of the central Sudan in the fifteenth and sixteenth centuries. *Journal of African History*, 19, 2: 173–93

1978c. Plantations in the economy of the Sokoto Caliphate. *Journal of African History*, 19, 3: 341–68

1979a. The characteristics of plantations in the nineteenth-century Sokoto Caliphate (Islamic West Africa). *American Historical Review*, 84, 4: 1267–92

1979b. Indigenous African slavery. *Historical Reflections/Refléxions historiques*, 6, 1: 19–61

1980a. *Caravans of Kola: The Hausa Kola Trade, 1700–1900*. Zaria

1980b. Kola in the history of West Africa. *Cahiers d'études africaines*, 20: 97–134

1981a. (ed.) *The Ideology of Slavery in Africa*. Beverly Hills

1981b. Slavery in the Sokoto Caliphate. In Paul E. Lovejoy, *The Ideology of Slavery in Africa*, pp. 200–43. Beverly Hills

1981c. Slavery in the context of ideology. In Paul E. Lovejoy, *The Ideology of Slavery in Africa*, pp. 11–38. Beverly Hills

1981d. The impact of the slave trade on Africa. *Trends in History*, 3,1

1982a. Polanyi's 'ports of trade': Salaga and Kano in the nineteenth century. *Canadian Journal of African Studies*, 16, 2.

1982b. The trans-Saharan trade and the salt trade of the central Sudan: a comparison of nineteenth century patterns. In Habib El-Hesnawi (ed.), *A History of the Trans-Saharan Trade Routes*. Tripoli

1982 c. The volume of the Atlantic slave trade: a synthesis. *Journal of African History*, 22, 4

forthcoming a. The salt industry of the central Sudan. In Mahdi Adamu (ed.), *Studies in the Economic History of the Central Savanna of West Africa*. Zaria

forthcoming b. The internal trade of West Africa before 1800. In J. F. Ade Ajayi and Michael Crowder (eds.), *History of West Africa* (3rd ed.) London

Lovejoy, Paul E. and Baier, S. 1975. The desert-side economy of the central Sudan. *International Journal of African Historical Studies*, 7, 4: 551–81

Lovejoy, P. E. and Hogendorn, J. S. 1979. Slave marketing in West Africa. In H. A. Gemery and J. S. Hogendorn (eds.), *The Uncommon Market: Essays in the Economic History of the Atlantic Slave Trade*, pp. 213–35. New York

Lugard, F. 1896. Slavery under the British flag. *The Nineteenth Century*, 39: 335–55

1906. *Instructions to Political and Other Officers, on Subjects Chiefly Political and Administrative*. London

MacCormack, Carol P. 1977. Wono: institutionalized dependency in Sherbro descent groups (Sierra Leone). In S. Miers and I. Kopytoff (eds.) *Slavery in Africa: Historical and Anthropological Perspectives*, pp. 181–204. Madison

MacDonald, Duff. 1882. *Africana* (2 vols.) London

MacGaffey, Wyatt. 1977. Economic and social dimensions of Kongo slavery (Zaire). In S. Miers and I. Kopytoff (eds.), *Slavery in Africa: Historical and Anthropological Perspectives*, pp. 235–57. Madison

MacKenzie, Donald. 1895. A report on slavery and the slave trade in Zanzibar, Pemba and the mainland of the British Protectorate of East Africa. *Anti-Slavery Reporter*, 4th series, 15: 69–96

McDougall, E. Ann. 1980. The 'desert and the sown' in pre-colonial history: a case study of Banamba, Mali. Unpublished paper, Centre for African Studies, Dalhousie University

McLoughlin, Peter F. M. 1962. Economic development and the heritage of slavery in the Sudan Republic. *Africa*, 32; 355–91

1966. Labour market conditions and wages in the Gash and Tokar deltas, 1900–1955. *Sudan Notes and Records*, 42: 111–26

1970. Labour market conditions in the three towns, 1900–1950. *Sudan Notes and Records*, 51: 105–18

McSheffrey, G. M. 1983. Slavery, indentured servitude, legitimate trade and the impact of abolition in the Gold Coast: 1874–1901. *Journal of African History*, 23

Madden, R. R. 1837. *Twelve Months Residence in the West Indies* (2 vols.) London

Malowist, Marian, 1966. Le Commerce d'or et d'esclaves au Soudan Occidentale. *Africana Bulletin*, 4: 49–72

1969. Les Débuts du système de plantations dans la période des grandes découvertes. *Africana Bulletin*, 10: 9–30

Mandala, Elias. forthcoming. An economic history of the Shire valley. Unpublished PhD thesis, University of Minnesota

Manning, Patrick. 1969. Slaves, palm oil, and political power on the West African coast. *African Historical Studies*, 2: 279–88

1975. Un document sur la fin de l'esclavage au Dahomey. *Notes africaines*, 147: 88–92

1979. The slave trade in the Bight of Benin, 1640–1890. In H. A. Gemery and J. S. Hogendorn (eds.), *The Uncommon Market: Essays in the Economic History of the Atlantic Slave Trade*, pp. 107–41. New York

1981. The enslavement of Africans: a demographic model. *Canadian Journal of African Studies*, 15, 3: 499–526

1982. *Slavery, Colonialism, and Economic Growth in Dahomey, 1640–1960*. Cambridge

Maquet, Jacques. 1970. Rwanda castes. In A. Tuden and L. Plotnicov (eds.), *Social Stratification in Africa*, pp. 93–124. New York

Marks, Shula and Atmore, Anthony (eds.) 1980. *Economy and Society in Pre-Industrial South Africa*. London

Martin, B. G. forthcoming. Ahmad Rasim Pasha and the suppression of the Fazzen slave trade. In J. R. Willis (ed.), *The Servile Estate*. London

Martin, Edmond B. and Ryan, T. C. I. 1977. A quantitative assessment of the Arab slave trade of East Africa. *Kenya Historical Review*, 5: 71–91

Martin, Gaston. 1931. *Nantes au XVIIIᵉ siècle: l'ère des négriers (1714–1774)*. Paris

Martin, Jean. 1973. Les Débuts du protectorat et la révolte servile de 1981 dans l'île d'Anjoun. *Revue française d'histoire d'outre-mer*, 60: 45–85

1976. L'Affranchissement des esclaves de Mayotte, décembre 1846 – juillet 1847. *Cahiers d'études africaines*, 16: 207–33

Martin, Phyllis. 1970. The trade of Loango in the seventeenth and eighteenth centuries. In Richard Gray and David Birmingham (eds.), *Pre-Colonial African Trade: Essays on Trade in Central and Eastern Africa before 1900*, pp. 139–62. London

1972. *The External Trade of the Loango Coast, 1576–1870*. Oxford

Marx, Karl. 1965. *Pre-Capitalist Economic Formations*, ed. Eric J. Hobsbawm. New York

Mason, Michael. 1969. Population density and 'slave raiding' – the case of the middle belt of Nigeria. *Journal of African History*, 10, 4: 551–64

1970. The *jihad* in the south: an outline of the nineteenth century Nupe hegemony in north-eastern Yorubaland and Afenmai. *Journal of the Historical Society of Nigeria*, 5, 2: 193–208

325

1973. Captive and client labour and the economy of the Bida Emirate, 1857–1901. *Journal of African History*, 14, 3: 453–71

1976. Trade and the state in nineteenth-century Nupe. Unpublished paper presented at Seminar on Economic History of the Central Savanna of West Africa, Kano

1981. Production, penetration and political formation: the Bida state, 1857–1901. In Donald Crummey and C. C. Stewart (eds.), *Modes of Production in Africa: The Pre-colonial Era*, pp. 204–26. Beverly Hills

Massing, Andreas Walter. 1977. Economic developments in the Kru culture areas. Unpublished PhD thesis, Indiana University

Mathew, Gervase. 1963. The East African coast until the coming of the Portuguese. In R. Oliver and G. Mathew (eds.), *History of East Africa*, vol. I, pp. 94–127. Oxford.

Mathieson, William Law. 1929. *Great Britain and the Slave Trade, 1839–1865*. New York

Matthews, T. I. 1981. Portuguese, Chikunda, and peoples of the Gwembe valley: the impact of the 'lower Zambezi complex' on southern Zambia. *Journal of African History*, 22, 1: 23–41

Maugham, Robin. 1961. *The Slaves of Timbuktu*. New York

Mauny, Raymond. 1961. *Tableau géographique de l'ouest africain au moyen âge*. Dakar

1974. Révoltes d'esclaves à Gorée au milieu du XVIIIᵉ siècle d'après Pruneau de Pommegorge. *Notes africaines*, 141: 11–13

Meillassoux, Claude. 1971. (ed.) *The Development of Indigenous Trade and Markets in West Africa*. London

1972. From reproduction to production. *Economy and Society*, 1: 93–105

1973. État et conditions des esclaves à Gumbu (Mali) au XIXᵉ siècle. *Journal of African History*, 14, 3: 429–52

1975a. (ed.) *L'Esclavage en Afrique précoloniale*. Paris

1975b. État et conditions des esclaves à Gumbu (Mali) au XIXᵉ siècle. In Claude Meillassoux (ed.), *L'Esclavage en Afrique précoloniale*, pp. 221–52. Paris

1976. *Femmes, greniers, et capitaux*. Paris

1977. Modalités historiques de l'exploitation et de la surexploitation de travail. *Connaissance du Tiers Monde*, 10: 135–53

1978a. Correspondence on slavery. *Economy and Society*, 7, 3: 321–31

1978b. Rôle de l'esclavage dans l'histoire de l'Afrique occidentale. *Anthropologie et Sociétés*, 2, 1: 117–48

1979. Historical modalities of the exploitation and over-exploitation of labour. *Critique of Anthropoligy*, 4, 13 and 14: 7–16

forthcoming *a*. Les Enfants du néant (essai sur l'esclavagisme). *Economy and Society*

forthcoming *b*. Female slavery. In Martin Klein and Claire Robertson (eds.), *Women and Slavery in Africa*. Madison

Mettas, Jean. 1975. La Traite portugaise en haute Guinée (1758–1797): problèmes et methodes. *Journal of African History*, 16, 3: 343–63

1978. *Répertoire des expéditions négrières françaises au xviiiᵉ siècle*, ed. Serge Daget. Nantes

Meyers, Allan. 1971. Slavery in the Hausa Fulani Emirates. In Daniel F. McCall and Norman R. Bennett (eds.), *Aspects of West African Islam*, pp. 173–84. Boston

1974. The 'Abid'l Buhari: slave soldiers and statecraft in Morocco. Unpublished PhD dissertation, Cornell University

1977. Class, ethnicity and slavery: the origins of the Moroccan Abid. *International Journal of African Historical Studies*, 10, 3: 427–42

Miers, Suzanne. 1975. *Britain and the Ending of the Slave Trade*. New York

Miers, S. and Kopytoff, I. (eds.) 1977. *Slavery in Africa: Historical and Anthropological Perspectives*. Madison

Miller, Joseph C. 1969. Cokwe expansion, 1850–1900. Occasional Paper No. 1, African Studies Program, University of Wisconsin

1970. Cokwe trade and conquest. In Richard Gray and David Birmingham (eds.), *Pre-Colonial African Trade: Essays on Trade in Central and Eastern Africa before 1900*, pp. 175–201. London

1973. Slaves, slavers, and social change in nineteenth century Kasanje. In Franz-Wilhelm Heimer (ed.), *Social Change in Angola*, pp. 9–29. Munich

1975. Legal Portuguese slaving from Angola: some preliminary indications of volume and direction, 1760–1830. *Revue française d'histoire d'outre-mer*, 42, 1–2: 135–76

1976a. The slave trade of Congo and Angola. In Martin L. Kilson and Robert Rotberg (eds.), *The African Diaspora*, pp. 75–113. Cambridge, Mass.

1976b. *Kings and Kinsmen: Early States among the Mbundu of Angola.* Oxford

1977. Imbangala lineage slavery (Angola). In S. Miers and I. Kopytoff (eds.), *Slavery in Africa: Historical and Anthropological Perspectives*, pp. 205–33. Madison

1978. *Slavery: A Comparative Teaching Bibliography.* Waltham, Mass.

1979. Some aspects of the commercial organization of slaving at Luanda, Angola, 1760–1830. In H. A. Gemery and J. S. Hogendorn (eds.), *The Uncommon Market: Essays in the Economic History of the Atlantic Slave Trade*, pp. 77–106. New York

1981a. Lineages, ideology and the history of slavery in western central Africa. In Paul E. Lovejoy (ed.), *The Ideology of Slavery in Africa*, pp. 40–71. Beverly Hills

1981b. Mortality in the Atlantic slave trade: statistical evidence on causality. *Journal of Interdisciplinary History*, 11: 385–423

forthcoming. The formation and transformation of the Mbundu states from the sixteenth to the eighteenth centuries. In Franz-Wilhelm Heimer (ed.), *The Formation of Angolan Society*

Mire, Lawrence. forthcoming. Al-Zubayr Pasha and the Zariba-based slave trade in the Bahr al Ghazal. In J. R. Willis (ed.), *The Servile Estate*. London

Mist, J. A. de. 1920. *The Memorandum of Commissary.* Cape Town

Molinari, G. de. 1889. La Question de l'esclavage africain et la conference de Bruxelles. *Journal des économistes*, 4th series, 48: 321–34

Mollien, Gaspard. 1820. *Travels in the Interior of Africa to the Sources of the Senegal and Gambia.* London

Monod, Th., da Mota, A. Texeira, and Mauny, R. (eds.) 1951. *Description de la côte occidental d'Afrique (Sénégal au Cape Monte, Archipels) par Valentim Fernandes (1506–1510).* Bissau

Moore, Francis. 1738. *Travels into the Inland Parts of Africa.* London

Moraes Farias, Paulo Fernando de. forthcoming. Models of the world and categorical models: the 'enslavable barbarian' as a mobile classificatory label. In J. R. Willis (ed.), *Islam and the Ideology of Enslavement.* London

Morton, Roger Frederic. 1976. Slaves, fugitives and freedmen on the Kenya coast, 1873–1907. Unpublished PhD dissertation, Syracuse University

Morton-Williams, Peter. 1964. The Oyo Yoruba and the Atlantic slave trade, 1670–1830. *Journal of the Historical Society of Nigeria*, 3, 1: 25–45

Muhammad, Akbar. forthcoming. The image of Africans in Arabic literature: some unpublished manuscripts. In J. R. Willis (ed.), *Islam and the Ideology of Enslavement.* London

Muller, Wilhelm. 1976. *Die Africanische Landschafft Fetu.* Hamburg

Murray, David R. 1980. *Odious Commerce: Britain, Spain and the Abolition of the Cuban Slave Trade.* Cambridge

Nachtigal, Gustav. 1971. *Sahara and Sudan*, vol. IV: *Wadai and Darfur*, trans. Allan G. B. Fisher and Humphrey J. Fisher. Berkeley and Los Angeles

Nair, Kannan. 1972. *Politics and Society in Southeastern Nigeria, 1841–1906.* London

Newbury, C. C. 1960. An early enquiry into slavery and captivity in Dahomey. *Zaire*, 14: 53–67

327

Bibliography

Newitt, M. D. D. 1972. Angoche, the slave trade, and the Portuguese c. 1844–1910. *Journal of African History*, 13, 4: 659–72

1973. *The Portuguese Settlement on the Zambezi*. London

Newton-King, Susan. 1980. The labour market of the Cape colony, 1807–28. In Shula Marks and Anthony Atmore (eds.), *Economy and Society in Pre-Industrial South Africa*, pp. 171–207. London

Nicholls, C. S. 1971. *The Swahili Coast: Politics, Diplomacy and Trade on the East African Littoral, 1798–1856*. New York

Nicholson, Sharon. 1978. Climatic variations in the Sahel and other African regions during the past five centuries. *Journal of Arid Environments*, 1: 3–24

Northrup, David. 1972. The growth of trade among the Igbo before 1800. *Journal of African History*, 13, 2: 217–36

1976. The compatibility of the slave and palm oil trades in the Bight of Biafra. *Journal of African History*, 17, 3: 353–64

1978. *Trade Without Rulers: Pre-Colonial Economic Development in South-Eastern Nigeria*. Oxford

1979. Nineteenth-century patterns of slavery and economic growth in south-eastern Nigeria. *International Journal of African Historical Studies*, 12, 1: 1–16

1981. The ideological context of slavery in southeastern Nigeria in the nineteenth century. In Paul E. Lovejoy (ed.), *The Ideology of Slavery in Africa*, pp. 100–22. Beverly Hills

forthcoming *a*. The slave trade to Calabar, 1800–1850. *Calabar Historical Journal*

forthcoming *b*. Land and tree tenure in southeastern Nigeria

Nwulia, Moses D. E. 1975. *Britain and Slavery in East Africa*. Washington, DC

Obichere, Boniface. 1978. Women and slavery in the Kingdom of Dahomey. *Revue française d'histoire d'outre-mer*, 65, 1: 5–20

Odoom, Kobina Osam. 1965. Slavery and the concept of man in the Qur'an. Unpublished MA thesis, McGill University

O'Fahey, R. S. 1971. Religion and trade in the Kayra Sultanate of Dār Fūr. In Yusuf Fadl Hasan (ed.), *Sudan in Africa*, pp. 87–97. Khartoum

1973. Slavery and the slave trade in Dār Fūr. *Journal of African History*, 14, 1: 29–44

1977. Slavery and Society in Dār Fūr. Unpublished paper presented at the Conference on Islamic Africa: Slavery and Related Institutions, Princeton University

O'Fahey, R. S. and Spaulding, J. L. 1974. *Kingdoms of the Sudan*. London

Ogedengbe, K. O. 1971. The Aboh Kingdom of the lower Niger, c. 1650–1900. Unpublished PhD thesis, University of Wisconsin

1977. Slavery in nineteenth-century Aboh (Nigeria). In S. Miers and I. Kopytoff (eds.), *Slavery in Africa: Historical and Anthropological Perspectives*, pp. 133–54. Madison

1980. Gods and slaves: an ideological interpretation of cult slavery among the Igbo of Nigeria. Unpublished paper presented at the Conference on the Ideology of Slavery in Africa, York University, Toronto

O'Hear, Ann. 1979. Weaving in Ilorin in the 19th and 20th centuries. Unpublished Seminar paper, Department of History, School of Basic Studies, Kwara State College of Technology, Nigeria

O'Laughlin, Bridget. 1977. Production and reproduction: Meillassoux's *Femmes, Greniers et Capitaux*. *Critique of Anthropology*, 2, 8: 3–32

Ol'derogge, D. A. 1957. Feodalizm v Zapadnom Sudane v 16–18 vv. *Sovietkaya Etnografia*, 4: 91–103

Olivier de Sardan, Jean Pierre. 1973. L'Esclavage d'échange et captivité familiale chez les Songhay zerma. *Journal de la Société des Africanistes*, 43, 1: 151–67

1975. Captifs ruraux et esclaves impériaux du Songhay. In Claude Meillassoux (ed.), *L'Esclavage en Afrique précoloniale*, pp. 99–134. Paris

1976. *Quand nos pères étaient captifs: récits paysans du Niger*. Paris

328

Oloruntimehin, B. Olatunji. 1971–2. The impact of the abolition movement on the social and political development of West Africa in the nineteenth and twentieth centuries. *African Notes*, 7, 1: 33–58

Olusanya, G. O. 1966. The freed slaves' homes – an unknown aspect of northern Nigerian social history. *Journal of the Historical Society of Nigeria*, 3, 3: 523–38

Omer-Cooper, J. D. 1969. *The Zulu Aftermath: A Nineteenth Century Revolution in Bantu Africa.* Evanston, Illinois

Oriji, J. N. 1982. A reassessment of the organization and benefits of the slave and palm produce trade amongst the Ngwa-Igbo. *Canadian Journal of African Studies*, 16, 3

Orlova, A. S. 1964. Institution de l'esclavage dans l'état du Congo au moyen âge. (XVIᵉ–XVIIᵉ siècles). In *VII Congrès International des Sciences Anthropologiques et Ethnologiques*, vol. IX. Moscow

Oroge, E. Adeniyi. 1971. The institution of slavery in Yorubaland with particular reference to the nineteenth century. Unpublished PhD thesis, University of Birmingham

1975a. The fugitive slave crisis of 1859: a factor in the growth of anti-British feelings among the Yoruba. *Odu*, 12: 40–53

1975b. The fugitive slave question in Anglo-Egba relations, 1861–1886. *Journal of the Historical Society of Nigeria*, 8, 1: 61–80

1975c. Iwofa: an historical survey of the Yoruba institution of indenture. Unpublished seminar paper, University of Ife

Ortoli, Henri. 1939. Le Gagé des personnes au Soudan français. *Bulletin de l'IFAN*, Series B, 1: 313–24

O'Sullivan, John. 1981. Slavery in the Malinke kingdom of Kabadougou (Ivory Coast). *International Journal of African Historical Studies*, 13, 4: 633–50

Ottenberg, Simon. 1958. Ibo oracles and intergroup relations. *Southwestern Journal of Anthropology*, 14: 295–317

Padgug, R. A. 1976. Problems in the theory of slavery and slave society. *Science and Society*, 40: 3–27

Palmer, H. R. 1928. *Sudanese Memoirs.* London

1936. *The Bornu Sahara and Sudan.* London

Pankhurst, Richard. 1961. *An Introduction to the Economic History of Ethiopia.* London

1962. 'Primitive money' in Ethiopia. *Bulletin de la Société des Africanistes*, 32, 2: 214–22

1964. The Ethiopian slave trade in the nineteenth and early twentieth centuries: a statistical inquiry. *Journal of Semitic Studies*, 9, 1: 220–8

1968. *Economic History of Ethiopia, 1800–1935.* Addis Ababa

1975. Ethiopian slave reminiscences of the nineteenth century. *Trans-african Journal of History*, 5: 98–110

1976. The history of Bareya, Sanquella and other Ethiopian slaves from the borderlands of the Sudan. Unpublished paper presented to Conference on Ethiopian Feudalism, Addis Ababa

Park, Mungo. 1971. *Travels in the Interior Districts of Africa in the Years 1795, 1796 and 1797.* London

Pasquier, R. 1967. A propos de l'emancipation des esclaves au Sénégal en 1848. *Revue française d'historie d'outre-mer*, 54: 188–208

Patenostre, Dr. 1930. La Captivité chez les peuhls du Fouta-Djallon. *Cahiers d'outre-mer*, 3: 241–54, 353–72

Patterson, Orlando. 1979. On slavery and slave formations. *New Left Review*, 117: 31–67

Perlman, Melvin L. The traditional systems of stratification among the Ganda and the Nyoro of Uganda. In A. Tuden and L. Plotnicov (eds.), *Social Stratification in Africa*, pp. 125–61. New York

Peroz, Marie Etienne. 1889. *Au Soudan français.* Paris

329

Perrot, Claude. 1975. Les captifs dans le royaume anyi du Ndényé. In Claude Meillassoux (ed.), *L'Esclavage en Afrique précoloniale*, pp. 351–88. Paris
    1969. Hommes libres et captifs dans le royaume agni de l'Indénié. *Cahiers d'études africaines*, 9: 482–501
Person, Yves. 1968–75. *Samori: une revolution Dyula* (3 vols.) Dakar
    1974. The Atlantic coast and the southern savannahs, 1800–1880. In J. F. Ade Ajayi and Michael Crowder (eds.), *History of West Africa*, vol. II, pp. 262–307. London
Peukert, Werner. 1978. *Der Atlantische Sklavenhandel von Dahomey 1740–1797: Wirtschaftsanthropologie und Sozialgeschichte*. Wiesbaden
Piault, Marc-Henri. 1975. Captifs du pouvoir et pouvoir des captifs. In Claude Meillassoux (ed.), *L'Esclavage en Afrique précoloniale*, pp. 321–50. Paris
Pignon, Jean. 1976. L'Esclavage en Tunisie de 1590 à 1620. *Cahiers de Tunisie*, 93–4: 143–65
Poku, K. 1969. Traditional roles and people of slave origin in modern Ashanti – a few impressions. *Ghana Journal of Sociology*, 6, 1: 34–8
Polanyi, Karl. 1966. *Dahomey and the Slave Trade: An Analysis of an Archaic Economy*. Seattle
Pollet, E. and Winter, G. 1968. L'Organisation sociale du travail agricole des Soninké (Djahunu, Mali). *Cahiers d'études africaines*, 8, 4: 509–34
    1971. *La Société soninké (Djahunu, Mali)*. Brussels
Postma, Johannes. 1972. The dimension of the Dutch slave trade from western Africa. *Journal of African History*, 13, 2: 237–48
    1975a. The Dutch slave trade: a quantitative assessment. *Revue française d'histoire d'outre-mer*, 42: 232–44
    1975b. The origin of African slaves: the Dutch activities on the Guinea coast, 1675–1795. In S. L. Engerman and E. D. Genovese (eds.), *Race and Slavery in the Western Hemisphere: Quantitative Studies*, pp. 33–49. Princeton
    1979. Mortality in the Dutch slave trade, 1675–1795. In H. A. Gemery and J. S. Hogendorn (eds.), *The Uncommon Market: Essays in the Economic History of the Atlantic Slave Trade*, pp. 239–60. New York
Pouncy, Hillard Warren. 1981. Colonial racial attitudes and colonial labor laws in British West Africa, 1815–1946. Unpublished PhD thesis, Massachusetts Institute of Technology
Prins, Pierre. 1907. Servitude et liberté dans les Sultanats du Haut-Oubangui. *Revue indigene*, 12: 126–36
Ratsimamanga, R. 1933. *De la condition de l'esclavage à Madagascar*. Montpellier
Rattray, R. S. 1929. *Ashanti Law and Constitution*. London
Rau, Virginia. 1970. The Madeiran sugar cane plantations. In H. B. Johnson, Jr (ed.), *From Reconquest to Empire: The Iberian Background to Latin American History*, pp. 71–84. New York
Rawley, James A. 1980. The port of London and the eighteenth century slave trade: historians, sources, and a reappraisal. *African Economic History*, 9: 85–100
Reefe, Thomas Q. 1981. *The Rainbow and the Kings: A History of the Luba Empire to 1891*. Berkeley and Los Angeles
Renault, François. 1971a. *Lavigerie, l'esclavage africain, et l'Europe 1868–1892* (2 vols.) Paris
    1971b. L'Abolition de l'esclavage au Sénégal: l'attitude de l'administration française 1848–1905. *Revue française d'histoire d'outre-mer*, 58: 5–81
    1976. *Libération d'esclaves et nouvelle servitude*. Abidjan
Rey, P. P. 1969. Articulation des modes de dépendance et des modes de reproduction dans deux sociétés lignagères (Punu et Kunyi du Congo-Brazzaville). *Cahiers d'études africaines*, 9: 415–40
    1971. *Colonialisme, neo-colonialisme, et transition au capitalisme*. Paris
    1973. *Les Alliances de classes*. Paris

1975a. L'Esclavage lignager chez les tsangui, les punu, et les kuni du Congo-Brazzaville. In Claude Meillassoux (ed.), *L'Esclavage en Afrique précoloniale*, pp. 509–28. Paris

1975b. The lineage mode of production. *Critique of Anthropology*, 3: 27–79

1979. Class contradiction in lineage societies. *Critique of Anthropology*, 4: 41–60

Rey-Hulman, Diana. 1975. Les Dépendants des maîtres tyolossi pendant la période précoloniale. In Claude Meillassoux (ed.), *L'Esclavage en Afrique précoloniale*, pp. 297–320. Paris

Reynolds, Edward. 1973. Agricultural adjustments on the Gold Coast after the end of the slave trade, 1807–1874. *Agricultural History*, 47, 4: 308–18

1974. *Trade and Economic Change on the Gold Coast, 1807–1874*. Harlow

1981. Abolition and economic change on the Gold Coast. In David Eltis and James Walvin (eds.), *The Abolition of the Atlantic Slave Trade*, pp. 141–51. Madison

Richard-Molard, J. 1952a. Notes démographiques sur la région de Labe. In P. Pélissier (ed.), *Hommage à Jacques Richard-Molard (1913–1951)*, special issue of *Présence africaine*, 15: 83–94

1952b. Les Densités de population au Fouta-Djallon. In P. Pélissier (ed.), *Hommage à Jacques Richard-Molard (1913–1951)*, special issue of *Présence africaine*, 15: 95–106

1952c. Essai sur la vie paysanne au Fouta-Djallon. In P. Pélissier (ed.), *Hommage à Jacques Richard-Molard (1913–1951)*, special issue of *Présence africaine*, 15: 155–251

Richards, W. A. 1980. The import of firearms into West Africa in the eighteenth century. *Journal of African History*, 31, 1: 43–59

Richardson, David. 1979. West African consumption patterns and their influence on the eighteenth-century English slave trade. In H. A. Gemery and J. S. Hogendorn (eds.), *The Uncommon Market: Essays in the Economic History of the Atlantic Slave Trade*, pp. 303–30. New York.

Riesman, Paul. 1974. *Société et liberté chez les Peuls Djelgôbé de Haute-Volta*. Paris

Rinchon, Dieudonne. 1938. *Le Trafic négrier, d'après les livres de commerce du capitaine gantois Pierre-Ignace-Liévin van Alstein*, vol. I. Paris

Roberts, Andrew. 1970a. Pre-colonial trade in Zambia. *African Social Research*, 10: 715–46

1970b. Nyamwezi trade. In Richard Gray and David Birmingham (eds.), *Pre-Colonial African Trade: Essays on Trade in Central and Eastern Africa before 1900*, pp. 39–74. London

Roberts, R. L. 1978. The Maraka and the economy of the middle Niger valley, 1790–1905. Unpublished PhD thesis, University of Toronto.

1980a. Production and reproduction in warrior states: Segu Bambara and Segu Tokolor. *International Journal of African Historical Studies*, 13, 3: 389–419

1980b. Long distance trade and production: Sinsani in the nineteenth century. *Journal of African History*, 21, 2: 169–88

1980c. Linkages and multiplier effects in the ecologically specialized trade of precolonial West Africa. *Cahiers d'études africaines*, 20, 1–2: 135–48

1981. Ideology, slavery and social formation: the evolution of Maraka slavery in the middle Niger valley. In Paul E. Lovejoy (ed.), *The Ideology of Slavery in Africa*, pp. 170–99. Beverly Hills

Roberts, Richard and Klein, Martin. 1981. The Banamba slave exodus of 1905 and the decline of slavery in the western Sudan. *Journal of African History*, 21, 3: 375–94

Robertson, Claire. forthcoming. Post proclamation slavery in Accra: a female affair. In Martin Klein and Claire Robertson (eds.), *Women and Slavery in Africa*. Madison

Rodney, Walter. 1966. Slavery and other forms of social oppression on the Upper Guinea Coast in the context of the Atlantic slave trade. *Journal of African History*, 7, 4: 431–43

1967. West Africa and the Atlantic slave trade. (Historical Society of Tanzania, Paper No. 2) Nairobi

Bibliography

1968. Jihad and social revolution in Futa Jallon in the eighteenth century. *Journal of the Historical Society of Nigeria*, 4, 2: 269–84

1969. Gold and slaves on the Gold Coast. *Transactions of the Historical Society of Ghana*, 10: 13–28

1970. *A History of the Upper Guinea Coast, 1545–1800*. Oxford

Romer, L. F. 1760. *Tilforladelig efterretning om kysten Guinea*. Copenhagen

Ronon, Dov. 1971. On the African role in the trans-Atlantic slave trade in Dahomey. *Cahiers d'études africaines*, 11, 1: 5–13

Ross, David A. 1965. The career of Domingo Martinez in the Bight of Benin, 1833–64. *Journal of African History*, 6, 1: 79–90

Ross, Robert. 1975. The 'White' population of South Africa in the eighteenth century. *Population Studies*, 29: 210–22

1978a. Sexuality and slavery at the Cape in the eighteenth century. In *Collected Seminar Papers on the Societies of Southern Africa in the Nineteenth and Twentieth Centuries* (Institute of Commonwealth Studies), vol. VIII, pp. 21–30. London

1978b. The occupation of slaves in eighteenth century Cape Town. Unpublished paper presented to Conference on Colonial Cities, Amsterdam

Rout, Leslie B., Jr. 1976. *The African Experience in Spanish America, 1502 to the Present Day*. Cambridge

Russell, M. 1976. Slaves or workers? Relations between Bushmen, Tswana, and Boers in the Kalahari. *Journal of Southern African Studies*, 2, 2: 178–97

Ryder, Alan. 1969. *Benin and the Europeans, 1485–1897*. London

Sahlins, Marshall. 1972. *Stone Age Economics*. Chicago

Salt, H. 1814. *A Voyage to Abyssinia*. London

Sanneh, L. O. 1976. Slavery, Islam, and the Jakhanke people of West Africa. *Africa*, 46, 1: 80–97

forthcoming. Islamic slavery in the African perspective. In J. R. Willis (ed.), *The Servile Estate*. London

Schoelcher, Victor. 1880. *L'Esclavage au Sénégal en 1880*. Paris

Schulz, A. and Hammar, A. 1897. *The New Africa: A Journey up the Chobe and down the Okavango Rivers: A Record of Exploration and Sport*. London

Seddon, David (ed.) 1978. *Relations of Production: Marxist Approaches to Economic Anthropology*. London

Sellnow, Irmgard. 1964. Die Stellung der Sklaven in der Hausa-Gesellschaft. *Mitteilungen aus den Institut fur Orientforschung*, 10, 1: 85–102

Shea, Philip James. 1975. The development of an export oriented dyed cloth industry in Kano Emirate in the nineteenth century. Unpublished PhD thesis, University of Wisconsin

Shepherd, Gill. 1980. The Comorians and the East African slave trade. In James L. Watson (ed.), *Asian and African Systems of Slavery*, pp. 73–99. Oxford

Sheriff, A. M. H. forthcoming. The slave mode of production along the East African coast. In J. R. Willis (ed.), *The Servile Estate*. London

Shorter, A. 1968. Nyungu-Ya-Mawe and the 'Empire of the Ruga-Ruga'. *Journal of African History*, 9, 2: 235–59

Siegal, Bernard J. 1945. Some methodological considerations for a comparative study of slavery. *American Anthropologist*, 47: 357–92

Silberbauer, George B. and Kuper, Adam J. 1966. Kgalagari masters and Bushmen serfs. *African Studies*, 25: 171–9

Smith, Mary F. 1955. *Baba of Karo: A Woman of the Moslem Hausa*. New York

Smith, M. G. 1954. Slavery and emancipation in two societies. *Social and Economic Studies*, 3, 3–4: 239–80

1955. *The Economy of Hausa Communities of Zaria*. London

Smith, Robert. 1970. The canoe in West African history. *Journal of African History*, 11, 4: 515–33

Snelgrave, William. 1734. *A New Account of Some Parts of Guinea and the Slave Trade*. London

Sousberghe, Leone de. 1961. *Deux palabres d'esclaves chez les Pende (Province de Leopold-ville, 1956)*. Academie Royale des Sciences d'Outre-Mer (Classe des sciences morales et politiques, Memoire, NS 25, 5). Brussels

Southall, Aidan W. 1970a. Stratification in Africa. In A. Tuden and L. Plotnicov (eds.), *Essays in Comparative Social Stratification*, pp. 231–72. Pittsburgh

1970b. Rank and stratification among the Alur and other Nilotic peoples. In A. Tuden and L. Plotnicov (eds.), *Social Stratification in Africa*, pp. 31–46. New York

Spaulding, Jay. 1982. Slavery, land tenure and social class in the northern Turkish Sudan, 1820–1881. *International Journal of African Historical Studies*, 15, 1: 1–20

Stein, Robert. 1978. Measuring the French slave trade, 1713–1792/3. *Journal of African History*, 19, 4: 515–21

1979. *The French Slave Trade in the Eighteenth Century: An Old Regime Business*. Madison

Strickland, D. A. 1976. Kingship and slavery in African thought: a conceptual analysis. *Comparative Studies in Society and History*, 18, 3: 371–94

Suret-Canale, Jean. 1969. Les Sociétés traditionalles en Afrique Tropicale et le concept de mode de production asiatiques. In Centre d'études et de recherches marxistes, *Sur le mode de production asiatique*, pp. 101–33. Paris

Swartenbroeckx, P. 1966. L'Esclavage chez les Yansi. *Bulletin de la Société Royale Belge d'Anthropologie et de Préhistoire de Bruxelles*, 77: 145–204

Swindell, Ken. 1980. Serawoollies, Tillibunkas and strange farmers: the development of migrant groundnut farming along the Gambia River, 1848–95. *Journal of African History*, 21, 1: 93–104

Tambo, David Carl. 1976. The Sokoto Caliphate slave trade in the nineteenth century. *International Journal of African Historical Studies*, 9, 2: 187–217

Tamuno, Takena N. 1964. Emancipation in Nigeria. *Nigeria Magazine*, 82: 218–27

Temperley, Howard. 1981. Anti-slavery ideology. In David Eltis and James Walvin (eds.), *The Abolition of the Atlantic Slave Trade*, pp. 21–35. Madison

Terray, Emmanuel. 1969. *Le Marxisme devant les sociétés 'primitives'*. Paris

1973. Review of Goody. *Annales*, 5: 1331–8

1974. Long-distance exchange and the formation of the state: the case of the Abron Kingdom of Gyaman. *Economy and Society*, 3: 315–45

1975a. La Captivité dans le royaume abron du Gyaman. In Claude Meillassoux (ed.), *L'Esclavage en Afrique précoloniale*, pp. 389–454. Paris

1975b. Classes and class consciousness in the Abron kingdom of Gyaman. In Maurice Bloch (ed.), *Marxist Analyses and Social Anthropology*, pp. 85–136. London

1976. Contribution à une étude de l'armée asante. *Cahiers d'études africaines*, 16: 297–356

1979. On exploitation: elements of an autocritique. *Critique of Anthropology*, 4, 13–14: 29–39

forthcoming a. Réflexions sur la formation du prix des esclaves à l'intérieur de l'Afrique de l'ouest précoloniale

forthcoming b. Production de l'or, travail des esclaves et intervention de l'état dans les sociétés akan précoloniales. In G. Dalton (ed.), *Research in Economic Anthropology*

Thomas, Robert Paul and Bean, Richard. 1974. The fishers of men – the profit of the slave trade. *Journal of Economic History*, 34, 4: 885–914

Thompson, Leonard. 1969a. Co-operation and conflict: the high veld. In Monica Wilson and Leonard Thompson (eds.), *The Oxford History of South Africa*, vol. I, pp. 391–446. Oxford

1969*b*. Co-operation and conflict: the Zulu Kingdom and Natal. In Monica Wilson and Leonard Thompson (eds.), *The Oxford History of South Africa*, vol. I, pp. 334–90. Oxford

Thornton, John. 1977. An eighteenth century baptismal register and the demographic history of Manguenzo. In *African Historical Demography*, pp. 405–15. Edinburgh

1979. The Kingdom of Kongo in the era of the civil wars, 1641–1718. Unpublished PhD thesis, UCLA

1980. The slave trade in eighteenth century Angola: effects on demographic structures. *Canadian Journal of African Studies*, 14, 3: 417–27

1981. Early Kongo–Portuguese relations: a new interpretation. *History in Africa*, 8: 183–204

forthcoming. The Kingdom of Kongo, ca. 1390–1678: history of an African social formation. *Cahiers d'études africaines*

Tilleman, E. 1904. *Enlidenenfoldig beretning om det landskab Guinea* (Copenhagen, 1697), as translated by Ove Jensen, *Journal of the African Society*, 4: 30–1

Tisserant, R. P. Charles. 1955. *Ce que j'ai connu de l'esclavage en Oubangui-Chari*. Paris

Tlou, Thomas. 1977. Servility and political control: Botlhanka among the Batawana of northwestern Botswana, ca. 1750–1906. In S. Miers and I. Kopytoff (eds.), *Slavery in Africa: Historical and Anthropological Perspectives*, pp. 367–90. Madison

Trapido, S. 1977. Aspects of the transition from slavery to serfdom: the South African Republic, 1842–1902. Unpublished paper presented at the Agrarian Labor Conference, Columbia University

Tuden, A. 1970*a*. Slavery and stratification among the Ila of central Africa. In A. Tuden and L. Plotnicov (eds.), *Social Stratification in Africa*, pp. 49–58. New York

Tuden, Arthur and Plotnicov, Leonard. 1970*b*. Introduction. In *Social Stratification in Africa*, pp. 1–29. New York

Turbet-Delof, Guy. 1968. Un texte antiesclavagiste publié en 1689. *Les Cahiers de Tunisie*, 16: 111–18

Tymowski, M. 1970. Les Domaines des princes du Songhay (Soudan occidental): comparaison avec la grande propriété foncière en Europe au début de l'époque féodale. *Annales: Economies, Sociétés, Civilisations*, 25–6: 1637–58

1973. L'Économie et la société dans le bassin du moyen Niger: fin du XVIe–XVIIIe siècles. *Africana Bulletin*, 18: 9–64

Uchendu, Victor. 1967. Slavery in southeast Nigeria. *Trans-Action*, 4: 52–4

1977. Slaves and slavery in Igboland, Nigeria. In S. Miers and I. Kopytoff (eds.), *Slavery in Africa: Historical and Anthropological Perspectives*, pp. 121–32. Madison

Udo, R. K. 1964. The migrant tenant farmer of eastern Nigeria. *Africa*, 34: 326–39

Usman, Yusufu Bala. 1974. The transformation of Katsina: *c*. 1796–1903: the overthrow of the *sarauta* system and the establishment and evolution of the emirate. Unpublished PhD thesis, Ahmadu Bello University

Uzoigwe, G. N. 1973. The slave trade and African societies. *Transactions of the Historical Society of Ghana*, 14, 2: 187–212

Vail, Leroy and White, Landeg. 1980. *Capitalism and Colonialism in Mozambique: A Study of Quelimane District*. London

Van den Boogart, Ernst and Emmer, Pieter C. 1979. The Dutch participation in the Atlantic slave trade, 1596–1650. In H. A. Gemery and J. S. Hogendorn (eds.), *The Uncommon Market: Essays in the Economic History of the Atlantic Slave Trade*, pp. 353–75. New York

Vansina, Jan. 1962. Long-distance trade-routes in central Africa. *Journal of African History*, 3, 3: 375–90

1966. *Kingdoms of the Savanna*. Madison

1973. *The Tio Kingdom of the Middle Congo, 1880–1892*. Oxford

1978. *The Children of Woot: A History of the Kuba Peoples*. Madison

Van Zwanenberg, R. M. A. 1976. Anti-slavery, the ideology of 19th century imperialism in East Africa. *Hadith*, 5: 110–29

Vaughan, James H., Jr. 1970. Caste systems in the western Sudan. In A. Tuden and L. Plotnicov (eds.), *Social Stratification in Africa*, pp. 59–92. New York

1977. Mafakur: a limbic institution of the Margi (Nigeria). In S. Miers and I. Kopytoff (eds.), *Slavery in Africa: Historical and Anthropological Perspectives*, pp. 85–102. Madison

Vellut, Jean-Luc. 1972. Notes sur le Lunda at la frontière luso-africaine. *Études d'histoire africaine*, 3: 61–166

1975. Le royaume de Cassange et les réseaux luso-africains (ca. 1750–1810). *Cahiers d'études africaines*, 15: 117–36

forthcoming. Essai d'histoire Lunda: des origines aux débuts du capitalisme colonial

Verger, Pierre. 1976. *Trade Relations between the Bight of Benin and Brazil, 17th–19th Century*, trans. Evelyn Crawford. Ibadan

Verlinden, Charles. 1950. La Colonie vénitienne de Tana, centre de la traite des esclaves au XIVe et au début XVe siècles. In *Studi in onore di Gino Luzzatto* (2 vols.), vol. ii, pp. 1–25. Milan

1955. *L'Esclavage dans l'Europe médiévale: péninsule Ibèrique-France*. Bruges

1967. Les Débuts de la traite portugaise en Afrique (1433–1448). In *Miscellanea mediaevalia in memoriam J. F. Niermeyer*, pp. 365–77. Groningen

1970. *The Beginnings of Modern Colonization: Eleven essays with an introduction*, trans. Yvonne Freccero. Ithaca and London

Vila Vilar, Enriqueta. 1977*a*. The large-scale introduction of Africans into Veracruz and Cartagena. In Vera Rubin and Arthur Tuden (eds.), *Comparative Perspectives on Slavery in New World Plantation Societies*, pp. 267–80. New York

1977*b*. *Hispanoamérica y el comercio de esclavos: los Asientos Portugueses*. Seville

Vogt, John L. 1973. The early São Tomé-Principé slave trade with Mina, 1500–1540. *International Journal of African Historical Studies*, 6, 3: 453–67

1979. *Portuguese Rule on the Gold Coast, 1469–1682*. Athens, California

Waddell, Hope. 1863. *Twenty-Nine Years in the West Indies and Central Africa: A Review of Missionary Work and Adventure, 1829–1858*. London

Walz, Terence. 1978. *Trade between Egypt and Bilād As-Sūdān, 1700–1820*. Cairo

Warburg, Gabriel. 1978. Slavery and labour in the Anglo-Egyptian Sudan. *Asian and African Studies*, 12: 221–45

1981. Ideological and practical considerations regarding slavery in the Mahdist state and in the Anglo-Egyptian Sudan, 1881–1918. In Paul E. Lovejoy (ed.), *The Ideology of Slavery in Africa*, pp. 244–69. Beverly Hills

Watson, James L. (ed.) 1980*a*. *Asian and African Systems of Slavery*. Oxford

1980*b*. Slavery as an institution, open and closed systems. In James L. Watson (ed.) *Asian and African Systems of Slavery*, pp. 1–15. Oxford

Weeks, John H. 1969. *Among the Primitive Bakongo*. New York

Weiskel, Timothy C. 1978. The precolonial Baule: a reconstruction. *Cahiers d'études africaines*, 18, 4: 503–60

1979. Labor in the emergent periphery: from slavery to migrant labor among the Baule peoples, c. 1880–1925. In Walter L. Goldfrank (ed.), *The World System of Capitalism: Past and Present*, pp. 207–33. Beverly Hills

White, C. M. N. 1957. Clan, chieftainship, and slavery in Luvale political organization. *Africa*, 27, 1: 59–73

Wilks, Ivor. 1957. The rise of the Akwamu Empire, 1650–1710. *Transactions of the Historical Society of Ghana*, 3: 99–136

1967. Abū Bakr al-Siddiq of Timbuktu. In Philip D. Curtin (ed.), *Africa Remembered:*

Narratives of West Africans from the Era of the Slave Trade, pp. 152–69. Madison

1971*a*. Asante policy towards the Hausa trade in the nineteenth century. In Claude Meillassoux (ed.), *The Development of Indigenous Trade and Markets in West Africa*, pp. 124–41. London

1971*b*. The Mossi and Akan states, 1500–1800. In J. F. Ade Ajayi and Michael Crowder (eds.), *History of West Africa*, vol. I, pp. 344–86. London

1975. *Asante in the Nineteenth Century: The Structure and Evolution of a Political Order.* Cambridge

1977. Land, labour, capital and the forest kingdom of Asante: a model of early change. In J. Friedman and R. M. Rowlands (eds.), *The Evolution of Social Systems*, pp. 487–534. London

1979. The golden stool and the elephant tail: an essay on wealth in Asante. *Research in Economic Anthropology*, 2: 1–36

Wirz, Albert. 1974. *Vom Sklavenhandel zum kolonialen Handel: Wirtschaftsraume in Kamerun vor 1914.* Freiburg

Wissmann, Hermann von. 1891. *My second Journey through Equatorial Africa from the Congo to the Zambesi*, trans. Minna J. A. Bergmann. London

Works, John Arthur. 1976. *Pilgrims in a Strange Land: The Hausa Communities in Chad, 1890–1970.* New York

Wright, Marcia. 1975. Women in peril: a commentary on the life stories of captives in nineteenth century east central Africa. *African Social Research*, 20: 800–19

Wright, William. 1831. *Slavery at the Cape of Good Hope.* London

Wrigley, C. C. 1971. Historicism in Africa: slavery and state formation. *African Affairs*, 70: 113–24

Wylie, Kenneth C. 1973. The slave trade in nineteenth century Temneland and the British sphere of influence. *African Studies Review*, 16, 2: 203–17

Zuccarelli, F. 1962. Le Régime des engagés à temps au Sénégal (1817–1848). *Cahiers d'études africaines*, 2: 420–61

Index

337